1993

The IUCN Species Survival Co

Conservation Biology of
Lycaenidae
(Butterflies)

Edited by T. R. New

The World Conservation Union   SPECIES SURVIVAL COMMISSION

WWF

Sultanate of Oman

Contents

iii

Preface

Butterflies have long been accorded 'special' status by many people who do not like insects. Ever since the ancient Greeks employed the same word (psyche) for 'soul' and 'butterfly', an aura of spiritual or aesthetic appreciation has enhanced their generally charismatic popularity, so that people to whom 'the only good insect is a dead insect' accept readily that butterflies merit conservation (New 1991). Perhaps the most widely appreciated butterflies are the swallowtails, birdwings and their allies (Papilionidae), which have recently received substantial conservation impetus through production of a global survey (Collins and Morris 1985) and a *Swallowtail Action Plan* (New and Collins 1991) based on this, and produced under the auspices of the IUCN Species Survival Commission's Lepidoptera Specialist Group.

Many other butterflies are much less well known than the swallowtails, and such a comprehensive appraisal of them would be difficult or impossible to achieve. But, especially in north temperate regions of the world, very substantial conservation effort has been directed to members of the largest family of butterflies, the Lycaenidae – the blues, coppers, hairstreaks, metalmarks and related forms. In 1989, I suggested that the Lepidoptera Specialist Group should seek to complement the swallowtail studies by an appraisal of the Lycaenidae, to 'round out' the emerging picture of butterfly conservation by gathering together some of the data on this family. Lycaenidae exemplify a wide spectrum of concerns: populations are often extremely localised with colonies occupying a few hectares or less; many are associated with early successional stages of vegetation in grasslands or herb associations; and many participate in subtle ecological associations with ants or (more rarely) Homoptera.

A number of species or subspecies of the Lycaenidae have been the targets of major conservation campaigns which have been vitally important in raising public awareness of insect conservation in areas where swallowtails are scarce, and it is no exaggeration to claim that they have been the most important butterfly family in fostering conservation concern in temperate regions.

This is not a Red Data Book but, rather, an introduction to the conservation biology of the Lycaenidae. It emphasises the very different knowledge base available for lycaenids compared with the swallowtails, and should be a salutary warning against feelings of complacency that butterflies are well known!

It draws on the expertise of many experienced practitioners of butterfly conservation, and on the large literature of lycaenid biology. The account consists of three sections. The first is a brief general introduction to the Lycaenidae and their place in butterfly conservation. The second is a series of regional overviews of lycaenids for several parts of the world where interest and knowledge has been sufficient to prepare such an essay; and the third is a series of selected case-histories or species accounts which range from the well known to the novel. This section is not in any sense encyclopedic, but provides a tentative basis for direction and for future synthesis and development of more general conservation strategies.

References

COLLINS, N.M. and MORRIS, M.G. 1985. *Threatened Swallowtail Butterflies of the World.* The IUCN Red Data Book, IUCN, Gland and Cambridge.

NEW, T.R. 1991. *Butterfly Conservation.* Oxford University Press, Melbourne.

NEW, T.R. and COLLINS, N.M. 1991. *Swallowtail Butterflies. An Action Plan for their Conservation.* IUCN, Gland.

Acknowledgements

The task of preparing this volume has been a pleasant one, leading me to appreciate very deeply the spirit of cooperation engendered by a common concern for the well being of butterflies. Most authors approached to contribute to the compilation agreed promptly and willingly, and I am very grateful for their participation and encouragement. Other people responded with constructive advice and suggestions in response to my queries, and most members of the Lepidoptera Specialist Group in 1989 and 1990 suggested possible species or candidate authors. Dr. Simon N. Stuart and his dynamic team, including Dr. Mariano Gimenez-Dixon and Ms Linette Humphrey, in the SSC Office in Gland, have been continually encouraging and supportive, and their rapid responses to my numerous questions have been appreciated greatly. Editorial advice from Dr. Alexandra Hails has also been welcomed.

Transformation of a miscellany of scripts into a relatively harmonic and consistent typescript was accomplished patiently by Mrs. Tracey Carpenter at La Trobe University; she also drew a number of the figures. The photographers are acknowledged individually in the photograph legends.

List of contributors

Dr. R.A. Arnold
Entomological Consulting Services Limited,
104 Mountain View Court,
Pleasant Hill,
California 94523,
U.S.A.

Dr. Z. Bálint
Zoological Department,
Hungarian Natural History Museum,
Baross utca 13,
Budapest, H-1008,
Hungary

Prof. E. Balletto
Dipàrtimento di Biologia Animale,
Università di Torino,
V. Accademia Albertina 17,
Torino,
Italy - 10123

Dr. J.W. Brown
Entomology Department,
San Diego Natural History Museum,
P.O. Box 1390,
San Diego,
California 92112,
U.S.A.

Dr. K.S. Brown, Jr.
Departmento de Zoologia,
Instituto de Biologia,
Universidade Estadual de Campinas,
C.P. 6109. Campinas,
São Paulo, 13. 081.
Brazil

Dr. C.J. Callaghan
Louis Berger International Inc.,
100 Halsted Street,
P.O. Box 270,
East Orange, NJ 07019,
U.S.A.

Dr. J. Hall Cushman
Center for Conservation Biology,
Department of Biological Sciences,
Stanford University,
Stanford, California 94305,
U.S.A.

Dr. H.A. Descimon
Laboratoire de Systématique évolutive,
Université de Provence,
3 place Victor Hugo,
13331 Marseille Cedex 3,
France

Ms E.M. Dexter
School of Australian Environmental Studies,
Griffith University,
Nathan,
Queensland 4111,
Australia

Dr. E. Duffey
Cergne House,
Church Street,
Wadenhoe,
Peterborough PE8 5ST,
U.K.

Dr. J.F. Emmel
26500 Rim Road,
Hemet,
California 92544,
U.S.A.

Dr. T.C. Emmel
Department of Zoology,
University of Florida,
Gainesville,
Florida 32611,
U.S.A.

Dr. D.K. Faulkner
Entomology Department,
San Diego Natural History Museum,
P.O. Box 1390,
San Diego,
California 92112,
U.S.A.

Mr. G.A. Henning
17 Sonderend Street,
Helderkruin 1724,
South Africa

Mr. S.F. Henning
5 Alexander Street,
Florida 1709,
South Africa

Dr. T. Hirowatari
Entomological Laboratory,
College of Agriculture,
University of Osaka Prefecture,
Sakai,
Osaka, 591
Japan

Prof. R.L. Kitching
School of Australian Environmental Studies,
Griffith University,
Nathan,
Queensland 4111,
Australia

Dr. J. Martin
Departamento de Biologia (Zoologia),
Facultad de Ciencias,
Universidad Autonoma de Madrid,
Madrid,
Spain

Dr. R.H.T. Mattoni
9620 Heather Road,
Beverly Hills,
California 90210,
U.S.A.

Dr. M.C. Minno
Department of Zoology,
University of Florida,
Gainesville,
Florida 32611,
U.S.A.

Dr. M.L. Munguira
Departamento de Biologia (Zoologia),
Facultad de Ciencias,
Universidad Autonoma de Madrid,
Madrid,
Spain

Dr. D.D. Murphy
Center for Conservation Biology,
Stanford University,
Stanford,
California 94305,
U.S.A.

Dr. T.R. New
Department of Zoology,
La Trobe University,
Bundoora,
Victoria 3083,
Australia

Dr. M.W. Parker
U.S. Fish & Wildlife Service,
San Francisco Bay National Wildlife Refuge Complex,
Newark,
California 94560,
U.S.A.

Dr. J.A. Powell
Department of Entomological Sciences,
201 Wellman Hall,
University of California,
Berkeley,
California 94720-0001,
U.S.A.

Dr. G.B. Prince
Department of Lands, Parks and Wildlife,
Mrs Macquarie's Road,
Hobart, Tasmania 7001,
Australia

Dr. P.R. Samson
Bureau of Sugar Experiment Stations,
P.O. Box 651,
Bundaberg,
Qld 4650,
Australia

Prof. M.J. Samways
Department of Zoology and Entomology,
University of Natal,
Pietermaritzburg 3200,
South Africa

Dr. D.P.A. Sands
Division of Entomology,
CSIRO,
Meiers Road,
Indooroopilly,
Qld 4068,
Australia

Dr. C.D. Thomas
School of Biological Sciences,
University of Birmingham,
Edgbaston,
Birmingham B15 2TT,
U.K.

Dr. Stuart B. Weiss
Center for Conservation Biology,
Department of Biological Sciences,
Stanford University,
Stanford, California 94305,
U.S.A.

PART 1. INTRODUCTION

Introduction to the biology and conservation of the Lycaenidae

T.R. NEW

Department of Zoology, La Trobe University, Bundoora, Victoria 3083, Australia

Introduction

The Lycaenidae, the 'blues', 'coppers', 'hairstreaks','metalmarks' and related butterflies, are the most diverse family of Papilionoidea and comprise between 30 and 40% of all butterfly species. They are mostly rather small. The world's smallest butterfly may be the lycaenid *Micropsyche ariana* Mattoni from Afghanistan with a wingspan of only about 7mm (although some individuals of *Brephidium exilis* (Boisduval) can have as small a wingspan as 6mm). A few Lycaenidae are relatively large: *Liphyra brassolis* Westwood has a wingspan of 8–9cm, and is the largest known species. The family occurs in all major biogeographical regions in temperate and tropical zones.

As with other Lepidoptera, the life cycle comprises egg, larva (caterpillar) passing through several instars, pupa and adult, with the cycle occupying several weeks to a year. Particularly in temperate regions, there may be a well-defined phenological break during winter which is passed in an inactive stage. The early stages of many taxa have been described, and a consideration of lycaenid conservation biology must include the biology of all of these life forms, from oviposition site selection by reproductive females to larval life and adult biology. In general, far more distributional and biological information is available on adults, which tend to be conspicuous and actively sought by collectors and photographers, than on the relatively inconspicuous and cryptic immature stages.

Many species have very precise environmental requirements, but the family occurs in many major biomes and vegetation associations from climax forests to scrublands, grasslands, wetlands and semi-arid desert communities, many of which could be viewed as early seres in terrestrial successions. Some lycaenids have considerable potential for use as indicator species as their incidence and abundance reflects rather small degrees of habitat change.

The larvae of some taxa feed on flowerbuds, flowers and fruits (Downey 1962), and thus may exert stronger selective pressures on their foodplants than many foliage feeders (Breedlove and Ehrlich 1968). Collectively, a very broad range of foods are utilised and many lycaenids have departed from the normal lepidopteran dependence on angiosperm plants to feed on lower plants or animal material. The extent of aphytophagy, which includes predacious and mutualistic relationships with ants and various Homoptera, is sometimes both pronounced and obligatory (Cottrell 1984), so that lycaenids, as a group, participate in a wider range of ecological interactions than perhaps any other Lepidoptera.

This ecological breadth has been the basis for designation of 'biological groups' in the family (Hinton 1951; Henning 1983). Together with the relatively comprehensive knowledge of the systematics and distribution of many temperate region taxa through longterm collector accumulation, this ecological breadth renders the family of very considerable value in conservation studies. Several species have been the targets of detailed practical measures related to their conservation in recent years, and many of these case histories are summarised in the third section of this volume.

This introductory chapter enlarges on some of the topics noted above, to provide a general background to the regional and species accounts which follow.

Taxonomy

In this volume the Lycaenidae is taken to include the Riodininae (= Nemeobiinae) and the Styginae, both of which have been given family status by some researchers.

Early classifications grouped the Riodinidae and Lycaenidae s. rest. as the superfamily Lycaenoidea. Clench (1955) divided the Lycaenoidea into three families: Lycaenidae s. str., Liptenidae and Liphyridae, to which Shirozu and Yamamato (1957) added the Curetidae. In contrast, Ehrlich (1958) considered the Lycaenoidea to be a single family with the major subfamiliar groupings of Riodininae, Styginae and Lycaeninae – the latter including the four families noted in the last sentence.

While the higher classification of the two 'problem' groups has proved to be controversial, the scheme proposed by Eliot (1973) (Figure 1a) has, with some modification, received strong support. As Eliot (1973) noted, no satisfactory classification for the whole of the Lycaenidae had been produced until then, despite notable attempts by Clench (1955) and

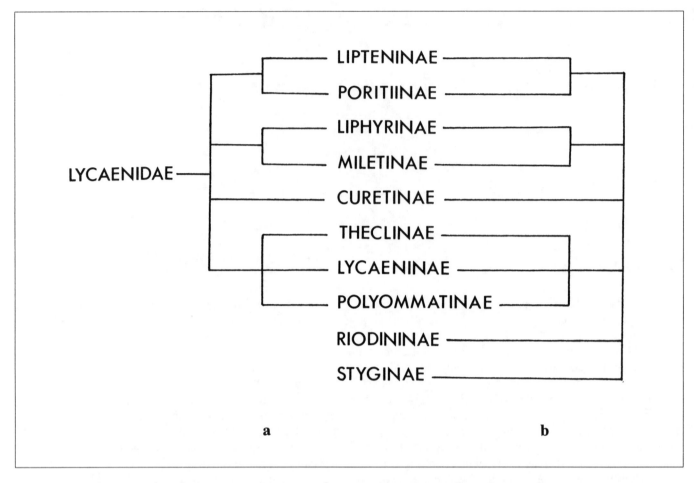

Figure 1. Classification of the Lycaenidae into major divisions: (a) after Eliot (1973); (b) after Ackery (1984).

Stempffer (1957, 1967). Other recent authorities (such as Harvey 1987), while maintaining the Riodinidae as distinct, have allied it with the Nymphalidae. However, yet others have retained the Riodinidae and Stygidae in a somewhat broader concept of the family (Ackery 1984 and Figure 1b). Thus the more recent classifications recognise eight (Eliot) or ten (Ackery) subfamilies (Figure 1). Eliot's (1973) more extensive 'tribal' divisions (Figure 2) have been more generally adopted as a working scheme by many researchers: while some of the formal divisions remain uncertain, the relationships implied appear to be valid.

There is a very wide range of chromosome numbers in the family, but the modal number appears to be $n = 24$ (Robinson 1971).

Diversity and distribution

The trio of Theclinae (hairstreaks), Riodininae (metalmarks) and Polyommatinae (blues) together comprise about 90% of the family. Some other subfamilies are small: Styginae, for example, (if recognised as distinct from Riodininae) includes only *Styx infernalis* Staudinger, from Peru. Theclinae, with well over 2000 species, is the most diverse section of the Lycaenidae.

The number of species of Lycaenidae can only be estimated. In a survey Robbins (1982) produced figures of 6000–6900, an estimate which placed Lycaenidae clearly ahead of the next most diverse family, Nymphalidae. Shields (1989) noted totals of 4089 Lycaenidae s.str. and 1366 'Riodinidae' for described taxa only. Bridges (1988) listed 16,475 species-group names and more than 4000 taxonomic publications for these groups.

Lycaenidae are most diverse in the tropics, especially the neotropics and southeast Asia, followed by Africa, and most species occur in tropical rainforest regions. For the neotropics, with 2650 ±350 spp., Riodininae and Theclinae are codominant, with only a few Polyommatinae, a single lycaenine, and very few others. The nearctic fauna, surprisingly, is not diverse, with only about half the number of species which occur in the Palaearctic. But, as any regional synopsis indicates, endemism at levels of both major geographical region and local community tends to be high.

Very few Lycaenidae are at all widely distributed. Exceptions include *Lampides boeticus* (L.) which extends from Europe to Australia and Hawaii, and *Celastrina argiolus* (L), which Eliot and Kawazoe (1983) regard as 'one of the world's commonest and most widespread butterflies'. The latter species occurs throughout most of the Palaearctic, Oriental and Nearctic

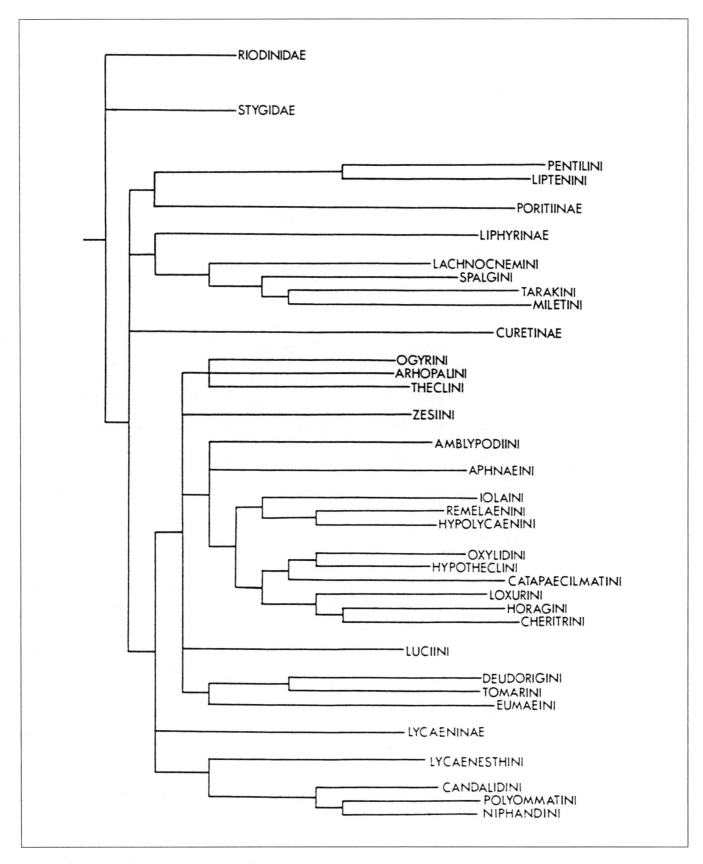

Figure 2. Classification of the Lycaenidae (after Eliot 1973).

regions, and has formed numerous putative subspecies over this broad range. The American subspecies have sometimes been regarded as separate species, *C. ladon* (Cramer) (Clench and Miller 1980).

Most lycaenids are not particularly vagile and some cannot cross even small spaces between habitat patches. Although a few are occasional migrants from Europe to Britain (*Lampides boeticus*, *Everes argiades* (Pallas), *Cyaniris semiargus* (Rottemburg)), these are apparently rather exceptional. Small Lycaenidae have apparently crossed oceanic barriers on occasion, but this process may have played only a minor role in their evolution: *Vaga* Zimmerman (in the Bonins and Hawaii) and *Hypojamides* Riley (in Tahiti) are putative examples. *L. boeticus* probably reached New Zealand from Australia (Gibbs 1980). A few lycaenids have been deliberately introduced to areas where they would not naturally occur. For example both *Strymon bazochi* Godart and *Tmolus echion* (L.) were introduced into Hawaii from Mexico early this century as potential agents for the control of lantana (Riotte and Uchida 1979).

Poor representation of many lycaenid groups in North America led Eliot (1973) to suggest that the fauna is derived from the Old World. Tentative explanations of present distribution patterns, sometimes involving a Gondwanan origin for the group with dichotomy into Riodininae and other tribes at the time of South American separation (Eliot 1973), are not wholly convincing. Anomalies occur, perhaps related to dispersal: 'coppers' (*Lycaena* F.) occur in New Zealand but not in Australia or southeast Asia, and their geographically nearest congenors are in the Himalaya. Other distribution patterns are perhaps easier to explain: *Udara (Vaga) blackburni* (Tuely) is one of only two endemic butterflies in Hawaii and it is thought that its ancestors may have progressively 'island-hopped' to this location. Members of another genus of small lycaenids, *Zizula* Chapman, may also have crossed substantial water barriers in the past; such dispersal by wind may be more frequent than commonly supposed. In Panama, Robbins and Small (1981) reported 128 species of hairstreaks being blown by the seasonal trade winds. More than 80% of these were blown through habitats where they do not normally occur.

In general, though, lycaenid faunas on remote islands are small, and climatic barriers (e.g. desert) may also counter dispersal on larger land masses. Colonisation of new habitats is clearly facilitated by the presence of larval foodplants and suitable ants, but there are few quantitative data on natural colonisation of islands or other 'new' habitats. However, on the Krakatau Islands (Indonesia), 24 species have been recorded since the sterilising volcanic eruptions of 1883: none were found in 1908, seven from 1919–1921, eight by 1928–1934, and 23 were present in the 1980s (New *et al.* 1988). Very few of these are habitual deep forest dwellers, and perhaps 15–18 of the species currently present there depend on early successional *Ipomoea pes-caprae* associations on accreting beach environments. Preservation of these rather transient associations on the islands appears to be a key theme to facilitate lycaenid colonisation from Java and/or Sumatra until more diverse vegetation is present. The eight species which have colonised

Anak Krakatau, last sterilised by volcanic activity in 1952, are all associated with such 'strand-line' vegetation. Natural opportunities to detect colonisation patterns of Lycaenidae on this scale are indeed rare.

Life histories and biology

Many species of Lycaenidae have very precise environmental needs, and a number of recent studies (especially in temperate regions) show that they may have considerable value as environmental indicators and, thus, an enhanced role in conservation studies. At this stage, though, the biology of most tropical taxa is almost entirely unknown, and a tendency to focus on the better understood temperate region forms is inevitable.

Myrmecophily

The life histories of slightly over 900 species (Downey 1962 noted 838 species) have been documented to varying extents. A remarkable feature of many of these is dependence on ants: 245 of the species noted by Downey had myrmecophilous larvae, and this dependency has attracted much attention. A tentative classification of different degrees of myrmecophily was proposed by Fiedler (1991a, 1991b).

The possible advantages of myrmecophily have been addressed by, *inter al.*, Henning (1983), Pierce (1984) and De Vries (1991a), and a broader overview of aphytophagy is given by Cottrell (1984). In general, the ants tend to protect the caterpillars from natural enemies (Pierce and Mead 1981; Pierce and Easteal 1986) and gain additional food from caterpillar secretions (Fiedler and Maschwitz 1988). Some of these mutualisms are very complex. In Panama, the ant *Ectatomma ruidum* protects caterpillars of *Thisbe irenea* (Stoll) (Riodininae) from attacks by predatory wasps, but not from tachinid fly parasitoids, for example (De Vries 1991b).

The caterpillars of *T. irenea* have an elaborate 'calling' system, and attract ants by producing sounds (De Vries 1990). Similar noises were recorded in other species, all of which depended on associations with ants to enhance their well being. The noises mimic vibrations used by the ants in their own communications. Stridulation is also well known in the pupae of many lycaenids, and one function of pupal sound production might also be to attract ants (Downey 1966).

Females of *Hypochrysops ignitus* (Leach) are attracted to colonies of ant-tended Membracidae (Sands 1986). Those of *Allotinus major* Felder & Felder lay eggs near or on membracids (probably a species of *Terentius*), using brooding adult female membracids as oviposition cues, and the caterpillars eat the membracid nymphs (Kitching 1987). Younger caterpillars sit on the membracids to feed and are thus exposed – unlike larvae of *Feniseca* Grote and *Taraka* Doherty which form silken retreats amongst their prey (Edwards 1886; Iwase 1953). Both the membracid and the caterpillars of *A. major* are tended by workers of the same ant, *Anoplolepis longipes* (Jerdon) (Kitching 1987).

In many cases, relationships between myrmecophily or aphytophagy and oviposition patterns are not as clear as in *Allotinus* Felder & Felder. Laying eggs in clusters ('clustering') in many Australian Lycaenidae is strongly associated with obligate myrmecophily (Kitching 1981), but this is not the case for neotropical Riodininae, in which myrmecophilous species lay eggs singly (Callaghan 1986). In the latter group, clustering is associated with gregarious behaviour. Myrmecophilous riodinine larvae are solitary, and gregarious larvae are not myrmecophilous. The latter may be aposematic and conspicuous, so that their protection against many predators is a function of their distastefulness. Many myrmecophilous larvae, in contrast, are rather cryptic, and accompanying ants may help to prevent them being attacked by predators and parasitoids.

Such relationships between caterpillars and ants are thus of central importance in considering the evolution and biology of Lycaenidae and have attracted much attention.

Myrmecophily and evolution in lycaenids

Symbiosis with ants may have been an early development in the evolution of Lycaenidae (Eliot 1973), and both Hinton (1951) and Malicky (1969) suggested that ancestral lycaenids were myrmecophilous. Contrary to Pierce's (1987) conclusion that the distribution of myrmecophily in Lycaenidae does not reflect phylogeny, Fiedler (1991a, 1991b) believed that there was a strongly phylogenetic relationship present.

However, there is some possible confusion over roles of myrmecophily in lycaenoid evolution as their influences on Riodinines and the other taxa may be markedly different (De Vries 1991a). Not only are they the most common basis for suggesting ecological groupings in the family (Henning 1983), but the evolution of lycaenid diversity itself may also be involved. Pierce (1984) suggested that lycaenid diversity may reflect speciation in relation to other butterfly families, and that this could be influenced by larvae/ant associations in two important ways:

1. Female lycaenids may adopt ants as oviposition cues (Fiedler and Maschwitz 1989, on *Anthene emolus* (Godart)) so that the presence of ants on a novel foodplant may induce a rapid host switch. Although few such 'oviposition mistakes' (Pierce 1984) may actually lead to range extensions, it may be more important for a given lycaenid to retain a particular ant association than a particular foodplant, and an increase in the number of ovipositions on different foodplants may increase the number of opportunities for subsequent speciation. Essentially, novel foodplant choices may be made by female lycaenids to an unusually high degree because they select for ants **as well as** for chemically and physically suitable foodplants. A 'new' hostplant may occupy a different ecological range from those utilised earlier, and population isolates could thus be formed.

2. The general non-vagility of many lycaenids results in their occurrence in small, semi-isolated populations with rather little regular genetic interchange between them. Pierce (1983) showed that a deme of the Australian *Jalmenus evagoras* (Donovan) may be restricted to a single *Acacia* tree, where males aggregate and compete for emerging females so that variability in male reproductive success effectively reduces population size further. Such patchy distributions (also noted in the North American *Glaucopsyche lygdamus* Doubleday: Pierce 1984) occur in spite of apparent continuous foodplant availability and it is quite possible that they result from selection of foodplant areas which are high in nitrogen, as well as having the required ants. Many myrmecophilous lycaenid larvae actively prefer nitrogen-rich foodplants and plant parts such as seed pods and flowers. This may be explained in part by the need to supply ants with amino acids as a 'nutrient reward' for tending the larvae (Pierce 1984).

Larval feeding

The overall importance of plant-feeding to caterpillars of Lycaenidae differs substantially between different subfamilies, and those of some groups rarely take plant food. As far as is known, all species of Poritiinae and Lycaeninae are normally phytophagous. Some Curetinae are phytophagous. Lipteninae are also plant feeders, but are highly unusual amongst butterflies in that larval food usually consists of algae, fungi or lichens (see Cottrell 1984, for summary). Most genera of the two largest subfamilies, Theclinae and Polyommatinae, appear to be phytophagous or opportunistically carnivorous with varying degrees of dependence on prey. *Maculinea* van Eecke and *Lepidochrysops* Hedicke larvae are phytophagous when young, but the late instars are obligate predators of ant larvae. Other aphytophagous genera are noted in Table 1. Both Liphyrinae and Miletinae appear to be entirely aphytophagous, and the unlisted genera in Table 1 reflect ignorance of their larval biology, rather than known phytophagy. *Liphyra* Westwood and *Euliphyra* Holland larvae are probably specific feeders on early stages of tree ants (*Oecophylla* spp): their larvae are flattened and have a heavily armoured cuticle which enables them to withstand ant attacks. The pupa of *Liphyra* remains inside the last larval skin, which thereby functions as a puparium.

Aslauga larvae are predators of Homoptera, at least as late instars. Eggs of Miletinae are typically laid near colonies of Homoptera, including aphids, coccids and membracids and some, at least, are found on a wide range of different hostplants. Although the larvae are predominantly predators, some younger instars may also feed on honeydew or other insect secretions such as aphid cornicle secretions.

Selection of foodplant species by phytophagous species, and their effects on foodplants, are difficult to study. Flower predation of a range of perennial herbaceous legumes by *Glaucopsyche lygdamus* in Colorado differed substantially between species (Breedlove and Ehrlich 1972), with either *Lupinus* or *Theropsis* being by far the most heavily attacked plant at each of a series of sites. On both plant genera, flower-feeding can markedly reduce seed-set (Breedlove and Ehrlich 1968, 1972). Whereas *G. lygdamus* females select inflorescences

Table 1. Lycaenidae with larvae which do not feed on plants (after Cottrell 1984, based on Eliot 1973).

Subfamily	Number of		Aphytophagous genera*
	Tribes	Genera	
Lipteninae	2	46	(none)
Poritiinae	1	7	(none)
Liphyrinae	1	5	(3) *Liphyra, Euliphyra, Aslauga*
Miletinae	4	12	(8) *Miletus, Allotinus, Megalopalpus, Taraka, Spalgis, Feniscea, Lachnocnema, Thestor*
Curetinae	1	1	(none)
Theclinae	19	241	(7) *Acrodipsas, Shirozua, Zesius, Spindasis, Oxychaeta, Trimenia, Argyrocupha*
Lycaeninae	1	18	(none)
Polyommatinae	4	149	(4) *Triclena, Niphanda, Maculinea, Lepidochrysops*

* Members of some genera are partially phytophagous, some only in the early instars (e.g. *Maculinea, Lepidochrysops*).

of less hairy *Lupinus* species on which to lay, the reverse trend is true of *Plebejus icarioides* Boisduval, which oviposits on the **most** hairy (non-floral parts) of *Lupinus* by preference (Downey 1962). Some caution is needed in extrapolating from laboratory feeding trials to the field – thus, captive larvae of *P. icarioides* will feed on any species of *Lupinus* proffered (Downey and Fuller 1961) but wild populations normally utilise only a few of the species available in their habitat. There may also be a pronounced seasonal variation in foodplant quality: *P. acmon* (Westwood) and related species utilise some foodplants only at particular times of the year (Goodpasture 1974). *J. evagoras* females preferred to oviposit on potted *Acacia* which had been given nitrogenous fertiliser rather than on similar plants given water alone (Baylis and Pierce 1991).

Comparatively few species of Lycaenidae seem to be markedly polyphagous and many clearly have very restricted ranges of foodplants. Broad taxonomic ranges of foodplants – such as the 30 or so species (representing the families Selaginaceae, Lamiaceae, Verbenaceae, Fabaceae and Geraniaceae) recorded for *Lepidochrysops* in Africa (Cottrell 1984) – are commonly recorded only for taxa which are later ant-feeders. However, there is evidence of more local host restriction for *Lepidochrysops*, so that in any one area only a single plant genus is used for oviposition (Cottrell 1984). In general support of this relationship between polyphagy and ant attendance, a broad foodplant range for *Hypochrysops miskini* (Waterhouse) in Queensland led Valentine and Johnson (1989) to suggest that rainforest lycaenids may be polyphagous because a narrow choice of plants may be restrictive and cancel out advantages of ant-attendance. In Queensland, rainforest species confined to single host plant species tend not to be ant-attended.

Rarely, different generations of the same species may utilise different foodplants: the first (spring) generation of *Celastrina argiolus* (L.) in Europe feeds on holly, while the second (summer) generation larvae eat ivy. This species also shows marked seasonal dimorphism, but it is not clear if this is food-related.

Nitrogen-rich plant feeding is a characteristic of many lycaenid taxa. Pierce (1985) has noted that caterpillars of lycaenids from Australia, South Africa and North America have been recorded feeding on most known non-leguminous, nitrogen-fixing plant families. Several species of Cycadaceae are included, and most Lipteninae are probably specialised lichen-feeders. There are, of course, exceptions: the non-myrmecophilous riodinine *Sarota gyas* (Cramer) in Panama and Costa Rica feeds exclusively on epiphylls (De Vries 1988), and those epiphylls tested were not nitrogen-fixers. Females of this species lay eggs on taxonomically disparate hostplants with old leaves covered by epiphylls. In many other lycaenids, though, ovipositions on reproductive structures of larval foodplants may reflect selection for high nitrogen levels in the future larval food.

Feeding on floral structures may itself engender polyphagy: Robbins and Aiello (1982) noted that the thecline *Strymon melinus* (Hübner) is one of the most polyphagous butterfly species known, and has been recorded feeding on flowers of 46 genera in 21 families of plants. Members of the genus *Callophrys* Billberg also feed on plants of some 11 families (Pratt and Ballmer 1991). Polyphagy of this sort might be an important ecological strategy for the lycaenids in exploiting and adjusting to changing environmental conditions and could be a correlate of *r*-selection. Flower-feeding could, perhaps, allow larval access to plants when the foliage is not available due to their chemical defences (Robbins and Aiello 1982), and it is likely that some lycaenids in the tropics have life cycles which are well adapted to exploit peak flowering seasons of putative foodplants. Robbins and Aiello cite data (Croat 1978) that peak flowering on Barro Colorado Island (Panama) occurs at the end of the dry season, a period corresponding with a marked increase in abundance of Lycaenidae but a decrease of many other butterflies. Such seasonal apparency may be an important feature facilitating the use of tropical lycaenids as indicators of habitat quality. It may also facilitate ecologically important dispersal, as the butterflies are abundant at the time of strong sustained dry season trade winds (Robbins and Small 1981). Samples were skewed heavily toward females, and many of the 128 species were being blown through habitats where they do not occur normally.

Most phytophagous lycaenid larvae are external feeders, either eating whole plant tissues or organs, or skeletonising foliage. However, *Callophyrys xami* (Reakirt) in Mexico feeds on fleshy-leaved Crassulaceae and, on *Echeveria gibbiflora*, caterpillars may burrow completely into the leaves and feed on the fleshy internal pulp. Wastes are expelled through the entrance hole (Ziegler and Escalante 1964). Larvae of some other *Callophrys* (such as *C. viridis* (Edwards)) feed on flowers of *Eriopsis* and, as with other larvae with similar habits, they resemble their foodplant flowers in coloration (Brown and Opler 1967). Variation in larval coloration occurs in other taxa, such as *Zizina labradus* (Godart) in Australia (Sibatani 1984).

Although it is clear that very considerable trophic specialisation occurs in many lycaenids – both in phytophagous and aphytophagous species where intricate and obligate relationships with other animals are common – little is known of the biology of most species of the family. The precise resource needs of many specialised species cannot yet be appreciated fully, but they are likely to render the species very susceptible to habitat change and consequent changes in resource supply.

Adult feeding

Adult lycaenids (of Theclinae, Lycaeninae and Polyommatinae) commonly seek nectar from flowers, although some Theclinae may depend more on aphid honeydew. In contrast, Lipteninae and Miletinae are not known to visit flowers, and depend on secretions from extrafloral nectaries or on homopteran honeydew. Adult *Liphyra* lack a proboscis and thus cannot feed. A few taxa may feed on secretions from the dorsal nectary organ of other ant-tended lycaenid larvae.

Adult sexual dimorphism

This is widespread in the family. Commonly, males are brighter (either the females are browner or have wider, dark borders to the wings). Indeed, in some taxa it is difficult to associate the sexes correctly because of relatively extreme dimorphism. Males may have modified scales or sex-brands on either surface of the forewing or on the upperside of the hindwing. These may be associated with hair-tufts but, more commonly, distinct sex brands are absent and androconia are scattered irregularly over the upper surface of the wings.

Adult behaviour

Males of some species are regular hill-toppers: some species of the '*Lycaenopsis*-group', for example, are rarely seen elsewhere,

and both sexes of some species of *Monodontides* Toxopeus appear to be hill-top residents (Eliot and Kawazoe 1983). Hill-topping may be common in riodinines (Shields 1967).

Protandry may occur regularly in some lycaenids. Males of *Polyommatus icarus* (Rottemburg) not only emerge before the females but also fly more strongly. Males of this genus interact strongly with other males, and it seems that the bright male colours may indeed be 'directed' at other males. Lundgren (1977) made the intriguing suggestion that the high frequency of the inter-male encounters may aid in regulating dispersal and population density, and this may occur also between groups of sympatric species with similar appearance.

Displays and pheromones both appear to be involved in ensuring conspecific matings in lycaenids living in the same area. The female anal hair-tuft of *Nordmannia* Tutt may play a role in courtship (Nakamura 1976). Multiple copulations can occur (Fujii, 1989, on *Shirozua janasi* (Janson)), and it is possible that copulatory mate guarding occurs in this thecline. The time of day for mating differs between species: *S. janasi* copulates during the day whereas two species of *Japonica* Tutt mate at dusk (Fujii 1989). There are occasional records of cross-taxon matings, sometimes even between subfamilies (Shapiro 1985), or even families (Shapiro 1982; Johnson 1984), usually between phenotypically similar butterflies.

'Perching' behaviour appears to be an important isolating mechanism in Riodininae (Callaghan 1979, 1983). Neotropical riodinines appear to have developed a range of different perching strategies which help to maintain specific isolation within the habitat. Habitat complexity is an important facet of this aspect of these forest butterflies, as the spacing of perching sites and positions of perching differ considerably between genera – by topographic features, by light/shadow regimes and by time of day. Following earlier accounts by Scott (1968) and Shields (1967), Callaghan suggested that perching (and hill-topping) species tend to have low population densities, and 'rendezvous' localities help such rarer species to find mates. Perching for short periods (an average of 2.4h in 10 riodinine genera) minimises exposure to predators. Different perching strategies are enhanced by ethological strategies such as displays. When males are scarce females may actively search out perching sites and await them if they are ready to mate. Ethological isolating mechanisms of this sort may be more important in taxa which are not strict deep forest dwellers.

Perching behaviour of different species of Cupressaceae-feeding *Callophrys* is distinctly non-random (Johnson and Borgo 1976). The insects apparently orientate to the position of the sun, and taller trees are most often selected for perching on. Perching posture in lycaenids, as in other butterflies, may have an important role in thermoregulation (Clench 1966).

Lycaenidae which are normally 'perchers' rather than 'patrollers' may at times undergo sustained flights and the down-valley flights of four such species of Theclini in Colorado and Arizona (Scott 1973) appeared to be a food-seeking behaviour. This may also be so for *Satyrium* Scudder in California (MacNeill 1967). Some species fly only at particular times of the day and, within a genus, species co-occurring at the same locality may not overlap in their flight periodicity (see Sibatani 1992, on *Favonius* Sibatani & Ito).

Some very small blues are extremely weak fliers, as suggested earlier. Some have elongated narrow wings which, at least in *Zizula hylax* (F.), enable the butterflies to crawl into the corollas of long-tubed flowers and obtain nectar (Ehrlich and Ehrlich 1972).

Defence against predators

It has been suggested that a few adult Lycaenidae participate in mimicry complexes, either with other blues or other kinds of Lepidoptera. I have netted specimens of *Udara* Toxopeus in stream beds in New Guinea in the belief that they were small members of one of the many species of *Delias* Hübner (Pieridae) in the same habitat; *Plebejus icarioides* may be a model for the noctuid moth *Caenurgina caerulea* Grote in North America (Downey 1965); and male *Lycaena heteronea* Boisduval may be a mimic of *G. lygdamus* and other sympatric blues (Austin 1972). The latter feed on plants containing alkaloids (*Lupinus*) or selenium (*Astragalus*), while the foodplants of the *Lycaena* (*Eriogonum*) apparently do not. However, experimental investigations of this scenario do not appear to have been made. In Sierra Leone, *Pseudaletis leonis* (Staudinger) may be a mimic of a similarly-patterned diurnal arctiid moth, or of a larger danaine (Owen 1991).

Other putative defences against predators include the chemical defence of *Eumaeus atala* (Poey). This species sequesters a deterrent defensive chemical (cycasin) from larval cycad foodplants, and this clearly renders the adults unpalatable to birds (Bowers and Larin 1989). Cycasin also deters attack by *Camponotus* ants. Adult *E. atala* are aposematic, and the genus is mimicked by several other Lepidoptera (including species of Castniidae and Noctuidae) in South America. Further examples of defence can be found at all growth stages: the 'false heads', including hindwing tails of many adults (Robbins 1980, 1981); the 'monkey head' pupae of *Spalgis* Moore (Hinton 1974); sound production by pupae of some taxa; unusual hairiness or thickened cuticle of some caterpillars; and the female anal hair-tuft of some species of *Nordmannia* which is used to cover eggs with long scales at the time of oviposition.

Even mode of hatching from the egg may be correlated with protection from natural enemy attack: caterpillars of *Maculinea alcon* (Denis & Schiffermüller) and *M. rebeli* (Hirschke) hatch through the base of the eggshell and emerge on the opposite side of the leaf (Thomas *et al.* 1991). The 'normal' exposed eggshells are unusually thick, perhaps to counter enemy attack.

Particularly in the tropics, lycaenid biology is almost unstudied at other than the most superficial levels. Most information, including that which has led to tentative generalisations for the family, has been derived from temperate region species. Even for the best-studied lycaenid faunas, there are many gaps in fundamental biological knowledge.

Endangering processes

In their review of threatened swallowtail butterflies, Collins and Morris (1985) enumerate a number of processes which may lead to the decline of these butterflies, and it is instructive to assess the effects of these processes on the ecologically very different Lycaenidae.

Collecting and trade

The effects of collecting are controversial and difficult to evaluate fully. Many lycaenids occur in small closed populations and because of this may be much more vulnerable to localised collector pressure than many other butterflies. There is at least some suggestion, for example, that the demise of the Large Copper, *Lycaena dispar* (Haworth), in Britain in the mid-nineteenth century was in part due to increased collector pressure on populations which had been rendered vulnerable by habitat destruction. In most cases collecting is probably the subsidiary rather than the prime cause of decline or extinction. Perhaps, especially in northern temperate regions, there is reason to suggest that this syndrome could occur for many localised taxa sought by collectors who visit the same colony year by year.

Even specialist collecting to help monitoring of restricted colonies for conservation assessment may cause direct damage to populations: Murphy (1989) has recently pointed out that conventional mark-recapture studies used to estimate population sizes of taxa of conservation interest may cause inadvertent damage, either by mutilation through handling, or by inducing changes in individual behaviour. Small delicate butterflies, such as most lycaenids, may be particularly vulnerable to such effects.

Commercial collecting is of considerably less importance for Lycaenidae than for large showy butterflies. Rare species from unusual localities will always find a market amongst wealthy collectors and museums, but the 'ornament' and 'souvenir' trades in Lycaenidae are very low. In Malaysia, for example, the vast bulk of this trade is in Papilionidae and Nymphalidae: in stores in Kuala Lumpur in 1988, I noticed only very few Lycaenidae (all relatively large species of *Arhopala* Boisduval and related genera). In general, for this trade, 'small' is distinctly not 'beautiful' or desirable.

Similarly, Lycaenidae are not particularly desired as exhibits in butterfly houses, and the difficulty of rearing many of the species may also be a deterrent in this context. Collins (1987a) lists only eight species of Lycaenidae (of 223 butterfly species in total) on show in a sample of 18 butterfly houses in Britain in 1986 (Table 2). Seven of these were obtained as pupae, but the Malaysian *Spindasis syama* (Horsfield) were apparently obtained as adults by the one exhibitor.

A total collecting ban is difficult to enforce, especially on unreserved public land – indeed, it is impossible without wardenship or other constant (and probably expensive) security measures. Even responsible, private collectors obeying voluntary restrictive quota codes may cause harm if they are in sufficient numbers. As Collins and Morris (1985) commented for Papilionidae 'there is a danger that collectors may be unable to recognise when they are depleting butterfly stocks below the threshold of recovery, particularly when they only visit the breeding area for short periods of time'. Although no Lycaenidae are currently listed in CITES Appendices, a number of rare or local species have received local legislative protection (if not more tangible conservation) through bans on collecting. In addition, over 40 species are mentioned in various country-based European legislation (Collins 1987b and Table 3) and 28 taxa are listed in the United States Federal Register of Endangered and Threatened Wildlife. The most prolific, and probably the least discriminating legislation is in India, where some 160 species are listed under the Wildlife Protection Act (Table 4). The Code of Conservation Responsibility adopted by commercial entomologists in Britain in 1974, restricts trade in a number of species (including *Maculinea arion* (L.), then still extant in Britain) to specimens already in 'circulation', so that the only legal way that a collector can purchase examples of these species is from the limited pool already in collections.

Seventy-nine lycaenid taxa are included in the IUCN Red List of Threatened Animals (1990) (Table 5). Many of these are also cited in various country-based legislations.

Habitat alteration and destruction

This is the prime threat to all lycaenid species with limited distributions and low vagility, and has already been the agent of major declines of many of these – as the examples discussed later in this volume attest. Lycaenid taxa are particularly susceptible to certain types of habitat alteration including: changes in forestry practices in tropical and temperate regions; conversion of shrublands to pasture and agricultural lands; wetland drainage; heathland succession; grassland management practices; the effects of grazing animals such as rabbits; and expanding urban, industrial and recreational land use.

In common with all other animals and plants, levels of concern therefore range from large-scale destruction of tropical rainforests whose biota have scarcely been documented (and in many cases never now can be), to small, local habitat changes

in 'ordinary' vegetation such as grassland or heathland. Such changes have, of course, occurred in many parts of the world, and in many major areas their effects have been both unheralded and undocumented so that we can merely infer, from the present status of taxa and knowledge of their biology as this accumulates, the magnitude of their effects. Only rarely outside northern temperate regions has conservation awareness for Lycaenidae progressed to the stage where concern can be shown in any practical manner. There, it is sometimes abundantly clear that decline of species or assemblages, and the initiation of concern for their conservation, has been engendered by particular localised human activities – sometimes as 'one-off' destructive events, sometimes more broadly. Many of the former apply to remnant populations which represent formerly much more widespread taxa which have become progressively vulnerable over a longer time. In other parts of the world, very many species have been recorded only from single or highly disjunct localities, and even sound demonstration of their abundance or dependence on particular habitats is difficult or impossible at this time. In short, status evaluation is difficult or impossible, and the option of habitat protection, in the interest of decreasing or eliminating perceived threats, is the most urgent option.

In contrast to most Papilionidae, grassland and other open vegetation types are vitally important habitats to many Lycaenidae. In Europe, calcareous grassland is a particularly important lycaenid habitat which has undergone large scale and sometimes dramatic changes. The extinction of *Cyaniris semiargus* (Rottemburg) in Britain as long ago as 1877 has been attributed to changes in grassland management (Heath 1981).

While 'traditional' methods of land and vegetation maintenance, such as coppicing of forests, may foster the well-being of some species, intensification of agricultural practices has caused concern for some. Wetlands are particularly vulnerable to such changes and a number of European wetland Lycaenidae are under threat. Some species of *Maculinea* and *Lycaena* restricted to this habitat are particularly endangered. Drainage of the fens in England last century was a prime cause of decline of *Lycaena dispar*.

Urbanisation has caused concern for lycaenids in places as far apart as Los Angeles, California and Melbourne, Australia.

Table 2. Lycaenidae flown in butterfly houses in Britain (Collins 1987a).

Species	Native range	Origin of material
Eumaeus atala	Caribbean	U.S.A.: Florida
Lampides boeticus	(widespread)	Sri Lanka, Malaysia
Lycaena helle	Europe, Asia	France
L. phlaeas	Europe, Asia	France
Narathura centaurus	Malaysia	Malaysia
Polyommatus icarus	Europe	U.K
Spindasis syama	Asia	Malaysia
Telicada nyseus	East Asia	Sri Lanka, Malaysia

Table 3. Lycaenidae protected by legislation in Europe (from Collins 1987b).

(i) Areas which protect Lycaenidae as part of 'all butterflies' or a similar ordinance, sometimes with exceptions for particular Pieridae stated. Date of legislation given in parentheses:

Austria: Niederösterreich (1978), Salzburg (1980), Steiermark (1936), Tyrol (1975), Öberösterreich (1982), Vienna (1985), Vorarlberg (1979).
Germany: (Law of German Democratic Republic 1984*).
Luxembourg: (1986).

(ii) Particular taxa

Taxon	Country	Date of legislation
Agrodiaetus admetus	Greece	(1980)
A. damon	Hungary	(1982)
A. ripartii	Greece	(1980)
Aricia agestis	Hungary	(1982)
A. crassipuncta	Germany (FR)	(1986)*
A. taberdiana	Germany (FR)	(1986)
Callophrys mystaphia	Germany (FR)	(1986)
C. suaveola	Germany (FR)	(1986)
Cupido osiris	Hungary	(1982)
Cyaniris helena	Greece	(1980)
Eumedonia damon	Hungary	(1982)
Freyeria trochylus	Greece	(1980)
Iolana iolas	Hungary	(1982)
Kretania eurypilus	Germany (FR)	(1986)
K. psylorita	Germany (FR)	(1986)
	Greece	(1980)
Lycaeides argyrognomon	Belgium: Wallone Region	(1985)
L. idas	Belgium: Flemish Region	(1980)
	Belgium: Wallone Region	(1985)
	Finland	(1976)
	France (females only)	(1979)
	Germany (FR)	(1986)
	Hungary	(1982)
	Netherlands	(1973)
L. helle	Belgium: Wallone Region	(1985)
	France (females only)	(1979)
	Germany (FR)	(1986)
	Hungary	(1982)
Lysandra bellargus	Belgium: Wallone Region	(1985)
	France (*L. b. coelestis*, females only)	(1979)
L. caucasica	Germany (FR)	(1986)
Maculinea alcon	Belgium: Flemish Region	(1980)
	Germany (FR)	(1986)
M. arion	Belgium: Flemish Region	(1980)
	Belgium: Wallone Region	(1985)
	Germany (FR)	(1986)
	United Kingdom	(1981)
M. nausithous	Germany (FR)	(1986)
	Hungary	(1982)
M. rebeli	Belgium: Wallone Region	(1985)
	Germany (FR)	(1986)

Continued...

Table 3 (cont.). Lycaenidae protected by legislation in Europe (from Collins 1987b).

Taxon	Country	Date of legislation
M. teleius	Belgium: Flemish Region	(1980)
	France (M. t. burdigalensis, females only)	(1979)
Neolycaena coelestina	Germany (FR)	(1986)
Nordmannia acaciae	Belgium: Wallone Region	(1985)
N. armenia	Germany (FR)	(1986)
N. marcidus	Germany (FR)	(1986)
N. sassanides	Germany (FR)	(1986)
Paleochrysophanus hippothoe	Hungary	(1982)
Plebejus pylaon	Hungary	(1982)
Polyommatus eros	Greece	(1980)
Pseudophilotes bavius	Germany (FR)	(1986)
Strymonidia pruni	Greece	(1980)
S. myrrhina	Germany (FR)	(1986)
Thersamonia thetis	Greece	(1986)
Tomares callimachus	Germany (FR)	(1986)
T. romanovi	Germany (FR)	(1986)
Turanana panagea	Greece	(1980)
Vacciniina optilate	Germany (FR)	(1986)
Zizeeria knysna	Greece (Z. k. cassandra)	(1980)

* FR = Federal Republic: it is not yet clear how the former laws for FRG and DDR will operate for a unified Germany.

Table 4. Lycaenidae listed in The Indian Wildlife (Protection) Act, 1972.
Note: the scientific names are given as spelled in the Act – a number of spelling errors are present in the listing.

1. Schedule 1. Part IV (Collection and trade, including gift, prohibited)

		Liphyra brassolis	Butterfly, moth
		Listeria dudgenni	Lister's hairstreak
Allotinus drumila	Darkie, crenulate/great	Logania watsoniana subfasciata	Mottle, Watson's
A. fabious penormis	Angled darkie	Lycaenopsis binghami	Hedge blue
Amblopala avidiena	Hairstreak, Chinese	L. haraldus ananga	Hedge blue, Felder's
Amblypodia ace arata	Leaf blue	L. puspa prominens	Common hedge blue
A. alea constanceae	Rosy oakblue	L. quadriplaga dohertyi	Naga hedge blue
A. ammonariel	Malayan bush blue	Nacaduba noreia hampsoni	Limeblue, white-tipped
A. arvina ardea	Purple brown tailless oakblue	Polymatus orbitulus leela	Greenish mountain blue
A. asopia	Plain tailless oakblue	Pratapa icetas mishmia	Royal, dark blue
A. comica	Comic oakblue	Simiskina phalena harterti	Brilliant, broadbanded
A. opalina	Opal oakblue	Sinthusa virgo	Spark, pale
A. zeta	Andaman tailless oakblue	Spindasis elwesi	Silverline, Elwe's
Biduanda melisa cyana	Blue posy	S. rukmini	Silverline, khaki
Callophyrs leechii	Hairstreak, ferruginous	Strymon mackwoodi	Hairstreak, Mackwood's
Castalius rosimon alarbus	Pierrot, common	Tajuria ister	Royal, uncertain
Charana cepheis	Mandarin blue, Cachar	T. luculentus nela	Royal, Chinese
Chlioria othona	Tit, orchid	T. yajna yajna	Royal, chestnut and black
Deudoryx epijarbas amatius	Cornelian, scarce	Thecla ataxua zulla	Wonderful hairstreak
Everes moorei	Cupid, Moore's	T. bieti mendera	Indian purple hairstreak
Gerydus biggsii	Bigg's brownie	T. letha	Watson's hairstreak
G. symethus diopeithes	Great Brownie	T. paona	Paona hairstreak
Heliophorus hybrida	Sapphires	T. pavo	Peacock hairstreak
Horaga albimacula	Onyxes	Virachala smilis	Guava blues
Jamides ferrari	Caeruleans		

Continued...

Table 4 (cont.). Lycaenidae listed in The Indian Wildlife (Protection) Act, 1972.

2. Schedule II. Part II. ('Special game': licence needed to collect or trade.)

Allotinus subviolaceous manychus
Amblypodia abetrans
A. aenea
A. agaba aurelia
A. agrata
A. alesia
A. apidanus ahamus
A. areste areste
A. bazaloides
A. camdeo
A. ellisi
A. fulla ignara
A. ganesa watsoni
A. paragenesa zephpreeta
A. paralea
A. silhetensis
A. suffusa suffusa
A. yendava
Apharitis lilacinus
Araotes lapithis
Artipe eryx
Bindahara phocides
Bothrinia chennellia
Castraleus roxus manluena
Catapoecilma delicatum
C. elegans myostina
Charana jalindra
Cheritrella truncipennis
Chliaria kina
Deudoryx hypargyria gaetulia
Enchrysops enejus
Everes kala
Helipphorus androcles moorei
Horaga onyx
H. viola
Hypolycaena nilgirica
H. thecloides nicobarica
Iraota rochana boswelliana
Jamides alectokandulana
J. exleodus para
J. coeruleus
J. kankena
Lampides boeticus
Lilacea albocaerulea
L. atroguttata
L. lilacea
L. melaena
L. minima
Logania massalia
Lycaenesthes lycaenina
Mahathala ameria
M. atkinsoni
Magisba malaya presbyter
Nacaduba aluta coelestis
N. ancyra aberrans
N. dubiosa fulva
N. helicon
N. herus major
N. pactolus
Neucheritra febronia

Niphanda cymbia
Orthomiella pontis
Pithecops fulgens
Polymmatus devanica devanica
P. metallica metallica
P. orbitulus jaloka
P. younghusbandi
Poritia erycinoides elisei
P. hewitsoni
P. plusrata geta
Pratapa bhetes
P. blanka
P. deva
P. icetas
Rapala buxaria
R. chandrana chandrana
R. nasaka
R. refulgens
R. rubida
R. scintilla
R. sphinx sphinx
R. varuna
Spindasis elima elima
S. lohita
S. nipalicus
Suasa lisidus
Surendra todara
Tajuria albiplaga
T. cippus cippus
T. culta
T. diaeus
T. illurgioides
T. illurgis
T. jangala andamanica
T. melastigma
T. sebonga
T. thyia
T. yajna istroides
T. callinara
Tarucus dharta
Thaduka multicaudata kanara
Thecla ataxus ataxus
T. bitel
T. icana
T. jakamensis
T. kabreea
T. khasia
T. kirbariensis
T. suroia
T. syla assamica
T. vittata
T. ziha
T. zoa
Una usta
Yasoda tripunctata

3. Schedule IV. ('Small game': small game hunting licence needed to collect.)

Tarucus ananda

Table 5. Lycaenidae included on the 1990 IUCN Red List of Threatened Animals.

Taxon	Status	Country
Alaena margaritacea	V	South Africa
Aloeides caledoni	V	South Africa
A. dentatis	R	South Africa
A. egerides	V	South Africa
A. lutescens	V	South Africa
Argyrocupha malagrida malagrida	V	South Africa
A. m. paarlensis	V	South Africa
Callophrys mossii bayensis	E	U.S.A.
Capys penningtoni	E	South Africa
Chrysoritis cotrelli	I	South Africa
C. oreas	I	South Africa
C. zeuxo	I	South Africa
Cyclyrius mandersi	I	Mauritius
Deloneura immaculata	Ex?	South Africa
D. millari millari	V	South Africa
Deudorix penningtoni	V	South Africa
D. vansoni	V	South Africa
Durbania limbata	V	South Africa
Erikssonia acraeina	R	South Africa
Eumaeus atala florida	V	U.S.A.
Everes comyntax texanus	Ex	(U.S.A.)
Glaucopsyche lygdamus palosverdesensis	Ex?	U.S.A.
G. xerces	Ex	(U.S.A.)
Hemiargus thomasi bethune-bakeri	I	U.S.A.
Icaricia icarioides missionensis	E	U.S.A.
I. i. moroensis	I	U.S.A.
I. i. pheres	I	U.S.A.
Lepidochrysops ariadne	E	South Africa
L. bacchus	V	South Africa
L. hypolia	Ex?	South Africa
L. loewensteini	V	South Africa
L. lotana	E	South Africa
L. methymna dicksoni	E	South Africa
L. titei	V	South Africa
Lycaeides argyrognomon lotis	E	U.S.A.
L. melissa samuelis	I	U.S.A.
Lycaena dispar	E	northern Europe
L. dorcas claytoni	I	U.S.A.
L. hermes	I	Mexico, U.S.A.
Maculinea alcon	V	Europe, USSR
M. arion	V	Europe, USSR
M. arionides	V	China, Japan, USSR

Continued...

Table 5. (cont.) Lycaenidae included on the 1990 IUCN Red List of Threatened Animals.

Taxon	Status	Country
M. nausithous	E	Europe, USSR
M. rebeli	V	south & central Europe
M. teleius	E	Europe, northern Asia
M. t. burdigalensis	E	France
Notarthrinus binghami	R	India
Oreolyce dohertyi	R	India
Ornipholidotos peucetia penningtoni	I	Mozambique, S. Africa
Oxychaeta dicksoni	E	South Africa
Panchala ganesa loomisi	E	Japan
Philotiella speciosa bohartorum	I	U.S.A.
Plebejus emigdionis	I	U.S.A.
P. icarioides missionensis	E	U.S.A.
Plebicula golgus	E	Spain
Poecilmitis adonis	V	South Africa
P. aureus	I	South Africa
P. endymion	V	South Africa
P. lyncurium	V	South Africa
P. nigricans	V	South Africa
P. rileyi	V	South Africa
Pseudalmenus chlorinda chlorinda	I	Australia: Tasmania
P. c. conara	I	Australia: Tasmania
Pseudiolaus lulua	V	South Africa
Shijimiaeoides battoides allyni	E	U.S.A.
S. b. comstocki	I	U.S.A.
S. enoptes smithi	E	U.S.A.
S. lanstoni	I	U.S.A.
S. rita mattoni	I	U.S.A.
Spindasis collinsi	V	Tanzania
Strymon acis bartrami	I	U.S.A.
S. avalona	K	U.S.A.
Thestor dicksoni dicksoni	V	South Africa
T. kaplani	V	South Africa
T. tempe	V	South Africa
Trimenia wallegrenii	V	South Africa
Uranothauma usambarae	V	Tanzania

(Categories defined in Appendix 1).

Increasing human recreational activities constitute another serious threat to many habitats all over the world and the following list, while far from exhaustive, gives some idea of the range of habitats involved:

- coastal sand dunes in California are threatened by off-road vehicles and trampling;
- alpine heathlands and meadows in Europe and southeastern Australia are threatened by the construction of ski-lifts, runs, access roads, car parks and resort accommodation and facilities;
- Pacific islands habitats are threatened by the proliferation of golf courses and by the exotic vegetation often introduced;
- mangrove swamps in eastern Australia are threatened by coastal resort development.

In many cases these recreational activities involve the degradation of particularly sensitive habitats which tend to support isolated, relict and often taxonomically discrete populations of lycaenids and other insects.

Examples could be multiplied several-fold, but the principle is well established, and the vital importance of suitable habitat and resources for conserving small animal and plant populations should not need further emphasis.

Pollution

The effects of chemical pollution on lycaenids are difficult to assess, but a number of declines of particular species in Europe have been attributed in part to atmospheric pollution, including acid rain. Such pollution is likely to affect the well being of sensitive foodplants and a wide spectrum of invertebrates associated with vegetation. Likewise, pesticide drift may cause occasional hazard, both in agricultural and forest environments.

Exotic introductions

No significant information is available on the deleterious effects of exotic taxa on native Lycaenidae in many parts of the world. The introduction of Dutch Elm Disease into Britain, with consequent large scale demise of *Ulmus* trees, led to a reduction in the numbers of the Whiteletter Hairstreak, *Strymonidia w-album* (Knoch). Similarly, the introduction of myxomatosis to Britain in the 1950s resulted in a drastic reduction of the intensity of rabbit grazing on chalk grasslands, with a resultant reduction in the numbers of several butterfly species, such as *Lysandra bellargus* (Rottemburg) and *Maculinea arion*. In New Zealand, Gibbs (1980) noted the trend towards decline of *Zizina oxleyi* (Felder & Felder) in parts of the South Island through hybridisation with the invasive Australian *Z. labradus* (both are sometimes treated as subspecies of *Z. otis* (F.) (Figure 3)). Claims that hybridisation with the introduced *Strymon melinus* Hübner could threaten the Avalon Hairstreak, *S. avalona* (Wright), on Santa Catalina Island, California, need further investigation (Wells *et al.* 1983).

In a rather different interaction between exotic and native species, Brown (1990) reported that the widespread *Leptotes marina* (Reakirt) had adapted well to urbanisation in North America with its range expansion largely due to a 'switch' to a South African larval foodplant (*Plumbago auriculata*), which is used widely in freeway landscaping and as an ornamental. Furthermore, larvae associate closely with the introduced Argentine ant, and the prime nectar source for adults is a Brazilian tree. *Leptotes* thus has benefited from the presence of several different exotic species.

Conservation of Lycaenidae

The major sequence of needs in order to effect conservation programmes for any form of terrestrial wildlife is as follows:

i) Documentation and education, to increase awareness at all levels and as a mode of communication between informed scientists and those who make practical decisions over priorities for land use;

ii) Detection of habitats supporting either critical faunas or single notable or vulnerable species which merit protection and the promotion of their continued protection in existing National Parks and other reserves;

iii) Investigation of the limits and/or wisdom of legislative protection for particular taxa or habitats, as an interim measure whilst additional documentation is obtained, and

iv) Autecological studies of selected taxa as a basis for formulating sound management plans, a step which can come only from a basis of substantial research rather than haphazard extrapolation and which is, therefore, costly.

v) Investigation of techniques for captive rearing, in case of need for *ex situ* conservation, or translocation. This should not be seen as a replacement option for *in situ* conservation.

The information contained in this volume has hitherto been scattered through a wide range of reports (of varying degrees of formality and distribution) and scientific papers. In dealing with such a diverse group of insects, this book cannot be as definitive as 'Threatened Swallowtail Butterflies' (Collins and Morris 1985), but the examples given reflect a growing number of detailed studies on lycaenids and concern over their conservation. It represents a useful starting point for the development of conservation programmes for the Lycaenidae and should help to focus attention on groups or geographical regions in need of urgent attention.

Public awareness

Most conservation projects to date have been species orientated and many of these have done much to improve public awareness of the threats to lycaenid species. The potential for reintroductions is demonstrated well by the recent project involving the successful liberation of the Large Blue, *Maculinea arion* L. in Britain. This case is discussed in detail by Elmes and Thomas (1992) and by New ('Large Blues', this volume). Attempts to introduce the continental subspecies of the Large Copper, *Lycaena dispar,* into Britain, are of long standing (Duffey 1977 and this volume). Both projects highlight the

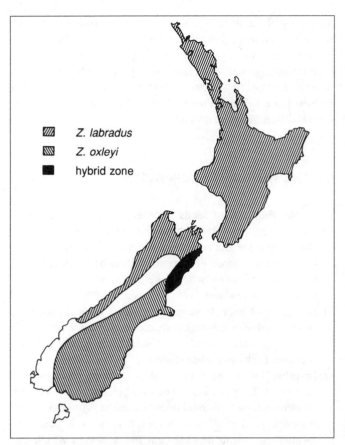

Figure 3. Distribution of *Zizina oxyleyi* (native) and *Z. labradus* (exotic) in New Zealand, and their hybrid zone (after Gibbs 1980).

need for substantial amounts of ecological information for such management initiatives and they have done much to improve public awareness of butterfly conservation issues.

There is no doubt that particular 'charismatic' butterflies amongst the Lycaenidae can do much to increase public awareness of conservation at a level which is otherwise difficult to realise, as witness the Large Blue campaign in Britain, the Mission Blue (*Plebejus icarioides missionensis* Hovanitz) in California and the more recent Eltham Copper (*Paralucia pyrodiscus lucida* Crosby) campaign in Australia.

However, such species-orientated conservation is essentially confined to well-developed countries. It could not be achieved practically in much of the rest of the world, where conservation of any sort is considered a luxury and where there are few skilled entomological or conservationist practitioners and little if any local funding or sympathy for insect well-being.

Any opportunity for promotion of significant species as 'local emblems' is worth pursuing. For example the appearance of butterflies on stamps might help to gain public sympathy: lycaenids have been depicted on postage stamps of nearly 70 countries (Coles *et al.* 1991 and Table 6) and these have included both less developed and developed countries.

Identification of threatened species and critical faunas

The identification of these is clearly an immediate need in lycaenid conservation. The information contained in this volume indicates that while the former is the main focus in the developed world it is the latter which may be the most relevant path to follow elsewhere. The largest group of oriental Polyommatini (the '*Lycaenopsis* group') was appraised by Eliot and Kawazoe (1983), and additional comprehensive studies of this sort would be of considerable value in setting conservation priorities on a faunistic basis. That study indicated a number of regions with high levels of diversity and/or endemism which could thus be considered as critical faunas (see Collins and Morris 1985 on Papilionidae, Ackery and Vane-Wright 1984 on Nymphalidae: Danainae).

Other examples of critical faunas can be cited: the Philippines support more species of the Polyommatini than any other area of comparable size and some are endemic; Sulawesi is less rich than the Philippines but about half the species there are relict endemics or have only a narrow range elsewhere; most taxa in the Papuan subregion are endemic; centres of diversity (?refugia) for Riodininae occur in the neotropics (see taxa accounts for South America, this volume) and of other taxa in various parts of the world. Many of these areas are undergoing substantial, rapid and irreversible changes at present, and the prime need is to increase reservation of ecologically representative areas as a prelude to more detailed studies of their needs. Unless additonal reserves are forthcoming the rich diversity of Riodininae in the neotropics (see essays by Brown and Callaghan, this volume) and the substantial numbers of unusual Polyommatinae in southeast Asia will be seriously reduced.

The emphasis on species-orientated lycaenid conservation is likely to occupy entomologists in temperate regions for some time to come. This has two important results. Firstly, detailed studies of particular taxa, which would be impossible in a broader context, may give a good basis for their proper management. Various projects on the reintroduction of species and successful management of threatened species, which are documented in the taxa accounts, attest to the depth of ecological knowledge necessary for the successful management of habitat for a particular species. In fact, for most Lycaenidae, preservation of suitable habitat is generally not in itself sufficient to ensure their long-term well-being: intricate management plans to conserve complex tripartite associations involving butterfly, ant and plant and to control seral succession by ensuring that some rapidly developing early stages may be continually available, are integral facets of successful conservation. Secondly, particular critical habitats may be reserved for the species and give benefit also to less obvious rare biota. However, few such studies result in reservation of large or well-buffered habitats. Systems akin to the British SSSI (Sites of Special Scientific Interest, history documented by Moore 1987) are not yet widespread elsewhere but merit serious attention in other parts of the world to ensure the adequate reservation of well-buffered habitats.

Table 6. List of Lycaenidae which have been depicted on postage stamps up to October 1991. (Data from Coles *et al.* 1991; identifications not checked further, authors' names omitted).

Species	Country, year of issue	Species	Country, year of issue
Aethiopana honorius	Ghana 1990	*Aricia agestis*	Cyprus 1983
Citrinophila erastus	Ghana 1990	*Brephidium exilis*	Cayman Islands 1990, Turks & Caicos Islands 1990
Hewitsonia boisduvali	Uganda 1989		
Mimacraea marshalli	Uganda 1989	*Catochrysops taitensis*	Samoa 1986
Pentila abraxas	Ghana 1990	*Celastrina argiolus*	Libya 1981
Telipna acraea	Ghana 1990	*Cupidopsis jobates*	Togo 1990
Ogyris amaryllis	Australia 1981	*Danis danis*	Netherlands New Guinea 1960
Aphnaeus questiauxi	Zambia 1980	*Glaucopsyche melanops*	Cyprus 1983, Libya 1981
Aphniolaus pallene	Uganda 1989	*Hemiargus ammon*	Cayman Islands 1988, Cuba 1991
Atlides polybe	Grenada 1975	*H. hanno*	Barbados 1983, British Virgin Islands 1978
Axiocerses amanga	Uganda 1989		
A. harpax	Mozambique 1953, Togo 1990	*H. thomasi*	Turks & Caicos Islands 1990
A. styx	Tanzania 1973	*Jamides bochus*	Tonga 1989
Bindahara phocides	Palau 1990	*J. cephion*	Solomon Islands 1980
Callophrys crethona	Jamaica 1978	*Lampides boeticus*	Ascension 1987, Fiji 1985, Vanuatu 1991
Chrysozephyrus mushaellus	China 1963		
Deudorix epijarbas	Samoa 1986	*Leptotes cassius*	St. Vincent 1989
Epamera handmani	Malawi 1966	*Luthrodes cleotas*	Vanuatu 1983, Wallis & Futuna Islands 1987
E. sidus	Kenya 1988		
Eumaeus atala	Cuba 1974	*Lycaeides idas*	Canada 1988
Evenus coronata	Ecuador 1970, Nicaragua 1986	*Lysandra albicans*	Libya 1981
E. dindymus	Grenadines of St. Vincent 1975	*L. bellargus*	Hungary 1959
E. regalis	Belize 1990, Brazil 1979, Nicaragua 1967	*L. coridon*	Switzerland 1952
		Maculinea arion	Gibraltar 1977, Great Britain 1981, Hungary 1969, Poland 1967
Hypokopelates otraeda	Mali 1964		
Hypolycaena antifaunus	Togo 1990	*Meleageria daphnis*	Bulgaria 1962, Hungary 1966, Rumania 1969
Japonica lutea	Laos 1986		
Lipaphnaeus leonina	Mali 1964	*Polyommatus icarus*	Guernsey 1981, Ireland 1985, Malta 1986
Loxura atymnus	China 1963		
Myrina silenus	Angola 1982, Mauritania 1966, Togo 1990, Sierra Leone 1979, Tanzania 1988	*Tarucus balkanicus*	Turkey 1958
		Uranothauma crawshayi	Malawi 1973
Narathura centaurus	Malaysia 1970	*Heliphorus epicles*	Hong Kong 1979, Macau 1985
Panthiades bathildis	Belize 1974	*Heodes solskyi*	China 1963
Pratapa ctesia	Laos 1986	*H. virgaureae*	Finland 1990, Hungary 1959, Mongolia 1977, Rumania 1960
Pseudalmenus chlorinda	Australia 1981		
Pseudolycaena marsyas	Grenada 1990, Grenadines of Grenada 1985, St. Vincent 1978	*Lycaena dispar*	Germany (F.R.) 1991
		L. helle	Germany (F.R.) 1991
Rapala arata	Korea (North) 1977	*L. salustius*	New Zealand 1970
Ritra aurea	Nicaragua 1986	*Palaeochrysophanus hippothoe*	Hungary 1974, Nicaragua 1986
Scoptes alphaeus	South Africa 1977	*Thersamonia phoebus*	Ifni 1963
Spindasis modesta	Zambia 1980	*T. thersamon*	Hungary 1969
S. natalensis	Swaziland 1987	*Abisara talantus*	Sierra Leone 1987
S. nyassae	Malawi 1984	*Ancyluris formosissima*	Guinea 1973, Hungary 1984
Strymon maesites	Dominica 1988, Turks & Caicos Islands 1982, Grenadines of St. Vincent 1989	*A. jurgenseni*	Nicaragua 1967
		Chorinea faunus	Guyana 1989
S. martialis	Cayman Islands 1988	*Dodona adonira*	China 1963
S. melinus	Honduras 1991	*Helicopis cupido*	Guyana 1983, Surinam 1971
S. rufofusca	Grenadines of Grenada 1985	*Melanis pixe*	Nicaragua 1967
S. simaethis	Grenada 1989, Grenadines of Grenada 1985	*Nymphidium mantus*	Guyana 1983
		Nymula orestes	Grenada 1975
Stugeta marmorea	Sierra Leone 1987	*Rhetus thia*	Nicaragua 1967
Tanuetheira timon	Congo 1971, Sierra Leone 1987	*R. sp.*	Honduras 1991
Thecla betulae	Bulgaria 1990	*Stalachtis calliope*	Guyana 1989, Surinam 1971
Agrodiaetus amanda	Finland 1990	*S. phlegia*	Surinam 1971
A. damon	Mongolia 1963		

Managing lycaenid populations

Various management plans for particular Lycaenidae have been produced, and these have several elements in common: habitat security; the need for management based on sound biological and ecological understanding of the target species; and the need for an understanding of the endangering processes. Increasing public awareness of the particular lycaenid is also commonly seen as important. The processes needed are well exemplified in a 'flow-chart' produced by Arnold (1983a) for Smith's Blue (*Euphilotes enoptes smithi* (Mattoni)) in California and augmented in his Recovery Plans for the Lotis Blue (*Lycaeides idas lotis* (Lintner) and other species (USFWS 1984, 1985), and this has been used as a basis for the scheme outlined in Table 7. It is clear from this that the basic information necessary to formulate sound management for any ecologically sensitive species cannot be gathered instantly. All too often the time available is insufficient once a decision has been taken to develop a habitat containing a threatened species or population.

The approach of 'Population Viability Analysis' (sometimes, 'Population Vulnerability Analysis'), PVA, is receiving substantial attention in assessing conservation needs of vertebrate animals. In general, the detailed demographic and reproductive data needed for such predictive modelling are not available for extending this approach to invertebrates. However, a North American lycaenid, the Karner Blue (*Lycaeides melissa samuelis* Nabokov) has recently (April 1992) been the focus of the first specialist workshop held to appraise an insect in this context. This species lives in fire-successional vegetation, and the metapopulations are associated with local extinctions and recolonisation or habitat shifts linked with climate and fire regimes (Cushman and Murphy, this volume). The outcome from this workshop may mark a substantial augmentation to current methods of formulating management programmes for insects of conservation concern.

Ex situ conservation

The controlled harvesting and ranching of Papilionidae to reduce pressure on natural populations and supply collector needs has proved to be an important conservation avenue for this group. It probably will never be achievable (or, indeed, needed) for lycaenids on any large scale, despite their uniqueness and vulnerability and their geographical overlap with areas where Papilionidae are also vulnerable. However, rearing of particular rare species in captivity does have some potential for augmenting field populations and for effecting translocations. The Atala Hairstreak, *Eumaeus atala*, has proved to be relatively easy to rear in captivity, and this practice is pursued by several butterfly houses in Britain using stock from Florida (Collins 1987a). Some success has been obtained with attempts to start new colonies of *E. atala* in the wild, and although the species continues to be regarded as vulnerable to habitat loss it has become more widespread in recent years (Lenczewski 1980). Some Japanese Theclini may be reared relatively easily from eggs collected in the field, and eggs of species which are otherwise very hard to collect have been found (Kuzuya 1959). The larval stage lasts for 3–4 weeks, as does the pupal period, and the only major problem in rearing was a tendency for older larvae to be cannibalistic.

Unlike most other butterflies, captive rearing of lycaenids may need to incorporate provision for ants, often of particular species for any given lycaenid, as well as foodplants.

Table 7. A pro-forma scheme for species-orientated conservation of Lycaenidae (after Arnold 1983a).

---

1. Preserve, protect and manage known existing habitat to provide conditions needed by the species.

    (a)   Preserve: prevent further degradation, development or environmental modification.

        Steps (some or all):
        (i)   Cooperative agreements with landowners/managers.
        (ii)   Memoranda or undertakings.
        (iii)   Conservation easements.
        (iv)   Site acquisition (purchase/donation): private land.
        (v)   Site reservation: public land.

    (b)   Maintain larval and adult resources at known habitat(s).

        Steps (some or all):
        (i)   Minimise use of toxic substances: herbicides, pesticides.
        (ii)   Minimise uncontrolled intrusion by humans: trampling, off-road vehicles, etc.
        (iii)   Minimise intrusion by domestic stock: cattle, horses, sheep, etc.
        (iv)   Minimise exotic vegetation planting.
        (v)   Minimise removal of native vegetation, unless controlled.

    (c)   Propose critical habitat (U.S.).

    (d)   If necessary, clarify taxonomic status of target lycaenid in habitat and, where known, outlier or other populations.

Continued...

18

Table 7 (cont.). A pro-forma scheme for species-orientated conservation of Lycaenidae (after Arnold 1983a).

---

2. Manage and enhance lycaenid population(s) by habitat maintenance and quality improvement, and reducing effects of limiting factors.

   (a)   Investigate and initiate habitat improvement methods as appropriate.

         Examples:
         (i)   Remove or control exotic weedy or noxious plants.
         (ii)   Promote natural establishment of foodplants and other natural vegetation – if necessary, propagate and transplant.
         (iii)   Promote particular grazing (grassland) or coppicing (woodland) regimes.

   (b)   Determine physical and climatic regimes/factors needed by species and relate to local habitat enhancement in overall site.

   (c)   Investigate ecology of the lycaenid species

         (i)   Life history and phenology; dependence on particular plant species/stages/organs.
         (ii)   Dependence on ants or other animals, and their role in protection from predators and parasites.
         (iii)   Population status; size, movement, degree of isolation, sex ratio, etc.
         (iv)   Adult behaviour: mating, oviposition cues and sites, activity rhythms.
         (v)   Determine predators, parasitoids and other factors which cause mortality or limit population growth.
         (vi)   Investigate possibility of captive rearing from local population enhancement or range extension.

   (d)   Investigate ecology of tending ant species and (if needed) homopterous prey.

   (e)   Investigate ecology of food plant species

         (i)   Life history and recruitment processes.
         (ii)   Mortality and debilitatory factors, including other consumer species.
         (iii)   Limiting factors – edaphic conditions, slope, exposure, etc.
         (iv)   If needed, horticultural studies to determine propagation techniques for transplantation/augmentation of food plant stocks.

3. Evaluate above, and incorporate into development of long-term management plan. Computer modelling may assist in making management decisions.

4. Monitor lycaenid populations to determine their status and to evaluate success of management.

   (a)   Determine sites to be surveyed, if choice available and/or logistics limited.

   (b)   Develop methodology to estimate population numbers, distribution and trends in abundance.

         Examples:
         (i)   Counts of larvae when feeding at night.
         (ii)   Counts of adults by transect patrols, mark-recapture, etc.

5. Throughout all above, increasing public awareness of the species by education/information programmes.

         Examples:
         (i)   Information signs at key sites (unless risk of inducing unwanted intrusion, collecting, etc.)
         (ii)   Interpretive tours, if secure sites permit without causing additional problems.
         (iii)   Audio and visual programmes, publications.
             – TV/radio interviews and information on the species and its management.
             – Conservation education programmes for schools and community groups.
             – 'Popular style' newspaper articles.
             – Continuing liaison with all interested parties.

6. Enforce available regulations and laws to protect species. Determine whether additional legal steps needed, and promote these if necessary.

References

ACKERY, P.R. 1984. Systematic and faunistic studies on butterflies. *In:* Vane-Wright, R.I. and Ackery, P.R. (Eds). *The Biology of Butterflies.* Academic Press, London. pp. 9–21.

ACKERY, P.R. and VANE-WRIGHT, R.I. 1984. *Milkweed Butterflies.* British Museum (Natural History, London and Cornell University Press, New York.

ARNOLD, R.A. 1983a. Conservation and management of the endangered Smith's blue butterfly, *Euphilotes enoptes smithi* (Lepidoptera: Lycaenidae). *J. Res. Lepid.* 22: 135–153.

ARNOLD, R.A. 1983b. Ecological studies of six endangered butterflies: island biogeography, patch dynamics and the design of nature reserves. *Univ. Calif. Publns Ent.* 99: 1–161.

AUSTIN, G.T. 1972. A possible case of mimicry between lycaenid butterflies (Lycaenidae). *J. Lepid. Soc.* 26: 63–64.

BAYLIS, M. and PIERCE, N.E. 1991. The effect of host-plant quality on the survival of larvae and oviposition by adults of an ant-attended lycaenid butterfly, *Jalmenus evagoras. Ecol. Entomol.* 16: 1–9.

BOWERS, M.D. and LARIN, Z. 1989. Acquired chemical defence in the lycaenid butterfly, *Eumaeus atala. J. Chem. Ecol.* 15: 1133–1146.

BREEDLOVE, D.E. and EHRLICH, P.R. 1968. Plant-herbivores coevolution: lupines and lycaenids. *Science* 162: 672–673.

BREEDLOVE, D.E. and EHRLICH, P.R. 1972. Coevolution: patterns of legume predation by a lycaenid butterfly. *Oecologia* **10**: 99–104.

BRIDGES, C.A. 1988. *Catalogue of Lycaenidae and Riodinidae (Lepidoptera: Rhopalocera)*. Urbana, Illinois.

BROWN, J.W. 1990. Urban biology of *Leptotes marina* (Reakirt) (Lycaenidae). *J. Lepid. Soc.* **44**: 200–201.

BROWN, R.M. and OPLER, P.A. 1967. Biological observations of *Callophrys viridis* (Lycaenidae). *J. Lepid. Soc.* **21**: 113–114.

CALLAGHAN, C.J. 1979. A new genus and a new subspecies of Riodinidae from southern Brazil. *Bull. Allyn Mus.* **53**: 1–7.

CALLAGHAN, C.J. 1983. A study of isolating mechanisms among neotropical butterflies of the subfamily Riodininae. *J. Res. Lepid.* **21**: 159–176.

CALLAGHAN, C.J. 1986. Notes on the biology of *Stalachtis susanna* (Lycaenidae: Riodininae) with a discussion of riodinine larval strategies. *J. Res. Lepid.* **24**: 258–263.

CLENCH, H.K. 1955. Revised classification of the butterfly family Lycaenidae and its allies. *Ann. Carneg. Mus.* **33**: 261–274.

CLENCH, H.K. 1966. Behavioral thermoregulation in butterflies. *Ecology* **47**: 1021–1034.

CLENCH, H.K. and MILLER, L.D. 1980. *Papilio ladon* Cramer vs. *Argus pseudargiolus* Boisduval & Le Conte (Lycaenidae): a nomenclatorial nightmare. *J. Lepid. Soc.* **34**: 103–118.

COLES, A., PHIPPS, T. and other Members of the Butterfly and Moth Stamp Society. 1991. *Collect Butterflies and other Insects on Stamps*. Stanley Gibbons, London and Ringwood.

COLLINS, N.M. 1987a. *Butterfly houses in Britain, the conservation implications*. IUCN, Cambridge.

COLLINS, N.M. 1987b. *Legislation to conserve insects in Europe*. Pamphlet **13**. Amateur Entomologists' Society, London.

COLLINS, N.M. and MORRIS, M.G. 1985. *Threatened Swallowtail Butterflies of the World*. IUCN, Gland and Cambridge.

COTTRELL, C.B. 1984. Aphytophagy in butterflies: its relationship to myrmecophily. *Zool. J. Linn. Soc.* **79**: 1–57.

CROAT, T.B. 1978. *Flora of Barro Colorado Island*. Stanford University Press, Stanford, California.

DE VRIES, P.J. 1988. The use of epiphylls as larval hostplants by the neotropical riodinid butterfly, *Sarota gyas*. *J. nat. Hist.* **22**: 1447–1450.

DE VRIES, P.J. 1990. Enhancement of symbiosis between butterfly caterpillars and ants by vibrational communication. *Science* **248**: 1104–1106.

DE VRIES, P.J. 1991a. Evolutionary and ecological patterns in myrmecophilous riodinid butterflies. *In:* Huxley, C.R. and Cutler, D.F. (Eds) *Ant-Plant Interactions*. Oxford University Press, Oxford, pp.143–156.

DE VRIES, P.J. 1991b. Mutualism between *Thisbe irenea* butterflies and ants, and the role of ant ecology in the evolution of larval-ant associations. *Biol. J. Linn. Soc.* **43**: 179–195.

DOWNEY, J.C. 1962. Host-plant relations as data for butterfly classification. *Syst. Zool.* **11**: 150–159.

DOWNEY, J.C. 1965. Mimicry and distribution of *Caenurgina caerulea* Grt. (Noctuidae). *J. Lepid. Soc.* **19**: 165–170.

DOWNEY, J.C. 1966. Sound production in pupae of Lycaenidae. *J. Lepid. Soc.* **20**: 129–155.

DOWNEY, J.C. and FULLER, W.C. 1961. Variation in *Plebejus icarioides*. I. Foodplant specificity. *J. Lepid. Soc.* **15**: 34–42.

DUFFEY, E. 1977. The re-establishment of the large copper butterfly *Lycaena dispar batavus* on Woodwalton Fen NNR, Cambridgeshire, England 1969–1973. *Biol. Conserv.* **12**: 143–158.

EDWARDS, W.H. 1886. On the history and preparatory stages of *Feniseca tarquinis* Fabr. *Can. Ent.* **18**: 141–153.

EHRLICH, P.R. 1958. The comparative morphology, phylogeny and higher classification of the butterflies. *Univ. Kans. Sci. Bull.* **39**: 305–370.

EHRLICH, P.R. and EHRLICH, A.H. 1972. Wing-shape and adult resources in lycaenids. *J. Lepid. Soc.* **26**: 196–197.

ELIOT, J.N. 1973. The higher classification of the Lycaenidae: a tentative arrangement. *Bull. Brit. Mus. Nat. Hist. (Ent.)* **28**: 373–506.

ELIOT, J.N. and KAWAZOE, A. 1983. *Blue butterflies of the Lycaenopsis group*. British Museum (Natural History), London.

ELMES, G.W. and THOMAS, J.A. 1992. Complexity of species conservation in managed habitats: interaction between *Maculinea* butterflies and their ant hosts. *Biodiv. and Conserv.* **1**: 155–169.

FIEDLER, K. 1991a. European and North West African Lycaenidae (Lepidoptera) and their associations with ants. *J. Res. Lepid.* **28**: 239–257 (1989).

FIEDLER, K. 1991b. Systematic, evolutionary and ecological implications of myrmecophily within the Lycaenidae. *Bonn. Zool. Monograph* **21**.

FIEDLER, K. and MASCHWITZ, U. 1988. Functional analysis of the myrmecophilous relationships between ants (Hymenoptera: Formicidae) and lycaenids (Lepidoptera: Lycaenidae). II. Lycaenid larvae as trophobiotic partners of ants – a quantitative approach. *Oecologia* **75**: 204–206.

FIEDLER, K. and MASCHWITZ, U. 1989. The symbiosis between the weaver ant, *Oecophylla smaragdina*, and *Anthene emolus*, an obligate myrmecophilous lycaenid butterfly. *J. nat. Hist.* **23**: 833–846.

FUJII, H. 1989. Repeated copulation in an orange hairstreak, *Shirozua janasi*: a case of mate guarding? *J. Lepid. Soc.* **43**: 68–71.

GIBBS, G.W. 1980. *New Zealand Butterflies*. Collins, Auckland.

GOODPASTURE, C. 1974. Foodplant specificity in the *Plebejus (Icaricia) acmon* group (Lycaenidae). *J. Lepid. Soc.* **28**: 53–63.

HARVEY, D.J. 1987. *The higher classification of the Riodinidae (Lepidoptera)*. Ph.D. Thesis, University of Texas, Austin. (not seen: referred to by De Vries, 1991a).

HEATH, J. 1981. *Threatened Rhopalocera in Europe*. Council of Europe, Strasbourg.

HENNING, S.F. 1983. Biological groups within the Lycaenidae (Lepidoptera). *J. ent. Soc. sth. Afr.* **46**: 65–85.

HINTON, H.E. 1951. Myrmecophilous Lycaenidae and other Lepidoptera – a summary. *Proc. Trans. S. Lond. ent. nat. Hist. Soc.* **1949–50**: 111–175.

HINTON, H.E. 1974. Lycaenid pupae that mimic anthropoid heads. *J. Entomol. (A)* **49**: 65–69.

IUCN, 1990. *The IUCN Red List of Threatened Animals*. Gland and Cambridge.

IWASE, T. 1953. Aberrant feeders among Japanese lycaenid larvae. *Lepid. News* **7**: 45–46.

JOHNSON, K. 1984. An attempted interfamilial mating (Lycaenidae-Nymphalidae). *J. Res. Lepid.* **28**: 291–292.

JOHNSON, K. and BORGO, P.M. 1976. Patterned perching behaviour in two *Callophrys (Mitoura)* (Lycaenidae). *J. Lepid. Soc.* **30**: 169–183.

KITCHING, R.L. 1981. Egg clustering and the southern hemisphere lycaenids: comments on a paper by N.E. Stamp. *Amer. Nat.* **118**: 423–425.

KITCHING, R.L. 1987. Aspects of the natural history of the lycaenid butterfly *Allotinus major* in Sulawesi. *J. nat. Hist.* **21**: 535–544.

KUZUYA, T. 1959. The breeding of the Theclini and collecting their eggs in winter. *J. Lepid. Soc.* **13**: 175–181.

LENCZEWSKI, B. 1980. *Butterflies of Everglades National Park*. Report **T–588**. National Parks Service, Florida.

LUNDGREN, L. 1977. The role of intra- and interspecific male: male interactions in *Polyommatus icarus* Rott. and some other species of blues (Lycaenidae). *J. Res. Lepid.* **16**: 249–264.

MACNEILL, C.D. 1967. A unidirectional mass movement by *Satyrium saepium* (Lycaenidae). *J. Lepid. Soc.* **21**: 204.

MALICKY, H. 1969. Versuch einer Analyse der ökologischen Beziehungen zwischen Lycaeniden und Formiciden. *Tidschr. Ent.* **112**: 213–298.

MOORE, N.W. 1987. *The Bird of Time*. Cambridge University Press, Cambridge.

MURPHY, D.D. 1989. Are we studying our endangered butterflies to death? *J. Res. Lepid.* **26**: 236–239.

NAKAMURA, I. 1976. Female anal hair tuft in *Nordmannia myratle*: egg-camouflaging function and taxonomic significance. *J. Lepid. Soc.* **30**: 305–309.

NEW, T.R., BUSH, M.B., THORNTON, I.W.B. and SUDARMAN, H.K. 1988. The butterfly fauna of the Krakatau islands after a century of colonisation. *Phil. Trans. R. Soc. Lond. B.* **322**: 445–457.

OWEN, D.F. 1991. *Pseudaletis leonis*: a rare mimetic butterfly in a West African rainforest (Lepidoptera: Lycaenidae). *Tropical Lepidoptera* **2**: 111–113.

PIERCE, N.E. 1983. *The ecology and evolution of symbioses between lycaenid butterflies and ants*. Ph.D. Thesis, Harvard University.

PIERCE, N.E. 1984. Amplified species diversity: case study of an Australian lycaenid butterfly and its attendant ants. *In:* Vane-Wright, R.I. and Ackery, P.R. (Eds) *The Biology of Butterflies.* Academic Press, London, pp. 197–200.

PIERCE, N.E. 1985. Lycaenid butterflies and ants: selection for nitrogen-fixing and other protein-rich foodplants. *Amer. Nat.* **125**: 888–895.

PIERCE, N.E. 1987. The evolution and biogeography of associations between lycaenid butterflies and ants. *Oxford Surv. evol. Biol.* **4**: 89–116.

PIERCE, N.E. and EASTEAL, S.I. 1986. The selective advantage of attendant ants for the larvae of a lycaenid butterfly *Glaucopsyche lygdamus. J. anim. Ecol.* **55**: 451–462.

PIERCE, N.E. and MEAD, P.S. 1981. Parasitoids as selective agents in the symbiosis between butterfly larvae and ants. *Science* **211**: 1185–1187.

PRATT, G.F. and BALLMER, G.R. 1991. Acceptance of *Lotus scoparius* (Fabaceae) by larvae of Lycaenidae. *J. Lepid. Soc.* **45**: 188–196.

RIOTTE, J.C. and UCHIDA, G. 1979. Butterflies of the Hawaiian islands according to the stand of late 1976. *J. Res. Lepid.* **17**: 33–39.

ROBBINS, R.K. 1980. The lycaenid 'false head' hypothesis: historical review and quantitative analysis. *J. Lepid. Soc.* **34**: 194–208.

ROBBINS, R.K. 1981. The lycaenid 'false head' hypothesis: predation and wing pattern variation of lycaenid butterflies. *Amer. Nat.* **118**: 770–775.

ROBBINS, R.K. 1982. How many butterfly species? *News Lepid. Soc.* **1982**: 40–41.

ROBBINS, R.K. and AIELLO, A. 1982. Foodplant and oviposition records for Panamanian Lycaenidae and Riodinidae. *J. Lepid. Soc.* **36**: 65–75.

ROBBINS, R.K. and SMALL, G.B. 1981. Wind dispersal of Panamanian hairstreak butterflies and its evolutionary significance. *Biotropica* **13**: 308–315.

ROBINSON, R. 1971. *Lepidoptera genetics.* Pergamon, Oxford.

SANDS, D.P.A. 1986. A revision of the genus *Hypochrysops* C. & R. Felder (Lepidoptera: Lycaenidae). *Entomonograph* No. **7**. Brill, Leiden.

SCOTT, J.A. 1968. Hilltopping as a mating mechanism to aid the survival of low density species. *J. Res. Lepid.* **7**: 191–204.

SCOTT, J.A. 1973. Down-valley flights of adult Theclini in search of nourishment. *J. Lepid. Soc.* **27**: 283–287.

SHAPIRO, A.M. 1982. An interfamilial courtship (Lycaenidae, Pieridae). *J. Res. Lepid.* **20 (1981)**: 54.

SHAPIRO, A.M. 1985. An intersubfamilial courtship (Lycaenidae). *J. Res. Lepid.* **24**: 195.

SHIELDS, O. 1967. Hilltopping. *J. Res. Lepid.* **6**: 69–178.

SHIELDS, O. 1989. World numbers of butterflies. *J. Lepid. Soc.* **43**: 178–183.

SHIROZU, T. and YAMAMOTO, H. 1957. Systematic position of the genus *Curetis* (Lepidoptera: Rhopalocera). *Sieboldia* **2**: 43–51.

SIBATANI, A. 1984. A remarkable polymorphism of mature larvae of *Zizina labradus* (Godart), common grass blue butterfly (Lepidoptera: Lycaenidae) from the Sydney area. *Aust. ent. Mag.* **11**: 21–26.

SIBATANI, A. 1992. Observations on the period of active flight in males of *Favonius* (Lycaenidae) in southern Primor'e, the Russian Federation. *Tyô to Ga* **43**: 23–34.

STEMPFFER, H. 1957. Les lepidoptères de l'Afrique noire francaise (3): Lycaenides. *Init. afr.* **14**: 1–228.

STEMPFFER, H. 1967. The genera of the African Lycaenidae (Lepidoptera: Rhopalocera). *Bull. Br. Mus. nat. Hist. (Ent.).* Supplement **10**, 322 pp.

THOMAS, J.A., MUNGUIRA, M.L., MARTIN, J. and ELLIS, G.W. 1991. Basal hatching by *Maculinea* butterfly eggs: a consequence of advanced myrmecophily? *Biol. J. Linn. Soc.* **44**: 175–184.

USFWS (U.S. Fish and Wildlife Service) 1984. *Recovery plan for the San Bruno Elfin and Mission Blue butterflies.* U.S. Fish and Wildlife Service, Portland, Oregon.

USFWS (U.S. Fish and Wildlife Service) 1985. *Recovery plan for the Lotis Blue butterfly.* U.S. Fish and Wildlife Service, Portland, Oregon.

VALENTINE, P.S. and JOHNSON, S.J. 1989. Polyphagy in larvae of *Hypochrysops miskini* (Waterhouse) (Lepidoptera: Lycaenidae). *Aust. ent. Mag.* **16**: 1–3.

WELLS, S.M., PYLE, R.M. and COLLINS, N.M. 1983. *The IUCN Invertebrate Red Data Book.* IUCN, Gland.

ZIEGLER, J.B. and ESCALANTE, T. 1964. Observations on the life history of *Callophrys xami* (Lycaenidae). *J. Lepid. Soc.* **18**: 85–89.

PART 2. REGIONAL ASSESSMENTS

Introductory comment

This section is important both for what it contains and for what it does not contain. It demonstrates that most of our knowledge of the status of particular Lycaenidae is derived from temperate regions, particularly in the northern hemisphere, and that the fauna of much of the Old World tropics (in particular) cannot yet be evaluated in this way. Much of the tropics supports a high diversity of butterflies, but few resident lepidopterists with the facilities for undertaking biological studies: much of what can be inferred is based less on ecological surveys and a detailed knowledge of biology and more on old collections and synoptic works. For example, books such as those by Corbet and Pendlebury (1978, Malaysia) and Seki *et al.* (1991, Borneo) give invaluable appraisals of those magnificent local faunas. The introduction to the latter includes passionate comment on conservation of butterflies in Borneo, and the text, photographs and keys facilitate identification of 379 species and subspecies – but the status of many of these is largely unknown, and the knowledge of their distribution often fragmentary. Many lycaenids there, as elsewhere, are indeed both rare and restricted – perhaps threatened by habitat alteration or destruction – but it is not possible to give a sound biological overview of these unique faunas, except in such very general terms.

There is abundant need to document lycaenid diversity in many of the nominal 'protected areas' in the tropics, and to ensure that the widest possible range of habitats is conserved, especially for the many specialist forest-frequenting taxa. Though few specific details are available, there seems little doubt that continuing forest destruction throughout the African and Asian tropics is adversely affecting these insects.

References

CORBET, A.S. and PENDLEBURY, H.M. 1978. *The Butterflies of the Malay Peninsula.* 3rd ed., revised by Eliot, J.N., Malayan Nature Society, Kuala Lumpur.
SEKI, Y., TAKANAMI, Y. and OTSUKA, K. 1991. *Butterflies of Borneo 2(1). Lycaenidae.* Tobishima Corporation, Tokyo.

Conservation biology of Lycaenidae: A European overview

Miguel L. Munguira[1], José Martin[1] and Emilio Balletto[2]

[1] *Departamento de Biología, Universidad Autónoma de Madrid, Cantoblanco, 28049 Madrid, Spain*
[2] *Dipartimento di Biologia Animale, Università di Torino, Via Accademia Albertina 17, 10123 Torino, Italy*

Biology of European Lycaenidae

The biology of European lycaenids is generally well known as a result of both general and specific studies. A review of central European species was made by Malicky (1969a) who dealt with larval foodplants, phenology and overwintering stages. Relationships with ants were also reviewed by Malicky (1969b) and Fiedler (1990a, 1991). Books on regional faunas including detailed ecological information on a species-by-species basis are available for Italy (Verity 1943), the Netherlands (Tax 1989), British Isles (Ford 1970; Emmet and Heath 1989) and Switzerland (SBN 1987). Specific autecological studies cover a wide range of species from almost every major group within the European fauna. Some of these studies are listed in Table 1, together with the geographic areas in which they were undertaken. Several studies in press or short notices have not been listed and a wider range of species is covered by these. Thus the information available covers roughly 50% of the European lycaenids. The Table clearly shows wider coverage of northern species and of the countries where the present authors are based (Italy and Spain), but nevertheless it gives a general idea of our knowledge of European lycaenids.

While most of the northern species are well known as far as their biology is concerned, information on most Mediterranean species is not available, even on such basic topics as foodplants or habitat preferences. Greece, with its 12 endemic species, is the area where basic studies are most urgently needed. High altitude species are also under-represented in ecological studies due to the difficulties of reaching their habitats for long-term studies, but their conservation seems to pose fewer problems than that of lowland species.

Synecological studies are generally less abundant and only refer to some geographic areas such as southern France (Cléu 1950; Bigot 1952, 1956; Dufay 1961, 1965–66), Hungary (Uherkovic 1972, 1975, 1976), Czechoslovakia (Kralichek and Povolny 1978), Italy (Balletto *et al.* 1977, 1982a–e, 1985, 1988, 1989), Switzerland (Erhardt 1985) and Germany (Kratochwil 1989a, 1989b, 1989c), or to some particular ecosystems (Fouassin 1961; Janmoulle 1965; Cléu 1957; Mikkola and Spitzer 1983; see also Ehrlich 1984).

Larval foodplants

Most of the European lycaenids are polyommatines (Kudrna 1986). The data on lycaenid larval foodplants in Table 2 clearly illustrate the fact that polyommatines have radiated in our area more than the other groups, using wider niches and evolving to produce a wider range of endemic species and peculiar ecotypes.

Life cycles

The most common strategy adopted by the European lycaenids to endure adverse seasons is larval quiescence. Most polyommatines hide away and spend the winter season (in northern Europe) or the summer and winter (in the Mediterranean areas) as second or third instar larvae. When the egg or pupa is the overwintering stage, a diapause normally takes place (e.g. *Iolana iolas* (Ochsenheimer), *Tomares ballus* (F): Munguira 1989, Jordano *et al.* 1990). Theclines typically overwinter as eggs, lycaenines and polyommatines as larvae. In the last case, however, there is considerable variation, again supporting the idea of a wider radiation of the group in our area. Table 3 summarises the data on overwintering stages for Spanish lycaenids (a sample covering 70% of European species).

There is one generation per year for most species. This seems to be a clear adaptation to temperate climates which have a favourable summer and a cold winter in which insect life comes through a dormant period. All the theclines follow this pattern, but again the polyommatines show some variation, having species with two generations (e.g. *Polyommatus* [or *Lysandra*] *bellargus* (Rottemburg), *Lycaeides idas* (L.)) or as many generations as weather allows (e.g. *Tarucus theophrastus* (F.), *Aricia cramera* Eschscholtz, *Polyommatus icarus* (Rottemburg)). It is possible that species with two generations are not 'fixed' to this condition, but constrained by food availability or unfavourable weather conditions. Thus, many species with a low number of generations may increase the number when resource limits change. An example of this is *Polyommatus icarus* with one generation in northern Britain, two in southern Britain (Emmet and Heath 1989) and four to five in Spain (Martin 1982).

Table 1. European Lycaenid species which have been the subject of thorough autecological studies, and the areas where these studies were made. Nomenclature here, and in the text follows Kudrna (1986).

Species	Area	Reference
Thecla betulae	U.K.	Thomas 1974
Satyrium pruni	U.K.	Thomas 1974
S. ilicis	Italy	Fiori 1957
Quercusia quercus	U.K.	Thomas 1975
Callophrys rubi	Germany	Fiedler 1990b
Tomares ballus	Spain	Jordano *et al.* 1990
Lycaena virgaureae	Sweden	Douwes 1975
L. phlaeas	U.K.	Dempster 1971; Emmet and Heath 1989
L. dispar	U.K.	Duffey 1968
Lampides boeticus	Spain	Martin 1984
Leptotes pirithous	Spain	Martin 1984
Glaucopsyche alexis	Spain	Martin 1981
G. melanops	Spain	Martin 1981
Maculinea rebeli	France	Thomas *et al.* 1989
	Spain	Munguira 1989
M. alcon	France	Thomas *et al.* 1989
	Spain	Munguira 1989
M. arion	U.K.	Thomas 1980
M. nausithous	France	Thomas 1984a
M. teleius	France	Thomas 1984a
Cupido minimus	U.K.	Morton 1985
C. lorquinii	Spain	Munguira 1989
Iolana iolas	Spain	Munguira 1989
Cyaniris semiargus	Spain	Rodriguez 1991
Plebejus argus	U.K.	Thomas 1985; Ravenscroft 1990
	Germany	Weidemann 1986
P. pylaon	Spain	Munguira 1989
	Hungary	Bálint and Kertész 1990
Lycaeides idas	Austria	Malicky 1961
	Sweden	Pellmyr 1983
	Belgium	Leestmans 1984
Aricia morronensis	Spain	Munguira and Martin 1988
A. agestis	U.K.	Jarvis 1958, 1959; Hoegh-Guldberg and Jarvis 1970
A. artaxerxes	U.K.	Hoegh-Guldberg and Jarvis 1970
	Denmark	
A. cramera	Italy	Balletto *et al.* 1981
A. nicias	Sweden	Wiklund 1977
A. eumedon	Spain	Munguira *et al.* 1988
Polyommatus golgus	Spain	Munguira and Martin 1989
P. dorylas	Spain	Munguira and Martin 1989
P. nivescens	Spain	Munguira and Martin 1989
P. thersites	France	Chapman 1914
P. bellargus	U.K.	Davis *et al.* 1958; Thomas 1983
P. albicans	France	Sourès 197;, Nel 1978
P. hispana		Schurian 1980
P. humedasae	Italy	Manino *et al.* 1987
P. galloi	Italy	Balletto and Toso 1979
P. icarus	Spain	Martin 1984
	U.K.	Dennis 1984
Agriades glandon	Spain	Munguira 1989
A. zullichi	Spain	Munguira 1989

Table 2. Larval foodplants in the European Lycaenidae.

Subfamily	Taxa	Food Plants
Polyommatinae	Most feed mainly on legumes	Fabaceae
	Some genera have shifted to other food plants, e.g. *Tarucus* Moore, *Celastrina* Tutt	Rhamnaceae, Aquifoliaceae, Cornaceae, Araliaceae
	Some *Maculinea* Ecke; *Pseudophilotes* Beuret *Maculinea arion* (L.)	Gentianaceae, Rosaceae, Lamiaceae
	Freyeria Courvoisier	Boraginaceae
	Scolitantides Hubner	Crassulaceae
	Plebejus argus (L.)	Fabaceae, Ericaceae, Cistaceae
	Vacciniina Tutt	Ericaceae
	Aricia Reichenbach	Geraniaceae, Cistaceae,
	Agriades Hubner	Primulaceae
	Cyaniris Dalman	Fabaceae, Plumbaginaceae
Theclinae	Most species feed mainly on trees and shrubs	Fagaceae, Rhamnaceae, Oleaceae, Ulmaceae, Ericaceae
	Some are adapted to legumes, e.g. *Tomares ballus* (F.), *Callophrys rubi* (L.)	Fabaceae
Lycaeninae	All species are restricted to:	Polygonaceae (*Rumex* and *Polygonum* spp.)

Table 3. Frequencies and percentages of species overwintering at different stages in the three subfamilies of Spanish Lycaenidae. Data taken from Martin (1982).

	Egg	Larvae	Pupae
Theclinae	9 (75%)	–	3 (25%)
Lycaeninae	1 (17%)	5 (83%)	–
Polyommatinae	4 (8%)	40 (78%)	7 (14%)
TOTAL	14 (20%)	45 (65%)	10 (15%)

European habitats of importance for lycaenids

Although conservation practice involves a battle for every piece of land containing wild animals or plants, some ecosystems in Europe are particularly important because they have become rare or support valuable species or communities (Blab and Kudrna 1982; Kudrna 1986; Balletto and Casale 1991). The following are some of the habitats of special importance for lycaenid conservation.

Woodlands

Apart from regions of the extreme north of Europe, woodlands represent the only stable ecosystems from sea level up to the high altitude vegetational stages. Nevertheless they have been subject to the most severe human pressures, and very few remain in their natural condition.

In the case of lycaenids, woodlands are generally used only by theclines which are mostly encountered on the borders of natural or artificial clearings. Whether this is the natural condition, or if theclines (as inhabitants of the canopy) can rarely be observed in closed woods, remains for the moment a matter of speculation.

Woodland damage has been particularly severe in central Europe (e.g. Germany), but the wide distribution of most theclines makes threats to whole individual species rather unlikely. Only some species such as *Satyrium pruni* (L.), *S. acaciae* (F.), *Thecla betulae* (L.), or *Callophrys avis* Chapman are locally rare or have declined in the last few decades (Heath 1981; Heath *et al.* 1984).

Screes

Rocky areas with sparse vegetation usually have a very interesting flora and fauna in Mediterranean countries. Limestone outcrops and schists are particularly interesting habitats for some rare endemics such as *Aricia morronensis* Ribbe. The most interesting areas are high altitude habitats where vegetation is sparse and the climate makes living conditions particularly severe for butterflies: here only a few well adapted species can survive. Some of the species living on these areas are among the rarest European endemics: *Agriades zullichi* Hemming and *Polyommatus golgus* (Hübner). *Turanana panagaea* (Herrich-Schaeffer), a rather widespread xerophilous species in Turkey, becomes extremely scarce and localised in Europe and although no appropriate habitat study has been made, it is possible that it may qualify as a member of this group on the western side of the Aegean.

Grasslands

Ecologically, grasslands can be subdivided into two major types on the basis of their being climacic or seral. The former occur typically in the far north of Europe and at high elevations of mountain ranges. The latter are found over a wider range of altitudes and generally represent the direct or indirect result of human activities. Within these grasslands some areas defined as 'seminatural' have conserved a very rich soil and diverse vegetation and are by far the most important habitats for lycaenid conservation.

Grassland management is changing dramatically throughout Europe, and the effects of this upon butterflies are just beginning to be understood. Erhardt and Thomas (1991) and Balletto *et al.* (1989) have dealt with the effect of grassland management on butterfly populations, stating that traditional land uses are the best way to preserve the existing butterfly diversity and are essential for the survival of several endangered species.

As far as butterfly conservation is concerned several types of grasslands can be considered although these categories are very heterogeneous from the vegetational point of view.

Dry grasslands and steppes are only found in Europe in some Mediterranean countries and in central east Europe. They often develop on stony, poor soils from the Mediterranean to the montane vegetation stage and are generally characterised by a comparatively low turf, or in some cases by the presence of one or more grass species of the genus *Stipa* from which some of them derive their name.

The xeric character of this type of vegetation is reflected in the structure of their butterfly communities which are dominated by grass feeders (Satyrinae and Hesperiidae). Some more or less restricted endemics and other interesting lycaenids occur in these habitats, the most notable of these species being undoubtedly *Plebejus pylaon* Fischer von Waldheim. In mountain areas these grasslands host many *Polyommatus* species of the subgenus *Agrodiaetus,* some of which are extremely local.

The conservation of these habitats is particularly important because traditionally they have been considered useless, and steppe landscapes are generally unattractive for the public and therefore given low priority for conservation. At low elevations, however, they have been used for sheep or goat grazing, mainly during the winter, or locally (e.g. Alps) as vineyards.

Mesophilous grasslands represent the lusher, more humid counterpart of dry grasslands. They generally develop on deeper, richer soils and are very rich in lycaenid butterflies. The rare species present in such areas include *Lycaena hippothoe* (L.), *Maculinea rebeli* (Hirschke), *M. arion*, *Aricia eumedon*, *Pseudophilotes bavius* (Eversmann), *Scolitantides orion* (Pallas) and *Lycaenides argyrognomon* (Bergsträsser).

Mountain meadows are maintained by extensive cattle or sheep grazing, or locally by seasonal mowing. As a consequence of the milk surplus in the EEC this management is changing to reafforestation for paper production, particularly in southern countries. On far too many occasions this management practice leads to plantations with alien tree species and to the total destruction of the original habitat.

It is important to point out that the greatest diversity of European lycaenids occurs in this kind of habitat, due to the ecotone nature of most meadows in which patches of trees, shrubs and grasslands occur in the same places. The beautiful, flowered meadows blooming with butterflies are disappearing very quickly in Europe and only some mountain areas such as the Alps or the Pyrenees act as refuge areas. The role of extensive grazing is crucial to conserve these habitats, and subsidies will probably soon be needed to support some of the less productive farming practices. Other aggressive uses related to skiing and the expansion of mountain tourism are deleterious for the conservation of these habitats.

High altitude grasslands are only present above the natural tree line, either at the highest elevations on the major mountains or in the extreme north of the continent. Their climacic character makes management less necessary and thus their conservation easier. An important number of the European rare lycaenids live in these habitats: all the *Agriades* species (including the extremely rare *A. zullichi* which is found in a habitat transitional with high altitude screes); *Albulina orbitulus* (Prunner), *Cyaniris helena* (Staudinger); and some subspecies of *Aricia morronensis*, *Polyommatus eros* (Ochsenheimer), *P. eroides* Firvaldszky, and *P. golgus*.

Threats to this type of environment are comparatively limited and are mainly represented by the spreading of ski resorts and mountain tourism, or to extensive overgrazing in southwest Europe.

Wet meadows and grasslands are azonal, like screes, in the sense that they can develop almost at any altitude where appropriate soil conditions are met (in this case a high humidity). Particularly at low elevations they are among the most endangered habitats in Europe. Species living on these grasslands are threatened throughout their range and examples of these are some of the most endangered species of *Maculinea*: *M. alcon* (Denis and Schiffermüller); *M. teleius* (Bergsträsser); and *M. nausithous* (Bergsträsser). Threats to this type of habitat are often related to land drainage and include changes in land management as a consequence of the very productive nature of these grasslands.

Shrublands

Shrublands normally grow as a consequence of the action of disturbing ecological factors such as strong winds, short vegetation times, human management or recurrent fires. They are interesting because some rare species are almost restricted to these formations.

True heathlands dominated by *Erica* species are the habitat of *Plebejus argus,* a species that has declined rapidly in England but which does not seem to have similar conservation problems in other countries.

Mediterranean shrublands (garigues or chaparral formations) also support interesting rare species such as *Iolana iolas*, a circum-Mediterranean species living on chaparral. Another peculiar type of Mediterranean shrubland is represented by heathlands (with *Erica arborea* and *E. scoparia*) found on the highest, windswept elevations of Corsica, Sardinia and Elba (France and Italy, Balletto *et al.* 1989). This is the exclusive habitat of the endemic *Lycaeides corsica* (Tutt).

    Kretania psylorita (Freyer) is a rare endemic living in Cretan shrublands dominated by an *Astragalus* species (Leigheb *et al.* 1990). Similar to these are some species living on biotopes dominated by *Thymus* species (called locally in Spain 'tomillares') where some endemics (*Cupido lorquinii* Herrich-Schaeffer) or rare species (*Pseudophilotes bavius, P. abencerragus* (Pierret) and *Scolitantides orion* (Pallas)) live.

Subalpine-type shrublands are found on mountains above the tree line. They are characterised by the presence of *Rhododendron* and *Vaccinium*, often in association with dwarf pine trees. Their butterflies are mainly boreal-alpine elements which include, in wet areas, *Aricia nicias* Meigen, and *Vacciniina optilete* (Knoch) among the lycaenids.

Wetlands

These are probably the most endangered among European habitats as a consequence of drainage either to control mosquitoes or to transform the habitat into agricultural land (particularly rice fields). Wetland drainage has affected huge areas, both in central Europe (see Kudrna 1986 for the case of Bohemia in the

16th century) and in the south of the continent (Italy in the 19th century). Typical lycaenids living on wetlands are *Lycaena dispar* (Haworth), *L. helle* (Denis and Schiffermüller) and at higher altitudes or latitudes, *Vaciniina optilete*. These three species are listed as threatened by Heath (1981) and *L. dispar* is listed in the Berne Convention as being one of the most endangered European lycaenids.

Causes of decline and extinction of European lycaenids

This subject has been considered by several authors when dealing with the broader topics of European butterflies (Heath 1981, Thomas 1984b, Kudrna 1986) and insects of the Mediterranean Basin (Balletto and Casale 1991). A considerable amount of information and a number of opinions are also available for individual countries (Blab and Kudrna 1982; Viedma 1984; Balletto and Kudrna 1985; SBN 1987; Gonseth 1987; Swaay 1990; Bàlint 1991; Kulfan and Kulfan 1991). Although no single review has dealt with the subject solely with reference to lycaenids, many papers pointing out causes of decline of individual species are now available (see Table 1 for references). An overview of the topic is provided in Table 4, where information on butterfly conservation at a European level is summarised.

Habitat alteration or destruction

All three authors referred to in Table 4, as well as various national reports, identify this factor as the most important one for butterfly decline throughout Europe. A change in habitat quality is the cause of all extinctions documented to have taken place. This applies also to the lycaenids *Lycaena dispar* and *Maculinea arion* in the United Kingdom (Duffey 1968; Thomas 1980) and *Lycaena hippothoe* (L.), *M. arion, M. nausithous* and *M. teleius* in The Netherlands (Heath 1981).

    Some examples of documented extinctions in Europe are given in Table 5. Wetland and grassland destruction or alteration are the main causes of recent extinctions.

    Butterfly declines are reaching an alarming scale in most central and north European countries where a high proportion of the fauna is experiencing dramatic range reductions (Heath *et al.* 1984). The range reductions of the following lycaenid species have been caused by habitat changes: *Plebejus argus* (United Kingdom, Ravenscroft 1990); *Polyommatus bellargus* (United Kingdom, Thomas 1983); *Satyrium pruni* (United Kingdom, Thomas 1974); *Lycaena dispar* and *L. helle* (Germany, Kudrna 1986); and *Polyommatus exuberans* Verity and *L. dispar* (Italy, Balletto *et al.* 1982a–e, Balletto in press).

    Habitat alterations can be quite subtle: for example, a slight change of growth in grass height on British *Maculinea arion* sites is enough to make the habitat unsuitable for the butterfly host ant (Thomas 1989). This change produced by grazing relaxation was sufficient to cause the disappearance of the

27

Table 4. Causes of decline or extinction of European butterflies in three different reviews of the topic. Similar causes (abbreviated) are listed on the same line.

Heath 1981	Thomas 1984b	Kudrna 1986
● Habitat destruction wetland drainage, changes in grassland management, forestry practices	● Habitat changes wetlands, woodlands, agricultural habitats ● Forestry management	● Wetland drainage ● Grassland management ● Afforestation
● Air pollution	● Air pollution	● Air pollution
● Pesticides	● Insecticides	● Weed & pest control
● Climatic change	● Weather & climate	
● Urbanisation		● Urbanisation
● Tourism		● Tourism & transport
● Collecting	● Butterfly collectors	● Overcollecting
● Commerce		
		● Earthworks
	● Isolation and area	

Table 5. Extinctions of European lycaenids documented to have taken place in individual countries with an indication of the total number of extinct butterfly species in each case.

Country	Extinct lycaenids	Species	Total extinct butterflies
United Kingdom	3	*dispar, arion, semiargus*	5
Netherlands	5	*arion, teleius, nausithous, hippothoe, semiargus*	15
Denmark	1	*dispar*	2
Luxembourg	3	*argiades, idas, dorylas*	8

butterfly from formerly suitable habitats. Extensive grazing is declining rapidly over almost all of Europe due to intensification of agricultural practices and abandonment of former grazing areas. Neither grazing relaxation nor the decline in extensive grazing is good news for butterflies because these insects have evolved in Europe over thousands of years together with man, and have probably benefited from the patchy structure of agrobiosystems in which grasslands, hedges and woodlands occur together. The apparent phenological synchronization observed in the Dolomites between butterfly cycles and traditional mowing cycles (Balletto *et al.* 1988) may be another example of such a process.

Air pollution

Almost every author identifies air pollution as a cause of butterfly decline, but this is not supported by detailed evidence in any case (Thomas 1984b). The effect of pollution on insects is better understood in soil or aquatic species, although it seems obvious that it may have a real effect upon terrestrial insects. A high diversity and population number have been recorded on road verges in the United Kingdom (Munguira and Thomas 1992), a habitat where pollution caused by car exhausts is expected to be particularly severe. This probably suggests that, at least for some species, direct effects of pollution are negligible, whereas indirect effects (for example, of acid rain on forests) may prove to be more important for butterfly populations.

Chemicals (pesticides, herbicides, fertilizers)

A negative effect on insect diversity is often attributed to any chemicals sprayed over natural or semi-natural habitats. The effect of pesticides has only been studied on common species, but it is also evident that no rare or endangered species can survive on heavily sprayed localities. Some indirect evidence for this can be found in the literature. In the Padano-venetian plains, Balletto *et al.* (1982e) found considerable differences between butterfly communities in heavily sprayed and traditionally managed rice fields. Whereas on average five butterfly species were observed on each of the relatively natural habitats which supported *Lycaena dispar*, only one or two species could be found in the more heavily sprayed fields and here *L. dispar* was totally absent. Other unpublished observations give further evidence of this effect. The conclusion is that chemicals can reduce butterfly diversity and that they may be implicated in the disappearance of *L. dispar* from vast areas in the region.

Erhardt (1985) showed a negative effect of grassland fertilization: whereas six lycaenids among 30 Lepidoptera were more abundant in an unfertilized meadow than in unfertilized areas only one lycaenid out of two Lepidoptera was more abundant in fertilized meadows. Butterfly diversity was also drastically reduced in fertilized compared with unfertilized meadows. Balletto *et al.* (1988), however, failed to demonstrate the same effect on six fertilized and three unfertilized plots in the Dolomites.

Climatic change

Any relationship between climate and butterfly fluctuations is also hard to establish. In the study of this process, authors have referred to short-term climatic fluctuations, which are the only ones we can analyse. Even this needs a database maintained over several years, and only the British Butterfly Monitoring Scheme (BMS) is now available for such studies. Pollard (1988) stated that some climatic parameters such as summer temperatures are correlated with high butterfly numbers. Climate can also represent an important factor when fluctuations in numbers occur in populations previously isolated by other means such as habitat destruction. The synergetic effect of both factors can certainly endanger populations that are already declining. For example, a coincidence of habitat damage and unfavourable weather accelerated the extinction of *Maculinea arion* in Great Britain (Thomas 1989). Long-term climatic changes normally represent a natural process, but it is now uncertain if the short-term fluctuations derived from the greenhouse effect will have any influence on butterfly populations. This certainly adds another factor probably having some effect on butterfly abundance or survival, particularly when considering rare species.

Tourism and urbanisation

Ever-expanding tourist facilities and advancing urbanisation are obviously among the factors that threaten many butterfly populations. Nevertheless their effects are far more restricted geographically than habitat destruction or alteration due to changes in land management practices. Tourism is particularly aggressive in some areas, such as the Mediterranean coast, the Alps or some parts of the Pyrenees, where huge areas have literally been covered by urbanisation or ski courses.

There is no particular lycaenid restricted to coastal areas around the Mediterranean, but the effect of tourism clearly makes the species' habitats smaller, acting together with other more extensive impacts. In northwestern Italy *Glaucopsyche melanops* (Boisduval) and *Satyrium esculi* (Hübner) are threatened by tourist resorts which are now spreading inland from the sea borders (already totally covered in tarmac and concrete). Some previously abundant populations of *Lycaena thesarmon* (Esper) have become extinct as a consequence of the spreading urbanisation around Rome.

High mountain habitats are particularly susceptible to the impact of expanding tourist facilities because they host scarce and ecologically specialised forms. One example is represented by *Vacciniina optilete* in the Alps, which is declining in many parts of its former range (Balletto in press). Another example is represented by *Agriades zullichi* and *Polyommatus golgus*, very rare endemic lycaenids in Sierra Nevada (southern Spain). Their range is already restricted by a road and a ski resort development, but they may now disappear from one of their localities if the planned redevelopments really take place.

Collecting and commerce

Again, every review on the causes of butterfly decline and extinction deals with this topic, but appropriate studies on the effects of collectors on butterfly populations remain wanting. The appeal of this topic probably has something to do with ethics and with the fact that treating some sophisticated and non-renewable products of nature as items of commerce is now unacceptable; neither does it seem correct to kill animals that other agencies are striving to conserve. Some collecting is still necessary in areas where our faunistic knowledge is poor.

Sometimes forbidding collection does little if any good for butterflies (Kudrna 1986). Results obtained from the enforcement of bans on butterfly collection in some cases have shown this to be an unsuccessful management practice: in Germany a ban on the collection of four butterfly species passed in 1936 has not prevented the dramatic decline of these species in the course of the last 55 years (Kudrna 1989).

In large populations the number of butterflies a collector can take is really negligible, not reaching 10% of the total daily population estimates, while small populations are normally of little interest to commercial collectors. To destroy one of these small populations by collection it is necessary to kill almost all the butterflies seen during the flight period: this represents a highly time-consuming job with slight rewards for the collector (Munguira *et al.* in press).

Legislation to protect species and habitats

In the last 30 years some European countries have passed laws protecting butterfly species. Heath (1981) reviewed this topic gathering data from 25 European countries, 13 (52%) of which had some legislation on the matter while only three countries (12%) included lycaenids among the protected species. In this review protected lycaenids were *Maculinea arion, M. alcon, M. teleius, Lycaena dispar, L. helle* and *Polyommatus bellargus*. Most of this legislation has been ineffective because it was based on the species themselves and paid little attention to habitats.

At the European level, the Council of Europe, an international organisation based in Strasbourg (France) that groups together almost all European countries, has endeavoured in recent years to provide collective tools for animal and plant conservation. This organisation sponsored the publication of Heath's *Threatened butterflies in Europe* (1981) and Collins and Wells' *Invertebrates in need of Special Protection in Europe* (1987). Partially as a result of these two reviews some invertebrates were included in the appendices to the Berne Convention (*Convention on the Conservation of European Wildlife and Natural Habitats*) in 1988. The Convention has been signed by 18 States and is important because it takes into account the need for habitat protection together with species protection. Appendix II of the Convention protects 24 lepidopteran species, five of which are lycaenids (*Lycaena dispar, Maculinea arion, M. teleius, M. nausithous* and *Polyommatus golgus*).

Another potentially useful international convention yet to be considered in this framework is the *International Convention for the Conservation of Wetlands* (Ramsar), 1971. Devised to ensure protection of all European important wetlands, Ramsar legislation is, in principle, an ideal instrument for the conservation of all wet meadows and wetlands including any threatened lycaenid species. The problem with this convention is that it was aimed at the conservation of birds and has been opened only in recent times to include other vertebrates (amphibians, reptiles). The possibility that butterflies may be also considered in the selection of Ramsar sites is unfortunately nowhere in sight, but insect conservationists should be aware that such a possibility exists for the future.

Species used as emblems, highlights of the fauna

Some individual species, generally characterised by a particularly striking appearance, have often been used to attract the attention of the general public toward conservation issues. These so-called 'panoramic species' have proved useful to promote the conservation of many animal groups.

Although the importance of lycaenids from this point of view is not as clear as with papilionids (e.g. *Parnasius apollo* (L.), *Papilio hospiton* Géné) some species have been instrumental in arousing considerable attention from the public towards butterfly conservation. The best example for this is *Maculinea arion* in Great Britain. During the 1970s the dramatic decline of this species in its few remaining biotopes was closely followed by many amateur lepidopterists and the topic appeared in several local and national press releases. A fund was established to support the preservation of the species and sponsor scientific research on its habitat requirements. Unfortunately all this interest came too late to save the species which became extinct in 1979 (Thomas 1989). However, this process helped in advancing the knowledge of the biology of the species to such an extent that it was successfully reintroduced to some sites a few years later. Since then, the

peculiarities of the biology of the 'large blue' and of the *Maculinea* species in general have fascinated the public and they are now certainly emblems of European efforts to preserve butterflies.

The reasons for the success of *Maculinea* species in this respect have something to do with their relatively large size and beauty among lycaenids, their obligate dependence on *Myrmica* ants and the fact that they are very sensitive to subtle changes in habitat quality (a perfect illustration of the reasons for butterfly decline in Europe). *Maculinea* species are subjects of conservation studies throughout Europe from Spain to Hungary and are being reintroduced in several countries where they had previously become extinct. They are also currently included in every European list of endangered Lepidoptera.

Another emblematic lycaenid, from the conservation point of view, is *Lycaena dispar*, the first butterfly whose extinction was documented in the United Kingdom as early as 1851. The habitat of this species consists of marshes, fens, wet meadows and oxbow lakes. Drainage of such biotopes has been the main cause of its decline throughout its range. It is protected by national laws in the following seven countries: United Kingdom, France, Netherlands, Hungary, Germany, Finland and Belgium; and also by all the Contracting Parties of the Berne Convention (Collins 1987). Apart from the United Kingdom it has also become extinct in Denmark and endangered in all the rest of its European range. *Lycaena dispar* is emblematic because it is sensitive to a very common practice in Europe, wetland drainage, and because it is conveniently large in size and colourful like the *Maculinea* species. It is the only lycaenid included by Kudrna (1986) in his short list of endangered European butterflies.

Species of economic importance as pests

There are no real pests among European lycaenids. Only some very common species can live on Mediterranean legume crops and could be considered as potential enemies of cultivated plants, but their presence has never caused serious problems. *Lampides boeticus* (L.) is occasionally listed among pests of peas, and together with *Polyommatus icarus* and *Leptotes pirithous* (L.) can also be a potential pest of alfalfa crops (Martin 1984).

Red Data List of European lycaenids

Any Red Data List is subjective and normally tends to be influenced by the authors' personal experience. Even the Red Data List concept is controversial and many authors have expressed opinions against it (Diamond 1988). Some authors have suggested that a list of endangered habitats may be far more useful than species orientated red data lists (Balletto and Casale 1991), and Kudrna (1986) has proposed that the latter should only include species which are in need of emergency action. In our opinion, policies concentrating on habitat conservation should be given priority over species-centred schemes although it must be remembered that it is sometimes easier for policy makers to focus on the protection of a species rather than the more complicated process of habitat protection. In general, we consider that our section on important habitats for lycaenids is more relevant than the present paragraph on threatened lycaenids.

In an attempt to make our list as impartial as possible we have pooled data from five European-level compilations of threatened species (Heath 1981; Kudrna 1986; Collins and Wells 1987; the Berne Convention (Appendix II, 1988) and an unpublished list drafted by Van der Made during the Wageningen Symposium on *Status of Butterflies in Europe* in 1989). For every species appearing on a list we have given a score depending on whether it was listed as endangered (3), vulnerable (2), or rare (1). Species appearing as indeterminate or other categories were not considered, and the Berne Convention species (Appendix II) have all been scored as 3. In this way the highest possible score for any species is 15 (if 'endangered' on all five lists) and the lowest is 1.

With a few exceptions that will be dealt with later the results shown in Table 6 are surprisingly consistent for the high ranking categories ('endangered' and 'vulnerable' in our list). All the species listed as 'endangered' have been accorded this status in at least one of the lists referred to above. Species in the 'rare' category are a more mixed group that can be interpreted as species on which different authors do not agree, or that are localised but common.

Such a list, however, is far from perfect, mainly because for the north and centre of Europe there is a long tradition in conservation studies, whereas in the south of the continent comparable research has long been neglected. *Polyommatus coelestinus* (Eversmann), for example, is categorised only as 'rare' because it is part of a complex which may be abundant in Anatolia and the Caucasus, but is certainly more than rare in other parts of Europe (e.g. Peloponnisos). There is a similar situation with *Turanana panagea*.

Another problem clearly under-ranking some species has to do with taxonomy (Daugherty *et al.* 1990). A number of *Polyommatus* of the subgenus *Agrodiaetus*, for instance, have been recognised as separate species only recently. Accordingly they were not included in older lists. Another case is *Agriades zullichi* which was considered a subspecies of the comparatively common *A. glandon* (Prunner), a fact that previously obscured the true endangered status of what is now considered a distinct species. As a consequence, we think that *Agriades zullichi*, *Polyommatus exuberans* and *P. humedasae* (Toso and Balletto) should be listed as 'endangered' and *Turanana panagea*, *Pseudophilotes barbagiae* Prins & Poorten, *Kretania psylorita*, *Polyommatus galloi* Balletto & Toso, *P. aroaniensis* Brown and *P. coelestinus* as 'vulnerable'.

Priorities in the conservation of European lycaenids

Some conclusions can be drawn from all that has been discussed in the preceding sections. Most butterfly conservationists agree that some general considerations are to be kept in mind if any conservation measure is intended to be effective. Therefore, the duty of ecologists and butterfly conservationists is to make these available in an understandable way to the people who make decisions.

The main considerations which emerge from our appraisal are:

(1) The fact that many lycaenid species are declining is supported by evidence derived from most European countries. Habitat destruction and changes in land use are apparently the two most important factors responsible for species decline. As a consequence, such alterations should be stopped in the areas where endangered species have their habitat.

(2) Vulnerable species suffer the same threatening factors on a more local scale, but any action liable to pose a threat for them should be carefully considered, and the status of the species over its distributional range taken into account.

(3) Wetlands and wet meadows are among the most vulnerable habitats in Europe. Accordingly, wetland lycaenids are unanimously regarded as the most endangered by butterfly specialists. A European wetland register is urgently needed and legislation passed in order to protect all European wetlands known to include populations of threatened species. As we have already said, the most suitable international framework for such an action is Ramsar which might be persuaded, at a future date, to incorporate butterfly data into the listing criteria.

(4) Traditional land practices have been compatible for centuries with the survival of species living on those sites and their continuation may occasionally prove necessary. They should be maintained wherever they are vital for the survival of declining species, and enhanced in those places where they gave way to more aggressive practices. Nevertheless, this fact cannot be generalised and some species will certainly do better in a totally natural habitat.

The policy of continuing with traditional practices may sometimes need subsidies, but may be enough to keep high standards of living in many areas as suggested by the IUCN conservation policies, and by several conservation specialists (Thibodeau and Field 1984). Abandonment of former extensive agricultural areas should be monitored, because this may eventually lead to changes in habitat as a result of natural succession and the resultant loss of many species adapted to traditional agrobiosystems.

(5) Nature reserves should only be declared for those habitats and species whose conservation cannot be assured by current land uses. Special care should be taken to satisfy the ecological requirements of protected species to ensure their survival. This will mean in many cases that management will have to oppose the natural succession of vegetation. Conflicts with the requirements of other endangered or rare species

Table 6. A Red Data List of European Lycaenidae, obtained by summing scores drawn from other previous lists (see text).

ENDANGERED (score 15–8)

Lycaena dispar	(15)
Maculinea teleius	(14)
M. nausithous	(14)
M. alcon	(9)
Polyommatus golgus	(9)
Maculinea arion	(8)

VULNERABLE (score 7–3)

Vacciniina optilete	(6)
Lycaena helle	(6)
Maculinea rebeli	(4)
Cupido lorquinii	(4)
Pseudophilotes bavius	(4)
Agriades pyrenaicus	(3)
Polyommatus humedasae	(4)
P. exuberans	(3)
Callophrys avis	(3)

RARE (score 2–1)

Plebejus pylaon	(2)
Polyommatus eroides	(2)
P. ainsae	(2)
P. galloi	(2)
P. violetae	(2)
Aricia morronensis	(2)
A. eumedon	(2)
Pseudophilotes baton	(2)
P. barbagiae	(2)
Agriades zullichi	(2)
Kretania psylorita	(2)
Turanana panagea	(2)
Cupido carswelli	(1)
Iolana iolas	(1)
Scolitantides orion	(1)
Kretania euripilus	(1)
Polyommatus aroaniensis	(1)
P. coelestinus	(1)
Thesarmonia thetis	(1)

should also be considered in order to make management decisions which ensure the conservation of all target species.

(6) Natural habitats where rare or endangered species live on climacic plant communities should also be preserved from any possible alteration by the creation of Natural or National Parks. Priority should be given to those places where extremely localised lycaenids are present, such as the high elevations of Sierra Nevada (Spain), or the Idhi Mountain (Crete). Climacic forests or shrublands must also be preserved when listed species live on them, but special effort should be made to ensure that the ecological requirements of target species are really those of the climax and do not depart from it in any way, however subtle.

(7) Finally, more research is still needed, even for the most well known among the European lycaenids. We suggest three topics of special relevance for lycaenid conservation:

● the creation of a European database of all the areas relevant for lycaenid conservation with special attention to the needs of endangered or rare species;

● the monitoring and mapping of each endangered or vulnerable species both on a national and European scale;

● the study of the ecological requirements of every target species so that sound recommendations can be made to ensure their long-term survival.

References

BÀLINT, Z. 1991. Conservation of butterflies in Hungary. *In:* Kudrna, O. (Ed.) Schutz der Tagfaltern in Osten Mitteleuropas: Böhmen, Mähren, Slowakei, Ungarn. *Oedippus* **3**: 5–36.

BÀLINT, Z. and KERTÉSZ, A. 1990. A survey of the subgenus *Plebejides* (Sauter, 1986) – A preliminary revision. *Linn. Belg.* **12**: 190–224.

BALLETTO, E. (in press). Butterflies in Italy: status, problems and prospects. *Proceedings of the International Congress 'Future of butterflies in Europe'*, Wageningen 1989.

BALLETTO, E., BARBERIS, G. and TOSO, G.G. 1982a. Lepidotteri ropaloceri dei littorali a duna dell'Italia meridionale. *Quaderni sulla 'Struttura dell zoocenosi terrestri' CNR, Roma* **3**: 153–158.

BALLETTO, E., BARBERIS, G. and TOSO, G.G. 1982b. Aspetti dell'ecologia dei Lepidotteri ropaloceri nei consorzi erbacei delle Alpi italiane. *Quaderni sulla 'Struttura dell zoocenosi terrestri' CNR, Roma* **2(II.2)**: 11–96.

BALLETTO, E. and CASALE, A. 1991. Mediterranean insect conservation: the importance of pleistocene refugia. *In:* Collins, N.M. and Thomas, J.A. (Eds): *The conservation of insects and their habitats.* Academic Press, London, pp. 121–142.

BALLETTO, E. and KUDRNA, O. 1985. Some aspects of the conservation of butterflies in Italy, with recommendations for a future strategy (Lepidoptera, Hesperiidae and Papilionoidea). *Boll. Soc. Entomol. Ital.* **117**: 39–59.

BALLETTO, E., LATTES, A. and TOSO, G.G. 1982d. Le comunità di Lepidotteri ropaloceri come strumento per la classificazione e l'analisi della qualità degli alti pascoli italiani. *Quaderni sulla 'Struttura dell zoocenosi terrestri' CNR, Roma* **2(II.2)**: 97–139.

BALLETTO, E., LATTES, A. and TOSO, G.G. 1985. An ecological study of the Italian rhopalocera. *Proc. 3rd Congr. eur. Lepid.* Cambridge: 7–14.

BALLETTO, E., LATTES, A., CASSULO, L. and TOSO, G.G. 1988. Studi sull'ecologia dei Lepidotteri ropaloceri in alcuni ambienti delle Dolomiti. *In:* Brandmayr, P. (Ed.) Le Dolomiti: Val di Fiemme – Pale di San Martino. Zoocenosi e Paesaggio I. *Studi trentini di Sci. nat.* **64**: (suppl.): 87–124.

BALLETTO, E. and TOSO, G.G. 1979. On a new species of *Agrodiaetus* (Lycaenidae) from Southern Italy. *Nota lepid.* 2: 13–25.

BALLETTO, E., TOSO, G.G. and BARBERIS, G. 1982c. Le comunità di Lepidotteri ropaloceri nei consori erbacei dell'Appennino. *Quaderni sulla 'Struttura dell zoocenosi terrestri' CNR, Roma* **2(II.1)**: 77–143.

BALLETTO, E., TOSO, G.G. and BARBERIS, G. 1982e. Le comunità di Lepidotteri ropaloceri di alcuni ambienti relitti della Padania. *Quaderni sulla 'Struttura dell zoocenosi terrestri' CNR, Roma* **4**: 45–67.

BALLETTO, E., TOSO, G.G., BARBERIS, G. and ROSSARO, B. 1977. Aspetti dell'ecologia dei Lepidotteri ropaloceri nei consorci erbacei alto Apenninici. *Animalia* **4**: 277–343.

BALLETTO, E., TOSO, G.G. and LATTES, A. 1989. Studi sulle comunità di Lepidotteri ropaloceri dell'littorale tirrenico. *Boll. Musei Ist. biol. Università Genova* **53**: 141–186.

BALLETTO, E., TOSO, G.G. and TROIANO, G. 1981. *Aricia cramera* (Escholtz, 1821) in Sardinia. *Nota lepid.* **4**: 81–92.

BIGOT, K. 1952. Biogéographie des lepidoptères de la Provence Occidentale. *Vie Milieu* **8**(3): 253–264.

BIGOT, K. 1956. Biogéographie des lepidoptères de la Provence Occidentale. *Vie Milieu* **8**(3): 253–264.

BLAB, J. and KUDRNA, O. 1982. Hilfprogram für Schmetterlinge. Ökologie und Schutz von Tagfaltern und Widderchen. Kild Verlag; *Naturschutz aktuell* **6**: 1–135.

CHAPMAN, T.A. 1914. A contribution to the life history of *Agriades thersites* Cantener. *Trans. ent. Soc. Lond.* **1914**: 285–308.

CLÉU, H. 1950. Les faunes entomologiques méditerranéennes dans le bassin du Rhône et leurs rapports avec les éléments de la flore. *Méms Mus. nation. Hist. nat. Paris* **30**: 243–266.

CLÉU, H. 1957. Lépidoptères et biocénoses des génévriers dans les peuplements du bassin du Rhône. *Ann. Soc. ent. Fr.* **126**: 1–29.

COLLINS, N.M. 1987. *Legislation to conserve insects in Europe.* Pamphlet 13. Amateur Entomologists' Society, London.

COLLINS, N.M. and WELLS, S.M. 1987. *Invertebrates in need of special protection in Europe.* Council of Europe, Strasbourg.

DAUGHERTY, C.H., CREE, A., HAY, J.M. and THOMPSON, M.B. 1990. Neglected taxonomy and continuing extinctions of tuatara (Sphenodon). *Nature* **347**: 177–179.

DEMPSTER, J. 1971. Some observations on a population of the small copper butterfly *Lycaena phlaeas* (Linnaeus) (Lep., Lycaenidae). *Entomologist's Gaz.* **22**: 199–204.

DAVIS, G., FRASER, J. and TYNAN, A. 1958. Population numbers in a colony of *Lysandra bellargus* Rott. (Lepidoptera). *Proc. R. ent. Soc. Lond.* **33**: 31–36.

DENNIS, R.L.H. 1984. Egg-laying sites of the common blue butterfly, *Polyommatus icarus* (Rottemburg) (Lepidoptera: Lycaenidae): the edge effect and beyond the edge. *Entomologist's Gaz.* **35**: 85–93.

DIAMOND, J.M. 1988. Conservation biology: red books or green lists? *Nature* **332**: 304–5.

DOUWES, P. 1975. Distribution of a population of the butterfly *Heodes virgaureae* (Lep., Lycaenidae). *Oikos* **26**: 332–40.

DUFAY, C. 1961. Faune terrestre et d'eau douce des Pyrénées Orientales. *Vie Milieu* **12** (1): suppl.

DUFAY, C. 1965–66. Contribution à la connaissance des peuplements en Lépidoptères de la Haute Provence. *Bull. mens. Soc. linn. Lyon,* 159pp.

DUFFEY, E. 1968. Ecological studies on the large copper butterfly *Lycaena dispar* Haw. *batavus* Obth. at Woodwalton Fen National Natural Reserve, Huntingdonshire. *J. appl. Ecol.* **5**: 69–96.

EHRLICH, P.R. 1984. The structure and dynamics of butterfly populations. *In:* Vane-Wright, R.I. and Ackery, P.R. (Eds) *The biology of butterflies.* Academic Press, London, pp. 25–40.

EMMET, A.M. and HEATH, J. (Eds) 1989. *The moths and butterflies of Great Britain and Ireland.* Vol. 7 (1). Harley Books, Colchester.

ERHARDT, A. 1985. Diurnal Lepidoptera – sensitive indicators of change in the semi-natural grassland. *J. appl. Ecol.* **22**: 849–62.

ERHARDT, A. and THOMAS, J.A. 1991. Lepidoptera as indicators of change in the semi-natural grasslands of lowland and upland Europe. *In:* Collins, N.M. and Thomas, J.A. (Eds) *The conservation of insects and their habitats.* Academic Press, London, pp. 213–236.

FIEDLER, K. 1990a. European and North West African Lycaenidae and their associations with ants. *J. Res. Lepid.* **28**: 239–57.

FIEDLER, K. 1990b. Bemerkungen zur Larvalbiologie von *Callophrys rubi* L. (Lepidoptera: Lycaenidae). *Nachr. entomol. Ver. Apollo* **11**: 121–41.

FIEDLER, K. 1991. Systematic, evolutionary, and ecological implications of myrmecophily within the Lycaenidae (Insecta: Lepidoptera: Papilionoidea). *Bonner Zool. Monographien* **31**: 1–210.

FIORI, G. 1957. *Strymon ilicis* Esp. (Lepidoptera: Lycaenidae). *Boll. Entom. Bologna* **22**: 205–56.

FORD, E.B. 1970. *Butterflies.* Collins, London.

FOUASSIN, M. 1961. Lépidoptères du littoral Belge. *Lambillionea* **61**: 65–71.

GONSETH, Y. 1987. *Atlas de distribution des papillons diurnes de Suisse (Lepidoptera: Rhopalocera).* Centre Suisse de Cartographie de la Faune, Neuchâtel.

HEATH, J. 1981. *Threatened Rhopalocera (Butterflies) in Europe.* Council of Europe, Strasbourg.

HEATH, J., POLLARD, E. and THOMAS, J.A. 1984. *Atlas of Butterflies in Britain and Ireland.* Penguin Books, Harmondsworth.

HOEGH-GULDBERG, O. and JARVIS, F.V.L. 1970. Central and North European *Aricia* (Lep., Lycaenidae): Relationships, heredity, evolution. *Natur. Jutlandica* **15**: 7–106.

JANMOULLE, E. 1965. Lépidoptères observés dans les dunes du littoral. *Lambillonea* **65**: 12.

JARVIS, F.V.L. 1958. Biological notes on *Aricia agestis* (Schiff.) in Britain. I. *Entomologist's Rec. J. Var.* **70**: 141–148, 169–178.

JARVIS, F.V.L. 1959. Biological notes on *Aricia agestis* (Schiff.) in Britain. III. *Entomologist's Rec. J. Var.* **71**: 169–178.

JORDANO, D., FERNÁNDEZ, J. and RODRIGUEZ, J. 1990. The effect of seed predation by *Tomares ballus* (Lep., Lycaenidae) on *Astragalus lusitanicus* (Fabaceae): determinants of differences among patches. *Oikos* **57**: 250–6.

KRALICEK, M. and POVOLNY, D. 1978. Versuch einer Characteristik der Lepidopterensynusien als primaren Konsumänten in den Vegetationsstufen der Tschekoslowakei. *Vestn. cekosl. Spolecn. Zool.* **42**: 273–288.

KRATOCHWIL, A. 1989a. Biozönotische Umschichtungen im Grünland durch Düngung. *Sonder. NNA. Ber.* **2**: 46–58.

KRATOCHWIL, A. 1989b. Community structure of flower visiting insects in different grassland types in Southern Germany. *Spixiana* 289–302.

KRATOCHWIL, A. 1989c. Erfassung von Blütenbesuchergemeinschaften verschiedener Rassengesellschaften in Naturschutzgebiet Taubergiessen (Oberrheinebene). *Sonderd. Ges. Ökol., Göttingen* **17**: 701–711.

KUDRNA, O. 1986. *Butterflies of Europe. Vol. 8. Aspects of the conservation of butterflies in Europe.* Aula-Verlag, Wiesbaden.

KUDRNA, O. 1989. Conservation of butterflies in the Federal Republic of Germany since 1980. *In:* Abstracts Int. Congress '*Future of butterflies in Europe: strategies for survival.*' Wageningen. Netherlands.

KULFAN, J. and KULFAN, M. 1991. Die Tagfalterfauna der Slowakei und ihr Schutz unter besonderer Berücksichtigung der Gebirgsökosysteme. *In:* Kudrna, O. (Ed.) Schutz der Tagfaltern in Osten Mitteleuropas: Böhmen, Mähren, Slowakei, Ungarn. *Oedippus* **3**: 75–102.

LEESTMANS, R. 1984. L'écologie et la biogéographie en Europe de *Lycaeides idas* (L., 1761). *Linn. belg.* **9**: 370–408.

LEIGHEB, G., RIBONI, E. and CAMERON-CURRY, V. 1990. *Kretania psylorita* Freyer (Lycaenidae). Discovery of a new locality in Crete. *Nota lepid.* **13**: 242–245.

MALICKY, H. 1961. Über die Ökologie von *Lycaeides idas* L., insbesondere über seine symbiose mit Ameisen. *Z. Arb. gem. Österr. Ent.* **13**: 33–49.

MALICKY, H. 1969a. Übersicht über praimaginalstadien, bionomie und ökologie der mitteleuropaischen Lycaenidae (Lepidoptera). *Mitt. Ent. Ges. Basel* **19**: 25–91.

MALICKY, H. 1969b. Versucht einer Analyse der ökologischen Beziehungen zwischen Lycaeniden (Lepidoptera) und Formiciden (Hymenoptera). *Tijdschr. Ent.* **112**: 213–298.

MANINO, Z., LEIGHEB, G., CAMERON-CURRY, P. and CAMERON-CURRY, V. 1987. Descrizione degli stadi preimarginali di *Agrodiaetus humedasae* Toso & Balletto, 1976 (Lepidoptera, Lycaenidae). *Boll. Mus. reg. Sci. nat. Torino* **5**: 97–101.

MARTÍN, J. 1981. Similtudes biológicas y diferencias ecológicas entre *Glaucopsyche alexis* (Poda) y *Glaucopsyche melanops* (Boisduval). (Lep. Lycaenidae). *Bol. Est. Central Ecol.* **10**: 59–70.

MARTÍN, J. 1982. La biología de los licénidos españoles (Lep. Rhopalocera). *Miscelánea Commemorativa Fac. Ciencias U. Autón. Madrid*: 1003–1020.

MARTÍN, J. 1984. Biología comparada de *Lampides boeticus* (L.), *Syntarucus pirithous* (L.) y *Polyommatus icarus* (Rot.) (Lep., Lycaenidae). *Graellsia* **40**: 163–93.

MIKKOLA, K. and SPITZER, K. 1983. Lepidoptera associated with peatlands in Central and Northern Europe: a synthesis. *Nota lepid.* **6**: 216–229.

MORTON, A.C. 1985. *The population biology of an insect with a restricted distribution: Cupido minimus.* PhD thesis, University of Southampton.

MUNGUIRA, M.L. 1989. *Biología y biogeografía de los licénidos ibéricos en peligro de extinción (Lepidoptera, Lycaenidae).* Serv. Publicaciones U. Autónoma de Madrid, Madrid.

MUNGUIRA, M.L. and MARTÍN, J. 1988. Variabilidad morfológica y biológica de *Aricia morronensis* (Ribbe), especie endémica de la Península Ibérica (Lepidoptera: Lycaenidae). *Ecología* **2**: 343–58.

MUNGUIRA, M.L. and MARTÍN, J. 1989. Paralelismo en la biología de tres especies taxonómicamente próximas y ecológicamente diferenciadas del género *Lysandra*: *L. dorylas, L. nivescens* y *L. golgus* (Lepidoptera, Lycaenidae). *Ecologia* **3**: 331–52.

MUNGUIRA, M.L. and THOMAS, J.A. (1992). Use of road verges by butterfly and burnet populations, and the effect of roads on adult dispersal and mortality. *J. appl. Ecol.* **29**: 316–329.

MUNGUIRA, M.L., THOMAS, J.A., MARTÍN, J. and ELMES, G.W. (in press). Population size, dispersal and the vulnerability to collectors of three endangered species of Maculinea butterfly. *Biol. Conserv.*

MUNGUIRA, M.L., VIEJO, J.L. and MARTÍN, J. 1988. Distribución geográfica y biología de *Eumedonia eumedon* (Esper, 1780) en la Península Ibérica (Lepidoptera: Lycaenidae). *Shilap Revta. lepid.* **16**: 217–229.

NEL, J. 1978. Un élevage de *Lysandra hispana* H.-S. (Lep. Lycaenidae). *Alexanor* **10**: 317–321.

PELLMYR, O. 1983. Plebian courtship revisited: Studies on the female-produced male behaviour-eliciting signals in *Lycaeides idas* courtship, (Lycaenidae). *J. Res. Lepid.* **21**: 147–57.

POLLARD, E. 1988. Temperature, rainfall and butterfly numbers. *J. appl. Ecol.* **25**: 819–828.

RAVENSCROFT, N.O.M. 1990. The ecology and conservation of the silver-studded blue butterfly *Plebejus argus* L. on the sandlings of East Anglia, England. *Biol. Conserv.* **53**: 21–36.

RODRÎGUEZ, J. 1991. Las mariposas del Parque Nacional de Doñana. *Biología y ecología de Cyaniris semiargus y Plebejus argus.* PhD thesis. Universidad de Córdoba.

SBN (Schweizerischer Bund für Naturschutz) 1987. *Tagfalter und ihre Lebensräume.* Holliger, Basel.

SCHURIAN, K.G. 1980. Dauerzuchtversuch mit *Lysandra hispana* (H.S., 1852) (Lepidoptera, Lycaenidae). *Alexanor* **11**: 196–199.

SOURÉS, B. 1974. Relations et facteurs de répartition de différentes espèces du genre *Lysandra* (Lépidoptères, Lycaenidae). *Entomops* **33**: 25–32.

SWAAY, C.A.M. van 1990. An assessment of the changes in butterfly abundance in The Netherlands during the 20th century. *Biol. Conserv.* **52**: 287–302.

TAX, M.H. 1989. *Atlas van der nederlandse dagvlinders.* Gravenland, Wageningen.

THIBODEAU, F.R. and FIELD, H.H. 1984. *Sustaining Tomorrow. A Strategy for World Conservation and Development.* University Press, New England.

THOMAS, C.D. 1985. The status and conservation of the butterfly *Plebejus argus*, L. (Lepidoptera: Lycaenidae) in North West Britain. *Biol. Conserv.* **33**: 29–52.

THOMAS, J.A. 1974. *Ecological studies of hairstreak butterflies.* PhD thesis, University of Leicester.

THOMAS, J.A. 1975. Some observations on the early stages of the purple hairstreak butterfly, *Quercusia quercus* (Linnaeus) (Lep., Lycaenidae). *Entomologist's Gaz.* **26**: 224–226.

THOMAS, J.A. 1980. Why did the large blue become extinct in Britain? *Oryx* **15**: 243–7.

THOMAS, J.A. 1983. The ecology and conservation of *Lysandra bellargus* (Lepidoptera: Lycaenidae) in Britain. *J. appl. Ecol.* **20**: 59–83.

THOMAS, J.A. 1984a. The behaviour and habitat requirements of *Maculinea nausithous* (the dusky large blue) and *M. teleius* (the scarce large blue) in France. *Biol. Conserv.* **28**: 325–47.

THOMAS, J.A. 1984b. The conservation of butterflies in temperate countries: past efforts and lessons for the future. pp. 333–353. *In:* Vane-Wright, R.I. and Ackery, P.R. (Eds), *The Biology of Butterflies*, London.

THOMAS, J.A. 1989. The return of the large blue butterfly. *British Wildlife* **1**: 2–13.

THOMAS, J.A., ELMES, G.W., WARDLAW, J.C. and WOYCIECHOWSKY, M. 1989. Host specificity among *Maculinea* butterflies in *Myrmica* ant nests. *Oecologia* **79**: 452–457.

UHERKOVICH, A. 1972. Adatok a Dravasik nagylepkefaunajanak (Makrolepidoptera) ismeeretéhez. *Vas. megvei Muz. Ert.* **5–6**: 115–145.

UHERKOVICH, A. 1975. Adatok Buranya nagylepkefaunajanak ismeeretéhez. iv. A Villanyi-hegiség nappali lepkëi. *Janus Pannonius Muz. Evk.* **17–18**: 33–42.

UHERKOVICH, A. 1976. Adatok a Dél-Dunanuntul nagylepkefaunajanak (Makrolepidoptera). *Folia ent. Hung.* **29**: 119–137.

VERITY, R. 1943. *Le Farfalle diurne d'Italia.* Vol. 2. Marzocco, Firenze.

VIEDMA, M.G. 1984. *Consideraciones acerca de la conservaación de especies de insectos.* Real Acad. Ciencias, Madrid.

WEIDEMANN, H.-J. 1986. *Tagfalter. Band I. Entwicklung, Lebensweise.* Neumann-Neudamm GmbH and Co. KG, Melsungen.

WIKLUND, C. 1977. Observationer över äggläggning födosöl och vila hos donzels blavinge, *Aricia nicias scandicus* Wahlgr. (Lep., Lycaenidae). *Entomol. Tidskr.* **98**: 1–4.

Overview of problems in Japan

Toshiya Hirowatari

Entomological Laboratory, College of Agriculture, University of Osaka Prefecture, Sakai, Osaka, 591 Japan

In Japan, there are about 240 resident butterfly species which comprise palaearctic and oriental faunal elements. Fortunately, none of them has been rendered completely extinct but many local butterfly colonies seem to have been totally eradicated.

The first legislation to protect butterflies as *'Tennen Kinenbutu'* or *'Natural monuments'* was promulgated by the national government in 1932 for *Panchala ganesa* (Lycaenidae, Arhopalini) in Nara City. Until now, a total of 37 species have been designated as *'Tennen Kinenbutu'* by the national and local governments. However, in some cases, legislation for the prohibition of collecting without any effective measures for conservation seems to have been ineffective, especially when a taxon is designated as a protected species rather than as a local population with a definable habitat or biotype. In fact, the Nara population of *P. ganesa* seems to have become extinct without any precise records because collectors lost interest in studying protected species. Another case is that of *Shijimia moorei* (Leech) (Lycaenidae, Polyommatini). This species had been known to occur in east Asia in places such as China and Taiwan. It was not until 1973 that this species was discovered in Kyushu,

Japan: its distribution is extremely local, feeding on *Lysionotus pauceflorus* (Gesneriaceae) which usually grows on *Quercus* trees (Fagaceae) in humid evergreen forest. Just after that, in 1975, this species was designated as *'Tennen Kinenbutu'* by the national government. In this case, the original colonies of Kyushu seem to have been conserved. However, there have been few additional records from other areas (except one from Nara, Honshu) because collectors do not publish records of protected species even if these are caught. It is believed that some populations of *S. moorei* other than that in Kyushu become extinct without any definite records of this.

Apart from *Shijimia moorei*, the decline of Japanese butterflies is attributable to alteration in land management practices and its effect on butterfly habitat. In Japan, most of the victims, such as *Shijimiaeoides divinus* Fixcen (Lycaenidae, Polyommatini), *Coreana raphaelis* Oberthur (Lycaenidae, Theclini) and *Fabriciana nerippe* C. & R. Felder (Nymphalidae), depend on habitats such as coppice or grassland which have been maintained by traditional agricultural practices such as slash and burn, periodical coppicing for fuels and charcoal

Table 1. Lycaenidae from Japan listed by Hama *et al.* (1989).

Species	Causes of decline	Locality
Artopoetes pryeri Murray	Urbanisation	Setagaya, Tokyo
Coreana raphaelis Oberthur	Urbanisation; deforestation	Kawanishi, Yamagata
Niphandra fusca Bremer	Urbanisation	Kiso, Nagano; Shiga
	Road construction	Kiso, Nagano; Shiga
	Larch forestation	Kiso, Nagano
Shijimiaeoides divinus Fixcen	Habitat degradation	Aomori
	Orchard and golf course construction	Aomori
	Agriculture and spraying	Azumino, Nagano
Tongeia fisheri Eversmann	Factory construction	Komagano, Nagano; Matsumato, Nagano
	Flood: foodplant extinction	
	Urbanisation	Matsumato, Nagano
	Succession	Azumino, Nagano
Lycaeides subsolana Eversmann	Flood control works	Minami-azumi, Nagano

production, grass-cutting, animal husbandry, and so on (Sibatani 1989; Ishii 1990).

In Japan, few projects on butterfly conservation are supported by governmental funding, but awareness is increasing in many local research groups. Primary interest on the decline of butterflies and campaigns for their conservation have mainly highlighted rather large and beautiful butterflies, i.e. the 'Luehdorfia Butterflies', *Luehdorfia japonica* Leech and *L. puziloi* Ehrschoff (Papilionidae) and the 'Great Purple' *Sasakia charonda* (Nymphalidae). However, urgent management is required for some lycaenid species which have survived in harmony with the traditional land management that is now being superceded.

In 1989, the Lepidopterological Society of Japan (LSJ) (a group with nearly 1500 members) published the first volume of 'Decline and Conservation of butterflies in Japan' (edited by Hama, Ishii and Sibatani 1989) which was the first systematic approach to the problem of butterfly conservation in Japan. Six species of Lycaenidae were included in that book (Table 1). Soon after publication, the LSJ held its first seminar on 'Conservation of Butterflies' in June 1990. We found that there are many more local extinctions of butterflies than we expected, and fewer conservation projects supported by adequate budgets.

Attempts to find adequate funds for protecting butterflies or their habitats and for monitoring and overseeing activities continue. In early 1990, a group of the LSJ was granted funds of JPY 3,450,000 from the Nippon Life Insurance Foundation for monitoring the latest states of distribution and changes in population size of Japanese butterflies as environmental indicators for quality of human life.

References

HAMA, E., ISHII, M. and SIBATANI, A. (Eds) 1989. *Decline and conservation of butterflies in Japan. I.* Lepidopterological Society of Japan, Osaka.

ISHII, M. 1990. What has led to the butterflies declining? *Shizen Hogo* (The conservation of Nature) **337**: 14–15. (In Japanese).

SIBATANI, A. 1989. Decline and conservation of butterflies in Japan. *In:* Hama, E., Ishii, M. and Sibatani, A. (Eds) *Decline and Conservation of Butterflies in Japan. I* Lepidopterological Society of Japan, Osaka, pp. 16–22.

Conservation of North American lycaenids – an overview

J. Hall Cushman and Dennis D. Murphy

Center for Conservation Biology, Department of Biological Sciences, Stanford University, Stanford, California 94305-5020, U.S.A.

Introduction

Two distinct patterns emerge when one examines the United States' Endangered Species List. First, although butterflies probably constitute less than 1% of global insect species richness, they are disproportionately represented on the list: 53% (14 of 26) of the insects currently afforded federal protection are butterflies. Second, members of the Lycaenidae (including the blues, coppers, hairstreaks and metalmarks) are disproportionately represented: the family comprises only 21% of the species-level butterfly fauna of North America (Scott 1986), but constitutes 50% of the listed butterfly taxa: see Table 1, (Federal Register 1991a).

This over-representation of lycaenids also extends to the list of candidate species awaiting protection, including some taxa at risk of imminent extinction (see Table 2). For the U.S. as a whole, lycaenids comprise 37% of all butterflies that are candidates for listing as endangered species, and this number rises to 49% if skippers (a group currently treated as a superfamily distinct from the 'true butterflies') are excluded (Federal Register 1991b). In California, lycaenids are substantially over-represented among those taxa listed as candidates for federal protection or known to be at particular risk, making up 10 of those 20 taxa, whereas the state contains only a third of the nation's lycaenid fauna (Murphy 1987a). In addition, the candidates list is dominated by taxa from California and/or Nevada, making up 71% of the candidates (20 of 28; Table 2). They include a subspecies of *Plebejus saepiolus* (Boisduval) (soon to be described) that is probably already extinct. Another undescribed subspecies of hairstreak, *Incisalia mossii* (Edwards), has been pushed towards extinction by overzealous collectors who have removed hostplants and larvae. Also included is a copper, *Lycaena hermes* (Edwards), that may be differentiated sufficiently from all known relatives to warrant its recognition as a monotypic genus. It has been extirpated in significant portions of its historical range on both sides of the California-Mexico border.

There are two opposing ways of viewing the lycaenid dominance of endangered and threatened species, and the list of candidates for this status. The first interpretation of this pattern is that it results from the biased study of U.S. butterfly families. It may be that non-lycaenid butterflies are just as endangered as lycaenids, but the latter have received more attention from biologists, and thus more is known about their imperilled state. While it is difficult to evaluate this contention, there are no obvious reasons why lycaenids should have received more attention than other families, given that they are small in size and not nearly as showy. We favour a second interpretation, which is that the patterns reflect ecological differences among the butterfly families.

Here, we first provide a brief overview of the taxonomic and geographic distributions of North American lycaenids. We then discuss five interrelated characteristics of lycaenids that we suspect are responsible for, or at least contribute to, the group's extreme susceptibility to endangerment and extinction. We conclude by summarising the ongoing efforts to conserve North American lycaenids. Throughout the chapter, we focus primarily on lycaenids and conservation programmes in the U.S. In part this is a reflection of our experience with lycaenids in this region. However, our restricted emphasis also occurs because insect conservation in Canada and Mexico is far less developed (see review by Opler 1991). Particularly in Mexico, a great number of insect taxa are at risk, but specific details are lacking.

Taxonomic and geographic distributions

Lycaenids are somewhat under-represented in North America and many of them just barely enter the United States from Mexico. The subfamily Riodininae (the metalmarks) is especially under-represented when compared to the equatorial latitudes in the New World, with just 20 species (14%) in North America. By comparison, riodinines make up about two-thirds of the local lycaenid fauna in equatorial lowland communities of South America. Indeed, the genera that include all but three of the North American species – *Apodemia* Felder & Felder, *Calephelis* Grote & Robinson, and *Emesis* F. – reach much greater species richness to the south of the United States.

The subfamily Lycaeninae (the harvesters, hairstreaks, coppers, and blues) is represented by more than 120 species,

Table 1. Lycaenid taxa that are listed as endangered by the U.S. government as of 15 July 1991 (Federal Register 1991a). CA = California state.

Species	Range	Food Plant
Apodemia mormo langei (Lange's Metalmark)	CA	*Eriogonum nudum*
Glaucopsyche lygdamus palosverdesensis (Palos Verdes Blue)	CA	*Astragalus trichopodus* var. *lonchus*
Euphilotes battoides allyni (El Segundo Blue)	CA	*Eriogonum parvifolium, E. cinereum, E. fasciculatum*
Euphilotes enoptes smithi (Smith's Blue)	CA	*Eriogonum latifolium, E. parvifolium*
Icaricia (=Plebejus) icarioides missionensis (Mission Blue)	CA	*Lupinus albifrons, L. formosus, L. variicolor*
Lycaeides argyrognomon (=idas) lotis (Lotis Blue)	CA	*Lotus formosissimus*
Incisalia (=Callophrys) mossii bayensis (San Bruno Elfin)	CA	*Sedum spathulifolium*

including some endemic species groups. *Feniseca* Grote is an endemic, monotypic genus of the small tribe of harvesters (Miletini) whose predaceous larvae feed on homopterans. Among the hairstreaks (Theclini) are a number of largely neotropical genera that are represented by one or just several species, including *Eumaeus* Hübner, *Atlides* Hübner, *Chlorostrymon* Clench, *Tmolus* Hübner, *Calycopis* Scudder, *Cyanophrys* Clench, *Strymon* Hübner, *Erora* Scudder and others. The genus *Callophrys* Billberg (sensu stricto) is holarctic. Genera that are largely restricted to North America (and mainly distributed in the west) include the species-rich *Satyrium* Scudder, *Mitoura* Scudder, and *Incisalia* Scudder (lumped with *Callophrys* by many), and the striking monotypic *Sandia* Clench & Ehrlich.

Representatives of the coppers (Lycaenini) are holarctic in distribution, but many representatives are endemic to North America. Two species are related to Old World species, *Lycaena cupreus* (Edwards) and *L. phlaeas* (L.), the latter being found also in Asia and Africa. Three other species are represented in eastern North America. The remaining eight species, with the exception of the aforementioned highly restricted *Lycaena hermes*, are distributed across the intermountain west.

Like the hairstreaks, the blues (Polyommatini) include a number of genera that are more diverse in the neotropics, just barely reaching into the U.S. (i.e. *Hemiargus* Hübner and *Leptotes* Scudder), and genera that share a similar distribution, but are also represented in Africa (i.e. *Brephidium* Scudder and *Zizula* Chapman). *Celastrina* Tutt and *Everes* Hübner are holarctic in distribution as functionally are *Glaucopsyche* Scudder and *Plebejus* Kluk (including *Agriades* Hübner, *Icaricia* Nabokov, *Lycaeides* Hübner, and *Plebulina* Nabokov), genera that show high affinity with many European genera (i.e. *Maculinea* van Ecke, *Aricia* Reichenbach, *Polyommatus* Kluk, *Plebicula* Higgins, *Lysandra* Hemming, and *Agrodiaetus* Hübner, among others). North American *Philotiella* Mattoni, the monotypic *Philotes* Scudder, and the highly subspeciated *Euphilotes* Mattoni are all related to Asian genera.

Regional numbers indicate that lycaenids make up a higher proportion of butterfly species richness in the far western portions of the continent. For example, they comprise 29 of the 162 (18%) butterfly and skipper species in Georgia (Harris 1972) and 46 of the 240 (19%) species in Colorado (Brown 1957, corrected for recent taxonomic changes). For southern California, Emmel and Emmel (1973) list 167 species of which 54 (32%) are lycaenids. On a narrower geographic scale, lycaenids make up 37 of the 122 (30%) butterfly species from the San Francisco Bay area (Tilden 1965) and 30 of the 91 (33%) species from Orange County in southern California (Orsak 1978).

Perhaps not surprisingly, it is in western North America – with its diverse topography, elevation, and vegetation types – where differentiation at or below the species level is greatest (see Scott 1986). Additionally, it is in this same region, which harbours the most diverse temperate-zone lycaenid genera at the species level (i.e. *Mitoura, Callophrys, Incisalia, Lycaena, Plebejus,* and *Euphilotes*), that geographically restricted taxa are receiving the most attention from conservation biologists.

Lycaenid characteristics and susceptibility to endangerment

Subspecific differentiation

As can be seen in Tables 1 and 2, 100% of the lycaenids currently protected under the U.S. Endangered Species Act (ESA), and 88% of the candidates for this status, are not full species. In a striking show of appreciation for the process of evolution, the U.S. Congress included both full species and subspecies as protectable taxonomic units (for vertebrates, even distinct populations at risk of endangerment or extinction are protected). Indeed, the most publicised extinction of a North

Table 2. Lycaenid taxa that are on the list of candidates for endangered status with the U.S. government.

Data are current as of 21 November 1991 (Federal Register 1991b). Abbreviations of U.S. states are as follows: California (CA), Florida (FL), Illinois (IL), Indiana (IN), Maine (ME), Massachusetts (MA), Michigan (MI), New Hampshire (NH), Nevada (NV), New York (NY), Ohio (OH), Oregon (OR), Pennsylvania (PA), and Wisconsin (WI). Status categories are as follows: 1 = sufficient information to support a proposal for listing as endangered or threatened; 2 = current information suggests that taxon is 'possibly appropriate' for listing as endangered or threatened; 3A = best available information indicates that the taxon is extinct; 3C = current information indicates that the taxon is more abundant or widespread than previously thought; S = a taxon known to have stable numbers, U = additional information is required to determine the taxon's current abundance trend, D = taxon with declining numbers and/or which is being subjected to increasing threats.

Species	Status	Range	Food plant
Eumaeus atala florida (Florida Atala)	2,S	FL	*Zamia pumila*
Euphilotes battoides spp. (Baking Powder Flat Blue)	2,U	NV	*Eriogonum* sp.
Euphilotes enoptes spp. (Dark Blue)	2,U	NV	*Eriogonum* sp.
Euphilotes rita spp. (Sand Mountain Blue)	2,U	NV	*Eriogonum* sp.
Euphilotes rita mattoni (Mattoni Blue)	2,U	NV	*Eriogonum* sp.
Hemiargus thomasi bethunebakeri (Miami Blue)	3C,U	FL	*Eriogonum* sp.
Icaricia (=Plebejus) icarioides spp. (Point Reyes Blue)	2,U	CA	*Lupinus* sp.
Icaricia (=Plebejus) icarioides spp. (White Mountains Icarioides Blue)	2,U	CA, NV	*Lupinus* sp.
Icaricia (=Plebejus) icarioides spp. (Spring Mountains Icarioides Blue)	2,U	CA, NV	*Lupinus* sp.
Icaricia (=Plebejus) icarioides fenderi (Fender's Blue)	2,U	OR	*Lupinus* sp.
Icaricia (=Plebejus) icarioides moroensis (Morro Bay Blue)	2,U	CA	*Lupinus chamissonis*
Icaricia (=Plebejus) icarioides pheres (Pheres Blue)	3A	CA	*Lupinus* sp.
Incisalia lanoraieensis (Spruce-Bog Elfin)	3C	ME,NY,NH, Canada	*Picea mariana*
Incisalia mossii ssp. ('hikupa') (San Gabriel Mountains Blue)	2,U	CA	*Sedum* sp.
Incisalia mossii ssp. (Marin Elfin)	2,U	CA	*Sedum* sp.
Lycaeides melissa samuelis (Karner Blue)	1,D	IN,MI,NH,NY,OH MA,IL,WI,PA.	*Lupinus perennis*
Lycaeides dorcas claytoni (Clayton's Copper)	2,S	ME	*Potentilla* sp.
Lycaena hermes (Hermes Copper)	2,U	CA, Mexico	*Rhamnus crocea*
Lycaena rubidus spp. (White Mountains Copper)	2,U	CA,NV	*Rumex* sp.
Mitoura gryneus sweadneri (Sweadner's Olive Hairstreak)	2,U	FL	*Juniperus silicicola*
Mitoura thornei (Thorne's Hairstreak)	2,U	CA	*Cupressus forbesii*
Philotiella speciosa bohartorum (Bohart's Blue)	2,U	CA	*Chorizanthe membranacea*
Plebulina emigdionis (San Emigdio Blue)	2,U	CA	*Atriplex canescens*
Plebejus saepiolus spp. (San Gabriel Mountains Blue)	2,U	CA	*Lupinus* sp.

Continued...

Table 2 (cont). Lycaenid taxa that are on the list of candidates for endangered status with the U.S. government.

Species	Status	Range	Food plant
Plebejus saepiolus spp. (White Mountains Saepiolus Blue)	2,U NV	CA,	*Lupinus* sp.
Plebejus shasta charlestonensis (Spring Mountains Blue)	2,D	NV	*Trifolium, Astragalus, Lupinus*
Satyrium auretorum fumosum (Santa Monica Mountain Hairstreak)	2,U	CA	*Quercus* sp.
Strymon acis bartrami (Bartram's Hairstreak)	2,U	FL	*Croton linearis*

American butterfly was a putative full species, the Xerces Blue (*Glaucopsyche xerces* (Boisduval)), a lycaenid that was probably a well-differentiated subspecies of the still widely distributed and highly variable *Glaucopsyche lygdamus* (Doubleday).

Lycaenids appear to have a high degree of subspecific variation and these differentiated populations (many formally recognized as subspecies) are particularly susceptible to endangerment and extinction. Analysis of Scott's (1986) taxonomically conservative treatment provides empirical support for this view. According to his classifications, the ratio of subspecies to species in North America is 2.4 times greater for lycaenids than for non-lycaenid butterflies (187/142 and 303/537 respectively). In addition, this ratio for those lycaenids largely restricted to western North America (i.e. *Mitoura, Callophrys* [including *Incisalia*], *Lycaena, Plebejus, Glaucopsyche* and *Euphilotes*) is 4.7 times higher than that for non-lycaenid butterflies (138/52).

Dispersal abilities

Dispersal is essential for the persistence of isolated populations. First, input of individuals from neighbouring areas can bolster populations whose numbers are dwindling, thereby preventing their extinction (the 'rescue effect' *sensu* Brown and Kodric-Brown 1977). Second, dispersal can provide an influx of genetically different individuals into a population, thereby increasing genetic diversity and presumably resulting in greater fitness and population viability (see review by Vrijenhoek 1985). Thus, taxa with limited dispersal abilities should be far more susceptible to local extinction events than taxa with well-developed dispersal abilities.

Although there have been numerous mark-recapture studies of North American butterflies (e.g. Ehrlich 1965, Arnold 1983, Murphy *et al.* 1986, Reid and Murphy 1986), few have focused on lycaenids. Despite the fact that many studies tend to underestimate mean dispersal distances, research to date indicates that lycaenids tend to move short distances between captures. For example, studies of the endangered Mission Blue (*Plebejus icarioides missionensis* Hovanitz) indicate that most adult movements are highly restricted: the majority of captures were in the immediate vicinity of larval hostplants and nectar resources (see Arnold 1983, Reid and Murphy 1986). However, studies have also shown a limited number of movements in the

order of hundreds of metres, as well as a single dispersal event between habitat patches (and distinct demographic units) of nearly 2 kilometres. Nevertheless, the tendency for lycaenids to be comparatively sedentary should result in less frequent recolonisation and rescue events as well as reduced gene flow between populations, leading to greater interpopulation differentiation.

Host specificity and successional stages

All lycaenids currently protected in the U.S. are specific to one or just several related hostplant species (Tables 1 and 2). Many of these plant species, particularly the commonly used *Eriogonum* and *Lupinus*, are found largely in early successional communities that are temporary and unpredictable. Butterflies that specialise on such plants must track an ephemeral resource base that itself may be dependent on unpredictable and perhaps infrequent ecosystem disturbances. For such species, suitable habitat can be a limited, ever-shifting fraction of a greater landscape mosaic. As a result, local extinction events are both frequent and inevitable.

The endangered Karner Blue (*Lycaeides melissa samuelis* Nabokov) is a prime example of the costs associated with such specialisation. Larvae of this subspecies feed exclusively on a lupine (*Lupinus perennis*) that is an early successional species restricted to pine-barren habitats (Zaremba 1991). The existence of these habitats is highly dependent on the occurrence of intermittent fires. However, in New York State, fire suppression and habitat loss have significantly reduced the size and number of this butterfly's patchily distributed populations.

Even when appropriate larval hostplants and successional stages are available, conditions may still be insufficient to sustain lycaenid populations. For example, the federally listed San Bruno Elfin (*Incisalia mossii bayensis* (Brown)) is not only restricted to a few rocky outcrops that support its narrowly distributed hostplant (*Sedum spathuliifolium*), but the butterfly apparently can only complete its life cycle on individual plants growing under highly exacting and uncommon topoclimatic environments (Weiss and Murphy 1990).

Sedentary behaviour combined with high levels of site-specific hostplant adaptation are likely to place many genetically distinct lycaenids at great risk of local and regional extinction. While no studies document the existence of genetically based host races in North American lycaenids, recent work details a genetic basis for larval hostplant preferences by adult butterflies in the rather sedentary nymphalid genus *Euphydryas*. Singer and colleagues have found significant differences in patterns of oviposition preference and tolerances for hostplants among phenotypically and geographically distinct populations, suggesting distinct adaptation at the population level (see Singer 1971; White and Singer 1974; Rausher 1982). More recently, Singer and colleagues have documented the existence of genetically based (i.e. heritable) differences between adjacent populations and within polyphagous populations (Singer 1983; Singer *et al.* 1988).

Species in the lycaenid genus *Euphilotes* exhibit similar patterns in the use of larval hostplants, thereby suggesting the possibility of genetic differentiation among populations for hostplant tolerance (see Pratt and Ballmer 1986). In southern California, *Euphilotes enoptes* (Behr) has been found to feed on five species of *Eriogonum*; the butterfly is monophagous at some locations, while it is polyphagous in others, with clear host preferences.

Association with ants

Roughly half of the lycaenid species world-wide associate with ants, and their larvae possess numerous distinctive structures that facilitate these interactions (Downey 1962; Atsatt 1981; Pierce 1987). Although a few of these associations are antagonistic, with butterfly larvae preying on ant brood (Cottrell 1984), the majority appear to be mutualistic (Pierce 1987). Lycaenids vary greatly in terms of their degree of dependence on ant associates and their degree of specificity for particular ant species.

We propose that butterfly species which associate with ants, and particularly those species with strong dependence on them, are far more sensitive to environmental changes and thus more prone to endangerment and extinction, than species that are not tended by ants. While this hypothesis remains untested, it seems probable because of two factors. First, such species simultaneously require the right food plant and the presence of particular ant species – a combination that occurs infrequently. These dual requirements of tended species should result in spatial distributions that are patchier than those for untended species. The degree of patchiness should increase as dependence and/or the species specificity of lycaenids increase. Second, we suspect that selection will favour reduced dispersal by myrmecophilous lycaenids, because of the difficulty associated with locating patches that contain the appropriate combination of food plants and ants. Thus, in addition to occurring as isolated populations of variable sizes, ant-tended species may express genetic traits associated with reduced outcrossing.

At this time, we cannot evaluate whether North American lycaenids that associate with ants are more vulnerable to endangerment or extinction than those without such dependencies. This is because there have been almost no studies of the ant associations of endangered lycaenid taxa. However, Downey (1962) observed that the Mission Blue was tended by the ant *Formica lasioides*, and suggested (but did not demonstrate) that ants may protect caterpillars from natural enemies and even transport them to their food plants. D.A. Savignano has studied the ant associations of the Karner Blue, but this work has yet to be published.

Numerous studies of non-endangered taxa in North America suggest that ants could be an important factor in the persistence of lycaenid populations. For example, parasitism levels of *Glaucopsyche lygdamus oro* (Scudder) (the Rocky Mountain subspecific relative of the federally listed Palos Verdes Blue, *G. lygdamus palosverdesensis* Perkins and Emmel) were 45–84% lower for ant-tended larvae than for untended larvae (Pierce and Mead 1981; Pierce and Easteal 1986). In Michigan, the work of Webster and Nielson (1984) also suggested that ant associates were beneficial for the Scrub-oak or Edward's Hairstreak, *Satyrium edwardsii* (Grote & Robinson). Clearly, we need to know much more about the ant associations of endangered lycaenids, as these interactions will be important considerations in management plans.

Although not from North America, the Large Blue (*Maculinea arion* (L.)) provides an important, sobering, example of the often dire consequences associated with a dependence on ants (see Thomas 1980; Cottrell 1984; New 1991). Despite considerable efforts to prevent its loss, in 1979 the Large Blue became extinct in its native Britain. While many factors undoubtedly contributed to this demise, the most prominent appears to have been the species' extreme dependence on ants. During early instars, *M. arion* larvae fed on wild thyme (*Thymus drucei praecox*) and, at the fourth instar, were carried by *Myrmica* ants into their nests, where the lycaenids fed on ant brood. The level of grazing in the blue's grassland habitats was progressively reduced from around 1950, largely due to changing agricultural practices and attempts to protect habitat of this endangered species. However, due to unforeseen complexities of the system, these altered grazing regimes had drastic effects on the lycaenid populations. The primary ant-species host (*M. sabuleti*) could persist only in fields that were closely cropped by livestock. Thus, even slight reductions in grazing allowed *M. scabrinodis*, a low-quality host, to exclude *M. sabuleti* from the area, thereby leading to the butterfly's subsequent demise.

Conservation planning in North America

Lycaenids have played a central role in the development of environmental interests over land-use policy. Although much less publicised than the Large Blue another lycaenid provides a further example of the kind of conservation efforts that are required to protect endangered butterflies.

The Mission Blue was conferred protection under the ESA in 1976, when the U.S. Fish and Wildlife Service formally recognized that encroaching urbanisation had virtually encircled the known distribution of this subspecies. More than half of the grassland habitat of the largest remaining known population on California's San Bruno Mountain had been lost during the 50 years preceding the listing. Furthermore, half of this remaining habitat (a quarter of the total) had been overtaken by invasive shrub and tree species. In 1978, developers and local government became aware that pending development would be prohibited by Section 9 of the ESA.

Given that the Mission Blue occurred primarily on private land and the ESA only offered remedies for taxa on public lands, there was a pressing need for an innovative plan that would balance biological and economic concerns. Such an approach was engineered by a committee composed of developers, environmentalists, government officials, and biological consultants. Using size estimates of the butterfly populations, distributional records for three lupine (*Lupinus*) larval hostplants, and information on the butterfly's natural history, the committee designed the first 'Habitat Conservation Plan' (HCP). This plan protected 80% of remaining habitat on San Bruno Mountain, provided funds for the management and restoration of this habitat, and allowed for the development of the remaining land. In 1982, the U.S. Congress institutionalised habitat conservation planning with amendments to the ESA, pointing to the Mission Blue conservation program as the model for this new process. Several dozen HCPs (many of them controversial) have been initiated in the ensuing decade.

In a second noteworthy case, a similar impasse between developers and environmentalists has focused on the Karner Blue in upstate New York. As mentioned earlier, this highly threatened subspecies, protected by the state but not the U.S. government, is restricted to fire-maintained gaps in early successional pitch-pine and scrub-oak barrens. The rather sedentary blue exists as a limited suite of metapopulations, consisting of collections of local populations that are dependent on a shifting mosaic of suitable habitat.

There has been an extensive, broad-based effort to conserve the remaining Karner Blue population (see review by Zaremba 1991). Primarily through the joint efforts of The Nature Conservancy and the New York State Department of Environmental Conservation, approximately 800ha of Karner Blue habitat have been protected as part of the Albany Pine Bush Preserve. In addition, the New York State Legislature established the Albany Bush Commission and charged the group with managing the remaining habitat. This and other ongoing programmes have involved prescribed burning, hostplant propagation, creation of effective dispersal corridors, and development of land-use practices to promote butterfly dispersal in areas adjacent to the preserve. Using the Karner Blue, Givnish *et al.* (1988) provided a model study for application of population viability analysis to conservation planning. Virtually identical in structure to an independently generated analysis of the well-studied nymphalid *Euphydryas editha* (Boisduval) (Murphy *et al.* 1990), this study broke from the traditional treatments of genetic threats and demographic stochasticity, and instead targeted environmental perturbations and metapopulation dynamics in an integrated scheme of reserve design and management.

Conservation planning for lycaenids has focused primarily on habitat management. All of the listed taxa, and many of the candidates, survive as remnant populations in small 'garrison' reserves embedded within largely urban areas with long histories of human settlement (Murphy 1987b). In such circumstances, opportunities to expand current distributions are few and conservation is less a matter of reserve design than reserve management. Heroic management efforts have brought Lange's Metalmark (*Apodemia mormo langei* Comstock) back from the brink of extinction. In 1976, the subspecies was listed as endangered by the U.S. government, as its remaining habitat was being threatened by sandmining and industrial development (see Opler 1991). The subspecies is restricted to the riparian sand dunes along the Sacramento and San Joaquin Rivers in central California. To prevent a further decline in numbers, in 1980, the U.S. Fish and Wildlife Service acquired all of the lycaenid's remaining habitat. While seriously degraded by sandmining and invasive plants, this 24ha region was incorporated into the San Francisco National Wildlife Refuge, and there have been considerable efforts to restore the habitat. After a number of unsuccessful attempts to increase butterfly numbers, managers found that disking portions of the habitat resulted in dramatic growth of the larval and adult foodplant (*Eriogonum nudum*). Since this action, the metalmark's abundance is estimated to have more than tripled, from fewer than 200 individuals in 1986 to more than 650 in 1989.

Conclusions

Extreme environmental events (such as drought, deluge, wildfire) can lead to dramatic fluctuations in the size of local butterfly populations, and in some well-documented cases, this has resulted in their extinction (e.g. Ehrlich *et al.* 1980; Murphy and Weiss 1988). For example, Ehrlich *et al.* (1972) reported that an early summer snowstorm caused the extinction of at least one subalpine population of *Glaucopsyche lygdamus* when it destroyed the entire standing crop of its larval food plant. Biotic factors, including the impact of natural enemies and ant associates, can also lead to significant variation in the size of lycaenid populations. However, as stressed throughout this volume, a long history of human-induced habitat alteration and destruction is responsible for the vast majority of declines and extinctions of lycaenids worldwide.

This has certainly been the case for North American lycaenids, as already discussed for a number of taxa in this chapter. The El Segundo Blue (*Euphilotes battoides allyni* (Shields)) is yet another example. This small lycaenid is restricted to the El Segundo sand dunes along the coast of southern California. While most of its habitat, perhaps more than 10,000ha in extent, has been destroyed by housing and commercial developments, small portions of the sand-dune ecosystem (which support its preferred larval hostplant *Eriogonum parvifolium*) still remain near the Los Angeles International Airport and a Standard Oil refinery (Arnold 1983). While noteworthy efforts have been made by Standard Oil to establish populations of the El Segundo Blue on their 1ha property, comparatively little has been done by the City of Los Angeles on the inhabitable sections of their 80ha airport site. Since the mid 1970s, there have been a number of unsuccessful attempts to develop much of the remaining site, several with revenue-generating activities linked to habitat management plans.

Pressure to develop and disturb lycaenid habitat in North America is likely to intensify in coming decades, and more listings of endangered and threatened species should be expected. Only an increase in the already considerable efforts to conserve lycaenids (and insects in general) will suffice to keep more of them from suffering the fate of the recently extirpated Palo Verdes Blue in southern California (see Arnold 1987). Establishment of the Xerces Society in 1971 has been an important step, as it has greatly increased the attention paid to insect conservation. The ESA of 1973 and the use of HCPs have also been instrumental in facilitating the protection of threatened and endangered lycaenids on both public and private lands. Unfortunately, the U.S. government has added only six insects to its list since 1981 (Opler 1991) – despite the fact that habitat degradation and the list of candidates have increased considerably during the intervening years. This reluctance to list species must be reversed, so that the power of the ESA and HCPs can have their designed effect (Murphy 1991).

Although the ESA and HCPs are powerful instruments of conservation planning and management, they are nevertheless 'stop-gap' measures designed to take effect *after* taxa are in trouble. As attention continues to be focused on these essential management efforts, considerable effort must also be directed towards more long-term objectives associated with dramatically reducing the environmental degradation that is leading to the endangerment and extinction of additional taxa. As outlined by Ehrlich and Ehrlich (1990), Gore (1991) and others, these long-term objectives include stabilisation and then reduction of the growth of human populations, rapid development and deployment of environmentally appropriate technologies, comprehensive changes in the system of economic accounting so as to accurately reflect the effects of our actions on the environment, and the development of a detailed scheme for environmental education and research.

References

ARNOLD, R.A. 1983. Ecological studies of six endangered butterflies (Lepidoptera, Lycaenidae): island biogeography, patch dynamics, and the design of habitat preserves. *Univ. Calif. Publns Entomol.* 99: 1–161.

ARNOLD, R.A. 1987. Decline of the endangered Palos Verdes blue butterfly in California. *Biol. Conserv.* 40: 203–217.

ATSATT, P.R. 1981. Lycaenid butterflies and ants: selection for enemy-free space. *Amer. Nat.* 118: 638–654.

BROWN, F.M. 1957. *Colorado butterflies.* Denver Museum of Natural History, Denver.

BROWN, J.H. and KODRIC-BROWN, A. 1977. Turnover rates in insular biogeography: effect of immigration on extinction. *Ecology* 58: 445–449.

COTTRELL, C.B. 1984. Aphytophagy in butterflies; its relationship to myrmecophily. *Zool. J. Linn. Soc.* 79: 1–57.

DOWNEY, J.C. 1962. Myrmecophily in *Plebejus (Icaricia) icarioides* (Lepid.: Lycaenidae). *Ent. News* 73: 57–66.

EHRLICH, P.R. 1965. The population biology of the butterfly, *Euphydryas editha.* II. The structure of the Jasper Ridge colony. *Evolution* 19: 327–336.

EHRLICH, P.R., BREEDLOVE, D.E., BRUSSARD, P.E. and SHARP, M.A. 1972. Weather and the 'regulation' of subalpine populations. *Ecology* 53: 243–247.

EHRLICH, P.R. and EHRLICH, A.H. 1990. *The population explosion.* Simon and Schuster, New York.

EHRLICH, P.R., MURPHY, D.D., SINGER, M.C., SHERWOOD, C.B., WHITE, R.R. and BROWN, I.L. 1980. Extinction, reduction, stability and increase: the response of Checkerspot butterfly (*Euphydryas*) populations to the California drought. *Oecologia* 46: 101–105.

EMMEL, T.C. and EMMEL, J.F. 1973. *The Butterflies of Southern California.* Natural History Museum of Los Angeles County, Los Angeles.

FEDERAL REGISTER 1991a. *Endangered and Threatened Wildlife and Plants.* U.S. Department of the Interior, Fish and Wildlife Service (15 July 1991).

FEDERAL REGISTER 1991b. *Endangered and threatened wildlife and plants; animal candidate review for listing as endangered or threatened species, proposed rule.* U.S. Department of the Interior, Fish and Wildlife Service (21 November 1991).

GIVNISH, T., MENGES, E and SCHWEITZER, D. 1988. *Minimum area requirements for long-term conservation of the Albany Pine Bush and Karner blue butterfly (Volume IV, Appendix T).* Report to the City of Albany, Malcolm Pirnie, Inc.

GORE, A. 1991. *Earth in the Balance: Ecology and the Human Spirit.* Houghton Mifflin, New York.

HARRIS, L. 1972. *Butterflies of Georgia.* University of Oklahoma Press, Norman.

MURPHY, D.D. 1987a. *A report of the California butterflies listed as candidates for endangered status by the United States Fish and Wildlife Service.* Report C-1755 to the California Department of Fish and Game.

MURPHY, D.D. 1987b. Challenges to biological diversity in urban areas. *In:* Wilson, E.O., (Ed.) *Biodiversity.* National Academy of Sciences Press, Washington, D.C., pp. 71–76.

MURPHY, D.D. 1991. Invertebrate conservation. *In:* Kohm, K.A. (Ed.) *Balancing on the Brink of Extinction: the Endangered Species Act and Lessons for the Future.* Island Press, Washington, D.C., pp. 181–198.

MURPHY, D.D., FREAS, K.E. and WEISS, S.B. 1990. An environment-metapopulation approach to population viability analysis for a threatened invertebrate. *Conserv. Biol.* 4: 41–51.

MURPHY, D.D., MENNINGER, M.S., EHRLICH, P.R. and WILCOX, B.A. 1986. Local population dynamics of adult butterflies and the conservation status of two closely related species. *Biol. Conserv.* 37: 201–223.

MURPHY, D.D. and WEISS, S.B. 1988. Ecological studies and conservation of the Bay Checkerspot butterfly, *Euphydryas editha bayensis. Biol. Conserv.* 46: 183–200.

NEW, T.R. 1991. *Butterfly Conservation.* Oxford University Press, Melbourne.

OPLER, P.A. 1991. North American problems and perspectives in insect conservation. *In:* Collins, N.M. and Thomas, J.A. (Eds). *The Conservation of Insects and their Habitats.* Academic Press, New York, pp. 9–32.

ORSAK, L.J. 1978. *The Butterflies of Orange County, California.* University of California Press, Irvine.

PIERCE, N.E. 1987. The evolution and biogeography of associations between lycaenid butterflies and ants. *In:* Harvey, P.H. and Partridge, L. (Eds). *Oxford Surveys in Evolutionary Biology, Volume 4.* Oxford University Press, Oxford, pp. 89–116.

PIERCE, N.E. and EASTEAL, S. 1986. The selective advantage of attendant ants from the larvae of a lycaenid butterfly, *Glaucopsyche lygdamus. J. Anim. Ecol.* 55: 451–462.

PIERCE, N.E. and MEAD, P.S. 1981. Parasitoids as selective agents in the symbiosis between lycaenid butterfly larvae and ants. *Science* 211: 1185–1187.

PRATT, G.F. and BALLMER, G.R. 1986. The phenetics and comparative biology of *Euphilotes enoptes* from the San Bernardino Mountains. *J. Res. Lepid.* 25: 121–135.

RAUSHER, M.D. 1982. Population differentiation in *Euphydryas editha* butterflies: larval adaptations to different host plants. *Evolution* 36: 581–590.

REID, T.S. and MURPHY, D.D. 1986. The endangered mission blue butterfly,

Plebejus icarioides missionensis. In: Wilcox, B.A., Brussard, P.F. and Marcot, B.G. (Eds). *The Management of Viable Populations: Theory, Application, and Case Studies.* Center for Conservation Biology, Stanford, California. pp. 147–168.

SCOTT, J.A. 1986. *The Butterflies of North America.* Stanford University Press, Stanford, California.

SINGER, M.C. 1971. Evolution of food-plant preferences in the butterfly *Euphydryas editha. Evolution* **35**: 383–389.

SINGER, M.C. 1983. Determinants of multiple host use by a phytophagous insect population. *Evolution* **37**: 389–403.

SINGER, M.C., NG, D. and THOMAS, C.D. 1988. Heritability of oviposition preference and its relationship to offspring performance within a single insect population. *Evolution* **42**: 977–985.

THOMAS, J.A. 1980. Why did the Large Blue become extinct in Britain? *Oryx* **15**: 243–247.

TILDEN, J.W. 1965. *Butterflies of the San Francisco Bay region.* University of California Press, Berkeley, California.

VRIJENHOEK, R.C. 1985. Animal population genetics and disturbance: the effects of local extinctions and recolonisation on heterozygosity and fitness. *In:* Pickett, S.T.A. and White, P.S. (Eds). *The Ecology of Natural Disturbance and Patch Dynamics.* Academic Press, New York, pp. 265–285.

WEBSTER, R.P. and NIELSON, M.C. 1984. Myrmecophily in the Edward's hairstreak butterfly *Satyrium edwardsii* (Lycaenidae). *J. Lepid. Soc.* **38**: 124–133.

WEISS, S.B. and MURPHY, D.D. 1990. Thermal microenvironments and the restoration of rare butterfly habitat. *In:* Berger, J. (Ed). *Environmental Restoration: Sciences and Strategies for Restoring the Earth.* Island Press, Washington, D.C., pp. 55–60.

WHITE, R.R. and SINGER, M.C. 1974. Geographical distribution of hostplant choice in *Euphydryas editha* (Nymphalidae). *J. Lepid. Soc.* **28**: 103–107.

ZAREMBA, R.E. 1991. Management of Karner blue butterfly habitat in a suburban landscape. *In:* Decker, D.J., Krasny, M.E., Goff, G.R., Smith, C.R. and Gross, D.W. (Eds). *Challenges in the Conservation of Biological Resources: a Practitioner's Guide.* Westview Press, San Francisco, pp. 289–302.

Neotropical Lycaenidae: an overview

Keith S. Brown, Jr.

Departamento de Zoologia, Instituto de Biologia, Universidade Estadual de Campinas, C.P. 6109 Campinas, São Paulo 13.081, Brazil

Introduction

The neotropical Lycaenidae are still only partly known and very little studied. They are here taken to include the Riodininae which are possibly closer to Nymphalidae than to other Lycaenids (Robbins 1988).The total of approximately 2300 species (Tables 1–3; Robbins 1982, 1992; Harvey 1987; Callaghan and Lamas in press) includes as many as 400 still to be described, and probably an equal number of well-known names which will be synonymised or joined with others as subspecies. With the exceptions of a single copper and about 60 blues, the species are divided almost equally between hairstreaks (all in the single tribe Eumaeini of the subfamily Theclinae) and metalmarks (Riodininae, with four neotropical tribes containing 1, 1, 137 and about 1100 named species; the last tribe is separable into at least eight subtribes (Harvey 1987)).

The neotropical fauna includes some of the most exquisite colours and bizarre patterns known in butterflies (Figure 1). It is perhaps fortunate that they attract little attention from collectors and dealers although as a result of this the body of biological and distributional information available is far less than for the swallowtails (Papilionidae, see Collins and Morris 1985) or some groups of Nymphalidae. A reasonable cross-section of phenotypes can be seen in colour in Hewitson's original descriptions and illustrations (1852–1872, 1863–1878), in Barcant's book on Trinidad butterflies (1970, Plates 5, 9, 11, 12, 27, 28 plus 22 and 23 in black and white), in Lewis's *'Butterflies of the World'* (1973), and in Seitz' *'Macrolepidoptera of the World'* (1916–1920, Plates 121–159, 110A, 113B, 193) but with many names outdated. Only minimal information can be unearthed in most general butterfly books (Smart, 1975, illustrates only 103 species) or local lists for the neotropics (de la Maza, 1988, shows only 118 species). The endemic Chilean lycaenid fauna is ignored in most publications, and many genera of South American hairstreaks have no name as yet.

Less than 20% of the neotropical Theclinae (Robbins 1993) and 10% of the Riodininae (Harvey 1987) have been subject to any biological study (e.g. population censuses, juvenile biology and host plants, myrmecophily, behaviour, voltinism). While a few species feed on plants of economic importance, especially Orchidaceae, Bromeliaceae, Leguminosae, Sapotaceae, Solanaceae, Myrtaceae, Anacardiaceae, Rubiaceae and Compositae, even these are rarely reared by entomologists. Highly diversified faunas in the high mountains (Theclinae) and lowland Amazonia (Riodininae) are so poorly sampled that even fundamental questions – on species relationships, generic assignments, distributions, resource partitioning, optional or obligatory relationships with ants, association of dimorphic females with their males, flight habits, seasonal variation in pattern and abundance, migration – remain to be answered.

In such a frame, the picture is ill-defined, begging for much new work by biologists who are not averse to meeting the small, the little-known, the variable and complex; all too few have accepted this challenge. Although it may be valid that 'A true connoisseur of neotropical Lepidoptera can always be distinguished by his love for the Lycaenids' (Brown 1973), this is still an affair destined for frustration.

Thus, the following attempts at generalisation and particularisation are very fragile, begging for more field work, laboratory study and experimentation. Very preliminary answers can be attempted for the following questions:

(1) Are neotropical Lycaenidae 'typical' members of the family, or do they show their own biological styles and syndromes?

(2) Do neotropical Lycaenidae show clear patterns of distribution, variation, behaviour, community structure, and ecological interaction?

(3) Are neotropical Lycaenidae useful as indicators of other animal and plant species, historical and ecological factors, system characteristics including degree of disturbance, and general community structure and function?

(4) Is it possible to identify threatened species or groups? Do they co-occur with endangered communities of other animals and plants? Can they be saved?

Most of the answers must be sought by patient and diligent field work in the neotropics. In the past few years, a few scientists have come to terms with the systematic tangles of the group and have begun to do careful studies of the biology of some species. Hopefully, their spectacular and fascinating results (see De Vries 1990, 1991a) will attract more workers to the family, to learn more about these small but disproportionately impressive, beautiful and varied insects (Figure 1).

Systematics and ecology

A summary of the recognized divisions of neotropical Lycaenidae down to the generic level (partial for the Theclinae) is presented in Tables 1–3, along with distributional, biological and bibliographic data. A number of outstanding and salient facts characterise the neotropical Lycaenidae:

- the small number of blues (Polyommatinae) in the region, with very widespread ocurrence of only three common species;
- the predominance of forest groups, with very few species dependent on non-forest, open or successional habitats as is more common in the northern hemisphere;
- the relatively low proportion of myrmecophilous species, and almost complete absence of lichen or fungus-eating species (although *Calycopis* larvae may often be detritivorous (Johnson 1985; Robbins 1992) and *Sarota* larvae feed on

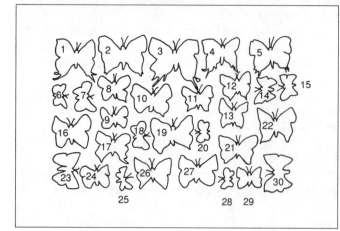

Figure 1. A pot–pourri of lycaenid diversity in the neotropics, all from Japi, São Paulo: (a) Theclinae.

Key to names:
1 'Thecla' phydela; 2 Atlides polybe; 3 Evenus regalis; 4 Arcas ducalis; 5 Panthiades phaleros; 6 Erora campa; 7 Chalybs hassan; 8 Chalybs chloris; 9 Arawacus tarania; 10 Cyanophrys acaste; 11 Cyanophrys bertha; 12 Cyanophrys remus; 13 Brangas ca. didymon; 14 Chlorostrymon simaethis; 15 Erora ca. opisena; 16 Ocaria cinerea; 17 'Thecla' deniva; 18 Ipidecla schausi; 19 Rekoa meton; 20 Ministrymon No.1.; 21 Rekoa meton Ventral; 22 Brangas silumena; 23 Ocaria thales; 24 Magnastigma hirsuta; 25 Chlorostrymon telea; 26 Parrhasius orgia; 27 'Thecla' elika; 28 Ministrymon No. 2.; 29 Thereus cithonius; 30 Parrhasius selika. Ventral side shown, except 19, 25, 26, 27, 28 dorsal.

epiphylls – liverworts and blue-green algae (De Vries 1988a)), and with only one case of carnivorous larvae known to date;

- the rarified distribution of most species – widespread but very sporadic;
- the small number of serious pest species considering the wide range of host plants;
- the presence of two monotypic tribes (Stygini and Corrachiini) in the Riodininae;
- the large number of monotypic genera and the existence of a few gargantuan genera (*Strymon, Calycopis, Euselasia,*

Mesosemia) (both perhaps due to insufficient study and the complexity of the family).

Some of these patterns may be altered when the groups are better known, but at the moment the 'flavour' is strongly that of typical forest butterflies. This may be due to the predominance of forest biomes in the neotropics, but even open-vegetation genera (*Rekoa, Strymon, Electrostrymon, Chlorostrymon, Calephelis, Ematurgina, Audre, Apodemia, Lemonias, Aricoris*) show biological syndromes much like those of their forest-inhabiting relatives and in contrast with other Lycaenidae which characterise successional habitats.

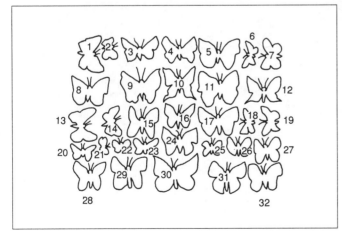

Figure 1. A pot-pourri of lycaenid diversity in the neotropics, all from Japi, São Paulo: (b) Riodininae and Polyommatinae.

Key to names:
1 *Lemonias glaphyra*; 2 *Calydna* sp. n. nr. *hemis*; 3 *Xenandra heliodes*; 4 *Symmachia arion* Female; 5 '*Mesosemia*' *acuta*; 6 *Mesene pyrippe*; 7 *Anteros lectabilis*; 8 *Napaea phryxe*; 9 *Emesis fastidiosa* Male Ventral; 10 *Chorinea licursis*; 11 *Emesis fastiosa* Female Ventral; 12 *Barbicornis basilis*; 13 *Notheme erota*; 14 *Charis cadytis*; 15 *Lasaia agesilas*; 16 *Caria plutargus*; 17 *Synargis brennus*; 18 *Calephelis brasiliensis*; 19 *Pterographium sagaris satnius*; 20 '*Everes*' *cogina* Female; 21 *Zizula cyna tulliola*; 22 *Baeotus johannae*; 23 *Adelotypa bolena*; 24 *Emesis fatimella*; 25 *Parcella amarynthina* Female; 26 *Theope thestias* ca. *discus*; 27 *Leucochimona matatha*; 28 *Panara soana trabalis*; 29 *Lemonias zygia epona*; 30 *Eurybia pergaea* var.; 31 *Riodina lycisca*; 32 *Mesosemia odice* Female. Dorsal aspect shown, except 1, 2, 7, 8, 9, 11, 14, 18, 24, 28, 32 ventral.

Table 1. Synopsis of neotropical Riodininae[a]; systematics and biology[b].

Taxonomic groups: SUBFAMILY (TRIBE), Subtribe or Group, *[†]Genus;	Plate numbers (Lewis 1973)	Approx. no. of spp.	Typical or well-known species	Distri-bution of genus[c]	Mim[d]	Myr[e]	Time of activity	Habitat (usual)[c]	Abn[f]	Larval host plants[q]	Biblio-graphy
RIODININAE[g] (STYGINI)											
Styx	78:33	1	infernalis	Peru And	?	–	PM	CloudF	1	Unknown	
(CORRACHIINI)											
Corrachia	71:42	1	leucoplaga	CR	–	–?	?	CloudF	1	Unknown	
(EUSALASIINI)											
*[†]Euselasia	73:4–32	134	mys, geon	NT, sp.AM	+–	–	AM,PM	HumidF	2–5	Myrt, Clusi.	1,2,3,23
Hades	74:1–2	2	noctula	TRAn	+	–	AM	RainF	3	Anacardi.	1
Methone	76:3	1	cecilia	AM–CR	++	–	AM	RainF	2	Unknown	
(RIODININI)											
Mesosemiiti[h]											
Perophthalma	77:22	1	tullius	NT	–	–	PM	HumidF	3	Rubi.	
Mesophthalma	75:16	1	idotea	AM	–	–	MD	HumidF	2	?	
*Leucochimona	74:24	9	mathata	NT	+	–	PM	HumidF	4	Rubi.	23
*Semomesia	78:19	8	capanea	AM–BA	–	–	PM	RainF	3	?	23
*[†]Mesosemia	72:4–5 75:14–37	120	cippus, telegone	NT	–	–	AM,PM	HumidF	2–5	Rubi.	23
*[†]Eunogyra	72:29	1	satyrus	AM–BA	–	+–?	AM	HumidF	3		
*Eurybia	72:30–4 73:1–3	20	nicaea	NT	–	+	LPM	RiverF	4	Marant.	4
[†]Alesa	70:1	6	prema, amesis	SAm	–	+	MD	RainF	2	Solan.	
Mimocastnia	76:4	1	rothschildi	AM	–	+	?	RainF	1	?	
*Teratophthalma	79:7–8	6	phelina	AM–And	+–?	–	PM	CloudF	3	?	23
*Ithomiola	74:12–3	3	floralis	AM	++	?	MD	HumidF	3	?	
Voltinia	79:31	2	radiata	TRAn	–	?	LPM	CloudF	2	?	
Hyphilaria	74:5–7	6	nicia	SAm	+–	–	AM	HumidF	3	Orchid.	23
Hermathena	74:9	2	candidata	NT	+?	?	PM	OpenF	2	?	
Cremna	71:43	5	actoris, thasus	NT	–	–	PM	RainF	3–4	?	
*[†]Napaea	76:7–8 :10–12	13	eucharila	NT	–	–	PM	HumidF	3	Orchid., Bromeli.	
Eucorna	–	1	sanarita	BR–SM	–	?	PM	CloudF	1	?	
Riodiniti[i,p]											
*Lyropteryx	75:1–2	4	apollonia	NT	+	–?	MD	RainF,Cd	2	?	
Necyria	76:5 :13–4	6	bellona	And–CR	+?	–?	MD	CloudF	4	?	
Cyrenia	72:1	1	martia	AM	–	–?	MD	HumidF	2	?	
*Ancyluris	70:4–12	21	aulestes	NT	+–	–	AM	HumidF	3	Melastomat.	23
Nirodia[j]	–	1	belphegor	BR–MG	–	–?	MD	CmpRup	2	?	
Rhetus	78:8,12	3	periander	NT	–	–	AM,MD	HumidF	4	?	
Chorinea	71:37	7	octauius	NT	+	–	MD	HumidF	3	Flacourti., Celastr.	
*Nahida	76:6	4	coenoides	EcAnd	++	–?	?	CloudF	2	?	
*Ithomeis	74:10–1	9	astraea	AM–CR	++	–?	PM	RainF	3	?	
*Panara	77:18	6	episatnius	AM–Atl	+–	–?	PM	RainF	3	?	23
Isapis	75:3	1	agyrtus	NT	–	–?	AM	RainF	3	?	
*Brachyglenis	71:2	5	esthema	NT	++	–?	AM	HumidF	2	?	
*Themone	79:10	4	pais, poecila	AM	++	–?	PM	RainF	2	?	

Continued...

Table 1 (cont). Synopsis of neotropical Riodininae[a]; systematics and biology[b].

Taxonomic groups: SUBFAMILY (TRIBE), Subtribe or Group, *†Genus;	Plate numbers (Lewis 1973)	Approx. no. of spp.	Typical or well-known species	Distri-bution of genus[c]	Mim[d]	Myr[e]	Time of activity	Habitat (usual)[c]	Abn[f]	Larval host plants[q]	Biblio-graphy
Notheme	76:19	1	erota	NT	–	–?	AM	HumidF	3	?	
Monethe	76:9	3	alphonsus	NT	–	–	MD	HumidF	3	?	
Paraphthonia	–	2	molione	Peru	?	?	?	?	?	?	
†Colaciticus	71:39	2	johnstoni	AM	–	–	PM	RainF	1	?	
Metacharis	76:1–2	9	ptolemaeus	NT	–	–	AM,PM	HumidF	4	Flacourti., Loranth.	5
†Cariomothus	71:19–20	4	erythromelas	SAm	–	–?	PM	HumidF	2	?	
*†Lepricornis	74:23	11	atricolor	SAm	+?	–	AM	HumidF	2	Combret.	
Pheles	77:29	1	heliconides	SAm	+	–?	MD	HumidF	2	?	
Barbicornis	70:38 71:1	1[k]	basilis	Atl	+–	–	AM	HumidF	4	Sapot., Ulm.	6
Syrmatia	79:9	4	nyx, aethiops	SAm	+–	–	EAM	RainF	4	Zinziber	
*Chamaelimnas	71:25–8	11	tircis, briola	NT	+	–	AM	HumidF	2	?	
Cartea	71:21	1	vitula	AM	++	–?	PM	RainF	4	?	
Crocozona	71:44	4	caecius	UpAM, BR–SM	–	–?	AM	HumidF	3	?	
†*Baeotis	70:23 :35–7	14	hisbon, zonata	NT	+	–?	AM	F, Cd	2	?	
Caria	71:15–8	14	ino, trochilus	NT	–	–	MD	HumidF	4	Ulm.	2,3,7
†*Chalodeta	71:22–3 :34	9	jessa, theodora	NT	–	–	MD	HumidF	3	Sterculi., Aster.	
Parcella	77:20	1	amarynthina	NT	–	–?	AM	HumidF	3	?	
†*Charis	72:23 71:29–31 :33	15	auius, cleonus	NT	–	–	MD	HumidF	5	?	
*Calephelis	(20:45–6)	32	nilus	NT(+NA)	–	–	MD	Cmp	5	Aster.	2,3,8
Amarynthis	70:2	1	meneria	AM	–	–?	MD	HumidF	4	?	
Amphiselenis	70:3	1	chama	Venez	–	–?	MD	CloudF	?	?	
*†Lasaia	74:14–6	11	agesilas	NT	–	–?	MD	RiverF	4	?	
†Exoplisia	76:15–7	4	cadmeis	SAm	–	–?	MD	RainF	2	?	
Riodina	78:13–5	3	lycisca	SAm	–	–?	MD	RiverF	4	?	23
*†Melanis :29–32	74:26–7	39	xarife, pixe	NT	+–	–	MD	HumidF	4	Legumin., Aster.	3
*†Siseme	78:24–8	10	aristoteles	And	–	–?	MD	RiverF	4	?	
†Comphotis	71:41	3	irrorata	AM	–	–?	PM	RainF	2	?	
Symmachiiti											
Lucillella	74:25	3	camissa	TRAn	–	–?	PM	CloudF	2	?	
*Mesene :10–4	75:5–6	28	phareus	NT	–	–	PM	HumidF	3	Sapind.	
†Mesenopsis	75:15	3	bryaxis	NT	+	–	PM	RainF	1	?	
†*Xenandra 79:35,38	74:28	9	heliodes	SAm	–	–?	MD	RainF	1	?	
†Xynias	79:36	4	cynosema	AM	++	–?	PM	RainF	1	?	
†*Esthemopsis	72:25–8	14	inaria	NT	++	–	PM	RainF	1	?	
Chimastrum	71:36	1	argenteum	TRAn	+–?	–?	PM	RainF	2	?	
†*Symmachia	78:10–1 :22,31 :34 79:1–6	45	probetor	NT	+–	–	PM	RainF	1–2	?	
†*Pterographium	78:21	9	sagaris	SAm	–	–	PM	HumidF	3	Melastom.	5,23
†*Phaenochitonia	77:25–6	12	cingulus	NT	–	–?	PM	HumidF	3	?	

Continued...

Table 1 (cont). Synopsis of neotropical Riodininae[a]; systematics and biology[b].

Taxonomic groups: SUBFAMILY (TRIBE), Subtribe or Group, *†Genus;	Plate numbers (Lewis 1973)	Approx. no. of spp.	Typical or well-known species	Distri-bution of genus[c]	Mim[d]	Myr[e]	Time of activity	Habitat (usual)[c]	Abn[f]	Larval host plants[q]	Biblio-graphy
†*Stichelia	77:24,28 78:18	7	bocchoris	SAm	–	–?	PM	F,Cd,Cmp	4	?	
Helicopiti[l]											
†*Sarota	71:32–3	11	gyas, chrysus	NT	–	–	N,AM	HumidF	4	Epiphylls	
†*Anteros	70:13–8	14	formosus	NT	–	–	AM	HumidF	2	Euphorbi.	3
Ourocnemis	77:14	2	archytas	AM	–	–?	?	RainF	?	?	
Helicopis[m]	74:3–4	4	cupido	AM–PB	+	–	AM	SwampF	4	Marant., Ar.	
Emesiti											
*†Argyrogrammana	70:21–2 :24–5 :27	18	holosticta	NT	–	–	PM	HumidF	2	Clusi.	
Callistium	71:5	1	cleadas	AM	–	–?	?	?	?	?	
†*Calydna	71:7–14 :38,40	25	thersander	NT	–	–?	MD	HumidF	3		
*†Emesis	72:18–22 :24	46	cerea, lucinda	NT	+–	+–	MD	F,Cd	4	Legumin., Myrt.	2,3,23
Pixus	–	1	corculum	Colomb	–	–	PM	RainF	3	?	17
†*Pachythone	77:15–7	14	gigas	NT	–	–?	PM	HumidF	2	?	
Pseudonymphidia	–	1	clearista	TRAn	–	–?	PM	HumidF	2	?	17
Roeberella	78:17	3	calvus	And	–	–?	?	CloudF	2	?	
Lamphiotes	–	1	velazquesi	Mexico	–	–?	?	HumidF	?	?	17
Apodemia	70:20?	12	mormo	Mexico	–	–	MD	Cd,Cmp	3	Ros., Legumin.	2,3
Zabuella	79:33	1	tenella	Argent	–	–?	?	?	?	?	
Dinoplotis	72:2	1	orphana	AM	–	–?	?	?	?	?	
Echenais	–	1	thelephus	AM	–	–?	PM	HumidF	?	?	
Imelda	74:8	3	mycea	Andes	–	–?	PM	CloudF	3	?	
Astraeodes	70:26	1	areuta	AM–PE	–	–?	?	?	?	?	
Dianesia	70:19	1	carteri	Bah,Cuba	–	–?	AM,PM	Coast Scrub	3	?	10
Mycastor		3	leucarpis	SAm	–	+?	PM	HumidF	2	?	21
Petrocerus	–	1	catiena	BR–SM	–	–	PM	CloudF	2	?	20
Lemoniiti[n]											
*Lemonias	74:19–20 :22	10	zygia	NT	–	+	PM	Cd,Cmp	4	Euphorbi.	11
Thisbe	79:27–30	4	irenea, molela	NT	–	+	PM	F,Cd	3	Legumin., Euphorbi.	18
Uraneis	79:32,37	3	hyalina	AM	++	+?	PM	HumidF	2	?	
Catocyclotis	71:23	1	aemulius	NT	–	+?	PM	HumidF	2	?	12
*†Juditha	74:17–8 78:7	6	azan, molpe	NT	+–	+	PM	HumidF	3	Legumin., Euphorbi. Simaroub.,	
*†Synargis	72:17 76:26–31 77:1–4	26	tytia, abaris	NT	+–	+	PM	HumidF	3	Legumin., Sterculi., Euphorbi.	23
Thyranota	79:34	1	galena	CBR	–	+?	MD	Cd,Cmp	4	Legumin.	
*†Ematurgina	72:14	5	axenus	SAm	–	+?	MD	Cd,Cmp	3	?	
†*Audre	70:28–34	22	epulus	SAm	+–	+	MD	Cd,Cmp	4	Legumin., Ros., Turner.	14
†Aricoris	77:13	2	tutana	SBR	–	+?	MD	Cd,Cmp	2	?	
Eiseleia	–	1	terias	Argent	–	+?	?	Chaco	2	?	19

Continued...

Taxonomic groups: SUBFAMILY (TRIBE), Subtribe or Group, *†Genus;	Plate numbers (Lewis 1973)	Approx. no. of spp.	Typical or well-known species	Distri-bution of genus[c]	Mim[d]	Myr[e]	Time of activity	Habitat (usual)[c]	Abn[f]	Larval host plants[q]	Biblio-graphy
Nymphidiiti											
Parnes	77:21	2	philotes	AM–Atl	–	+?	PM	RainF	2	?	
Periplacis	77:23	1	glaucoma	SAm	–	+?	PM	HumidF	2	?	
†Menander	75:4,7–9 78:9	8	hebrus	NT	–	+	PM	HumidF	2	Marcgravi.	15
*Zelotaea	79:39	2	phasma	BR	+	+	PM	RainF	1	?	
Pandemos	77:19	2	pasiphae	NT	–	+?	PM	HumidF	1	?	16
†*Dysmathia	72:6	7	portia	AM	–	+?	PM	RainF	1	?	
Joiceya	–	1	praeclara	BR–MT	–	+?	?	Cd	1	?	22
Rodinia	78:16	1	calpharnia	AM	–	+?	?	?	1	?	
Calociasma	71:6	4	lilina	NT	–	+?	PM	OpenF	2	?	
†*Calospila	71:3–4 :21,74 77:27 :30–5 78:1–6	40	emylius, zeanger	NT	+–	+	PM	HumidF	4	Malpighi.	
†*Adelotypa	72:3,7–12 :15–6	31	senta, bolena	NT	–	+	PM	HumidF	4	?	
*†Setabis (=Orimba)	77:5–12 78:20,33	29	epitus, lagus, cruentata	NT	++	+?	PM	RainF	2	Sterculi.[o]	
†*Theope	79:11–26	45	terambus	NT	+–	+	PM	F,Cd	2	Legumin., Sterculi.	
†*Nymphidium	76:18 :20–5	34	lisimon	NT	+–	+	PM	HumidF	4	Legumin., Sterculi.	5
Stalachtiti											
Stalachtis	78:29–30 :32,35	8	phaedusa	SAm	++	+	MD	F,Cd,Cmp	4	Simaroub., Legumin.	23,24

Notes:

* Genus in which 'species' names will probably be united, reducing total number of species.

† Genus in which new species will be described, increasing total number of species (If both symbols present, the first one should predominate – overall increase or reduce).

a Does not include primarily Nearctic species extending into Mexico.

b Information on Riodininae from Callaghan and Lamas (1994) and Harvey (1987)

c AM = Amazon; And = Andes; Ant = Antilles; Argent = Argentina; Atl = Atlantic; BA = Bahia; Bah = Bahamas; BR = Brazil; CBR = Central Brazil; Cd = Cerrado; Cl = Cloud; Colomb = Colombia; Cmp = Campo; CR = Costa Rica; EcAnd = Ecuadorian Andes; F = Forest; Hu = Humid; MG = Minas Gerais; MT = Mato Grosso, Brazil; NA = North America; NT = Neotropics; PE = Pernambuco, NE Brazil; SAm = South America; SBR = Southern Brazil; Sec = Secondary forests; SM = Serra do Mar; sp.AM = especially the Amazon; TRAn = TransAndean; upAM = Upper Amazon basin; Venez = Venezuela.

d Mim = mimicry of distasteful or venomous species; '++' = strongly present or characteristic, '+' = present, '+–' = weak, variable or sometimes present.

e Myr = larva myrmecophilous.

f Abn = usual abundance when found: 1 = very scarce, 2 = scarce, 3 = uncommon, 4 = common, 5 = abundant.

g Maintained at family level by Harvey and others; subfamilies = Styg, Corrach, Hamear, Eus, Rio.

h Divided by Harvey into Mesosemiini (first 5 genera), Eurybiini (nos 7,8,9), 'incertae sedis' (Eunogyra and rest).

i Divided by Harvey into 'Ancyluris section' (first 17 genera) and 'Riodina section' (remaining 23).

j Probably part of Rhetus, isolated in high mesic rockfields (see Figure 3 and species account).

k United into a single species by Azzará (1973); probably 3 species at most.

l Divided by Harvey into Sarotini and Helicopini (this tribe monotypic).

m Callaghan maintains 20 species, but 4 (Harvey) is more likely.

n Divided by Harvey into a 'Lemonias-section' (first 3 genera), a 'Synargis-section' (next 4), and an 'Audre-section' (last 5 genera).

o Larvae have been reported feeding on Membracidae (carnivorous), the only case of aphytophagy known in the neotropical Lycaenidae to date. (Harvey, pers. comm., indicates probable aphytophagy in Mimocastnia).

p A single fossil genus (near Rhetus) and species have been described: Riodinella nympha Durden and Rose 1978, from the middle Eocene, about 48 million years ago.

q Plant family names abbreviated by omission of standard ending.

Bibliography cited in right-hand column:
1 Harvey 1989; 2 Downey and Allyn 1980; 3 Kendall 1976; 4 Horvitz et al. 1987; 5 Callaghan 1989; 6 Azzara 1978; 7 Clench 1967; 8 McAlpine 1971; 9 Clench 1972; 10 Harvey and Clench 1980; 11 Ross 1964, 1966; 12 Callaghan 1982b; 13 Callaghan 1986b; 14 Schremmer 1978; 15 Callaghan 1977, 1978; 16 Harvey and Gilbert 1988; 17 Callaghan 1982b; 18 De Vries 1988b, 1991b; 19 Miller and Miller 1972; 20 Callaghan 1979; 21 Callaghan 1983b; 22 Talbot 1928; 23 Dias 1980; 24 Callaghan 1986a.

Table 2. Synopsis of systematics and biology of neotropical coppers and blues.

SUBFAMILY (TRIBE) Section Genus	Plate nos (Lewis)	No. of spp.	Typical species	Distribution[a]	Habitat[a]	Abundance[a]	Larval Hosts
LYCAENINAE							
Heliophorus section							
Iophanus	62:34[e]	1	*pyrrhias*	CAm	CloudF	2	?
POLYOMMATINAE (POLYOMMATINI)[b]							
Leptotes section							
Leptotes	(19:34)	8	*cassius*	NT	Cmp, Sec	5	Legumin.
Zizula section							
Zizula	69:51	2	*cyna*	NT	Swamp	3	Legumin.?
Brephidium section							
Brephidium	(19:17)	1	*exilis*	CAm–Ven	Estuary	4	Various
Everes section							
Everes	(19:13)	1	*comyntas*	CAm	Cmp	3	Legumin.
'*Everes*'[c]	–	2	*cogina*	BR–SM	Cmp	3	Legumin.?
Lycaenopsis section							
Celastrina	(19:11)	1	*ladon*	CAm	Cmp, Forest	4	Legumin.
Polyommatus section							
Hemiargus (+2 subgenera)	(19:23) 67:18	9	*hanno*	NT	Cmp, Scrub	4	Legumin.
Pseudochrysops	–	1	*bornoi*	Ant	Scrub	2	
Madeleinea[d] (*Itylos* auctt.)	–	>8	*pelorias*	SAnd	Scrub	2	
Paralycaeides[d]	–	4	*inconspicua*	SAnd	Scrub	2	
Pseudolucia[d]	67:25–6	19	*chilensis*	SAnd	Puna	3	
Nabokovia[d]	–	2	*faga*	SAnd	Scrub	2	
Itylos[d] (*Parachilades* auctt.)	67:23	4	*titicaca*	SAnd	Scrub, Puna	2	
Polytheclus[d]	–	2	*sylphis*	SAnd	Scrub	2	

Notes

a   The conventions and abbreviations in these categories follow those in Table 1.

b   Does not include North American (Nearctic) species invading northern Mexico.

c   Dr. Heinz Ebert gave a new name to this genus, still unpublished; may be true *Everes*. The species *griqua* Schaus was renamed as *Pseudolucia parana* by Bálint (1993), but Dr. Ebert regarded this taxon as belonging to the *Everes* section and congeneric with *cogina*.

d   Following Bálint 1993.

e   This figure number from de la Maza 1988.

General references for neotropical Polyommatinae include Nabokov 1945; Clench 1964; and the very useful catalogue of Bridges 1988.

Notes to Table 3 (opposite).

a   Table composed with the help of Dr. R.K. Robbins. A number of well-known genera of Eumaeini are either little-known biologically, or with infrageneric relationships still poorly defined, and thus are not included in this Table. Genera briefly described by Johnson (1991a) are also omitted, for lack of complete information on their scope and position; the same applies to the 20 new neotropical genera and 88 new species proposed by Johnson (1992) 'based on adult wing pattern, tergal morphology and male and female genitalia' (all of these show great variation in some populations), and to the two new genera and 29 new species added by Johnson and coauthors, in numbers 23 (1992, with five separate papers) and 24–29 (1993, including a review of *Pseudolucia* and two new genera of Polyommatinae, see Table 2. The well known genera not included here include: *Theritas, Mithras, Allosmaitia, Thereus* (=*Noreena*), *Ocaria, Parrhasius, Michaelus, Oenomaus, Symbiopsis* (Nicolay 1971b), *Calycopis s.l.* (=*Calystryma, Femniterga, Tergissima* and 15 of the other genera described in Johnson 1991a; the other seven new 'Outgroup' genera also include several segregates from well-known genera mentioned here), *Electrostrymon, Lamprospilus, Theclopsis, Siderus, Contrafacia* (=*Orcya*), *Ipidecla, Hypostrymon, Nesiostrymon* (see Johnson 1991b, including its citations of most previous papers of that author), *Paiwarria* and *Theorema*.

b   The conventions and abbreviations in these categories follow those in Table 1.

c   References: 1 Robbins 1987; 2 Nicolay 1971a; 3 Robbins 1980, 1985; 4 Robbins 1991; 5 Nicolay 1980 and Johnson 1989; 6 Nicolay 1977; 7 Clench 1944, 1946; 8 Nicolay 1980 and Callaghan 1982; 9 Nicolay 1982; 10 Miller 1980; 11 Robbins and Venables 1991.

Table 3. Synopsis of the systematics and biology of selected neotropical hairstreaks (better defined genera, including about 30% of known species)[a].

SUBFAMILY (TRIBE), Genus	Plate numbers (Lewis)	No. of spp.	Typical species	Distribution[b]	Habitat[b]	Abundance	Larval hosts	Myr.[b] ?	Refs[c]
THECLINAE (EUMAEINI)									
Eumaeus	67:17	6–7	minijas	Ant–AM	F, Scrub	3	Cycad.	–	
Thestius	69:7	1–3	pholeus	AM	HumidF	2			
Micandra	67:47,51 69:8	8–10	platyptera	CAm–And	CloudF	2	Legumin.	–	1
Evenus	69:13,19 :25,45	13	regalis	NT	Cl, HumidF	2	Sapot.	–	
Atlides	66:12 :14–6	13	polybe	NT	Cl, Humid RainF	2	Loranth.	–	
Arcas	68:8 69:44,46	7	imperialis	NT	Cl, Humid RainF	3	Laur., Anacardi.	–	2
Pseudolycaena	68:39	4–6	marsyas	NT	F, Cd, Scrub	4	Polyphagous	–	
Arawacus (=Polyniphes, Dolymorpha)	66:9–11 67:24 68:26 69:17,21	16–20	aetolus dumenilii	NT	F, Cd, Scrub	4	Solan.	+	3
Rekoa (=Heterosmaitia)	67:45 68:12,44,48 69:9	7	meton marius palegon	NT	F, Cd, Cmp	4	Polyphagous	+	4
Chlorostrymon	67:30–1	5	simaethis	NT	F, Cd, Cmp	2	Sapind.	+	5
Magnastigma		6	julia, hirsuta	NT	Hu, RainF, Cd	2			6
Cyanophrys	67:29,36 68:15 :23–4 :34	19–22	herodotus bertha acaste	NT	HumidF	3	Polyphagous	+?	7
Panthiades (=Cycnus)	67:22,44 68:5	8	bitias, phaleros	NT	Cl, Hu, RainF	3	Polyphagous	+	8
Olynthus	–	10	punctum, fancia	CR–SBR	Cl, RainF	2	Lecythid.	+	9
Strymon	66:18 67:1,3 :28 68:19,53 69:40 :47–8	40–70	ziba mulucha	NT	F, Cd, Cmp	4	Polyphagous	+	
Tmolus	69:49,52	10–11	echion	NT	Hu, RainF, Cd	3	Polyphagous	+	
Ministrymon	67:2,15 :27 68:41 69:38	18–22	azia una	NT	HumidF, Scrub	2	Legumin.		
Brangas	66:13	18–20	getus, silumena	NT	Cl, Hu, RainF	2	Loranth., Sapind.		
Chalybs	68:27	3	janias	NT	HumidF	2	Legumin.		
Erora	68:20	>40	aura, phrosine	NT	Cl, Hu, RainF	2	Polyphagous		10
Trichonis	–	2	hyacinthinus	AM	RainF	1	?		1
Iaspis	69:18,27 :41	11–12	temesa,talayra	NT	Forest	2	Sterculi.	+	
Janthecla	68:38	10	janthina, rocena	NT	Cl, Hu, RainF	3	?		11

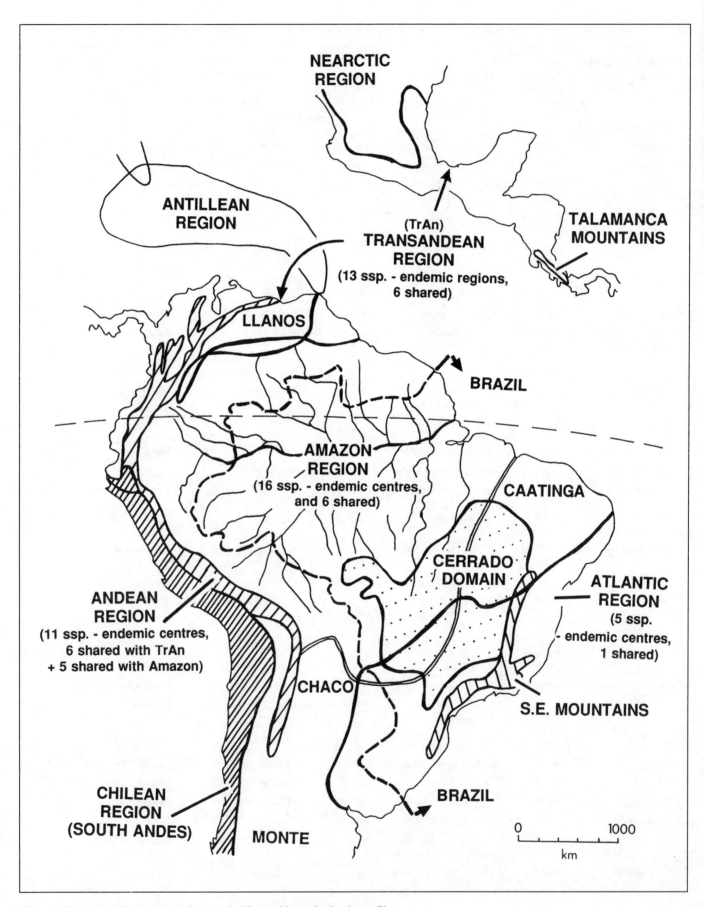

Figure 2. Biogeographical patterns of neotropical Lycaenidae and other butterflies.

On the basis of four foreleg characters, Robbins (1988) has advocated separation of the Riodininae from the Lycaenidae, suggesting affinity with the Nymphalidae. The considerable variation of some leg characters leads to difficulty and disagreement about their interpretation in many groups and in this case further integration with other sets of characters would be helpful before a final decision is reached.

Distribution and variation

As noted above, three species of neotropical blues (*Hemiargus hanno*, *Leptotes cassius* and *Zizula cyna*) are very widespread indeed despite their minute size and weak flight, especially *Zizula cyna* which struggles to rise above the grasses in the sites it inhabits throughout tropical America. *Leptotes* and *Hemiargus* are also known from distant oceanic islands (Galapagos and Fernando de Noronha), as well as all islands in the Caribbean. Robbins and Small (1981) have shown that most Theclinae are also widespread and undifferentiated, and suggest that this is due to mass, long-range, community dispersal during the dry season, like Pieridae and Hesperiidae, ranging over the entire region. Riodininae may be at the opposite extreme of the spectrum, most being extremely local (even in more widespread species) and often well-differentiated geographically (especially in *Eurybia*, *Mesosemia*, *Nymphidium* and the mimetic groups).

Largely endemic thecline faunas are found in high mountains in southeastern Brazil, the Andean cloud forests and the Central American highlands, while local riodinine assemblages inhabit wet lowland forests (Callaghan 1983a, 1985). A largely endemic fauna (Table 2) inhabits the extremely long, narrow 'island' forming the Republic of Chile, isolated by desert (N), high-altitude rocks (E), ice (S) and ocean (W). There are contiguous areas in southwestern Bolivia and Peru extending up the semi-arid 'puna' as far as southern Ecuador in some cases. In the Brazilian Atlantic region (Figure 2) much endemism is seen in cerrado species (central plateau) in addition to montane and coastal forms; in the overall region, 49% of the Theclinae, 44% of the Riodininae, and two congeneric blues are endemic. These levels are slightly higher than for skippers, nymphalids or pierids (all 39%) or papilionids (42%), but they may drop when proper links can be discovered between Atlantic and Amazonian or Andean sister-groups (species or subspecies).

Robbins (pers. comm.) has suggested a list of 25 thecline species or superspecies which are 'widespread, common in many regions and habitats, and likely to be recorded on a quick trip to the neotropics': *Theritas mavors/triquetra*, *Pseudolycaena* supersp. *marsyas*, *Arawacus* supersp. *aetolus*, *Rekoa meton*, *R. marius*, *R. palegon*, *Tmolus echion*, *Oenomaus ortygnus*, *Panthiades bitias/hebraeus*, *Parrhasius polibetes*, *Cyanophrys herodotus*, *Electrostrymon* supersp. *endymion*, *Calycopis isobeon*, *C. cerata*, *Chlorostrymon simaethis*, *Ministrymon una*, *M. azia*, *Strymon mulucha*, *S. bazochii*, *S. ziba*, and '*Thecla*' (catch-all genus for the majority of species still not assigned to existing generic names) *hemon*, *hesperitis*, *syllis*,

celmus and *tephraeus*. In South America, *Arcas imperialis*, *Panthiades phaleros* and some other forest species could be added to this list.

At the other extreme, one or two specimens are known from a single locality (such as two new *Atlides* species from a single 2200m hilltop west of Cali, Colombia), and perhaps over a hundred (about 10%) are known from fewer than ten specimens in museum collections. In April 1991, Robbins took the fourth known specimen of a striking thecline, without generic or specific identification, on *Mikania* flowers invading this author's backyard; the first three were in a single Brazilian collection, awaiting description. So for these species, and perhaps for over 50% of Riodininae, much information is still waiting in the wings before any idea of distribution, biology, affinities or importance can be assigned. The general patterns of biogeography of neotropical Lycaenidae are very similar to those known in other insects, as shown in Figure 2.

Mimetic species that join 'rings' of similar and distasteful heliconians, ithomiines, arctiids, dioptids and other Lepidoptera vary in parallel with these (mostly in 16 genera of Riodininae, Table 1) and are just as useful as their models for identifying centres of endemism at the infraspecific level in the lowland neotropical forests (Figure 2). Many other Lycaenidae show strong geographic variation, often regarded today as at the species rather than the subspecies level. Probably about half of any local lycaenid fauna will contain some information about region and habitats.

Behaviour and juvenile host plant relations

Most neotropical blues and hairstreaks have the usual rapid, darting flight of these groups. Especially impressive are the larger hilltopping species of *Arcas*, *Evenus*, *Atlides* and *Brangas*, but they are surely no faster than some of the small species which are completely lost by the eye on each flight and are only seen again when they land back on the same perch.

Riodinine flight varies from the same rapid, darting pattern (*Theope*, many *Euselasia*, *Charis*, *Mesene*, *Symmachia*, *Stichelia*, *Calydna*, *Calospila*) through a more usual and slower, erratic flight (always returning to a chosen perch) to the very casual, dipping or fluttering flight of mimetic species imitating their distasteful models (*Methone*, *Ithomiola*, *Ithomeis*, *Brachyglenis*, *Themone*, *Chamaelimnas*, *Cartea*, *Uraneis*, *Stalachtis*, and females of *Esthemopsis* and *Setabis*). A few species may imitate wasps with a 'buzzy' flight (*Chorinea*, *Syrmatia*, some *Rhetus*), while ground-perching species may rise in spirals when disturbed. *Styx* has a very weak, almost falling flight (*fide* G. Lamas).

Adults usually visit small flowers, and many riodinines (principally males) are also found on damp sand or mud (*Lyropteryx*, *Riodina*, *Rhetus*, *Necyria*, *Barbicornis*, *Parcella*, *Notheme*, *Monethe*, *Lasaia*, *Chamaelimnas*, *Caria*, *Siseme*). All vertical levels of the habitat, and also adjacent non-forest areas, are included in usual foraging surveys.

Adults of the genus *Eumaeus*, locally common from southern Florida to central-west Brazil, incorporate toxic cycasins from their larval foodplants (mostly *Zamia* but often other Cycadaceae) (Rothschild *et al.* 1986; Bowers and Larin 1989). They are brightly marked models for mimicry rings, flying very slowly and liberating cyanide gas when crushed; their larvae are gregarious and also highly aposematic, having a delicate relationship with the phenology of their hosts (Clark and Clark 1991). No other adult neotropical Lycaenidae have yet been shown to be similarly protected against predators.

Mass movements of Riodininae communities have not been reported, though populations often appear suddenly in a new habitat as a few worn individuals and are later replaced by a large endogenous generation if foodplants are found. Theclinae seem to move over large regions in loose, multispecific groups (hundreds of individuals of dozens of species), or sometimes migrate unidirectionally or erratically as dense populations of a single species (*Pseudolycaena* and *Calycopis*), principally during the dry season when flowers are scarce. Sunny clearings can attract such concentrations, which can at times contain nearly a hundred species. Especially interesting areas to find these assemblages are sheltered sites on low or high ridges, on dry, sunny or windy days (Robbins and Small 1981).

Territorial perching and area defence by males are widespread and easily demonstrated by marking neotropical Lycaenidae (see also Bates 1859). In open fields, males perch on the tips of the highest grass blades, driving off with their rapid forays other males, many other butterflies and even insect predators, bird predators and collectors. In forests, perching may be in the canopy (only in the morning since canopy species descend to the cooler understorey at noontime), on forest edges, in small clearings, on tree trunks in the sun or shade, on top of or under leaves at all levels (with distinct partitioning, Callaghan 1983a), along rivercourses or trails, or on hilltops and rocks (especially in mountains), almost always in an exposed, often sunlit spot. Territories defended vary from less than one to many dozens of cubic metres. As might be expected, hilltopping (or ridge-topping or edge-seeking) is very common in male Lycaenidae in wait for females of their sparse populations. More than one hundred species may accumulate at a favoured hilltop in late morning to mid-afternoon, colouring the sky in their territorial battles. Early morning 'leks' of many males have been seen in *Euselasia*, *Barbicornis*, *Sarota* and *Syrmatia*.

When not exhibiting territorial behaviour, theclines perch on the tops of leaves or on twigs in the forest undergrowth, in shade or sun-flecks, 'rubbing' their hindwings in the usual manner to call attention to their 'false head' (Figure 3 and Robbins 1980, 1985) (this also occurs in the riodinines *Anteros* and *Sarota*). Whilst doing this, they fly upon the slightest provocation, usually landing quite far away.

Riodinines usually perch under leaves with wings flat open (most genera) or closed (Euselasiini, *Sarota, Anteros, Themone, Helicopis, Theope*, most *Setabis*); some perch on tops of leaves with wings half-open (*Mesosemia, Semomesia* and relatives, also *Eurybia* at dusk). Particular underleaf perches are used repeatedly and insistently by the same individual, and by members of the same population. If the resident individual is removed from a leaftop territorial perch or an underleaf resting station, a series of conspecific males will then occupy the same perch; depending upon the genus, these can be progressively younger and more splendid, or older and more worn than the first resident.

Courtship can have both aerial and perched components, either of which can be very complex. They are presumably accompanied by diverse pheromonal signals and responses which are produced by scent-spots or pads, androconial brushes or patches. In *Helicopis cupido* (observed in Guyana) the male alternates rapid wing flutters (to 40° open) with short 220° wing opened phases (one-second cycles), whilst perched right behind the female (who maintains her wings closed) on top of a sloping large leaf of the larval foodplant (*Montrichardia*, Araceae); he then moves directly in to initiate mating.

Oviposition is not often observed, but as with most butterflies, occurs in short bouts which involve appreciable searching, inspection, and tactile evaluation (foreleg 'drumming') of the exact site. Off-hostplant egg-laying is not common but has been observed, as in other butterflies. Eggs are often placed in axils and other tight places, and are very rarely found; they are often pincushion-shaped and highly sculptured (Downey and Allyn 1979, 1980, 1981, 1984), but in four small tribes of Riodininae, they are smooth and barrel-shaped (Harvey 1987). Myrmecophilous species may lay their eggs along ant foraging routes (*Stalachtis, Lemonias, Mycastor, Nymphidium*) or even visually encourage ants to directly remove eggs as they are expelled (*Adelotypa senta; Audre domina*, Robbins and Aiello 1982).

Larvae may be smooth (especially if myrmecophilous), tubercled, spiny or hairy, often in relation to their habitat. They are usually highly cryptic, even when on flowers (a habit common in Theclinae, rare in Riodininae), and may be polymorphic, probably incorporating pigments from the flowers on which they feed (Monteiro 1991). Some larvae and many pupae are found in 'nests' inside rolled leaves. Pupae are quite variable in shape, with systematic significance in the Riodininae (Harvey 1987). These biological characters are quite similar to those of other Lycaenidae, though some riodinine larvae are unique.

Myrmecophily is quite frequent in Theclinae, perhaps in 50% of species (De Vries 1990; Malicky 1970), but in Riodininae has been reported in only three subtribes with 283 species: Eurybiiti; Lemoniiti; and Nymphidiiti (Harvey 1987; De Vries 1991a). *Stalachtis*, in a fourth monogeneric subtribe, is optionally myrmecophilous, even in a single population (*susanna, phlegia, lineosa*, on Simaroubaceae; Callaghan 1986; Benson, Francini and Brown, unpublished).

Ant-associated larvae have easily recognisable specialised glands (Cottrell 1984). In Lycaenidae these include a dorsal nectary organ on the seventh abdominal segment and a pair of tentacle organs on the eighth segment. All known ant-associated riodinine larvae have a pair of glands (tentacle nectary organs) on the eighth segment. These secrete a solution which may be

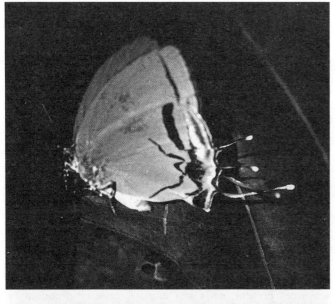

Figure 3. Pictures of Riodinines and Theclines in life, to show behaviour and habitat.
(a) *Paiwarria telemus* (Manaus) [top left]; (b) *Arawacus meliboeus* (Japi, São Paulo) [top right]; (c) *Strymon oreala* (Santa Teresa, Espírito Santo) [middle left]; (d) *Nirodia belphegor* (Serra do Cipó, Minas Gerais) [middle right]; (e) *Helicopis acis* (Belém, Pará) [bottom]. (Photos: K.S. Brown Jr., except (d) Ivan Sazima.)

very rich in amino acids (De Vries 1988b; De Vries and Baker 1989). Larvae of Lemoniiti and Nymphidiiti have two additional myrmecophilous organs (Harvey 1987): a pair of anterior tentacle organs on the metathorax which produce chemicals affecting ant behaviour (De Vries 1988b); and a pair of vibratory papillae on the anterior margin of the prothorax, which produce sound to call ants (De Vries 1988b, 1990), also seen in other lycaenids (De Vries 1991a, 1991b).

Food resources of larvae are exceedingly varied, with at least 50 plant families recorded more than once; no pattern can be discerned except for certain tendencies for given species, genera or tribes to use the same resource over a wide geographical range. In contrast, some species are extremely polyphagous, especially those that feed on flowers (mostly Theclinae: Robbins and Aiello 1982; Monteiro 1991).

The normally Myrtaceae-feeding and rare *Euselasia eucerus* in Brazil has taken to imported *Eucalyptus* leaves and becomes extremely abundant and destructive in commercial plantations of these Australian trees. The riodinine *Audre campestris*, the thecline *Michaelus jebus*, and some blues may be pests of cultivated beans and other legumes, and *Strymon ziba* can become a serious pest on pineapples, but in general few Lycaenidae have achieved such notoriety.

Lycaenids as indicator species

The extremely sporadic distribution of most neotropical Lycaenidae, not only in collections but also in the field in both time and space, was noted by early naturalists (Bates 1859) and amply confirmed by all later observers. Riodinines are especially local, confined to a very narrow microhabitat, and active only at a particular time of day and level of forest; they are often greatly reduced in diversity and numbers in highly variable or unpredictable climates. Some are even nocturnal: *Euselasia clesa* was seen flying in typical territorial behaviour under a black light at 4 a.m., one hour before dawn and *Sarota chrysus* flies during the night and often comes to light (see also Miller 1970). Most species, however, pick a time slot in the early morning or mid-afternoon to be active, with the latest species often being those of *Nymphidium* and *Eurybia*, the earliest *Euselasia, Syrmatia* and *Sarota*. While many species are present year round, great seasonal variation in both presence and abundance is the rule (as for Theclinae), with species often peaking either in mid-summer, late fall or late spring in higher to lower elevations. At least one species in perhumid tropical forest (*Euselasia zara* in southeastern Brazil) has been seen only in November (in lowlands) to February (in uplands) and seems to be univoltine, as has also been suggested for *Audre domina* in Panama (Robbins and Aiello 1982).

All this natural fluctuation leads to serious problems in establishing baseline data for lycaenids, or recognising any significant tendencies to change or vary coherently in different habitats. When added to the great difficulty in collecting and identifying most species, the tendency to move about over the landscape, and the chaotic state of the systematic and biological data, these characters greatly diminish the utility of neotropical Lycaenidae as ecological indicators at the present time.

This does not mean that they are not potentially very useful in surveys and monitoring of natural and altered systems. Riodinines compose nearly half the daily list of butterflies in most parts of the Amazon Basin, and each species seems to be delicately tuned into a large number of physical and biological factors in its environment, which are therefore faithfully indicated by the species' presence (though not excluded by its absence). Some species may feed on a single plant genus or family as larvae or may be associated with certain ant species, thus necessitating the presence of these resources which may be harder to find and recognize than flying adult butterflies. The overall richness and diversity of the local lycaenid fauna offers excellent opportunities for correlation with different systems in varying stages of naturalness. Even a partial list can lead to hypotheses about ecological factors, history of the region, resources present, soils and climate, primary productivity, importance of other communities, and stability of the whole system. The routine and very propitious use of Lycaenidae as indicators in the neotropics only awaits the resolution of the systematic picture in order to produce useable manuals for identification, and wider biological studies in order to expand the knowledge of indicator parameters possible with diverse species and groups.

Threatened neotropical lycaenids

Insects that are highly stenoecious – with many narrow environmental requirements or specialised interactions necessary for their survival – may be easily reduced or eliminated locally by minor habitat alteration through natural or human disturbance. This applies to many neotropical Lycaenidae populations. With this local extinction, local adaptive genes will disappear, reducing the biodiversity and biosynthetic capacities of life.

On the other hand, winged insects are often migratory and accustomed to seeking out the narrow environmental conditions needed for growth and reproduction, and are already adapted to normal levels of natural disturbance; they are likely to be widespread even though local, and very persistent in the regional species pool. Thus, a definition of 'threat' to a neotropical lycaenid should consider its ecological characteristics, geographical distribution, aptitude for mobility and colonisation, density of colonies, usual population size, voltinism (are adults always around to be able to flee destruction and colonise elsewhere?), and the kind, degree and extent of local or regional disturbance patterns – both natural (on long and short time-scales) and artificial.

In principle, essentially all lycaenid species should survive transformation of primitive mosaic habitats (in areas of complex topography) into anthropic mosaics with 10–30% of the original vegetation maintained in large patches. Such is the case in the

Brazilian Atlantic forests, where reduction of the original forest to 12% of its former area has not caused detectable extinction of lycaenids or indeed of any other insects or vertebrates monitored (Brown 1991; Brown and Brown 1991). In ecologically more homogeneous areas, reduction of natural habitat to 10% or less of its original area may still not lead to overall species extinction, though much genetic variation will be lost with local populations (and less vagile species in some groups can be eliminated). Most lycaenids will survive even in smallish habitats (0.1–100ha) as long as the edge effects (Lovejoy et al. 1986; Janzen 1984, 1986) do not overwhelm the essential habitat characteristics: isolated areas of 10ha may be dramatically transformed within a year, and appreciable effects can be seen up to 250m from an edge in larger patches of experimental fragments in the central Amazon (Brown 1991). However, local disturbance can have a positive effect: it often brings in many new species of sun-loving lycaenids to the more diverse successional community (Hutchings 1991).

In regions subjected to large-scale commercial conversion (to pasture, monoculture, silviculture, agrosilviculture or timber production), many lycaenids may not find new habitat and more large-scale regional extinction is possible. If a species is confined to the region, it might become extinct, especially if the habitat is very specialised and different from neighbouring areas (a basin, mountain top, headwater system, lakeshore or marsh, seasonally flooded region, or other natural 'island'). Thus, land-use patterns could make a large difference in the genetic erosion and threat to lycaenid species in tropical forests (Brown and Brown 1991).

Brazil includes half the forest area, two of the four species-endemic regions and 19 of the 45 subspecies-endemic centres in the neotropics; it has about 425 species of Theclinae and 700 species of Riodininae (Brown 1982, 1991). A new official list of fauna threatened with extinction in Brazil was prepared by the Zoology Society in 1989 (Bernardes et al. 1990). It includes 23 butterflies, only one of which is a lycaenid: *Joiceya praeclarus,* an inconspicuous monotypic genus known only from a small area in central Mato Grosso, and not seen there since its original discovery in the 1920s. This would represent the syndrome of 'restricted to a limited area, isolated, under intense large-scale human occupation', though it is probably preserved in the four conservation units established recently in the area. However, at least one population of the species must be found before its survival can be assured or even dealt with.

A second list, prepared by the Zoology Society, recommending 'further study', includes another five species of Lycaenidae and also six genera of little-known Riodininae which include mostly rare, extremely local and sometimes geographically limited species – the syndrome of 'widespread but extremely sporadically recorded' (*Alesa, Colaciticus, Esthemopsis, Mesenopsis, Symmachia* and *Xenandra*). To the generic list could be added *Petrocerus, Erora,* and other groups of riodinines and theclines confined to high-elevation habitat islands in southeastern Brazil (same syndrome as *Joiceya,* but somewhat more widespread).

The five species of Lycaenidae on the second list represent further syndromes of rarity and threat, which need some more study before inclusion on the official Brazilian list of threatened fauna. They include the theclines *Arcas ducalis* (widespread but local in hills and mountains, mostly on hilltops) and *Arawacus aethesa* (highly restricted geographically to a lowland area under intensive deforestation); and the riodinines *Eucorna sanarita* (few localities in high mountains), *Nirodia belphegor* (a monotypic genus possibly part of *Rhetus* from natural rockfields in mountains of central Minas Gerais), and *Helocopis cupido* nr. *lindeni* (a few coastal swamps in the northeast). Other rare or restricted species may be added in the coming years to this list.

Outside Brazil, the best candidates for threatened status may be island species or high-altitude groups, with most members still very little known. The primitive, taxonomically isolated *Styx infernalis* is but rarely seen at medium high elevations in Peruvian cloud forests. These and some further Brazilian cases are treated in the species accounts in this book.

Acknowledgements

Dr. Robert K. Robbins of the U.S. National Museum (Washington) kindly criticised the text of this chapter and produced the final version of Table 3, as well as providing extensive unpublished information on Theclinae. Drs Donald J. Harvey of the same institution, and Curtis John Callaghan of Búzios, Rio de Janeiro and the Museu Nacional, furnished unpublished catalogues and extensive information on Riodininae. Reprints of papers and further notes on Lycaenidae were provided by Kurt Johnson of the American Museum of Natural History (New York) and Stan S. Nicolay of Virginia Beach. Dr. Olaf H.H. Mielke of the Departamento de Zoologia, Universidade Federal do Parana, Curitiba has helped greatly in knowledge of the Brazilian butterfly fauna over the past 30 years, and curated a very rich and complete collection which has greatly aided in understanding systematics and biogeography.

References

AZZARÁ, M.L. 1978. Revisão do gênero *Barbicornis* Godart, 1824 (Lepidoptera, Lycaenidae, Riodininae). *Acta Biol. Paran., Curitiba* **7**: 23–69.

BÁLINT, Z. 1993. A catalogue of the polyommatine Lycaenidae (Lepidoptera) of the xeromontane oreal biome in the Neotropics as represented in European collections. *Repts Mus. Nat. Hist. Univ. Wisc. (Stevens Point)* **29**: 1–36.

BARCANT, M. 1970. *Butterflies of Trinidad and Tobago.* Collins, London, 314pp.

BATES, H.W. 1859. Notes on South American butterflies. *Trans. ent. Soc. London N.S.* **5**: 1–11.

BERNARDES, A.T., MACHADO, A.B.M. and RYLANDS, A.B. 1990. *Fauna Brasileira Ameacada de Extinção.* Fundação Biodiversitas/IBAMA, Belo Horizonte, 65pp.

BOWERS, M.D. and LARIN, Z. 1989. Acquired chemical defence in a lycaenid butterfly, *Eumaeus atala. J. Chem. Ecol.* **15**: 1133–1146.

BRIDGES, C.A. 1988. *Catalogue of Lycaenidae and Riodinidae (Lepidoptera: Rhopalocera).* Printed by the author, *vii* + 8 x *ii* + 888pp.

BROWN JR., K.S. 1973. *A Portfolio of Neotropical Lepidopterology.* Rio de Janeiro, 28pp.

BROWN JR., K.S. 1979 *Ecologia Geográfica e Evolução nas Florestas Neotropicais.* Universidade Estadual de Campinas, *xxxi* + 265 + 120pp.

BROWN JR., K.S. 1982. Historical and ecological factors in the biogeography of aposematic Neotropical butterflies. *Amer. Zool.* **22**: 453–471.

BROWN JR., K.S. 1991. Conservation of Neotropical palaeoenvironments: insects as indicators. *In:* Collins, N.M. and Thomas, J.A. (Eds), *Conservation of Insects and their Habitats.* Academic Press, London, pp.349–404.

BROWN JR., K.S. and BROWN, G.G. 1991. Habitat alteration and species loss in Brazilian forests: economic, social, biological and geological determinants. *In:* Whitmore, T.C. and Sayer, J.A. (Eds), *Deforestation and Species Extinction in Tropical Forest,* IUCN, Gland, Switzerland.

CALLAGHAN, C.J. 1977. Studies on restinga butterflies. I. Life cycle and immature biology of *Menander felsina* (Riodininae), a myrmecophilous metalmark. *J. Lepid. Soc.* **31**: 173–182.

CALLAGHAN, C.J. 1978. Studies on restinga butterflies. II. Notes on the population structure of *Menander felsina* (Riodininae). *J. Lepid. Soc.* **32**: 87–94.

CALLAGHAN, C.J. 1979. A new genus and a new subspecies of Riodinidae from Southern Brazil. *Bull. Allyn Mus.* **53**: 1–7.

CALLAGHAN, C.J. 1982a. Notes on immature biology of two myrmecophilous Lycaenidae: *Juditha molpe* (Riodininae) and *Panthiades bitias* (Lycaeninae). *J. Res. Lep.* **20**: 36–42.

CALLAGHAN, C.J. 1982b. Three new genera of Riodininae from Mexico and Central America. *Rev. Soc. Mex. Lep.* **7**: 55–63.

CALLAGHAN, C.J. 1983a. A study of isolating mechanisms among Neotropical butterflies of the subfamily Riodininae. *J. Res. Lep.* **21**: 159–176.

CALLAGHAN, C.J. 1983b. A new genus of Riodinine butterflies. *Bull. Allyn Mus.* **78**: 1–7.

CALLAGHAN, C.J. 1985. Notes on the zoogeographic distribution of butterflies in the subfamily Riodininae in Colombia. *In:* Proc. 2nd Symp. on Neotropical Lepidoptera. *J. Res. Lep.*, Supplement **1**: 50–69.

CALLAGHAN, C.J. 1986a. Notes of the biology of *Stalachtis susanna* (Lycaenidae: Riodininae) with a discussion of Riodininae larval strategies. *J. Res. Lep.* **24**: 258–263.

CALLAGHAN, C.J. 1986b. Restinga butterflies: biology of *Synargis brennus* (Stichel) (Riodinidae). *J. Lepid. Soc.* **40**: 93–96.

CALLAGHAN, C.J. 1989. Notes on the biology of three Riodinine species: *Nymphidium lisimon attenuatum, Phaenochitonia sagaris satnius* and *Metacharis ptolemaeus* (Lycaenidae: Riodininae). *J. Res. Lep.* **27**: 109–114.

CALLAGHAN, C.J. and LAMAS, G. (in press). A checklist of the subfamily Riodininae. Atlas of Neotropical Lepidoptera.

CLARK, D.B. and CLARK, D.A. 1991. Herbivores, herbivory and plant phenology: patterns and consequences in a tropical rain-forest cycad. *In:* Price, P.W., Lewinsohn, T.M., Fernandez, G.W. and Benson, W.W. (Eds), *Plant-Animal Interactions: Evolutionary Ecology in Tropical and Temperate Regions,* John Wiley and Sons, N.Y., pp. 209–225.

CLENCH, H.K. 1944. Notes on Lycaenid butterflies. (a) The genus *Callophrys* in North America; (b) The *acaste*-group of the genus *Thecla. Bull. Harv. Mus. Comp. Zool.* **94**: 217–245.

CLENCH, H.K. 1946. Notes on the *amyntor* group of the genus *Thecla* (Lepidoptera: Lycaenidae). *Entomologist* **79**: 152–157, 185–191.

CLENCH, H.K. 1964. A synopsis of the West Indian Lycaenidae with remarks on their zoogeography. *J. Res. Lep.* **2**: 247–270.

CLENCH, H.K. 1967. A note on *Caria domitianus* and *ino* (Riodinidae), with description of a new subspecies. *J. Lepid. Soc.* **21**: 53–56.

CLENCH, H.K. 1972. A review of the genus *Lasaia* (Riodinidae). *J. Res. Lep.* **10**: 149–180.

COLLINS, N.M. and MORRIS, M.G. 1985. *Threatened Swallowtail Butterflies of the World: The IUCN Red Data Book.* IUCN, Gland, 401pp.

COTTRELL, C.B. 1984. Aphytophagy in butterflies: its relationship to myrmecophily. *Zool. J. Linn. Soc.* **79**: 1–57.

DE VRIES, P.J. 1988a. The use of epiphylls as larval hostplants by the neotropical riodinid butterfly, *Sarota gyas. J. nat. Hist.* **22**: 1447–1450.

DE VRIES, P.J. 1988b. The larval ant-organs of *Thisbe irenea* (Lepidoptera: Riodinidae) and their effects upon attending ants. *Zool. J. Linn. Soc.* **94**: 379–393.

DE VRIES, P.J. 1990. Enhancement of symbiosis between butterfly caterpillars and ants by vibrational communication. *Science* **248**: 1104–1106.

DE VRIES, P.J. 1991a. Evolutionary and ecological patterns in myrmecophilous riodinid butterflies. *In:* Huxley, C.R. and Cutler, D.F. (Eds) *Ant-Plant Interactions,* Oxford University Press, Oxford, pp. 143–156.

DE VRIES, P.J. 1991b. Mutualism between *Thisbe irenea* butterflies and ants, and the role of ant ecology in the evolution of larval-ant associations. *Biol. J. Linn. Soc.* **43**: 179–195.

DE VRIES, P.J. and BAKER, I. 1989. Butterfly exploitation of a plant-ant mutualism: adding insult to herbivory. *J. New York ent. Soc.* **97**: 332–340.

DIAS, M.M. 1980. Morfologia da pupa de alguns Riodinidae brasileiros (Lepidoptera). *Rev. bras. Entomol.* **24**: 181–191.

DOWNEY, J.C. and ALLYN, A.C. 1979. Morphology and biology of the immature stages of *Leptotes cassius theopus* (Lucas) (Lepidoptera: Lycaenidae). *Bull. Allyn Mus.* **55**: 1–27.

DOWNEY, J.C. and ALLYN, A.C. 1980. Eggs of Riodinidae. *J. Lepid. Soc.* **34**: 133–145.

DOWNEY, J.C. and ALLYN, A.C. 1981. Chorionic sculpturing in eggs of Lycaenidae. Part I. *Bull. Allyn Mus.* **61**: 1–29.

DOWNEY, J.C. and ALLYN, A.C. 1984. Chorionic sculpturing in eggs of Lycaenidae. Part II. *Bull. Allyn Mus.* **84**: 1–44.

DURDEN, C.J. and ROSE, H. 1978. Butterflies from the middle Eocene: the earliest occurrence of fossil Papilionoidea (Lepidoptera). *Pearce-Sellards Series, Texas Memorial Museum* **29**: 1–25.

HARVEY, D.J. 1987. The higher classification of the Riodinidae (Lepidoptera). Ph.D. dissertation, University of Texas, Austin, 216pp.

HARVEY, D.J. 1989. Perforated cupola organs on larvae of Euselasiinae (Riodinidae). *J. Lepid. Soc.* **34**: 127–132.

HARVEY, D.J. and CLENCH, H.K. 1980. *Dianesia,* a new genus of Riodinidae from the West Indies. *J. Lepid. Soc.* **34**: 127–132.

HARVEY, D.J. and GILBERT, L.E. 1988. Ant association, larval and pupal morphology of the neotropical Riodinid butterfly, *Pandemos palaeste.* Unpublished manuscript.

HEWITSON, W.L. 1852–1872. *Illustrations of New Species of Exotic Butterflies.* Five volumes, van Voorst, London, v + 124, iv + 124, iv + 124, iii + 118, iv + 127pp., 60, 60, 60, 60 and 60 plates.

HEWITSON, W.L. 1863–1878. *Illustrations of Diurnal Lepidoptera: Lycaenidae,* in eight parts. Van Voorst, London. x + 229 pp., 108 plates.

HORVITZ, C., TURNBULL, C. and HARVEY, D.J. 1987 The biology of immature *Eurybia elvina* (Lepidoptera: Riodinidae), a myrmecophilous metalmark butterfly. *Ann. Ent. Soc. Amer.* **80**: 513–519.

HUTCHINGS, R.W. 1991. *Dinâmica de tres comunidades de Papilionoidea (Insecta: Lepidoptera) em fragmentos de floresta na Amazônia central.* M.Sc. dissertation, Instituto Nacional de Pesquisas da Amazônia/Fundação Universidade de Amazonas, xii + 65pp.

JANZEN, D. 1984. No park is an island: increase in interference from outside as park size increases. *Oikos* **41**: 402–410.

JANZEN, D. 1986. The eternal external threat. *In:* Soulé, M.E. (Ed.), *Conservation Biology: the Science of Scarcity and Diversity,* Sinauer, Sunderland, Mass., pp. 286–303.

JOHNSON, K. 1989. Revision of *Chlorostrymon* Clench and description of two new austral Neotropical species (Lycaenidae). *J. Lepid. Soc.* **43**: 120–146.

JOHNSON, K. 1991a. Neotropical Hairstreak Butterflies: Genera of the '*Calycopis/Calystryma* grade' of Eumaeini (Lepidoptera, Lycaenidae, Theclinae) and their diagnostics. *Repts Mus. Nat. Hist., Univ. Wisc., Stevens Point* **21**: iv + 128pp.

JOHNSON, K. 1991b. Cladistics and biogeography of two trans-Caribbean hairstreak butterfly genera, *Nesiotrymon* and *Tetra* (Lepidoptera, Lycaenidae). *Amer. Mus. Novitates* **3011**: 1–43.

JOHNSON, K. 1992. Genera and species of the Neotropical 'Elfin'-like hairstreak butterflies (Lepidoptera, Lycaenidae, Theclinae). *Repts Mus. Nat. Hist. Univ. Wisc. (Stevens Point)* **22**: 1–279 (2 vols).

JOHNSON, S. 1985. Culturing a detritivore, *Calycopis isobeon* (Butler & Druce). *News Lepid. Soc.* 41–42.

KENDALL, R.O. 1976. Larval foodplants and life history notes for some metalmarks (Lepidoptera: Riodinidae) from Mexico and Texas. *Bull. Allyn Mus.* **32**: 1–12.

LEWIS, H.L. 1973. *Butterflies of the World*. Follett, Chicago, xviii + 312pp.

LOVEJOY, T.E., BIERREGAARD, R.O., RYLANDS, A.B., MALCOLM, J.R., QUINTELA, C.E., HARPER, L.H., BROWN JR., K.S., POWELL, A.H., POWELL, G.V.N., SCHUBART, H.O.R. and HAYS, M.B. 1986. Edge and other effects of isolation on Amazon forest fragments. *In:* Soulé, M.E. (Ed.) *Conservation Biology: the Science of Scarcity and Diversity*, Sinauer, Sunderland, Mass., pp. 257–285.

MALICKY, H. 1970. New aspects on the association between Lycaenid larvae (Lycaenidae) and ants (Formicidae, Hymenoptera). *J. Lepid. Soc.* **24**: 190–202.

DE LA MAZA, R.R. 1988. *Mariposas Mexicanas*. Fondo de Cultura Economica, Mexico, 302pp.

MCALPINE, W.S. 1971. A revision of the butterfly genus *Calephelis* (Riodinidae). *J. Res. Lep.* **10**: 1–125.

MILLER, L.D. 1970. Multiple capture of *Caria ino melicerta* (Riodinidae) at light. *J. Lepid. Soc.* **24**: 13–15.

MILLER, L.D. 1980. A review of the *Erora laeta*-group, with description of a new species (Lycaenidae). *J. Lepid. Soc.* **34**: 209–216.

MILLER, L.D. and MILLER, J.Y. 1972. A new riodinid from northern Argentina (Riodinidae). *Bull. Allyn Mus.* **4**: 1–5.

MONTEIRO, R.F. 1991. Cryptic larval polychromatism in *Rekoa marius* Lucas and *R. palegon* Cramer (Lycaenidae: Theclinae). *J. Res. Lepid.* **29**: 77–85.

NABOKOV, V. 1945. Notes on Neotropical Plebejinae (Lycaenidae: Lepidoptera). *Psyche* **52**: 1–61, 8 plates.

NICOLAY, S.S. 1971a. A review of the genus *Arcas* with descriptions of new species (Lycaenidae, Strymonini). *J. Lepid. Soc.* **25**: 87–108.

NICOLAY, S.S. 1971b. A new genus of hairstreak from Central and South America (Lycaenidae, Theclinae). *J. Lepid. Soc.* **25** (Suppl. 1): 1–39.

NICOLAY, S.S. 1976. A review of the Hubnerian genera *Panthiades* and *Cycnus* (Lycaenidae: Eumaeini). *Bull. Allyn Mus.* **35**: 1–30.

NICOLAY, S.S. 1977. Studies on the genera of American hairstreaks. 4. A new genus of hairstreak from Central and South America (Lycaenidae: Eumaenini). *Bull. Allyn Mus.* **44**: 1–24.

NICOLAY, S.S. 1980. The genus *Chlorostrymon* and a new subspecies of *C. simaethis*. *J. Lepid. Soc.* **34**: 253–256.

NICOLAY, S.S. 1982. Studies in the genera of American hairstreaks. 6. A review of the Hubnerian genus *Olynthus* (Lycaenidae: Eumaeini). *Bull.*

Allyn Mus. **74**: 1–30.

ROBBINS, R.K. 1980. The Lycaenid 'false head' hypothesis: historical review and quantitative analysis. *J. Lepid. Soc.* **34**: 194–208.

ROBBINS, R.K. 1982. How many butterfly species? *News Lepid. Soc.* 40–41.

ROBBINS, R.K. 1985. Independent evolution of 'false head' behaviour in Riodinidae. *J. Lepid. Soc.* **39**: 221–225.

ROBBINS, R.K. 1987. Evolution and identification of the New World hairstreak butterflies (Lycaenidae: Eumaeini): Eliot's *Trichonis* section and *Trichonis* Hewitson. *J. Lepid. Soc.* **49**: 138–157.

ROBBINS, R.K. 1988. Comparative morphology of the butterfly foreleg coxa and trochanter (Lepidoptera) and its systematic implications. *Proc. Ent. Soc. Wash.* **90**: 137–154.

ROBBINS, R.K. 1991. Evolution, comparative morphology, and identification of the Eumaeine butterfly genus *Rekoa* Kaye (Lycaenidae: Theclinae). *Smith. Contr. Zool.* **498**, 64pp.

ROBBINS, R.K. 1993. (in preparation). (Manuscript on larval foodplants of Neotropical Eumaeini).

ROBBINS, R.K. and AIELLO, A. 1982. Foodplant and oviposition records for Panamanian Lycaenidae and Riodinidae. *J. Lepid. Soc.* **36**: 65–75.

ROBBINS, R.K. and SMALL, G.B. 1981. Wind dispersal of Panamanian hairstreak butterflies (Lepidoptera: Lycaenidae) and its evolutionary significance. *Biotropica* **13**: 308–315.

ROBBINS, R.K. and VENABLES, B.A.B. 1991. Synopsis of a new Neotropical hairstreak genus, *Janthecla*, and description of new species (Lycaenidae). *J. Lepid. Soc.* **45**: 11–33.

ROSS, G.N. 1964. Life history studies on Mexican butterflies. III. Early stages of *Anatole rossi*, a new myrmecophilous metalmark (Lepidoptera: Riodinidae). *J. Res. Lep.* **3**: 87–94.

ROSS, G.N. 1966. Life history studies on Mexican butterflies. IV. The ecology and ethology of *Anatole rossi*, a myrmecophilous metalmark (Lepidoptera: Riodinidae). *Ann. Ent. Soc. Amer.* **59**: 985–1004.

ROTHSCHILD, M., NASH, R.J. and BELL, E.A. 1986. Cycasin in the endangered butterfly *Eumaeus atala florida*. *Phytochemistry* **25**: 1853–1854.

SCHREMMER, F. 1978. Zur Bionomie und Morphologie der myrmecophilen Raupe und Puppae von der neotropischen Tagfalter-Art *Hamearis erostratus* (Lepidoptera: Riodinidae). *Entomologica Germanica* **4**: 113–121.

SEITZ, A. 1916–1920. *Die Grossschmetterlinge der Erde 5: Die Amerikanischen Tagfalter*. pp. 617–738 ('Erycinidae'); pp. 744–812 ('Lycaenidae', written by M. Draudt), Plates 121–159, 110A, 113B, 193, Stuttgart.

SMART, P.M. 1975. *The International Butterfly Book*. Thomas Crowell, N.Y., 274pp.

TALBOT, G. 1928. List of Rhopalocera collected by Mr. C.L. Collenette in Matto Grosso, Brazil. *Bull. Hill Mus.* **2**: 192–220.

Threatened Lycaenidae of South Africa

Michael J. Samways

Department of Zoology and Entomology, University of Natal, Pietermaritzburg 3200, South Africa

Southern African geology and geography

To appreciate the conservation biology of lycaenids in South Africa, it is necessary to introduce the characteristic geology and geography of the area. About 180 million years B.P., the great supercontinent of Pangaea began to split. By 135 million years B.P., the southern tip of Africa looked very much in outline as it does today. Since that time, uplifting and erosion has led to the appearance of 22 physiographic regions, each characterised by altitude and surface form (Figure 1). These regions fall naturally into two groups. The first group, of 12 regions, is the Interior Plateau. The second group, of 10 regions, is the Marginal Zone, which is divided from the Interior Plateau by the great divide known as the Great Escarpment.

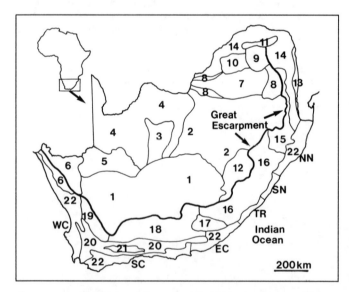

Figure 1. The 22 physiographic regions of South Africa.
1. Upper Karoo; 2. Highveld; 3. Kaap Plateau; 4. Southern Kalahari; 5. Bushmanland; 6. Namaqualand Highlands; 7. Bushveld Basin; 8. Bankveld; 9. Pietersburg Plateau; 10. Waterberg Plateau; 11. Soutpansberg; 12. Lesotho Tableland; 13. Lebombo Hills; 14. Lowveld; 15. Middelveld; 16. Eastern Midlands; 17. Winterberg Mountains; 18. Great Karoo; 19. Doring Karoo; 20. Cape Folded Mountains; 21. Little Karoo; 22. Coastal Belt.

Sub regions: NN = Northern Natal; SN = Southern Natal; TR = Transkei; EC = Eastern Cape; SC = Southern Cape; WC = Western Cape.

The Interior Plateau is the southern tip of the great African Plateau, and its altitude varies from a minimum of slightly under 900m in the Kalahari Desert, to almost 3500m in the Lesotho Highlands. Here, the thick Karoo sediments of the Carboniferous to Triassic ages were covered in the Jurassic by thick lava flows, which, on cooling to a hard layer of basalt, protected the underlying softer rocks from weathering, giving rise to the high mountains of southern Africa.

The Marginal Zone between the Great Escarpment and the coast, varies in width from 60km in the west to 240km in the east. Its elevation varies from sea-level to a maximum of 2300m in the Swartberg Range south of the Great Escarpment. In turn, the Great Escarpment is composed of several distinct mountain ranges, giving southern Africa a distinctive and varied topography.

Off the coast, the northward flowing cold Benguela Current moves up the west coast, and the southward flowing warm Agulhas Current flows down the east coast. These flow patterns, along with topography and global wind patterns, influence the area's rainfall regimes. There are three distinct rainfall regions in southern Africa: summer, winter and all-season rainfall areas. The varied topography and climate has resulted in nine climatic zones (Figure 2).

Species richness and threatened species

The long period of geographical isolation in southern Africa, lack of glaciation, varied topography and climate has produced a wide range of biotypes and high levels of endemism and species richness in both plants and animals (Huntley 1989). Vári and Kroon (1986) list 8300 species of Lepidoptera in southern Africa (i.e. south of the Zambezi River), while Pinhey (1975) estimates that the final total will exceed 10,000.

In South Africa (i.e. south of the Limpopo River), 632 species of butterfly (Papilionoidea and Hesperioidea) so far have been described. Of these, 102 (16%) are under some level of threat (Henning and Henning 1989). If subspecies are included, the total number of threatened taxa is 14%.

Vári and Kroon (1986) list 389 lycaenid species in southern Africa. Of these, 310 occur in South Africa, and 105 species and

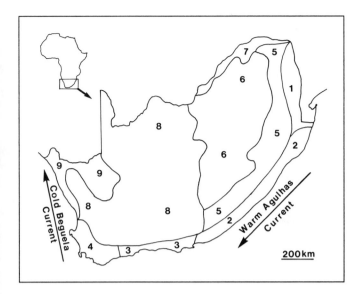

Fig. 2. The nine climatic zones in South Africa.
1. Subtropical Lowveld; 2. Subtropical Coast; 3. Temperate Coast;
4. Mediterranean; 5. Plateau Slopes; 6. Temperate Eastern Plateau;
7. Subtropical Plateau; 8. Semi-arid Plateau; 9. Desert.

subspecies are in some way threatened (Henning and Henning 1989) (Table 1 and Figure 3). This is 75% of all threatened butterflies in the country. Two species of lycaenid are now Extinct, and another one species and one subspecies are Endangered (Table 1 and Figure 3).

Particularly significant is that 96% (101) of the threatened species (71% species and 25% subspecies) are endemic to South Africa (Clark and Dickson 1971; Henning and Henning 1989; Murray 1935). These figures are high for a portion of a continental land mass, but not unusual for other biotic groups in the subcontinent. Of the remaining four species, only one is widespread in Africa, while the other three have limited distributions or are on the edge of a range just extending into South Africa.

Geographical distribution of threatened species

Figure 4 illustrates that by far the richest area for rare endemics is the Cape Fold Mountains (physiographic areas 19, 20 and 21 in Figure 1). Most occur on mountain slopes, but some inhabit ridges (e.g. *Poecilmitis wykehami*, *Thestor dicksoni dicksoni*), peaks (e.g. *Lepidochrysops outeniqua*, *P. endymion*, *P. balli*)

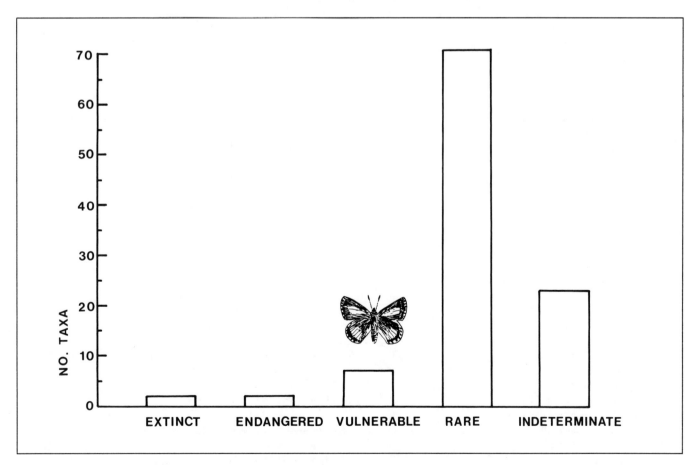

Figure 3. Status of South Africa's 105 threatened lycaenid species and subspecies using the official IUCN categories (Data from Henning and Henning, 1989).

63

Table 1. Status of threatened lycaenid species and subspecies in South Africa (from the South African Red Data Book, Henning and Henning 1989).

Lipteninae	
Alaena margaritacea Eltringham	V
Deloneura immaculata Trimen	Ex
Durbania amakosa albescens Quickelberge	R
Durbania amakosa flavida Quickelberge	I
Ornipholidotos peucetia penningtoni (Riley)	R
Liphyrinae	
Aslauga australis Cottrell	R
Miletinae	
Thestor brachycerus (Trimen)	I
Thestor compassbergae Quickelberge & McMaster	I
Thestor dicksoni calviniae Riley	R
Thestor dicksoni dicksoni Riley	R
Thestor dryburghi Van Son	I
Thestor kaplani Dickson & Stephen	R
Thestor montanus pictus Van Son	I
Thestor pringlei Dickson	R
Thestor rossouwi Dickson	I
Thestor stepheni Swanepoel	I
Thestor strutti Van Son	R
Thestor swanepoeli Pennington	I
Thestor tempe Pennington	R
Thestor yildizae Koçak	R
Theclinae	
Aloeides caledoni Tite & Dickson	R
Aloeides carolynnae Dickson	R
Aloeides clarki Tite & Dickson	R
Aloeides dentatis dentatis (Swierstra)	R
Aloeides dentatis maseruna (Riley)	I
Aloeides egerides (Riley)	R
Aloeides kaplani Tite & Dickson	I
Aloeides lutescens Tite & Dickson	R
Aloeides merces Henning & Henning	R
Aloeides nollothi Tite & Dickson	I
Aloeides nubilus Henning & Henning	R
Aloeides pringlei Tite & Dickson	I
Aloeides rossouwi Henning & Henning	R
Aloeides trimeni southeyae Tite & Dickson	R
Argyrocupha malagrida cedrusmontana Dickson & Stephen	R
Argyrocupha malagrida malagrida (Wallengren)	V
Argyrocupha malagrida maryae Dickson & Henning	V
Argyrocupha malagrida paarlensis (Dickson)	R
Bowkeria phosphor borealis Quickelberge	R
Bowkeria phosphor phosphor (Trimen)	R
Capys penningtoni Riley	R
Chrysoritis oreas (Trimen)	R
Chrysoritis cottrelli Dickson	E
Erikssonia acraeina Trimen	V
Hypolycaena lochmophila Tite	I
Iolaus (Epamera) aphnaeoides Trimen	R
Iolaus (Epamera) diametra natalica Vári	R
Iolaus (Pseudiolaus) lulua Riley	R
Oxychaeta dicksoni (Gabriel)	V
Phasis pringlei Dickson	R
Phasis thero cedarbergae Dickson & Wykeham	R
Poecilmitis adonis Pennington	R
Poecilmitis aureus Van Son	R
Poecilmitis azurius Swanepoel	R
Poecilmitis balli Dickson & Henning	R
Poecilmitis brooksi tearei Dickson	R
Poecilmitis daphne Dickson	R
Poecilmitis endymion Pennington	R
Poecilmitis henningi Bampton	R
Poecilmitis hyperion Dickson	R
Poecilmitis irene Pennington	R
Poecilmitis kaplani Henning	R
Poecilmitis lyncurium (Trimen)	R
Poecilmitis lyndseyae Henning	I
Poecilmitis nigricans nigricans (Aurivillius)	I
Poecilmitis nigricans zwartbergae Dickson	I
Poecilmitis orientalis Swanepoel	I
Poecilmitis pan Pennington	I
Poecilmitis penningtoni Riley	R
Poecilmitis pyramus Pennington	R
Poecilmitis pyroeis hersaleki Dickson	R
Poecilmitis rileyi Dickson	R
Poecilmitis stepheni Dickson	R
Poecilmitis swanepoeli Dickson	R
Poecilmitis trimeni Riley	I
Poecilmitis wykehami Dickson	R
Trimenia wallengrenii (Trimen)	R
Polyommatinae	
Anthene minima (Trimen)	R
Cyclyrius babaulti (Stempffer)	I
Lepidochrysops bacchus Riley	R
Lepidochrysops badhami Van Son	R
Lepidochrysops balli Dickson	R
Lepidochrysops hypopolia (Trimen)	Ex
Lepidochrysops jamesi classensi Dickson	R
Lepidochrysops jamesi jamesi Swanepoel	R
Lepidochrysops jefferyi (Swierstra)	R
Lepidochrysops littoralis Swanepoel & Vari	R
Lepidochrysops loewensteini (Swanepoel)	R
Lepidochrysops lotana Swanepoel	V
Lepidochrysops methymna dicksoni Tite	E
Lepidochrysops oosthuizeni Swanepoel & Vari	R
Lepidochrysops oreas oreas Tite	R
Lepidochrysops outeniqua Swanepoel & Vari	R
Lepidochrysops penningtoni Dickson	R
Lepidochrysops pephredo (Trimen)	R
Lepidochrysops poseidon Pringle	I
Lepidochrysops pringlei Dickson	R
Lepidochrysops quickelbergei Swanepoel	R
Lepidochrysops swanepoeli Pennington	R
Lepidochrysops titei Dickson	I
Lepidochrysops victori Pringle	R
Lepidochrysops wykehami Tite	I
Orachrysops ariadne (Butler)	R
Orachrysops niobe (Trimen)	V
Tuxentius melaena griqua (Trimen)	R

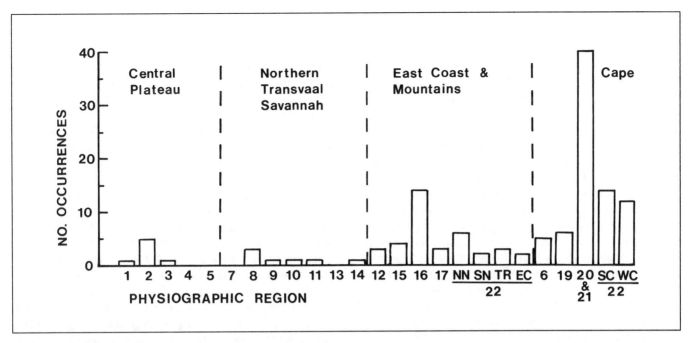

Figure 4. Distribution of South Africa's threatened lycaenid taxa across the 22 physiographic regions. (N.B. A few taxa occur in more than one region).

and gullies (e.g. *P. azurius*). Some species, despite the harsh winter conditions of the Cape, can be found at high elevations (e.g. *Argyrocupha malagrida cedrusmontana* at 1900m and *Aloeides pringlei* at 2072m). The lower elevations of the Cape (physiographic subregions 22SC and 22WC) are also rich in localised endemics (Figure 4) illustrating the wide range of biotopes occupied by this group of butterflies in the topographically varied and geologically stable area on the southern tip of Africa.

The next richest area in rare, threatened lycaenids is the east coast and hinterland. Most of the blue butterflies in these areas are fairly abundant, and the mountain peaks do not have the same richness of localised endemics as in the Cape. One species (*Lepidochrysops lowensteini*) occurs at about 2800m in the Lesotho Tableland, while the middle altitudes support 14 threatened taxa. The lower altitudes of the east coast are also relatively rich in threatened endemics. When the four east coast subregions of physiographic region 22 are added together (Figure 4), the coastal plain from Mozambique in the north to Port Elizabeth in the south hosts 13 taxa.

The Central Plateau (regions 1, 2, 3, 4, and 5) and the Northern Transvaal savannah (regions 7, 8, 9, 10, 11, 13, and 14) are poor in localised, threatened endemics, with regions 4, 5, and 13 supporting none. The reason for this is uncertain, but with the monotonous landscape and little opportunity for topographic isolation, it is possible that competition from more vigorous species has taken place. This may even have happened in recent times with *Lepidochrysops hypopolia*. One of the two original localities for this species is Potchefstroom on the Highveld, where it was found in 1879: today the habitat is occupied by the closely-related *L. praeterita*, with *L. hypopolia* not having been recorded for over 110 years.

Threats leading to taxon extinction

Overcollecting

There appear to be no verified cases of butterfly species going extinct through overcollecting (New 1984, Pyle *et al.* 1981). Many of the lycaenids in South Africa are in remote rugged localities which are not readily accessible. Some of the lowland species are more easily collected, but there is no verified case of overcollecting affecting a population level permanently.

Invasive species

Many plant species of the Cape fynbos heaths and shrublands have their seeds dispersed and buried by ants. At the turn of the century, the exotic Argentine ant (*Iridomyrmex humilis* (Mayr)) appeared in South Africa and recently has invaded the fynbos and has begun to supplant indigenous ants (Bond and Slingsby 1984). For blue butterflies of the Cape this is a serious development for two reasons. Firstly, *I. humilis* does not disperse and bury the seeds as do the native ants: this will eventually lead to the alteration of the habitat through loss of Cape Proteaceae species by gradual attrition of seed reserves. Secondly, because many lycaenids depend directly on certain indigenous ant species as hosts, the loss of native ants must inevitably have serious long-term repercussions for the survival of many of the lycaenids.

By late 1978, *I. humilis* had reached the Highveld, but to date has not been recorded from Natal. Should further increase in the range of *I. humilis* occur, which is probable, many lycaenids throughout the country could be affected. This may be inevitable as there are no known methods of arresting the expansion or controlling the population levels of this aggressive, invasive ant.

Apart from the very serious threat from the Argentine ant, none of the other ant species or other hosts associated with lycaenids are under threat. In fact, most species are widespread and abundant (e.g. *Anoplolepis custodiens* (Smith), *Crematogaster* spp., *Camponotus* spp.).

The invasive spread of alien trees and shrubs has also been significant for most South African biomes (Macdonald *et al.* 1986). For blue butterflies, genera such as *Pinus*, *Acacia*, *Eucalyptus*, *Solanum* and *Rubus* pose the greatest threat by partial or total alteration of the habitat. Without containment, these weeds are likely to be increasingly threatening to lycaenid populations (Figure 5). The habitat of *Argyrocupha malagrida malagrida* is already being heavily invaded by alien vegetation, as is the habitat of one of the populations of *Poecilmitis pan*.

There is no evidence that classical biological control programmes have had any adverse effect upon lycaenid conservation, or even upon any other threatened insect species in South Africa (Samways 1988).

Change in landscape use

Loss of habitat is a complex issue and involves more than simply loss of natural areas to agriculture and urbanisation. For example, the increased subdivision of the landscape by vehicle tracks and roads prevents the spread of natural fires which are an important natural influence preventing the succession from grassland to scrub (Tainton and Mentis 1984). The savannah is burnt to simulate the effects of lightning strikes and maintain habitats in a relatively pristine state. Conversely, accidental fires that are more intense or regular than would normally be the case in nature can be a threat in their own right. This is particularly the case adjacent to urban or commercially forested areas. Such a fire threat, as well as direct habitat loss, faces, for example, *Thestor yildizae* on Table Mountain in Cape Town.

The majority of taxa are included in the butterfly Red Data Book (Henning and Henning 1989) because of their extremely limited natural distribution (Figure 5) particularly in mountainous areas. However, agricultural and urban developments are major threats for many lycaenids, particularly those at low elevations. In the case of *Orachrysops ariadne*,

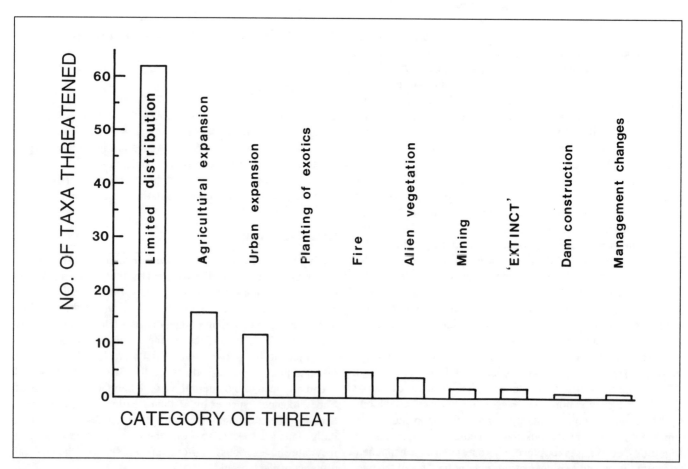

Figure 5. Major threats, in decreasing magnitude, to South Africa's 105 rare lycaenid taxa. (N.B. Some lycaenids are threatened by more than one category.)

Many are not threatened but simply have strictly limited distributions. All are threatened by global warming and increased radiation from the southern hole in the ozone layer. 'Extinct' is the IUCN categorisation; other categories are the actual threats. It is not known what the threats were to the Extinct species. (Data calculated from identified and listed threats for all red-listed species in Henning and Henning, 1989).

although its site is privately protected, absence of large herbivores and lax management of vegetation is posing a threat to the long-term security of the species.

Many of the threat categories are interrelated, e.g. urban expansion and fire hazards or dam construction. The overall root cause is the same: increased human population pressure which is particularly threatening to the lowland species but not so much to those of the rugged, relatively inaccessible, Cape mountains.

Global warming and thinning of the ozone layer

In the long term, these threats may outweigh all others. The earth's temperature may rise by 3°C by the year 2050, and models predict that although there will be little change at the equator, the poles may be 7°C warmer (Pearman 1988). Besides a rise in sea level, there may also be a shift in seasons. For South Africa, projections are for a generally warmer, drier situation, where soil moisture conditions in the Highveld might be 11–18% drier than at present (Huntley et al. 1989). The exceptionally species-rich Cape fynbos would be particularly affected, with the possible risk of a collapsing domino effect with many localised invertebrates disappearing along with their plant hosts. Additive upon these general effects will be an increase in inclement conditions such as droughts, hailstorms and hurricanes. Adding further stress will be the growing hole in the ozone layer of the stratosphere over the South Pole, with depletion in parts of up to 50% (Brunke 1988). South Africa, with its southerly geographical position, is likely to be particularly affected by the increased levels of ultraviolet radiation. Already, in 1989, there was a 45% depletion (Scourfield et al. 1990).

All these adverse environmental pressures bode ill for many lycaenids with their localised distributions and specialised life-cycles (many of which are still to be determined). Temperature falls by 0.6°C for every 100m rise in altitude, which suggests that to maintain the same local thermal environment, species must move up the mountainside by at least 500m by the middle of next century. Such movement would be difficult for species whose habitat has been partitioned by roads, buildings, etc. (Siegfried 1989). Further, as many of the South African lycaenids occur on isolated ridges and peaks, they cannot go higher and must adapt or die. In the short term, genetic adaptation is unlikely, and these ecological pressures may be too great for survival.

Conservation measures

The production of the Red Data Book on butterflies (Henning and Henning 1989) has been an important step forward (Samways 1989a). Although not all the species and subspecies listed may be truly threatened (apart from the effects of significant global events) with many further populations awaiting discovery, the book has focused on the rarity of many butterflies, particularly lycaenids, and is a major stepping stone for further research.

Few insects are protected by law in South Africa, and each province has its own ordinances. To date no specific species or subspecies is protected by law in Natal or the Orange Free State. In the Cape Province, according to Ordinance 19 of 1974, Schedule 2, Protected Wild Animals may not be hunted, killed, captured or kept in captivity without a permit from the Department of Nature and Environmental Conservation. Amendment of Schedule 2 (13 February 1976) gives full protection to: *Aloeides egerides, A. lutescens, Argyrocupha malagrida malagrida, Trimenia wallengrenii, Oxychaeta dicksoni, Lepidochrysops bacchus, Poecilmitis endymion, P. lyncurium, P. nigricans nigricans, P. rileyi, Thestor dicksoni dicksoni* and *T. kaplani*. In the Transvaal, by Ordinance 12 of 1983, Section 45 (Schedule 7) (Protected Wild Animals), *Poecilmitis aureus* is protected.

The 582 nature reserves in southern Africa total 7×10^6ha, 5.8% of the land surface (Huntley 1989). Siegfried (1989) estimated that 74% of vascular plant species and over 90% of each of the vertebrate groups are represented in nature reserves. Such comparative data is not available for insects, but of the threatened lycaenids listed by Henning and Henning (1989), two are extinct, and only 24 (23%) occur in nature reserves or wilderness areas, all but one state owned. Apart from the protection ordinances, this means that 75% are not geographically protected in nature reserves. For many of these, apart from global atmospheric threats, they are relatively safe as their localities are in remote terrain. Given the extent of remote terrain there is also the possibility of the occasional new species being found from time to time.

In recent years there has been an increase in invertebrate conservation awareness in South Africa. *Aloeides dentatis dentatis* in particular has become quite a celebrity as the Roodepoort City Council has established the 12ha Ruimsig Entomological Reserve specifically for the butterfly (Henning and Henning 1985).

Although such authorities as the National Parks Board, the Natal Parks Board, the Defence Force, the Universities of Natal, Pretoria and Stellenbosch have a strong interest in conservation and support invertebrate conservation projects, only the Transvaal Provincial Administration has a full-time Invertebrate Conservation Officer. This is encouraging, but still inadequate bearing in mind that there are about 80,000 described species of insect in South Africa (Prinsloo 1989) and that this may only be a quarter of the total percentage, including a large proportion of endemics. The emphasis to date has been on the conservation of large vertebrates, while the Wildlife Society principally supports the conservation of habitats and whole natural areas. It is well known that vertebrates are not good indicator or umbrella species for invertebrate conservation. Other invertebrates with specific habitat requirements and appropriately sized home ranges are better as flag species (Samways 1989b).

Although the setting aside of game and nature reserves has given refuge to the great majority of vertebrates, it applies to less than one-quarter of the blue butterflies. Nature reserves nevertheless are playing a role. Acquisition of much more land for state-owned nature reserves is unlikely, as most land is firmly accounted for. This means that invertebrate zoologists, entomologists and naturalists must monitor areas where blue butterfly populations are still maintaining a foothold, and lobby for conservation of that patch of land. As these habitat patches are indeed small (tennis court size in the case of *Argyrocupha malagrida malagrida*) it is a feasible proposition, as shown by the Henning brothers and the Roodepoort City Council in the setting aside of the Ruimsig Entomological Reserve.

Summary

Southern Africa, with its long stable geological history and highly varied topography and climate, is rich in insect species. In South Africa, 632 species of butterfly have been described, of which 102 (16%) are under some sort of threat. There are 389 lycaenid species in southern Africa, with 310 species occurring in South Africa. A total of 105 species and subspecies of lycaenid are threatened, 75% of all threatened butterfly taxa in the country. Of the 105 threatened species two lycaenid species are Extinct; one species and one subspecies are Endangered; seven taxa are Vulnerable; 71 are Rare; and 23 are Indeterminate. A high proportion of the threatened lycaenid taxa (71% species + 25% subspecies = 96% total) are endemic. Most of the threatened taxa occur in the Cape fold mountain area, usually on mountain slopes, and sometimes at high elevations (up to 1,800m). Many of the rare lycaenids also occur along the east coast and hinterland, including one at 2800m. The Central Plateau and Northern Transvaal savannah are poor in localised endemics.

Overcollecting is not a threat. Of great seriousness is the invasive Argentine ant (*Iridomyrmex humilis*) which is supplanting native ant hosts for lycaenids, the key species in maintaining the character of the habitats through seed burial. Invasive exotic plant species are also a threat for several lycaenids, as is fire, mining, dam building, forestry, and, for one species, neglectful management. For the lowland species, agricultural and urban expansion are the greatest threats, but for many of the species, which generally inhabit mountainous areas which are rugged or remote, it is simply that they have an extremely limited distribution.

Of great concern in southern Africa is the overall effect of global warming and the hole in the ozone layer. Projections indicate that most species will need to shift in elevation by 500m by the year 2050 if they are to remain at the same temperature. For most species, especially those that inhabit hilltops, such a shift would be ecologically and genetically impossible.

Twelve lycaenid taxa are protected by law in the Cape Province, and one species in the Transvaal. None are protected in the Orange Free State or Natal. Only 23% of threatened lycaenids occur within nature reserves or wilderness areas, compared with over 90% for each of the vertebrate groups and 74% for vascular plants. One species, *Aloeides dentatis*, has been allocated a 12ha reserve of its own. Further acquisition of patches of land for specific lycaenid populations is a feasible short-term approach to further the cause of invertebrate conservation.

Acknowledgements

The Foundation for Research Development and the University of Natal Research Fund provided financial assistance. Messrs. Stephen and Graham Henning kindly criticised the text and Mrs Ann Best and Mrs Myriam Preston kindly processed the manuscript.

References

BOND, W. and SLINGSBY, P. 1984. Collapse of an ant-plant mutualism: The Argentine ant (*Iridomyrmex humilis*) and myrmecochorous Proteaceae. *Ecology* **65**: 1031–1037.

BRUNKE, G.C. 1988. Tropospheric background measurements of $CFCl_3$(F-II) conducted at Cape Point, South Africa, since 1979. *In:* Macdonald, I.A.W. and Crawford, R.J.M. (Eds), *Long-term Data Series relating to southern Africa's Renewable Natural Resources.* South African National Scientific Programmes Report No. 157. Foundation for Research Development, Council for Scientific and Industrial Research, Pretoria. pp. 434–435.

CLARK, G.W. and DICKSON, C.G.C. 1971. *Life Histories of South African Lycaenid Butterflies.* Purnell, Cape Town. 272pp.

HENNING, S.F. and HENNING, G.A. 1985. South Africa's endangered butterflies. *Quagga* **10**: 16–17.

HENNING, S.F. and HENNING, G.A. 1989. *South African Red Data Book – Butterflies.* South African National Scientific Programmes Report No. 158. Foundation for Research Development, Council for Scientific and Industrial Research, Pretoria. 175pp.

HUNTLEY, B.J. (Ed.) 1989. *Biotic Diversity in Southern Africa: Concepts and Conservation.* Oxford University Press, Cape Town. 380pp.

HUNTLEY, B.J., SIEGFRIED, R. and SUNTER, C. 1989. *South African Environments into the 21st Century.* Human and Rousseau Tafelberg, Cape Town. 127pp.

MACDONALD, I.A.W., KRUGER, F.J. and FERRAR, A.A. (Eds) 1986. *The Ecology and Management of Biological Invasions in southern Africa.* Oxford University Press, Oxford. 324pp.

MURRAY, D.P. 1985. *South African Butterflies. A Monograph of the Family Lycaenidae.* Staples Press, London. 195pp.

NEW, T.R. 1984. *Insect Conservation – An Australian Perspective.* Junk, Dordrecht. 184pp.

PEARMAN, G.I. (Ed.) 1988. *Greenhouse: Planning for Climate Change.* CSIRO, Melbourne.

PINHEY, E.C.G. 1975. *Moths of Southern Africa.* Tafelberg, Cape Town. 273pp.

PRINSLOO, G.L. 1989. Insect identification services in South Africa. Proceedings of the Seventh Entomological Congress organized by the *Entomological Society of southern Africa, Pietermaritzburg 10–13 July 1989.* p.107.

PYLE, R.M., BENTZIEN, M.M. and OPLER, P.A. 1981. Insect conservation. *Ann. Rev. Entomol.* **26**: 233–258.

SAMWAYS, M.J. 1988. Classical biological control and insect conservation: Are they compatible? *Env. Conserv.* **15**: 349–354.

SAMWAYS, M.J. 1989a. Amnesty for insects. *S. Afr. J. Sci.* **85**: 571–572.

SAMWAYS, M.J. 1989b. Insect conservation and landscape ecology: A case-history of bush crickets (Tettigoniidae) in southern France. *Env. Cons.* **16**: 217–226.

SCOURFIELD, M.W.J., BODEKER, G., BARKER, M.D., DIAB, R.D. and SALTER, L.F. 1990. Ozone: the South African connection. *S. Afr. J. Sci.* **86**: 279–281.

SIEGFRIED, W.R. 1989. Preservation of species in southern African nature reserves. *In:* Huntley, B.J. (Ed.) *Biotic Diversity in Southern Africa: Concepts and Conservation.*

TAINTON, N.M. and MENTIS, M.T. 1984. Fire in grassland. *In:* Booysen, P. de V. and Tainton, N.M. (Eds). *Ecological Effects of Fire in South African Ecosystems.* Springer-Verlag, Berlin. pp.115–147.

VARI, L. and KROON, D. 1986. *Southern African Lepidoptera: A Series of Cross-referenced Indices.* Lepidopterists' Society of southern Africa and the Transvaal Museum, Pretoria. 198pp.

Australian Lycaenidae: conservation concerns

T.R. NEW

Department of Zoology, La Trobe University, Bundoora, Victoria 3083, Australia

Introduction

The Lycaenidae of Australia comprise about 140 described species (Table 1, Figure 1). The family is most diverse in the northern tropical parts of the country, where the fauna of northern Queensland has strong relationships with that of New Guinea and parts of the Oriental Region. Indeed, Eliot (1973) chose to follow Gressitt (1956) in considering the northern tip of Queensland, Cape York Peninsula, as part of the Oriental Region in delimiting areas for considering lycaenid distribution patterns.

Taxonomic appraisal of the fauna, at least of the adult stages, is relatively complete (Common and Waterhouse 1981) and it is possible to provide a reasonably sound appraisal of the status and broad scale distribution of all species. Dunn and Dunn (1991) give maps of the documented distribution of Australian butterflies. A few further species undoubtedly remain to be discovered, but most future changes in taxonomy are likely to be made at the species/subspecies interface, with some subspecies being elevated in status as more information becomes available. Not surprisingly for a large continent extending from the humid tropics to cold temperate regions and with large arid and semiarid zones, the distribution of many lycaenid species is circumscribed, and there is room for considerably more research to clarify the precise ranges and status of many of the more elusive resident taxa.

Only one riodinine (*Praetaxila segecia punctaria* (Fruhstorfer)) extends into Australia, where it is confined to the

Table 1. Taxonomic summary of the Australian Lycaenidae (data from Dunn and Dunn 1991).

Subfamily	No. genera	No. species
Liphyrinae	1	1
Riodininae	1	1
Theclinae	15	75
Polyommatinae	22	65
Total	39	142

extreme north of Queensland; its close relatives are found in New Guinea. Intriguingly, four species of Lycaeninae occur in New Zealand, but none in Australia. In general, the Australian Lycaenidae show some attenuation in diversity from those of New Guinea and Malaysia, and the number of subfamilies is smaller. This is particularly obvious at the tribal level: Australia has 32 species of Luciini compared with about a hundred in New Guinea, and only four Arhopalini compared with 38 in New Guinea and slightly more than a hundred in Malaysia. Of the generally widespread subfamilies four are absent: Miletinae; Curetinae; Lycaeninae; and Poritiinae. The two predominant subfamilies in Australia are Polyommatinae and Theclinae, and endemism is high in both (Polyommatinae: 4/22 genera, 22/65 species; Theclinae: 6/15 genera, 25/75 species). Theclini, in particular, are a major radiation in the Australian butterfly fauna (Kitching 1981). These figures for endemism do not include numerous putative subspecies which are clearly restricted to Australia and often have very limited distributions. The biological status of most of these is by no means clear and some, at least, may constitute sibling species complexes.

Many endemic taxa are very rare. Several, indeed, are known only from one or two localities. For example, *Hypochrysops piceatus* Kerr, McQueen & Sands has only been found in two small colonies in southern Queensland and only one of these now remains. *Jalmenus aridus* Graham & Moulds, one of very few butterflies believed to be endemic to Australia's interior arid zone, is known from one colony in Western Australia. A number of subspecies of *Ogyris* Westwood and *Candalides* Hübner, inter al., also have very limited distributions. Some of these, such as the 'O. idmo group' in Western Australia, are taxonomically more complex than currently documented (Field 1992), and perhaps of greater conservation concern than suspected at present.

It is notable that ant-dependence to differing extents occurs in virtually all the genera which are diverse and widespread. This habit may have been instrumental in leading to diversification of Lycaenidae in some semiarid regions where plant growth is very irregular and the spectrum of food plants limited. Larval feeding habits differ considerably between various genera. Additional foodplant records continue to be accumulated (e.g. Valentine and Johnson 1988). In *Ogyris*

70

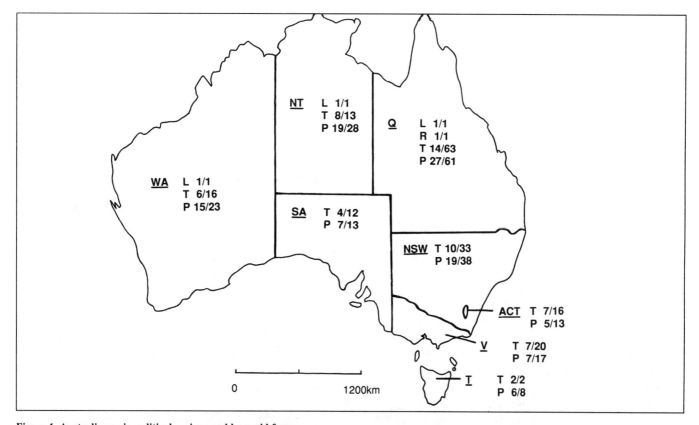

Figure 1. Australia: main political regions and lycaenid fauna.
Regions denoted by initial letters: ACT, Australian Capital Territory; NSW, New South Wales; NT, Northern Territory; SA, South Australia; T, Tasmania; V, Victoria; WA, Western Australia. Lycaenid subfamilies: L, Liphyrinae; P, Polyommatinae; R, Riodininae; T, Theclinae. Figures are no. of included genera/species.

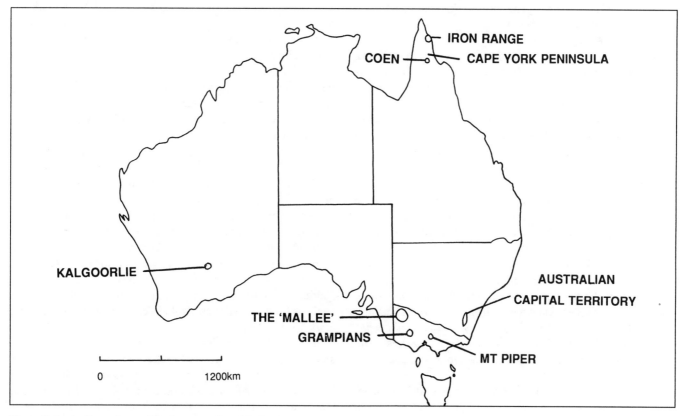

Figure 2. Australia: main specific places mentioned in the text.

caterpillars of some species may live in ant nests throughout their lives.

By contrast many other *Ogyris* larvae feed on mistletoes (Loranthaceae, Viscaceae), and this unusual host plant group may have been a major basis for speciation in this genus. In contrast, *Hypochrysops* has exploited a taxonomically diverse range of flora, so that diversification has occurred in these genera by using contrasting ecological strategies. However, very few lycaenids feed directly on one dominant tree genus, *Eucalyptus*.

The Australian fauna

Some highlights of the Australian fauna are described below with much of the information gleaned from the extensive data summarised by Common and Waterhouse (1981).

- The widespread oriental species *Liphyra brassolis major* Rothschild is rather rare in northern tropical Australia, where it occurs in association with *Oecophylla* ants.
- In the Luciini, many taxa are very local. For example, *Lucia limbaria* Swainson occurs in isolated localities in the south and east of mainland Australia.
- Several species of *Acrodipsas* Sands (formerly referred to *Pseudodipsas* C. & R. Felder) are also rare and localised: *A. arcana* (Miller & Edwards) is known from only one hilltop in New South Wales, and *A. hirtipes* Sands from a hilltop near Coen (northern Queensland) (Figure 2) where it occurs with *A. melania* Sands. The latter is known also from a single specimen captured at the very tip of Cape York Peninsula. *A. brisbanensis cyrilus* (Anderson & Spry) is a local subspecies in Victoria and *A. b. brisbanensis* (Miskin), although more widely distributed along the east coast, is also regarded as rare. Indeed, none of the seven species of *Acrodipsas* is common.
- *Paralucia* Waterhouse & Turner contains three species of which two are rare: *P. spinifera* Edwards & Common (see Dexter and Kitching, this volume) is one of our rarest lycaenids, and is known only from one restricted area of New South Wales; and *P. pyrodiscus lucida* Crosby has recently aroused considerable conservation interest in Victoria (see New 1992, and New, this volume).
- *Hypochrysops* C. & R. Felder is the most speciose lycaenid genus in Australia, and many of the 18 species are rare and local (Sands 1986 and Sands, this volume). It is absent from Tasmania, and most of the species are northern or east central in distribution. Several New Guinea (or closely related) species are known only from northern Cape York, and the only species in Western Australia is *H. halyaetus* Hewitson. As with *Philiris* Rober and *Arhopala* Boisduval, Australian subspecies of some New Guinea species have developed.
- *Ogyris*, with 12 endemic Australian species, also occurs in New Guinea but is of considerable biological interest in Australia. Several species include a number of named infraspecific taxa and many of these are local and rare forms attractive to collectors. Both subspecies of *O. idmo* Hewitson are extremely rare, as are *O. otanes* C. & R. Felder, *O. ianthus* Waterhouse, and *O. iphis* Waterhouse & Lyell. All merit strenuous conservation measures, in common with several more widespread forms.
- *Jalmenus* Hubner contains 10 species. *J. pseudictinus* is regarded as very local in parts of eastern Queensland, as is *J. lithochroa* Waterhouse in southern South Australia. *J. clementi* Druce is known from a very small region of northwestern Australia, and *J. aridus* from a colony near Kalgoorlie (Figure 2).
- The single species of *Pseudalmenus* Druce, *P. chlorinda* (Blanchard) is confined to southeastern Australia, and seven subspecies have been described. Four of these are from Tasmania (see Prince, this volume), where populations separated by only a few kilometres have very different wing markings. *P. c. fisheri* Tindale, from Western Victoria, is also very local.
- Some other lycaenids are not regarded as rare but are very clearly restricted to particular geographical regions or ecological communities: *Neolucia hobartensis* (Miskin), with two subspecies, is an alpine/subalpine species of southeastern Australia.

Distributional and diversity patterns

The distribution patterns (Dunn and Dunn 1991) reveal several trends relevant to the consideration of lycaenid conservation in Australia. The northern part of Queensland, as for many other biota, supports a large number of taxa on the southernmost fringes of their Oriental/New Guinea distributions. Remnant rainforests in this region are particularly important butterfly habitats (Monteith and Hancock 1977) and the individual patches may be viewed as an 'archipelago' of these in northern Queensland.

Lycaenid diversity is greatest around the eastern and southeastern fringe of the Australian mainland, with a smaller number of species in the west or southwest. Very few species occur in the climatically inhospitable inland.

A very high proportion of Australian Lycaenidae are forest and open woodland-frequenting taxa. A few herb/shrub community taxa, such as *Lampides boeticus* (L.), *Theclinesthes serpentata* (Herrich-Schäffer) and *Zizina labradus* (Godart), are amongst the most widely distributed lycaenids in Australia. Habitat relationships in the southeast are exemplified by an analysis for the Australian Capital Territory (Table 2: Kitching *et al.* 1978).

Most of the non-endemic species belong to oriental genera, and essentially constitute the 'younger northern element' of the fauna. Endemism at the generic level is distinctively more southern (and, especially, southeastern), with the implication that some, at least, may represent speciation from earlier colonisers than those taxa which occur solely in the north; a

Table 2. Habitat relationships of 25 species of Lycaenidae recorded from the Australian Capital Territory. Figures given are numbers of species. Data from Kitching *et al.* 1978.

No. Habitat	Total	No. species shared with habitat				Not shared
		2	3	4	5	
1 Lowland savannah	5	5	5	2	1	–
2 Savannah woodland	16		12	5	1	4
3 Dry sclerophyll forest	15			6	2	2
4 Wet sclerophyll forest	11				4	3
5 Alpine zone	4					–

similar situation occurs in Australian Satyrinae (New in press). Couchman and Couchman (1977) considered Tasmanian forms of *P. chlorinda* to be 'evidently of very ancient origin'. Centres of endemism, local 'critical faunas', can thus be delimited with some degree of reliability.

Conservation

Lycaenid diversity is highest in those parts of Australia which are subject to substantial, rapid and largely irreversible changes by European people. Thus diversity is highest in the eastern and southeastern fringe of the Australian mainland, with smaller numbers of species in the west or southwest and very few in the climatically inhospitable inland. Environmental changes through human activities have accelerated in recent decades and show little sign of abating or slowing in the near future: assessing threats to taxa at both local and national levels becomes essential if the loss of species and notable subspecies is to be avoided.

For some parts of the country it is not possible to determine if some taxa were formerly more widespread than they are at present. Inferences on past endangering processes, including habitat change and loss, thus contain a large element of historical supposition.

As stated earlier, local 'critical faunas' can be delimited with some degree of reliability. In addition, there are a number of 'critical habitats' for Lycaenidae which can be identified. These occur on a macroscale (isolated pockets of rainforest – as in northern Queensland, alpine or mallee vegetation) and also as specific sites which support one or more narrow endemics and which may be especially vulnerable – several of the hilltops referred to in the taxonomic summary are good examples of this. Because of their restricted or sporadic distributions over this vast island continent, a substantial number of endemic lycaenids on the Australian mainland must be considered vulnerable to continuing habitat change, even though they are not directly or imminently threatened.

Threatened taxa

In a preliminary survey of threatened insects in Australia, Hill and Michaelis (1988) included nine species of Lycaenidae, five of which were known only from one or two sites. The survey was based on a questionnaire circulated widely to entomologists in Australia, seeking information on priorities for insect conservation. In all, 24 taxa of Lycaenidae (Table 3) were noted by respondents and these included three subspecies of *P. chlorinda*, two of which occurred in Tasmania. Tasmanian taxa were noted as of concern by other respondents, so that conservation concern for native Lycaenidae has a broad geographic base within Australia.

It is notable that the Hill and Michaelis list includes threatened Lycaenidae from all mainland states except the Northern Territory, where documentation is relatively incomplete.

Nadolny (1987) noted that the most endangered butterfly in New South Wales is likely to be *Paralucia spinifera*, which is

Table 3. Taxa of Lycaenidae in Australia which may be threatened. Data from Hill and Michaelis (1988), digested from respondents to survey conducted by Australian National Parks and Wildlife Service, closing February 1985. States abbreviated as in Figure 1.

Taxon	State(s)
Acrodipsas arcana (Miller & Edwards)	Q,NSW
A. brisbanensis brisbanensis (Miskin)	Q,NSW
A. illidgei (Waterhouse & Lyell)	Q
A. n.sp.	WA
A. myrmecophila (Waterhouse & Lyell)	Q,NSW,V
Hypochrysops apollo Miskin	Q
H. cleon Grose-Smith	Q
H. epicurus Miskin	Q,NSW
H. hippuris Hewitson	Q
H. ignitus ignitus (Leach)	SA,NSW,V
H. piceatus Kerr, Macqueen & Sands	Q
Jalmenus lithochroa Waterhouse	SA
Jamides cytus claudia (Waterhouse & Lyell)	Q
Ogyris amaryllis meridionalis Bethune-Baker	SA
O. idmo halmaturia Tepper	SA,V
O. idmo idmo Hewitson	WA
O. otanes C. & R. Felder	SA,NSW,WA
Paralucia spinifera Edwards & Common	NSW
Philiris azula Wind & Clench	Q
P. ziska titeus D'Abrera	Q
Pseudalmenus chlorinda chlorinda (Blanchard)	T
P. c. barringtonensis Waterhouse	NSW
P. c. conara Couchman	T
Theclinesthes albocincta (Waterhouse)	SA

of considerable phylogenetic importance in possibly linking *Paralucia* with related genera. *P. spinifera*, the Bathurst Copper, has recently been the subject of more detailed study in the State (Dexter and Kitching, this volume).

However, in general there are few detailed accounts of range contractions of taxa other than on a very local scale or by inferences from older collectors who claim that some species are now scarcer or more restricted than in the past. More survey work, particularly in poorly documented areas, is needed to identify all threatened taxa of the Australian Lycaenidae.

Major threats to Australian lycaenids

The survey by Hill and Michaelis (1988) identified some of the major threats to Australian lycaenids and these are listed below, together with other threats specified in the literature:

- land clearing, sometimes by fire, for agriculture and urban development;
- urbanisation and tourist resort development;
- pest fly control;
- roadworks;
- mining;
- collecting (individual and commercial);
- agricultural practices, e.g. pasture improvement.

Examples of species threatened by the ecological processes follow; others can be found in the literature. Any of these species might also be susceptible to overcollecting.

(i) The best known and most accessible site for *H. piceatus* is a small patch of mistletoe-bearing *Casuarina* along some 200m of road verge, which could be eliminated easily and inadvertently by road widening.

(ii) *O. otanes*, recently (July 1989) the first butterfly to be nominated for listing under the Victorian Flora and Fauna Guarantee Act, is known in Victoria from a single hilltopping site in the arid northwest of the state which has been the subject of physical disturbance during the establishment of a trigonometric survey point, by vehicles on sand-dunes. Other populations of *O. otanes* were known in the 1970s but were destroyed by collecting.

(iii) One of the very few sites at which *Acrodipsas myrmecophila* occurs, and the only one known in Victoria at present, is currently the target of mining exploration. Additionally, it is not clear whether the two species of *Acrodipsas* described from a hill near Coen breed on the hill or in nearby lowland vegetation and then hilltop. In both cases, much nearby land is currently subject to mining exploration and this could pose a threat. Several such hilltops in Australia are among the classic collecting localities favoured by butterfly collectors, and such rare species could be rendered additionally vulnerable by uncontrolled collecting.

(iv) The several species associated with coastal mangrove vegetation are vulnerable as drainage occurs for urban or tourist resort development.

(v) The detailed appraisal of *P. chlorinda* in Tasmania (Couchman and Couchman 1977), which has recently been updated (Prince 1988), claims that it has been eliminated over whole areas where one or other of its required major resources (a eucalypt, an *Acacia* – normally *A. dealbata* – and an *Iridomyrmex* ant) have been destroyed. Couchman and Couchman located the species in more than 50 localities in the years following 1945 but at the time of writing their account found it difficult to think of more than 10 localities where *P. chlorinda* might then survive. 'Pasture improvement' with removal of all mature eucalypts and acacias in paddocks badly affected *P. c. conara*, and most of the habitat of the eastern *P. c. chlorinda* has been clearfelled for woodchips. Two other forms are extinct, one because of local tree clearing and one because of housing development and clearing/burning, and some existing forms are highly localised (see Prince, this volume).

(vi) Of the three species of *Acrodipsas* listed as threatened by Hill and Michaelis (1988), *A. arcana* is threatened by fires and clearing, *A. illidgei* (a mangrove-frequenting species, see Samson this volume) by urbanisation and use of insecticides against mosquitoes, and a third (undescribed) species is subject to habitat destruction by clearing for agriculture.

Geographical areas of importance for lycaenids

While it is essential to identify threatened species as foci for conservation attention, some larger geographical areas also merit particular attention by harbouring diverse or unusual faunal groups. Worthy of note are:

i) Cape York Peninsula. This is a major region of faunal interchange between Australia and New Guinea, with many northern Lycaenidae not extending further into Australia. This northern element includes some 75 species (more than half the Australian Lycaenidae) and, whereas a number of these extend further down the east coast or elsewhere, many species are both rare and restricted to the 'far north', often to forested areas. The number of rainforest Lycaenidae decreases latitudinally from about 32 species at Iron Range to none in the cool temperate forests of Victoria and Tasmania. Tropical rainforests are a key habitat for maintaining the integrity of tropical fauna in Australia.

ii) Southern Queensland. Kitching (1981) highlights the very high diversity of Lycaenidae in southern Queensland, and suggests that this reflects the confluence of northern and southern faunas. Thus, many of the northern taxa reach their southern limits here and the putatively older southern forms, their most northern range extensions. There are also a number of rare species found only in this region, which supports around half the Australian lycaenid species.

iii) Western Victoria, particularly the Grampians ('Gariwerd') mountains and the 'Mallee region'. A number of rare inland forms occur in these areas, and some taxa from semiarid regions are scarce or non-existent elsewhere.

These regions include substantial areas of National Park or other reserves: Iron Range and the Grampians ('Gariwerd') National Parks are two examples. In situations where the prime conservation need is security of habitat and our state of knowledge of particular species does not permit intervention to markedly influence management, protection of these reserves and their enhancement is the most important step which can be taken. Presence of rare Lycaenidae, such as *P. chlorinda fisheri* in the Grampians ('Gariwerd') can here augment pressures for habitat protection and maintenance of the integrity of reserves. The role of insects in such planning in Australia is in its infancy, and the limited work on lycaenid conservation to date has been almost entirely species-targeted.

In the current Australian political climate, demands for multiple land use, sometimes involving substantial intrusion into National Parks, are not uncommon.

Legislation

None of the threatened lycaenids identified by Hill and Michaelis (1988) is formally listed as endangered in any state other than Victoria and Queensland, so there is no legal mechanism for their protection other than their fortuitous and largely undocumented/unmonitored incidence in nominally safe 'Reserves'.

The issue of 'species listing' is a controversial one in Australia. In the past a number of insect species have been gazetted as 'protected' in various States, with little apparent reason. This practice has in some instances alienated concerned collectors and others who are in a position to help very positively with the documentation needed to clarify the status and well being of the taxa involved. In no case until 1989 had 'listing' of an insect species been accompanied by any form of formal undertaking or provision for study of the biology of the species.

The single species listed in Queensland legislation, *Acrodipsas illidgei* (see Samson, this volume) was designated in 1990 as 'permanently protected fauna', an extraordinarily high level of nominal protection placing it on a par with some charismatic vertebrates.

The recent legislation enacted in Victoria in 1988 and known as the 'Flora and Fauna Guarantee' is pioneering in scope. Taxa can be nominated for listing, and made subject to an 'interim conservation order' – a legal hiatus which provides the opportunity for a more formal appraisal of the status of the species during a period when it is nominally protected from further intensification of the threatening processes such as habitat destruction. Essentially, the onus then falls on the State Department for Conservation and Natural Resources to investigate the species, and to clarify its need for conservation. If identified as threatened, a management plan must be produced to clarify the major steps needed to protect the species. Clearly, this is limited to within Victorian State boundaries, but many conservationists are hoping that despite its utopian and possibly impracticable (because of restricted logistic capability) ideals, the Guarantee will tangibly safeguard rare Victorian endemics and isolated remnant or outlying populations of taxa more common in other parts of the country.

As noted earlier, *O. otanes* was the first species to be listed in Victoria and this was followed by nominations for a number of other lycaenids (*Acrodipsas myrmecophila, A. brisbanensis, Paralucia pyrodiscus lucida*, as further candidates. The isolated

hill on which *A. myrmecophila* occurs in Victoria, Mt Piper, also supports *A. brisbanensis* and has been listed (as Butterfly Community No. 1) for investigation as a 'threatened community', again a pioneering step for butterfly conservation in Australia, on the basis of this unique co-occurrence. Very few lycaenid species have thus been accorded consideration for legal protection in Australia.

Both *O. otanes* and *O. idmo* have been placed, for some 10 years, on a 'voluntary restricted collecting code' list of the Entomological Society of Victoria. This 'code', heeded by the great majority of responsible collectors, restricts the numbers of adults which can be taken by any person to two each year, and deters the collection of early stages. Because *Ogyris* larvae pupate in groups under the loose bark of eucalypts, this stage is undoubtedly vulnerable to overcollecting: it is the easiest one to obtain in order to procure first class cabinet specimens, and collectors tend to take a surfeit of pupae to counter losses due to parasitoids.

Although particular lycaenids are highly sought after by collectors in Australia, the extent of commercial dealing in butterflies is rather low. A few local forms have appeared in dealers' lists in Australia in recent years, including various subspecies of *Pseudalmenus* and *Ogyris*. Prices have been in the order of $5–10/specimen, rarely more, and the market does not appear to be large. No information is to hand on numbers of specimens sold to overseas collectors as opposed to those in Australia, but a number of the rarer taxa have been listed as 'ex-pupa', implying their wild origin.

The future for the Australian Lycaenidae

Habitat alteration in many parts of Australia has continued at an accelerating pace in recent years. In some documented cases habitat degradation has resulted in serious range contractions for lycaenids (Hill and Michaelis 1988; Couchman and Couchman 1977, updated by Prince 1988). There are undoubtedly other undocumented cases amongst the Australian lycaenids. There is clearly still a very long way to go to improve knowledge of biology and local distributions. Even for Victoria, perhaps the best documented mainland state, distribution maps are incomplete on a fine scale and progress towards improving this condition is slow.

However, there are some encouraging signs. There is, for example, the improved legislation pioneered by Victoria, which has produced the legal mechanisms necessary for protection of invertebrate species in this State and has taken this beyond mere prohibition of collecting to provision for sound scientific management. Another encouraging sign in recent years is that an increasing number of biologists and others are becoming aware of the effects of habitat alteration on insects, are seeking to counter them at all levels, and to document more fully the distribution of butterflies in Australia. Finally, there is evidence of an increasing awareness of the importance of invertebrates in ecosystems and natural community dynamics. Butterflies are playing their part as 'invertebrate ambassadors' in promoting this awareness: the Eltham Copper (see New, this volume) has, more than any other single invertebrate species, helped to bring the plight of many insects to wide public and government attention in Victoria. *A. illidgei* in Queensland (see Samson, this volume) has also been a key factor in saving some important coastal areas from poorly planned development.

The topic of insect conservation is now widely discussed in Australia, and many of the themes of concern are addressed by New (1984, 1992) and Greenslade and New (1991). A more general appraisal of the Australian environment and the widespread changes that have occurred during only 200 years of European settlement are included in Jeans (1986). The factors and processes exemplified above for lycaenids are of much wider concern in affecting much of the endemic Australian biota.

References

COMMON, I.F.B. and WATERHOUSE, D.F. 1981. *Butterflies of Australia*. 2nd ed. Angus and Robertson, Sydney.

COUCHMAN, L.E. and COUCHMAN, R. 1977. The Butterflies of Tasmania. *Tasmanian Year Book 1977*: 66–96.

DUNN, K.L. and DUNN, L.E. 1991. *Review of Australian Butterflies: Distribution, Life History and Taxonomy. Part 3. Lycaenidae*. Power Press, Bayswater, Victoria.

ELIOT, J.N. 1973. The higher classification of the Lycaenidae: a tentative arrangement. *Bull. Brit. Mus. nat. Hist. (Ent.)* 28: 373–506.

FIELD, R. 1992. [Research Grant Report on 'Life history studies and species determination of the *Ogyris idmo* Hewitson (Lepidoptera: Lycaenidae) complex in Western Australia']. *Myrmecia* 28 (4): 12–17.

GREENSLADE, P. and NEW, T.R. 1991. Australia: conservation of a continental insect fauna. *In:* Collins, N.M. and Thomas, J.A. (Eds) *Conservation of Insects and their Habitats*. pp. 33–70. Academic Press, London.

GRESSITT, J.L. 1956. Some distribution patterns of Pacific Island Fauna. *Syst. Zool.* 5: 11–32.

JEANS, D.N. (ed.) 1986. *Australia – a Geography. Vol. 1. The Natural Environment*. Sydney University Press, Sydney.

HILL, L. and MICHAELIS, F.B. 1988. *Conservation of insects and related wildlife*. Occasional Paper No. 13. Australian National Parks and Wildlife Service, Canberra.

KITCHING, R.L. 1981. The geography of the Australian Papilionoidea. *In:* Keast, A. (Ed.) *Ecological Biogeography of Australia*. W. Junk, The Hague, pp. 979–1105.

KITCHING, R.L., EDWARDS, E.D., FERGUSON, D., FLETCHER, M.B. and WALKER, J.M. 1978. The butterflies of the Australian Capital Territory. *J. Aust. ent. Soc.* 17: 125–133.

MONTEITH, G.B. and HANCOCK, D.L. 1977. Range extensions and notable records of butterflies of Cape York Peninsula, Australia. *Aust. ent. Mag.* 4: 21–38.

NADOLNY, C. 1987. *Rainforest Butterflies in New South Wales: their Ecology, Distribution and Conservation*. NSW National Parks and Wildlife Service, Sydney.

NEW, T.R. 1984. *Insect Conservation: an Australian Perspective*. W. Junk, Dordrecht.

NEW, T.R. 1992. Conservation of butterflies in Australia. *J. Res. Lepid.* 29: 237–253.

NEW, T.R. (in press). The evolution and characteristics of the Australian butterfly fauna. *In:* Jones, R.E., Kitching, R.L. and Pierce, N.E. (Eds) *Biology of the Australian Butterflies*. CSIRO, Melbourne.

PRINCE, G.B. 1988. The conservation status of the Hairstreak Butterfly *Pseudalmenus chlorinda* Blanchard in Tasmania. (Report to Department of Lands, Parks and Wildlife. Hobart, Tasmania).

SANDS, D.P.A. 1986. A revision of the genus *Hypochrysops* C. & R. Felder (Lepidoptera: Lycaenidae). *Entomonograph* No. 7. E.J. Brill, Leiden.

VALENTINE, P.S. and JOHNSON, S.J. 1988. Some new larval food plants for north Queensland Lycaenidae (Lepidoptera). *Aust. ent. Mag.* 14: 89–91.

PART 3. ACCOUNTS OF PARTICULAR TAXA OR COMMUNITIES

Introductory comment

The following examples complement and extend points raised in the previous section. The series of case-histories presented includes some which are classics in insect conservation and which have necessitated considerable research over many years, and some which are regarded as priorities for future study and appraisal. They range from the well-known to the speculative. Most are taxon-based, but several neotropical assemblages regarded as 'threatened communities' are included also.

For two of the taxon studies which have been of critical importance in advancing the knowledge and practice of lycaenid conservation, authors were not found. Rather than ignore these and impoverish the perspective which I hope this book will provide, I have included accounts of these abstracted from published papers and reports. The 'species accounts' are, therefore at two levels: those attributed to particular authors who have usually played leading roles in the study of the particular species and non-attributed accounts which give a more historical perspective from an 'outsider'. These latter accounts may be open to update and revision.

Several species are discussed in substantial detail in the previous section, and accounts of the Mission Blue and Karner Blue (see Cushman and Murphy, this volume) are of the utmost importance in insect conservation in North America. Likewise, Bálint (this volume) provides short accounts of 17 further eastern European taxa, mostly little known but which can act as foci for future attention in that region. Despite lack of current detailed information on such taxa, appraisals such as those presented for these taxa are invaluable in demonstrating the scope of regional needs. Some taxa have been especially significant in raising public awareness of butterfly conservation (New 1991). The Large Blue (*Maculinea arion*) in Britain and the Mission Blue (*Plebejus icarioides missionensis*) in the United States are, perhaps, the most widely known. The Xerces Blue (*Glaucopsyche xerces*) became extinct in California shortly before the Second World War, and is commemorated in the name of the Xerces Society, a leading body for the promotion of invertebrate conservation in North America and elsewhere. Foundation of the Society in December 1971 was, indeed, stimulated by the plight of the Large Blue in Britain (Pyle 1976).

Many of the most informative and influential cases of lycaenid conservation in the northern hemisphere have involved conservation of subspecies, sometimes of remnant populations or those close to the edge of a species' range.

As far as possible, a standard sequence of subheadings is adopted in this section, to facilitate comparison between taxa. Comments on 'Status', unless otherwise made clear, refer to the geographical range or country indicated, and not necessarily the entire species range. ('Red List') denotes that the species is listed by IUCN (1990). The abbreviation 'UTM', used in several European species accounts, refers to 'Universal Transverse Mercator' projection.

References

IUCN 1990. *IUCN Red List of Threatened Animals*. IUCN, Cambridge.

NEW, T.R. 1991. *Butterfly Conservation*. Oxford University Press, Melbourne.

PYLE, R.M. 1976. Conservation of Lepidoptera in the United States. *Biol. Conserv.* **9**: 55–75.

The mariposa del Puerto del Lobo
Agriades zullichi Hemming (= *nevadensis* Zullich)

M.L. Munguira and J. Martin

Departamento de Biologia (Zoologia), Facultad des Ciencìas, Universidad Autonoma de Madrid, Madrid, Spain

Country: Spain (southeast).

Status and Conservation Interest: Status – vulnerable.

This species is probably one of Europe's rarest butterflies. Restricted to the high altitude schist screes of the Sierra Nevada (Granada Province), it is threatened in part of its range by a planned redevelopment of the ski station already built within its range. Its collection has only been reported five times although the area in which it lives is a classical collecting site. Nevertheless, a recent survey (Munguira 1989) found it was still abundant in one locality.

Taxonomy and Description: The species was regarded as a subspecies of *Agriades glandon* (de Prunner) for almost 50 years after it was described as a new species. This fact has prevented it from being listed separately by Heath (1981) and Viedma and Gomez (1976, 1985).

Recent studies consider it to be a true species (Kudrna 1986; Munguira 1989) based on features of larval and adult morphology, geographical isolation and its distinct ecology. There are two other species of this genus in Europe including *A. glandon* which is common in the Pyrenees, Alps and Scandinavian tundra and *A. pyrenaicus* Boisduval which lives in several high altitude ranges in southern Europe. These two species have been listed as 'endemic' (Viedma and Gomez 1976, 1985) and 'vulnerable' (Heath 1981) respectively.

Distribution: *A. zullichi* has only been found in three localities in the Sierra Nevada (southern Spain), each one in a different 10 x 10km UTM square (Munguira 1989). One suitable area for the species is a 40km long and 5–10km wide area on the higher altitudes of the Sierra, but the butterfly is only present in small scattered patches due to the distribution of its foodplant. A thorough study of the whole area has not been made, and all the available information comes from two classic sites (Puerto del Lobo and Veleta). The altitudinal range of the species is 2600 to 2900m.

Population Size: Population numbers seem to be high in the type locality (Puerto del Lobo) where at least several hundred adults were collected in 1968 (Fernandez-Rubio 1970). In a larval survey from this locality we recorded 56 larvae in 0.5ha giving a rough estimate of 3000 butterflies for the total population in the area. On the other hand, the most endangered colony in the Veleta probably only supports *c.*100 adults, and in a thorough larval survey we only found 12 larvae.

Habitat and Ecology: The species is restricted to schist screes on wind-exposed hill ridges where the vegetation cover is poor. The climatic vegetation is a grassland of the *Erigeronto frigidi – Festuceto clementei* series. The foodplant (*Vitaliana primuliflora*) grows in tight cushions 10 to 40cm across and 5cm high, in three patches in the Veleta (of 25, 900 and 1500 square meters respectively) and is abundant over an area of 8ha in the Puerto del Lobo.

The female lays eggs singly inside the leaf rosettes of the foodplant. The first instars feed on the parenchyma of the needle-like leaves and are of a purple colour resembling the dead leaves of the plant, among which they usually rest. Overwintering takes place inside the plant cushions at the third

Agriades zullichi (photo by M.L. Munguira).

Habitat of *A. zullichi*: S. Juan, Sra Nevada, 2760 m, May 1987 (photo by M.L. Munguira).

instar. The last two instars feed on flowers, especially on the corolla and developing fruits. Their colour is green with yellow, black and white markings, making them difficult to see in their colourful environment. They reach their full grown condition (fifth instar) at the end of May after 10 months at the larval stage. The species is never associated with ants. This fact was reported by Chapman (1911) for *A. glandon* that, like *A. zullichi*, lacks the dorsal nectary organ found in other lycaenids. Pupation takes place under stones and adults emerge a month later (mid-July).

Threats: Development of tourist resorts clearly threatens the survival of the Veleta colony: redevelopment of the existing ski station could easily cause the extinction of this population. While the other populations are not threatened by this particular development they are unprotected at the moment, making future developments in their areas possible. Collecting could probably damage the Veleta colony, whose very low population numbers make it sensitive to any aggression. Large scale collecting should be banned, because the low total population numbers of the species make any reduction in numbers dangerous for its future.

Conservation: The declaration of Sierra Nevada as a Man and Biosphere Reserve and Natural Park has proved to be ineffective in protecting the Veleta area from tourist developments. We suggest that the area be declared a National Park. This would conserve not only its five endemic butterflies (Munguira and Martin 1989), but also the unusual richness of exclusive insects and plants of the area.

The distribution of the food plant should be carefully mapped, in order to identify other possible areas where the butterfly might be found or introduced if necessary.

Access to the species' habitat should be limited. Particularly, the construction of new roads in the proximity of the main population should be controlled if at all permitted.

Other management practices for habitat improvement are not needed because of the climatic character of the plant communities in which it lives. Therefore the correct policy for the species conservation is to reduce impacts to a minimum, and leave the habitat as undisturbed as possible.

References

CHAPMAN, T.A. 1911. On the early stages of *Latiorina (Lycaena) orbitulus*, an amyrmecophilous Plebeiid Blue butterfly. *Trans. ent. Soc. London*, **1911**: 148–159.

FERNANDEZ-RUBIO, F. 1970. Redescubrimiento de una rara mariposa en Sierra Nevada. Nota sobre la captura del Lycaenido: *Plebejus glandon zullichi* Hemming, 1933 (=*nevadensis* Zullich y Reisser, 1928). *Arch. Inst. Aclimatacion Almeria* **15**, 161–167.

HEATH, J. 1981. *Threatened Rhopalocera (butterflies) in Europe*. Council of Europe, Strasbourg.

KUDRNA, O. 1986. *Butterflies of Europe. 8. Aspects of the Conservation of Butterflies in Europe.* Aula Verlag, Wiesbaden.

MUNGUIRA, M.L. 1989. *Biologia y biogeografia de los licenidos ibericos en peligro de extincion (Lepidoptera, Lycaenidae).* Ediciones Univ. Autonoma de Madrid, Madrid.

MUNGUIRA, M.L. and MARTIN, J. 1989. Biology and conservation of the endangered lycaenid species of Sierra Nevada, Spain. *Nota lepid.,* **12** (**suppl. 1**): 16–18.

VIEDMA, M.G. and GOMEZ, M.R. 1976. *Libro Rojo de los lepidopteros ibericos.* ICONA, Madrid.

VIEDMA, M.G. and GOMEZ, M.R. 1985. *Revision del Libro Rojo de los lepidopteros ibericos.* ICONA, Monografias no. **42**, Madrid.

The Large Copper (Dutch – Grote Vuurvlinder), *Lycaena dispar* Haworth

E. DUFFEY

Cergne House, Church Street, Wadenhoe, Peterborough PE8 5ST, U.K.

Area: Europe to eastern Asia.

Status and Conservation Interest: Status – *L. d. dispar*: extinct; *L. d. batava*: rare; *L. d. rutila*: not threatened at present, (Red List).

A widely distributed wetland species with several described subspecies. It was first recorded in 1795 in the Huntingdonshire fens, England. This distinctive and very local subspecies, *L. d. dispar*, became extinct in about 1851, at least partly due to excessive collecting of the very locally distributed larvae (Duffey 1968). The Dutch race, *L. d. batava*, which is very similar to *L. d. dispar*, was introduced to Woodwalton Fen Nature Reserve, England, in 1927 and still survives there.

Taxonomy and Description: *L. dispar* was first described by Haworth (1803) and the much more widely distributed *L. d. rutila* by Werneburg in 1864. The Dutch race, *L. d. batava*, was discovered in 1915 and described by Oberthür in 1923. However, Higgins and Hargreaves (1983) combine the extinct British race with the Dutch race under the name *L. d. dispar*, presumably because these two races are very difficult to distinguish unless a series of each is available. *L. d. dispar* and *L. d. batava* are generally larger and have more brilliant colours than *L. d. rutila*. (See Bink 1970 for further discussion about the subspecies.)

In the following account the generally used name for the Dutch population, *L. d. batava*, is retained.

Distribution: The extinct British population appeared to be confined to a few fen areas in Huntingdonshire, Cambridgeshire and Norfolk, although specimens were occasionally taken elsewhere. The Dutch population of *L. d. batava* is confined to a few localities in the provinces of Friesland and Overijssel (Bink 1972 and pers. comm. 1991) and has declined in recent years so that very few colonies survived in 1991. *L. d. rutila* is widely but locally distributed in Europe (eastern Germany, Poland, Baltic countries, Hungary and Russia) but is said to be declining in the west of its range due to drainage and reclamation of wetlands (Higgins and Hargreaves 1983).

Population Size: The Dutch population of *L. dispar* has declined markedly in recent years and only one strong colony is known, although small numbers occur elsewhere (F.A. Bink, pers. comm.). The decline is said to be due to lack of management of the habitat which becomes unfavourable as succession proceeds. If this situation does not improve, the Dutch population may become seriously endangered.

The introduced *L. d. batava* in Britain is very insecure as it is confined to only about 30ha of about 214ha at Woodwalton Fen. It has been shown that it is vulnerable to excessive summer flooding (Duffey 1977) and that without protection for the larvae the population gradually declines to extinction over a number of years. This population has survived since 1927 either by protecting a large proportion of the larvae from predators by rearing in muslin cages, or else by maintaining a captive population so that reintroductions can be made when numbers become dangerously low.

Although the *L. d. rutila* population has declined in recent years, it is still widely distributed and not thought to be in danger.

Habitat and Ecology: Bink (1970, 1972, 1986) has shown that *L. d. batava* in the Netherlands occurs in an area of overgrown peat cuttings where the female lays her eggs on the great water dock *Rumex hydrolapathum* in open reed or sedge beds. At Woodwalton Fen in England it has been shown (Duffey 1977) that when the foodplants become hidden in taller vegetation the ovipositing females often fail to find them. The preferred type of *Rumex hydrolapathum* is often of moderate size, and large plants are avoided, especially if growing by open water. Nevertheless, in years when the butterflies are numerous, eggs may be laid on all size groups. *L. d. batava* is single-brooded but may produce a second brood in warm summers. *L. d. rutila* is normally double-brooded. A large female *L. d. batava* is capable of producing up to 700 eggs but under natural conditions in the field, production averages 60 per female (Bink 1986) and, at Woodwalton Fen, 114 per female (Duffey 1968). Bink (1986) has shown that *L. d. batava* reaches its highest pupal weight on host plants growing at pH 5.5–6.5. Below pH 5.5 the foodplants suffer from acidity stress, resulting in a reduction in the protein content of the leaves. The insects reared on such plants are smaller and lay fewer eggs. Nevertheless, there is no convincing evidence that ovipositing females select plants of the best quality.

Eggs are laid singly or in lines, usually along a leaf midrib, on the underside. However, scattered single eggs are not infrequent on the upper side of the leaves of the foodplant. The larvae hatch after 7–10 days, and graze the leaf surface, forming 'windows'. They hibernate as third-instar larvae in dead leaves around the base of the water dock plants. During hibernation the larvae are unaffected by winter flooding. In the spring, depending on weather and the regrowth of the docks, the larvae emerge in late April or early May to feed until they pupate about mid-June. In July the adults are on the wing, with males usually being the first to emerge. When a second brood is recorded in *L. d. batava* the adults are smaller than the first brood and fewer eggs are produced. The double broods of *L. d. rutila* have flight periods of May–June and August–September.

Threats: The decline of *L. dispar*, especially in central and western Europe, is due to the loss of wetland habitats where the preferred foodplant grows. In the Netherlands Bink (1986) has shown that succession in the fens leads to oligotrophic conditions which reduces growth and nutrient quality of the foodplant. Fenland reserves in the Netherlands require effective management to preserve the best conditions for *L. dispar*. In England the species is at risk because it occurs at only one locality and a captive population has to be maintained as an insurance against extinction.

Conservation: Vigorous efforts to protect wetlands are being made throughout Europe by the International Union for the Conservation of Nature and the International Council for the Protection of Birds, but not specifically for invertebrates. The British population of *L. d. batava* is the responsibility of the Nature Conservancy Council for England (English Nature) and although a permanent wild population cannot survive in the small area available without larval protection or reintroductions, no serious attempt has yet been made to assess whether other suitable areas can be found in the East Anglian wetlands. The most secure population in the Netherlands is in the Weerribben fen area. This region could provide a nucleus for re-establishment in neighbouring fens providing they are maintained in a favourable condition. There is no doubt that the best prospects for *L. d. batava* are in the Netherlands, if the appropriate authorities could be persuaded to manage suitable fenland areas more effectively.

Throughout most of continental Europe where conservation work is effective, the main emphasis is on habitat protection for plants and for vertebrates. More attention should be given to invertebrates, particularly declining populations such as *L. d. batava* and *L. d. rutila*. The former may soon be endangered and although the latter is not threatened at present, it may become so in the future.

References

BINK, F.A. 1970. A review of the introductions of *Thersamonia dispar* Haw. (Lep., Lycaenidae) and the speciation problem. *Ent. Ber. Amst.* **30**: 179–83.

BINK, F.A. 1972. Het onderzoek naar de grote vuurvlinder (*Lycaena dispar batava* (Oberthur)) in Nederland (Lep., Lycaenidae). *Ent. Ber. Amst.* **32**: 225–39.

BINK, F.A. 1986. Acid stress in *Rumex hydrolapathum* (Polygonaceae) and its influence on the phytophage *Lycaena dispar* (Lepidoptera: Lycaenidae). *Oecologia, Berl.* **70**: 447–451.

DUFFEY, E. 1968. Ecological studies on the large copper butterfly *Lycaena dispar* Haw. *batavus* Obth. at Woodwalton Fen National Nature Reserve, Huntingdonshire. *J. appl. Ecol.* **5**: 69–96.

DUFFEY, E. 1977. The re-establishment of the large copper butterfly *Lycaena dispar batava* Obth. on Woodwalton Fen National Nature Reserve, Cambridgeshire, England, 1969–73. *Biol. Conserv.* **12**: 143–258.

HIGGINS, L. and HARGREAVES, B. 1983. *The Butterflies of Britain and Europe*. Collins, London.

The Adonis Blue, *Lysandra bellargus* Rottemburg

Country: England.

Status and Conservation Interest: Status – locally extinct in Britain, some rapid decline of other colonies: threatened.

Intensive surveys of *Lysandra* (or *Polyommatus*) *bellargus* in the early 1970s revealed that this local species had declined substantially, and had become rare over much of southern England, the northern fringe of its European range. Rapid losses occurred in the 1950s and the late 1970s and the butterfly had become extinct on many sites. These included some which continued to support the Chalkhill Blue, *Lysandra coridon* (Poda). In some cases the sites had been destroyed or the foodplant eliminated by agricultural practices, but disappearance also from areas of unimproved farmland implied that other effects – perhaps related to grazing regimes – might be involved. Cool weather was also suggested to be a factor inducing decline. A study of the ecology of the species (Thomas 1983) revealed some unexpected subtleties relevant to the conservation and management of open grassland species, and of taxa in marginally suitable climatic regimes.

Distribution: *L. bellargus* occurs over much of Europe, where populations have generally not declined as conspicuously as in Britain. In England, it is confined to calcareous grassland in the south.

Population Size: This species forms discrete colonies which commonly contain from about 150–850 individuals. Most adults do not stray far from the colonies and the populations are effectively closed; many are isolated from their nearest neighbour colony by tens of kilometres, and no interchange is likely to occur between colonies even a kilometre or so apart.

Population size within a colony can vary greatly. Heath *et al.* (1984) note one Dorset population increasing from fewer than 50 adults to more than 60,000 between 1977 and 1982. Such variations provide evidence of resilience of populations to extinction (Morris and Thomas 1989) but can also reveal likelihood of extinction: one colony declined from 3400 adults to extinction in only three years. In the past, *L. bellargus* has been recorded from all calcareous formations in southern England. Extinctions include several colonies in nature reserves.

Habitat and Ecology: *L. bellargus* has two generations each year. Eggs laid in late August or September hatch into overwintering caterpillars which mature to adults by around late May to early June. Offspring of this spring generation develop more rapidly to reach the adult stage in only around 2–3 months. Eggs are laid singly on the foodplant foliage. Larvae are day-feeders, and all stages from the second instar onward are tended by ants, mainly *Myrmica sabuleti* and *Lasius alienus*. Larvae and pupae are often buried by ants, which continue to tend them.

Larvae feed only on one foodplant species, the horseshoe vetch *Hippocrepis comosa*, which occurs much further north in England than the butterfly does, and is still present in many southern areas from where *L. bellargus* has disappeared.

Nearly all populations occur on steep south-facing slopes, mainly on closely cropped, unimproved pasture. Females prefer to oviposit in short turf and in sheltered sun-spots. In sites where there is sward of varying heights, oviposition is restricted almost entirely to short (1–4 cm) vetch, areas which (because of high insolation) are both warm and support numerous ants.

Threats: Colony extinction has been due mainly to habitat change. About one-third of colonies were lost because of loss of *Hippocrepis* due to ploughing or 'agricultural improvement'. However, *Hippocrepis* persists abundantly on some other sites, and grazing incidence and intensity are important factors in the butterfly's well being. Closely cropped sites were very suitable, although very heavy grazing is harmful. Some major extinctions coincided with the onset of myxomatosis in the 1950s, which resulted in massive loss of rabbits and a resultant decline in grazing intensity on much chalk grassland. Reduction in grazing intensity appeared to be a major factor leading to extinction, and many surviving colonies are on ground grazed by cattle. 'Improved' or lightly grazed sites have only small populations. However, it is not profitable to graze unimproved pasture closely, and some hillsides have been abandoned or are grazed very irregularly – factors likely to lead to a further decline of *L. bellargus* on such sites. Cessation of grazing can lead to development of coarse grasses and 'choking out' of *Hippocrepis*.

The butterfly's close association with short swards is evident from its oviposition behaviour, but the reasons behind this are not clear. *L. bellargus* is common in tall pasture in parts of Europe, for example, and dependence on hotter areas on the fringe of its range might also be a factor influencing site suitability. Warmth might be important both for the butterfly itself and for its influence on ants, so that details of their association with *L. bellargus'* early stages might be very subtle.

Pasture improvement by drilling, herbicides and fertilisers remains a threat. Until recently, steeper hillsides have not been ploughed, but some are now cultivated, despite their very thin soil.

Conservation: The above ecological observations (Thomas 1983) emphasise that there is little alternative for practical conservation of the Adonis Blue but to manage sites actively for its specialised ecological requirements – either on nature reserves or on commercial farmland, in which case subsidy agreements may be necessary to ensure site security. Merely reserving habitat of *L. bellargus* is not sufficient, although reserves are clearly recommended as a basis for management regimes. For new reserves, preference may be accorded to ones which support more than one colony. Management, probably involving rotational grazing or mowing, must seek to ensure the availability of short sward on south-facing slopes, and that habitats are not overly fragmented or have barriers (such as valleys or areas of tall scrub) imposed between them. Much *Hippocrepis* has been converted into a form suitable for *L. bellargus* during the last decade by increased rabbit and stock grazing and, if accessible to a founder population, some such sites have been colonised successfully.

Thomas (1983) also suggested that the carrying capacity of many sites for *L. bellargus* could be increased by creating more south-facing 'sun-spots', perhaps by using explosives or earth-moving equipment, and that such methods could be used to construct sites in previously unsuitable areas.

Another consideration is to introduce *L. bellargus* to new areas, or to sites from which it had earlier disappeared, once these have been rendered suitable again by management. Thus, *L. bellargus* was re-introduced in 1981 to Old Winchester Hill National Nature Reserve, where it had become extinct in the 1950s (Thomas 1989). It increased rapidly in numbers and was still present after 16 generations (Thomas 1991). Only the shortest *Hippocrepis* were utilised, and the breeding sites circulated in pattern with successive paddocks being grazed heavily in rotation.

References

HEATH, J., POLLARD, E. and THOMAS, J.A. 1984. *Atlas of Butterflies in Britain and Ireland*. Viking Books, Harmondsworth.

MORRIS, M.G. and THOMAS, J.A. 1989. Reestablishment of insect populations, with special reference to butterflies. pp. 22–36 In Emmet, A.M. and Heath, J. (Eds) *The Moths and Butterflies of Great Britain and Ireland* Vol. 7, Part 1. Harley Books, Great Horkesley.

THOMAS, J.A. 1983. The ecology and conservation of *Lysandra bellargus* (Lepidoptera: Lycaenidae) in Britain. *J. appl. Ecol.* **20**: 59–83.

THOMAS, J.A. 1989. Ecological lessons from the re-introduction of Lepidoptera. *Entomologist* **108**: 56–68.

THOMAS, J.A. 1991. Rare species conservation: case studies of European butterflies. pp. 149–197 *In:* Spellerberg, I.F., Goldsmith, F.B. and Morris, M.G. (Eds) *The Scientific Management of Temperate communities for Conservation*. Blackwell, Oxford.

Large Blues, *Maculinea* spp.

Area: England, France, elsewhere in Europe.

Status and Conservation Interest: Status – *M. arion, M. alcon, M. teleius:* vulnerable (Wells *et al.* 1983); *M. nausithous:* endangered (Wells *et al.* 1983); *M. teleius:* endangered (Red List).

Large Blues were noted by Wells *et al.* (1983) as 'some of the most rapidly declining butterflies in Europe, and probably in Asia too'. All are threatened with extinction in Europe, because of land use changes (Elmes and Thomas 1992). The Large Blue, *M. arion* (L.), became extinct in Britain in 1979 despite valiant long-term efforts to save it, and is extinct also in the Netherlands, Belgium and parts of northern France. The Alcon Large Blue, *M. alcon* Denis & Schiffermueller, is also extinct in many former European localities. The Scarce Large Blue, *M. teleius* Bergstrasser, is apparently declining throughout its European and east Palaearctic range, and is extinct in Belgium and the Netherlands. The Dusky Large Blue, *M. nausithous* Bergstrasser, is also undergoing local extinctions. Elmes and Thomas (1992) assessed the five European species as 'Endangered'. Thomas (1984) referred to *M. teleius* and *M. nausithous* as 'among the world's rarest butterflies' and it has been recommended that research into *Maculinea* biology be given top priority in butterfly conservation programmes (Heath 1981). See also Bálint (this volume), for notes on Carpathian taxa. *M. arion* in Britain is the best documented conservation case, and a European subspecies is currently the subject of translocations into Britain. This is one of very few such international translocation programmes (see also Duffey, this volume, on translocation of *L. dispar*). *M. arion* has been the target of conservation efforts in Britain since the 1920s, latterly coordinated by a Large Blue Committee, and full-time ecological work on the British *M. arion* has been pursued since 1972. Substantial biological information relevant to conservation of some other species has also accumulated (Thomas 1984; Elmes and Thomas 1992).

Maculinea species are protected legally in Britain, Belgium and France.

Taxonomy and Description: The British form of *M. arion* was subspecies *eutyphron* (Fruhstorfer), and recent successful translocation attempts (Thomas 1989) involve the Swedish *M. a. arion*. Rebel's Large Blue, *M. rebeli* Hirschke, has sometimes been treated as a subspecies of *M. alcon*, but is distinct biologically (Elmes and Thomas 1987).

Distribution: *Maculinea* is Palaearctic. *M. arion* occurs from western Europe to southern Siberia, Armenia, Mongolia and China; *M. teleius* occurs from Spain to China and parts of Japan; *M. nausithous* is confined to Europe. The Greater Large Blue, *M. arionides* Staudinger, occurs only in China and Japan and its status is unclear. Wells *et al.* (1983) list it as 'Vulnerable' but surveys have not been undertaken in the alpine forest regions it frequents.

Because several species have been studied in detail they are treated separately below. Much recent work and synthesis on the conservation needs of *Maculinea* in western Europe is included in Elmes and Thomas (1992).

(i) *M. arion*

Population Size: About 90 sites for *M. arion* were known in the southern half of England, mainly concentrated in six areas. The colonies were all circumscribed and most comprised a few tens to a few hundred adults: the largest probably contained up to 2000–5000 adults in their 'best' years (Thomas and Emmet 1989). In general, colonies were isolated from each other and closed, as adult dispersal ability is poor.

Extinction of the colonies in the six main English areas occurred as follows: colonies in Northamptonshire died out around 1860; the last definite record from south Devon was in 1906; colonies in Somerset survived until the late 1950s; periodic declines in the Cotswolds culminated in the last known colony disappearing in 1960–1964; the last colony from the Atlantic coast of Devon and Cornwall died out in 1973; and those in Dartmoor disappeared in the 1970s. Only two sites remained by 1972, and the butterfly finally became extinct in Britain in 1979 when the reared female offspring of the last remaining female died before any males emerged which could mate with them (Thomas 1980).

Habitat and Ecology: *M. arion* occurs on unimproved grassland and is ecologically specialised. It is univoltine and adults are relatively short-lived. Females lay eggs on the flower buds of wild thyme, *Thymus praecox*. The first three caterpillar instars feed on the thyme flowers and the last (fourth) drops to the ground and thereafter depends on the attentions of *Myrmica* ants. As with other *Maculinea* species, caterpillars are carried into *Myrmica* nests, where they feed on ant eggs, larvae and prepupae; this is its major growth stage. Caterpillars hibernate and pupate inside ant nests, and the adult *M. arion* emerges in late June to mid July.

Any species of *Myrmica* ant will tend the larvae when they leave the foodplant, but *M. arion* is essentially specific to *Myrmica sabuleti* for successful rearing. Two species of *Myrmica, sabuleti* and *scabrinodis,* are common where *Thymus* grows, but a high density of *sabuleti* with thyme within 2m of their nest entrances is needed for the well-being of *M. arion*, and the size of a Large Blue colony was correlated with the number of *sabuleti* nests present.

The largest colonies in England covered 10–20ha with a few thousand thyme plants and *sabuleti* nest densities of one every 1–2m^2. Small colonies occurred on areas of less than 1ha if 60% of the ground was occupied by *sabuleti*. Thomas (1991) believed that a 'safe' population of 400–1000 *M. arion* adults could be supported on 1ha under ideal conditions: populations with less than 400 adults (reflecting around 2500 usable *sabuleti* nests) might undergo periodic extinctions. Suitable colony sites were south-facing areas with short-grazed (to about 2cm) turf so the ground could be sun-baked (Thomas 1980, 1991). Sward height was important: if grazing was removed so that the height exceeded about 4cm, *sabuleti* declined substantially, and *scabrinodis* became relatively more abundant.

The precise biotope of *M. arion* varies slightly in different parts of Europe, but is always narrow (Thomas 1991).

Threats: Site alienation through improvement for agriculture (by treatment with herbicides or fertilisers, or more direct conversion by ploughing or drilling) destroyed about half the sites and exterminated the colonies on them. The other sites were mainly abandoned for agriculture, with the resultant cessation of domestic stock grazing, aided in the 1950s by the spread of myxomatosis and removal of rabbit grazing. Although *M. sabuleti* disappeared rapidly from high sward the thyme could persist in sward up to 10cm, but it declined in abundance and few seedlings became established. Several populations of *M. arion* on nature reserves disappeared because of lack of appreciation of the need for grazing management. In hindsight, with the knowledge now available, it is very likely that extinction in Britain could have been prevented.

Collecting could have played a role in extinction of some small colonies over the years.

Conservation: With knowledge gained in recent years, through the studies of Thomas (1991 and references therein), sites in Britain suitable for *M. arion* have been prepared by prescription grazing and *M. sabuleti* populations have thereby been increased

substantially on several sites as a basis for attempts to reintroduce *M. arion*. This commenced in the early 1980s, using Swedish stock. This was chosen because of its phenological suitability: female butterfly emergence had to coincide with the development of *Thymus* flower buds in Britain for oviposition. It was in fact the only suitable stock available since the *Thymus*-feeding races of *M. arion* are all rare in northern Europe. A trial introduction in 1983 was followed by a major release on one site in 1986. Seven butterflies emerged in 1984 from the 1983 release and small numbers were present also in 1985 and 1986. About 200 additional larvae were imported in 1986: some 75 adults emerged in 1987 and 150–200 in 1988. By 1991, it was estimated (Thomas 1991) that the main site could support around 600–750 adult butterflies. Introductions have now been made to other sites and populations will be monitored for several years. Changes in farming practices (EEC farming subsidies in the 1980s) and return of rabbit grazing have rendered some of the former sites again suitable for *M. arion*. The reintroduction has been adjudged successful (Morris and Thomas 1989; Elmes and Thomas 1992).

Before its extinction in 1979, it had already been anticipated that reintroduction might be needed, and the work was coordinated through the 'Joint Committee for the Conservation of the Large Blue', with several commercial firms providing sponsorship. The butterfly had already became a familiar emblem for much other conservation work on British butterflies. It appeared on stamps and received wide media coverage. One possible role for a reintroduced colony in due course may be to serve as a tourist attraction, with controlled access, thus serving as an important avenue for education on butterfly conservation.

(ii) *M. nausithous and M. teleius*

Population Size: The small amount of published information suggests that colonies are discrete, closed and generally small with no more than a few hundred individuals.

Habitat and Ecology. These two species coexist on some sites. They both breed in marshland, and females oviposit on flowerbuds of the same foodplant, great burnet, *Sanguisorba officinalis*. Because of the observed coexistence, it had been assumed generally that the ecology of the two species was very similar (Thomas 1984) but each has specialised individual requirements (Elmes and Thomas 1987). As in other species of *Maculinea*, larvae feed on the plant for the first three instars and then feed on *Myrmica* brood in ant nests. Larval sizes of the two species differ markedly at the time of leaving the plant: an average larva of *M. nausithous* weighs 1.15mg, and that of *M. teleius*, 4.32mg. The principle host ant species differ (Thomas *et al.* 1989): for *M. nausithous* it is *Myrmica rubra* and for *M. teleius, M. scabrinodis,* and this segregation helps to explain why populations of *Maculinea* species have always been localised in areas where *Myrmica* ants and foodplants are abundant. In areas where the butterflies coexist (mainly wetlands around bogs or in swampy fields) high densities of both host *Myrmica* species occur.

Threats: Habitat alienation has been attributed to development and drainage of wetlands (Wells *et al.* 1983); even if the main reedy areas survive, the drier fringes (where breeding occurs) may be lost. All known sites for both species in the Rhône Valley were damaged by reservoir construction in 1981. More subtle site changes, affecting the abundance and well-being of the ants, are also likely to occur: extinction occurs if the density of the particular ant becomes too low and this is occurring because traditional methods of hay and reed cutting are being abandoned (Thomas 1991). *Myrmica scabrinodis* is abundant only in short vegetation, and *M. teleius* is relatively common there. *M. nausithous* gradually replaces it as succession proceeds and the vegetation becomes taller (4–7 years since establishment). It may later disappear.

Conservation: Reserve establishment to safeguard habitat is a priority for both species, with management to conserve plagioclimax conditions. Thomas (1991) notes that high densities of both *M. scabrinodis* and *Sanguisorba* can be maintained in moist hay meadows cut once a year in parts of France and Poland, and there is little doubt that habitats suitable for both species can be created easily. Translocation may well be a practical conservation option in the absence of natural colonisation of new habitats. Large populations of the butterflies can be supported on small land areas, and vegetation cutting on a 3–year rotation may be sufficient to maintain site suitability.

(iii) *M. alcon and M. rebeli*

Population Size: Confusion in the past over the relative status of these two taxa means that much of the historical and detailed distribution of each is not wholly clear. Both species occur in small colonies: many colonies of *M. alcon* contain fewer than 100 individuals.

Habitat and Ecology. The two species can coexist, but *M. rebeli* can occur at much higher altitudes than *M. alcon* and extends to 1000m in the Swiss alps (Elmes and Thomas 1987). Eggs of both species are laid on *Gentiana* – those of *M. alcon* on *G. pneumonanthe* and *G. asclepiadea*, and of *M. rebeli* on *G. cruciata* and *G. germanica*. Only large, vigorous plants are suitable, and the general life history is similar to that of other *Maculinea*. The main host ant of *M. alcon* is *Myrmica ruginodis*, and for *M. rebeli*, *M. schencki*.

Threats: Major threats are various forms of habitat destruction, predominantly through agricultural changes, but *M. alcon* is also threatened to some extent from urbanisation. Elmes and Thomas (1987) cite specific threats for Swiss populations.

Conservation: As for other *Maculinea*, habitats can be created by particular mowing or grazing regimes, and reservation with correct management is needed. A survey of the species' range to detect the best habitats is needed, especially to detail the distribution of *M. rebeli* in the alps. Recent work by Elmes *et al.* (1991a, b) has led to greater understanding of the interaction between the *M. rebeli* caterpillar and its ant hosts.

References

ELMES, G.W. and THOMAS, J.A. 1987. Le genre *Maculinea*. pp. 354–368 *In: Les Papillons de Jour et leurs Biotopes*. Ligue Suisse pour la Protection de la Nature, Basle.

ELMES, G.W. and THOMAS, J.A. 1992. Complexity of species conservation in managed habitats: interaction between *Maculinea* butterflies and their ant hosts. *Biodiv. and Conserv.* **1**: 155–169.

ELMES, G.W., THOMAS, J.A. and WARDLAW, J.C. 1991(a). Larvae of *Maculinea rebeli*, a large-blue butterfly, and their *Myrmica* host ants: wild adoption and behaviour in ant-nests. *J. Zool.* **223**: 447–460.

ELMES, G.W., WARDLAW, J.C. and THOMAS, J.A. 1991(b). Larvae of *Maculinea rebeli*, a large-blue butterfly and their *Myrmica* host ants: patterns of caterpillar growth and survival. *J. Zool.* **224**: 79–92.

HEATH, J. 1981. *Threatened Rhopalocera in Europe*. Council of Europe, Strasbourg.

MORRIS, M.G. and THOMAS, J.A. 1989. Re-establishment of insect populations, with special reference to butterflies. *In:* Emmet, A.M. and Heath, J. (Eds) *The Moths and Butterflies of Great Britain and Ireland*. Vol. 7, Part 1. Harley Books, Great Horkesley, pp. 22–36.

THOMAS, J.A. 1980. Why did the large blue become extinct in Britain? *Oryx* **15**: 243–247.

THOMAS, J.A. 1984. The behaviour and habitat requirements of *Maculinea nausithous* (the dusky large blue butterfly) and *M. teleius* (the scarce large blue) in France. *Biol. Conserv.* **28**: 325–347.

THOMAS, J.A. 1989. The return of the Large Blue butterfly. *Brit. Wildlife* **1**: 2–13.

THOMAS, J.A. 1991. Rare species conservation: case studies of European butterflies. *In:* Spellerberg, I.F., Goldsmith, F.B. and Morris, M.G. (Eds) *The Scientific Management of Temperate Communities for Conservation*, Blackwell, Oxford, pp. 149–197.

THOMAS, J.A., ELMES, G.W., WARDLAW, J.C. and WOYCIECHOWSKI, M. 1989. Host specificity among *Maculinea* butterflies in *Myrmica* ant nests. *Oecologia* **79**: 452–457.

THOMAS, J.A. and EMMET, A.M. 1989. *Maculinea*. In: Emmet, A.M. and Heath, J. (Eds) *The Moths and Butterflies of Great Britain and Ireland*. Vol. 7, Part 1. Harley Books, Great Horkesley, pp 171–175.

WELLS, S.M., PYLE, R.M. and COLLINS, N.M. 1983. *The IUCN Invertebrate Red Data Book*. IUCN, Gland.

Polyommatus humedasae (Toso & Balletto)

E. BALLETTO

Dipàrtimento di Biologia Animale, Università di Torino, V. Accademia Albertina 17, Torino, Italy – 10123

Country: Italy (northwest).

Status and Conservation Interest: Status – vulnerable.

This is one of the most well known, endemic species living in a very rare and endangered type of habitat, known to be occupied by a number of other restricted insects (Magistretti and Ruffo 1959, 1960) and plants (Peyronnel 1964). Even though one or two additional biotopes will probably be discovered in the future it is doubtful whether those populations will be as well represented as they are in the species' type locality.

Taxonomy and Description: *Polyommatus humedasae* is a species of the subgenus *Agrodiaetus* that has been described in comparatively recent times (Toso and Balletto 1976). Even though doubts on its species-level identity were initially expressed by some authors (Higgins and Riley 1983), these were finally dispelled (Higgins and Hargreaves 1983) by the study of its haploid chromosome complement (*n* = 38: Troiano *et al.* 1979).

The most closely related species, judging by external morphology, is the Greek *Polyommatus aroaniensis* (Brown 1976), an endemic of the mountains of Peloponnesos (Aroania Ore, i.e. Mt. Chelmos) and characterised by a lower number in its haploid chromosome complement (*n* = 15–16).

Distribution: *Polyommatus humedasae* lives in a particularly small area of a dozen hectares by Pondel (= Pont d'Ael) in the Val d'Aosta region (northwest Italy). The average altitude of the biotope is 1100m and it lies in the montane vegetational zone.

Population Size: The population structure is probably closed. Even though the biotope currently known may not be the only one where this species lives, there is but scanty evidence that this is the case, mostly based on a single and old museum specimen and 'entomological gossip'.

Surveys of adult specimens demonstrated a reasonably high population vigour with an average density of 11 specimens/ hectare and at least 110 animals instantaneously present at the site over a period of one month. Although no studies focused on

the estimation of the total population number are available, it may be represented by a few thousand adults.

Habitat and Ecology: *Polyommatus humedasae* lives in xero-thermophilous environments of the *Festucetalia vallesiacae (Stipo-Poioncarniolocae)* vegetational formations; the detailed association was never investigated to a sufficient detail at the phyto-sociological level. The geological substrate is represented by ophiolitiferous calco-schists of a Jurassic age (Balletto *et al.* 1982). As these schists are very fissured and fragmented, they play a fundamental role in providing a xeromorphic character to this biotope, irrespective of the orientation, which is to the northeast.

Adults are often concentrated on what appear to be the remnants of some now abandoned alfalfa fields, whose flowers represent a good nectar source for all 'blues' of the genus *Polyommatus*. No male territorial behaviour has been described or observed.

Eggs are laid singly on the lower surface of the leaves of *Onobrychys montana* Lam. & DC. In a laboratory study in 1982, oviposition started in mid-August and peaked between August 15–21. Hatching starts in the last half of September (Manino *et al.* 1987). Newly-hatched larvae, 1mm long, feed for a few weeks and then shelter for hibernation. Hibernation takes place at the first instar, in the litter at the plant base. Feeding starts again in mid-April, and the second moult takes place in the first half of May. Moults are carried out within the litter at the base of the foodplant. Each moult takes a few days to perform. Each of the successive instars lasts about 15 days. Full-grown larvae (mid-June) are green and 15mm long. Pupation also takes place in the litter and lasts about 20–25 days.

No relationship with ants has, so far, been described.

Adults fly from mid-July to mid-August. The butterfly community of Pondel is particularly rich and includes about 30 other species flying synchronously in the same biotope (Balletto *et al.* 1982).

Apart from *Medicago sativa*, adult nectar sources include *Sedum ochroleucum* spp. *montanum* and *Onobrychys montana*, the larval food plant. Actual and potential nectar sources are very abundant throughout the period when imagines are flying

88

and nectar does not seem to represent a limiting factor of population size.

Threats: Potential threats are of a rather varied and contrasting nature. Since the only biotope known for this species is situated in the montane ecological zone its climax is represented by woodland. No adult specimens of *Polyommatus humedasae*, however, have been observed in the woods on any of five surveys carried out in different years. A few small alfalfa fields that used to be cultivated in this biotope until about ten years ago have now been abandoned. It seems most likely, therefore, that if natural succession was to continue towards the climax vegetation the biotope would disappear, probably together with the animal. As with many other butterflies, in fact, this appears to be an ecotonal species, taking advantage of the intermediate stages of the recolonisation of sun-exposed landslides. It seems unlikely, however, that in the present situation this 'blue' will colonise new biotopes by a natural process.

As with many other endemics, another threat is over-collecting. Even though the exact location of the site was not divulged in the original description in order to prevent such a threat, collectors soon discovered the place and many of them can often be met in a single day on the biotope.

Conservation: The biotope lies a few hundred metres from the outer edge of the Parco Nazionale del Gran Paradiso, Italy's largest protected area and one of the most strictly regulated. It seems therefore obvious that a first measure for the conservation of *Polyommatus humedasae* would be to extend the northern boundary of the Gran Paradiso National Park to include this biotope (Balletto and Kudrna 1985). The reason why this step has not yet been taken is apparently that the general area is heavily under pressure by the conflicting interests of the inhabitants of the valleys of Cogne and Aosta, who do not want to renounce rights for agricultural and chamois-stalking practices. Site management, even though not yet needed, may become necessary in the future, to interrupt the natural trend of the vegetation towards a closed woodland.

References

BALLETTO, E., BARBERIS, G. and TOSO, G.G. 1982. Aspetti dell'ecologia dei Lepidotteri ropaloceri nei consorzi erbacei delle Alpi italiane. Collana *'Promozione della qualita dell'ambiente': Quaderni sulla 'struttura delle Zoocenosi terrestri'* **II.2**: 11–96.

BALLETTO, E. and KUDRNA, O. 1985. Some aspects of the conservation of butterflies in Italy, with recommendations for a future strategy. *Boll. Soc. ent. ital.* **117 (1–3)**: 39–59.

BROWN, J. 1976. Notes regarding previously undescribed European taxa of the genera *Agrodiaetus* Hubner, 1822 and *Polyommatus* Kluk, 1801. *Entomologist's Gaz.* **27**: 27–83.

HIGGINS, L.G. and HARGREAVES, B. 1983. *The butterflies of Britain and Europe.* Collins, London.

HIGGINS, L.G. and RILEY, N.D. 1983. *A field guide to the butterflies of Britain and Europe*, 5th ed., 384pp. Collins, London.

MAGISTRETTI, M. and RUFFO, S. 1959. Primo contributo alla conoscenza della fauna delle oasi xerotermiche prealpine. *Mem. Mus. civico St. nat. Verona* **7**: 99–125.

MAGISTRETTI, M. and RUFFO, S. 1960. Secondo contributo alla conoscenza della fauna delle oasi xerotermiche prealpine. *Mem. Mus. civico St. nat. Verona* **8**: 223–240.

MANINO, Z., LEIGHEB, G., CAMERON-CURRY, P. and CAMERON-CURRY, V. 1987. Descrizione degli stadi preimmaginali di *Agrodiaetus humedasae* Toso & Balletto, 1976 (Lepidoptera, Lycaenidae). *Boll. Mus. regionale Sci. nat. Torino* **5(1)**: 97–101.

PEYRONNEL, B. 1964. Escursione della Societa Botanica Italiana in Val d'Aosta. *Giorn. bot. ital.* **71**: 183–196.

TOSO, G.G. and BALLETTO, E. 1976. Una nuova specie del genere *Agrodiaetus* Hubn. (Lepidoptera: Lycaenidae). *Annali Mus. civico Sty. nat. G. Doria, Genova* **81**: 124–130.

TROIANO, G., BALLETTO, E. and TOSO, G.G. 1979. The karyotype of *Agrodiaetus humedasae* Toso & Balletto (Lepidoptera: Lycaenidae). *Boll. Soc. ent. ital.* **111(7–8)**: 141–143.

Polyommatus galloi (Balletto & Toso)

E. Balletto

Dipàrtimento di Biologia Animale, Università di Torino, V. Accademia Albertina 17, Torino, Italy – 10123

Country: Italy (south)

Status and Conservation Interest: Status – rare.

This is one of the few relatively well known species living in a very rare and endangered type of habitat, known to be inhabited by a number of exclusive insects and plants (Gavioli 1936; Avena and Bruno 1975).

Taxonomy and Description: *Polyommatus galloi* is another species of the subgenus *Agrodiaetus* Hübner described in comparatively recent times (Balletto and Toso 1979). Its species-level distinction from *Polyommatus ripartii* (Freyer) (south France, northwest Italy) was confirmed by the study of the haploid chromosome complement ($n = 66$: Troiano 1979, instead of $n = 90$ as in *P. ripartii*: Lesse 1960).

The most closely related species, from both external morphology and haploid chromosome complement, is apparently *Polyommatus demavendi* (Pfeiffer), distributed from Turkey to north Iran and characterised by a slightly larger number of chromosomes ($n = 70–71$: Lesse 1960).

Distribution: *Polyommatus galloi* lives over an area of several square kilometres shared between the southern Italian regions of Calabria and Lucania, on Mt Pollino and on the Orsomarso mountain range. The altitude of biotopes inhabited by this species ranges from 1800 to 2200m.

Population Size: The population structure is relatively closed in that specimens at high altitudes on Mt Pollino are unlikely to be able to reach the Orsomarso chain, and vice versa. Each of the two main sets of biotopes contain an apparently small number of metapopulations. Even though the biotopes currently known may not be the only ones where this species lives, there is currently no evidence that this is the case.

Surveys of adult specimens demonstrated a reasonably high population density with an average 6–7 specimens/hectare simultaneously present at the same site over a period of about one month. On the whole this species may be represented by several thousand adults/year.

Habitat and Ecology: *Polyommatus galloi* lives in xeromorphic environments, at the highest elevations reached in the southern Italian Apennines by the vegetational formations of the Alliance *Bromion erecti*. The particular Sub-Alliance represented here (*Seslerio-Xerobromenion apennium*) is considered somewhat transitional to the *Seslerietalia apenninae* present at the high elevations of the central Apennines in otherwise similar ecological conditions (Avena and Bruno 1975). The geological substrate is represented by Lower Cretaceous grey limestones, or by Jurassic calcitutites and limestones (Balletto *et al.* 1982).

Adults are generally concentrated on the flowerheads of the nectar sources. No male territorial behaviour has been described or observed. No particular study has been devoted to the reproductive biology of this species but females have been observed to lay eggs on the lower surface of the leaves of *Onobrychis caputgalli*. (L.) Lam. Adults fly from mid-July to mid-August.

No relationship with ants has, so far, been described or observed.

Apart from *Lavandula angustifolia* ssp. *angustifolia*, a good nectar source for most xerophilous species of *Polyommatus*, adults feed on the flowerheads of *Sedum album, Picris hieracioides, Echinops ritro, Cirsium afrum* and *Onobrychis caputgalli*. The latter also represents the larval foodplant. Actual and potential nectar sources are very abundant throughout the period when imagines are flying and nectar is not likely to represent a limiting factor for population size.

Threats: A study conducted in 1977 and again in 1980–81 (Balletto *et al.* 1982) has shown that this species is particularly sensitive to the adverse influence of grazing. Even though the effect of sheep overgrazing is particularly severe, even slight grazing by domestic stock can result in considerably diminished population densities, which soon fall well below 50% of normal. A potential threat is over-collecting although for the time being this is not an issue.

Conservation: The most important thing would be to reverse the negative effects of sheep grazing.

Mt. Pollino is included in a Natural Park, one of the largest in southern Italy, but unfortunately not one having particularly strict regulations with regard to stock rearing practices (Balletto and Kudrna 1985). The main reason why, up until now, steps in this direction have not yet been taken, is that the general area is under pressure from the conflicting interests of the local shepherds, who do not want to renounce, or even reduce their grazing rights.

In the Mediterranean area, where summer rainfall is episodic, overgrazing causes the soil moisture to evaporate very quickly and in the long run can easily elicit severe transformations of the habitat of this species.

Site management, even though not yet needed, may become necessary on a local basis, to interrupt the natural trend of the vegetation towards a closed woodland.

References

AVENA, G. and BRUNO, F. 1975. Lineamenti della vegetazione del Masiccio del Pollino (Appennino calabro-lucano). *Not. Fitosoc.* **10**: 131–153, Roma.

BALLETTO, E. and KUDRNA, O. 1985. Some aspects of the conservation of butterflies in Italy, with recommendations for a future strategy. *Boll. Soc. ent. ital.* **117(1–3)**: 39–59.

BALLETTO, E. and TOSO, G.G. 1979. On a new species of *Agrodiaetus* (Lycaenidae) from Southern Italy. *Nota lepid.* **2(1/2)**: 13–25.

BALLETTO, E., TOSO, G.G. and BARBERIS, G. 1982. Le comunita di Lepidotteri ropaloceri nei consorzi erbacei dell'Appennino. Collan *'Promozione della qualita dell'ambiente': Quaderni sulla 'struttura delle Zoocenosi terrestri'* **II.1**: 77–143.

GAVIOLI, O. 1936. Ricerche sulla distribuzione altimetrica della vegetazione in Italia: 3°. Limiti altimetrici delle formazioni vegetali nel gruppo del Pollino (Appennino calabro-lucano). *N. Giorn. bot. ital.*, n.s. **43**.

LESSE, H. (de) 1960. Les nombres de chromosomes dans le groupe d'*Agrodiaetus ripartii* Freyer (Lepidoptera Lycaenidae). *Revue fr. Ent.* **27(3)**: 240–264.

TROIANO, G. 1979. Karyotype. *In*: Balletto E., & Toso G.G., On a new species of *Agrodiaetus* (Lycaenidae) from Southern Italy. *Nota lepid.* **2(1/2)**: 13–25.

The Sierra Nevada Blue, *Polyommatus golgus* (Hübner)

M.L. Munguira and J. Martin

Departamento de Biologia (Zoologia), Facultad des Ciencìas, Universidad Autonoma de Madrid, Madrid, Spain

Country: Spain (southeast).

Status and Conservation Interest: Status – vulnerable (listed as endangered (Viedma and Gomez 1985) or vulnerable (Heath 1981)).

This species, also known as the Niña de Sierra Nevada, and *Agriades zullichi* are flagship representatives of a very peculiar and endangered habitat. They live in an area with 53 endemic plant species and at least 50 exclusive insects (including three endangered Orthoptera). Several authors have supported the idea of protecting the area as a National Park (Gómez-Campo 1987; Munguira and Martin 1989a), but part has been developed as a ski station, creating a conflict between conservation and development in an area where job creation and investment are badly needed.

P. golgus is listed in Appendix II of the Berne Convention of which Spain is a Contracting Partner.

Taxonomy and Description: Hübner described *golgus* as a distinct species, but it was considered by many authors to be a subspecies of *P. dorylas* (Denis & Schiffermuller) (Agenjo 1947). Lesse (1960) studied the chromosome numbers of the *dorylas* group and stated that *golgus* had a lower number (*n* = c. 131–134) than the other species. This has been used by other authors (Gómez and Arroyo 1981) as evidence in favour of it being a true species.

Another closely related species, *P. nivescens* (Keferstein), with *n* = c. 190–191 (one of the highest chromosome numbers in the animal kingdom) is endemic to Spain and also lives in the Sierra Nevada at lower altitudes; and an ecologically similar species (*P. atlantica* (Elwes)) is endemic to the Atlas Mountains in Morocco.

Distribution: Restricted to four 10 x 10km UTM squares in the Sierra Nevada (Granada Province, southeast Spain). It lives at heights ranging from 2500 to 2900m in the oromediterranean and crioromediterranean zones (the Mediterranean equivalents of subalpine and alpine zones).

Population Size: Population structure is not closed and small numbers of adults can be seen all around the suitable area. Larval surveys revealed a very low population density, but the populations occupied a very extensive area. Adult males are concentrated in wet places where they defend perching sites against other conspecific males in a behaviour similar to lek behaviour (Munguira and Martin 1989b). The population studied probably had several thousand adults, but no accurate estimate has been made. Records of the species from 1838 to 1986 show it as abundant in the habitat to which it is restricted.

Habitat and Ecology: Present in grassland communities growing among dwarf junipers (*Genisto baeticae-Junipereto nanae*) and at higher altitudes on climax grasslands (*Erigeronto frigidi-Festuceto clementei*) growing among schist screes (Munguira 1989; Munguira and Martin 1989b). Due to the very harsh weather conditions (with snow cover for nine months) the plants growing in the area are strong rooted perennials with aerial parts growing close to the ground. One of these plants is *Anthyllis vulneraria arundana*, the butterfly's foodplant, which is also endemic to the area.

P. golgus, in cop., Sierra Nevada, July 1985 (photo by M. Munguira).

Figure 2. Habitat of *P. golgus*, Sierra Nevada, Veleta, September 1986 (M. Munguira).

Eggs are laid singly on the upperside of curled leaves of the plant, whose parenchyma is used as food by the caterpillars. The species overwinters in its third larval instar. Larvae are regularly tended by *Tapinoma nigerrimum* ants, that often have their nests close to the foodplants. Pupation takes place in June, after five larval instars, in the ground near the foodplant. Adults fly in July in a single generation.

Nectar sources include *Arenaria tetraguetra, Silene rupestris, Jasione amethystina* and *Hieracium pilosella*. The flowers of these plants and many others are abundant in the area during the flight period, and therefore nectar does not seem to be a limiting factor for the species.

Threats: Tourism-related development is the major threat for the butterfly. A metalled road crosses one of the areas and a ski station actually exists in part of the butterfly's habitat. Redevelopment of the ski station poses the greatest threat, involving construction of new roads and buildings and reshaping of slopes for ski courses. These would have great impact on the butterfly's habitat and make other further impacts (pollution, refuse accumulation) more likely.

Conservation: The climax character of the plant communities in which the butterfly lives is a great advantage for conservation practice: the only necessary action is to protect the area and try to reduce impacts to their minimum. The declaration of a National Park in the area seems necessary, at least to protect one of the richest mountain ranges in Europe as far as endemic plants is concerned (Blanco 1989), as well as the five endemic butterflies (*Parnassius apollo nevadensis* Oberthur, *Erebia hispania* Butler, *Polyommatus golgus, Agriades zullichi, Aricia morronensis ramburi*) and other insects. New developments in the Monachil and Dilar valleys should be stopped and any job-creating alternatives studied so that conservation does not necessarily involve refusal to develop a depressed area. Sierra Nevada was declared in 1986 a reserve of the Man and Biosphere (MAB) project, and in 1989 it became a Natural Park, but this conservation status has not prevented the area from being damaged.

The inclusion of *P. golgus* in the appendices of the Berne Convention probably assures its protection in the long term but no short-term actions have been undertaken, and the developments currently taking place have not been stopped despite legislation against them.

This is one of the most obvious cases in which the importance of education should be stressed. Unlike other National Parks, in which the conservation interests are geological formations, remarkable forests or vertebrate faunas, the principal values of

93

Sierra Nevada are its small endemic invertebrates and plants. Its high altitude and geographical location makes it the southernmost limit for many northern and alpine plants and animals. Its populations are therefore of key importance in conserving the genetic diversity of these species. It is therefore necessary to enhance awareness among the general public of the great scientific and conservation interest of this apparently unattractive area.

References

AGENJO, R. 1947. Catálogo ordenador de los lepidópteros de España. Sexagesima novena familia. *Graellsia* **5**.

BLANCO, E. 1989. Areas y enclaves de interés botánico en España (Flora silvestre y vegetación). *Ecologia* **3**: 7–21.

GÓMEZ, M.R. and ARROYO, M. 1981. *Catálogo sistemático de los lepidópteros ibéricos*. Ministerio de Agricultura y Pesca, Madrid.

GÓMEZ-CAMPO, C. (Ed.) 1987. *Libro rojo de especies vegetales amenazadas de España peninsular e Islas Baleares*. ICONA, Madrid.

HEATH, J. 1981. *Threatened Rhopalocera (butterflies) in Europe*. Council of Europe, Strasbourg.

LESSE, H. De. 1960. Spéciation et variation chromosomique chez les lépidoptères rhopalocères. *Ann. Sci. Nat. Zool. Biol. Anim.* **2**: 1–223.

MUNGUIRA, M.L. 1989. *Biologia y biogeografia de los licénidos ibéricos en peligro de extinción (Lepidoptera, Lycaenidae)*. Ediciones Universidad Autónoma de Madrid, Madrid.

MUNGUIRA, M.L. and MARTIN, J. 1989a. Biology and conservation of the endangered lycaenid species of Sierra Nevada, Spain. *Nota lepid.* **12** (suppl. **1**): 16–18.

MUNGUIRA, M.L. and MARTIN, J. 1989b. Paralelismo en la biologia de tres especies taxonómicamente próximas y ecológicamente diferenciadas del género *Lysandra: L. dorylas, L. nivescens* y *L. golgus* (Lepidoptera, Lycaenidae). *Ecologia* **3**: 331–352.

VIEDMA, M.G. and GOMEZ, M.R. 1985. *Revisión del Libro Rojo de los lepidópteros ibéricos*. ICONA, Madrid.

Le Faux-Cuivre smaragdin*, *Tomares ballus* F.

Henri A. Descimon

Laboratoire de Systématique évolutive, Université de Provence, 3 place Victor Hugo, 13331 Marseille Cedex 3, France

Country: Western Mediterranean (France).

Status and Conservation Interest: Status – not thought to be threatened at the present time.

This species may be a test one, facing both the impetus of economic development in the Mediterranean region, especially in the coastal belt where its habitats occur, and the abandonment of traditional land occupation, which provides its chief haunts.

Taxonomy and Description: The Genus *Tomares* Rambur is limited to the western Palaearctic region. Three of the six species recognized are distributed around the Mediterranean basin. *T. ballus* occurs as two subspecies: the nominal one, from north Africa and southern Spain, and *catalonica* Sagarra, from Spanish Catalonia and southeast France. The latter is characterised by a yellowish-green hue of the hindwing underside while the nominal subspecies is bluish-green.

Distribution: *T. ballus* is widely distributed in Maghreb and the southern half of Spain (Gomez-Bustillo and Fernandez-Rubio 1974). In France, it is limited to a nucleus disjunct from the main area in the littoral region of the Var and Alpes-Maritimes, with some recently discovered colonies in Bouches-du-Rhône. Although still widespread in the Var department and able to colonise available habitats rapidly, the species has undergone some restriction of its geographical range in France. It no longer exists in the Alpes Maritimes, where it was present until the 1970s at Cannes and Vallauris. It has also been eliminated in its classical localities close to Hyeres.

Population Size: In southern Spain, the species is often very abundant (Jordano *et al.* 1990a) and widespread. In France, the colonies are patchy and unstable, although they appear to be dense (several hundreds/ha, according to the author's visual estimations). However, the species displays obvious colonising abilities, and starts thriving in new available habitats within a very few years. Episodical colonisation of localities outside its normal breeding range is occasionally reported (de Laever 1954).

Habitat and Ecology. Throughout its area of distribution, the species is confined to open landscapes, either steppe vegetation formation, or forest clearings of a sufficient size, where the vegetation covering is sparse. In France, it is confined to calcareous substrates. In this country, there are two main kinds of habitat: forest clearings of the live oak-Aleppo pine forest; and semi-neglected orchards of olive trees and vines, where by far the more abundant colonies are to be found.

Foodplants differ according to the geographical region but always belong to Fabaceae: in northern Africa, mainly *Erophaca baetica* (Powell in Oberthur 1910); in southern Spain *Astragalus lusitanicus* (Sierra Morena) and *Medicago polymorpha* (Guadalquivir Valley) (Jordano *et al.* 1990a, 1990b); in France, either *Bonjeana hirsuta* (Chapman 1904) or predominantly *Anthyllis tetraphylla*, which is also used in northern Morocco (Descimon and Nel 1986). *B. hirsuta* is chiefly confined to the woodland clearings habitat, while *A. tetraphylla* used to thrive in cultivated areas where weeding was regular enough to prevent scrub invasion but sparse enough to allow annuals, therophytes and hemicryptophytes to grow.

Feeding behaviour appears to be highly opportunistic and depends upon the compatibility between the vegetative cycle of the plant and the developmental stage of the butterfly. Fine adjustment of the latter to the constraints imposed by the various host-plant cycles is evident.

In France, eggs are laid singly or in very small groups, while in Sierra Morena, they are laid in clumps of several tens. The caterpillars prefer to consume flowers and seedpods, but can also attack leaves. In France, the duration of the caterpillar stage is 50–60 days, depending on yearly climate. Pupation occurs under stones present in the habitat. Pupal duration is about 10 months.

Threats: In France, near the seashore, the only cause of disappearance of *T. ballus* is the rampant urbanisation of the strip of land bordering the crowded beaches of the Mediterranean sea. On the mainland, improved cultivation techniques quickly cause the disappearance of 'weeds' such as *Anthyllis tetraphylla*. In woodland areas, the dramatically increased frequency of

---

* A name contrived recently by G.C. Luquet.

fires (of course due to urbanisation) is also a cause of the extinction of some colonies, in particular those close to Hyeres. However, in this case, the return of the butterfly following resprouting of its foodplants can be rapid if nearby colonies are preserved. In all zones, nibbling ('moth-eating' in French!) of the countryside by private houses and their gardens specifically attacks the chief haunt of *T. ballus*: sunny, terraced, sparsely cultivated landscapes. In the zones not yet struck by building speculation (and they become scarce, since, under the southern sun, every piece of land is under threat), land abandonment causes the open therophytic landscapes to be invaded by scrub and then continuous pine forest with no more suitable habitats available to *T. ballus*.

The low yield of traditional Mediterranean cultivation practices does not now allow for continuing a landscape maintenance regime which, in the past, provided a high floristic and faunistic diversity.

Collecting does not play any role in the decline of the species: even in the limited areas where overcollecting was exercised by collectors when the habitats remained ecologically preserved, a decrease in the species' abundance was scarcely observed.

Conservation: At present, no legal measures for protection are taken in France. Should such measures be taken, they would probably be limited to prohibiting collection. Such provisions prove extremely inefficient – especially in a country of Latin and Mediterranean tradition – and can even be counterproductive: professional entomologists waste much time in satisfying administrative formalities; honest amateur entomologists are discouraged and give up butterfly watching; dishonest collectors ignore the laws completely; and unscrupulous dealers continue to enjoy the increased prices of 'black market' specimens.

The problem of conservation of a large, semi-continuous and widespread population of *Tomares ballus* in southern France is closely linked to the general problem of overall conservation of biological diversity and even of human living quality in this region. Up to the present time, in spite of some pungent attacks through urbanisation of the seashore region, southern France has been relatively safe from the 'economic development syndrome' which rages in northern Europe and involves intensified exploitation of profit-earning zones, abandonment of other zones, overurbanisation and general pollution (Descimon 1990).

At the present time, perhaps the most effective strategy to conserve *T. ballus* habitat would be an educational effort directed towards private landowners in 'moth-eaten' countryside: such efforts could maintain parts of the traditional Meditteranean landscape, such as olive orchards, with a low level of 'cleaning'.

In Spain, where the species is more abundant, and Maghreb (Thomas and Mallorie 1985), the problems are less serious but probably basically the same.

References

DE LAEVER, E. 1954. *Tomares ballus* Fabr. dans les Basses Alpes. *R. fr. Lépidoptérologie* **14**: 165.

DESCIMON, H. and NEL, J. 1986. *Tomares ballus* F. est-il une espéce vulnérable en France? *Alexanor* **14**: 219–231.

DESCIMON, H. 1990. Pourquoi y a-t-il moins de papillons aujourd'hui? *Insectes* **77**: 6–10.

GOMEZ-BUSTILLO, M.R. and FERNANDEZ-RUBIO, F. 1974. *Mariposas de la Peninsula iberica. Ropaloceros (II)*. Ministerio de Agricultura, Madrid. 258pp.

JORDANO, D., HAEGER, J.F. and RODRIGUEZ, J. 1990a. The effect of seed production by *Tomares ballus* (Lepidoptera: Lycaenidae) on *Astragalus lusitanicus* (Fabaceae): determinants of differences among patches. *Oikos* **57**: 250–256.

JORDANO, D., HAEGER, J.F. and RODRIGUEZ, J. 1990b. The life-history of *Tomares ballus* (Fabricius, 1787) (Lepidoptera: Lycaenidae): phenology and host plant use in southern Spain. *J. Res. Lepid.* **28**: 112–122.

THOMAS, C.D. and MALLORIE, H.C. 1985. Rarity, species richness and conservation: butterflies of the Atlas mountains in Morocco. *Biol. Conserv.* **33**: 95–117.

The Silver-studded Blue, *Plebejus argus* L.

C.D. THOMAS

Centre for Population Biology, Imperial College at Silwood Park, Ascot, Berks SL5 7PY, U.K.

Country: U.K.

Status and Conservation Interest: Status – *P. a. masseyi*: extinct; *P. a. cretaceus*: not threatened but few colonies survive; *P. a. caernensis*: not threatened; *P. a. argus*: not threatened but few colonies survive.

   P. argus has virtually disappeared from four-fifths of its former British range (Heath *et al.* 1984; Thomas and Lewington 1991). Studies have been undertaken in north Wales (C.D. Thomas 1985a,b, 1991; Thomas and Harrison 1992), Devon (Read 1985), Suffolk (Ravenscroft 1986, 1987, 1990), Norfolk (N.Armour-Chelu, pers. comm.), and Dorset (J.A. Thomas 1991). *P. argus* is regarded as an important indicator of vigorous heathland habitats, and has been severely affected by habitat fragmentation, and by the cessation of traditional management which maintains the heathland successions required by this insect. Many of the British populations of *P. argus* are already on reserves, and English Nature, the Countryside Council for Wales, The Royal Society for the Protection of Birds (RSPB), the National Trust, the County Naturalist Trusts, and Local Councils actively foster this species.

Taxonomy and Description: *P. argus* has formed several local races in Britain, and although these probably do not warrant the formal status of subspecies (C.D. Thomas 1985a), they do provide extra conservation interest. Race *masseyi* was found on the mosslands at the southern margin of the Lake District, and had blue females (de Worms 1949). Scottish populations were similar. Race *caernensis* is restricted to limestone grasslands in north Wales. They are very small, and have blue females. Heathland populations in north Wales look similar to *caernensis*, but are slightly larger, and a mossland population in north Wales is similar but distinctly larger (C.D. Thomas 1985a). Race *cretaceus* occupies calcareous grasslands in southern England; it is large with relatively pale males. Race *argus* is found elsewhere.

Distribution: Europe and temperate Asia. In Britain, *P. argus* survives in Wales and southern England but is extinct in Scotland.

Population Size: Race *cretaceus* has suffered a reduction in range and is only recorded now at Portland Bill (Dorset), where the remaining colonies are in good health (Warren 1986; Thomas and Lewington 1991). Race *caernensis* is thriving, despite its restricted range in north Wales. In 1983, the peak emergence was about 250,000 in 10 colonies on the Great Orme, and about 30,000 in 16 colonies in the Dulas valley: the total emergence was perhaps three times greater (C.D. Thomas 1985b). Numbers were similar at both localities in 1990. An introduced population was established near Prestatyn in 1983, and was vigorous by 1990 (Thomas and Harrison 1992). Heathland populations in north Wales are mostly smaller than those on the limestone, but one large population (about 40,000 at peak in 1983) occurs on the RSPB Reserve of South Stack Range. *P. argus* did not decline on heathlands in north Wales between 1983 and 1990 (Thomas and Harrison 1992). The mossland population in north Wales contained about 5000 adults at peak in 1983, and was similar in 1990.

   Race *argus* populations occur predominantly on heathland, where it is mostly a story of continuing attrition. Only one population is left in the Midlands, and just a handful survive in East Anglia and south Wales. On the Sandlings of Suffolk, six of nine colonies contained more than 500 individuals at peak in 1986, yet only one or possibly two still contained this number by 1990, and two colonies were on the verge of extinction: the total 1990 Sandlings population was estimated to be just 23% of that in 1986, flying over 53% of the 1986 area (Ravenscroft 1986, 1987, 1990, pers. comm.). Similarly, in Devon *P. argus* is practically confined to one area of heathland (Read 1985). It is only in the Poole Basin, New Forest, and on the west Surrey heaths that race *argus* remains numerous (Thomas and Lewington 1991). A few populations survive on sand dunes in Cornwall.

Habitat and Ecology: *P. argus* occurs on heathlands, calcareous grassland, sand dunes and mossland, and the larvae feed on a wide variety of hosts in the Leguminosae, Ericaceae and Cistaceae (C.D. Thomas 1985a,b; Jordano *et al.* in press). Despite the apparent breadth of biotopes and host plants, *P. argus* is local because it has other specialised requirements. In the north, particularly, *P. argus* is restricted to warm microclimates: it occurs on sites that contain plenty of hot, bare ground, mostly on south-facing slopes. The eggs are laid at the margins of bare ground and vegetation, and the larvae feed on the tender growth of their host plants. Further south, vegetation edges seem to be less important, but relatively short successional vegetation is still favoured (Ravenscroft 1990; Thomas and Lewington 1991; Jordano *et al.* in press, N. Armour-Chelu, pers. comm.).

Eggs are laid in midsummer, in response to ants (N. Armour-Chelu, pers. comm.), and these overwinter and hatch in spring. The hatchling larvae are attractive to, and are usually picked-up by, the workers of *Lasius niger* or *Lasius alienus*, and they are taken back to the nest (Ravenscroft 1990; Jordano and C.D. Thomas in press). Quite what happens to the first instar larvae in the nest is unknown, but the later instars feed on foliage above ground, constantly tended by *Lasius* (C.D. Thomas 1985a; Ravenscroft 1990; Jordano and C.D. Thomas in press). The ants are pugnacious in defence of larvae and, if provoked, will pick up and retreat with any that are small enough to carry. Pupae can be found under stones, where they are always tended by *Lasius*, and as often as not they are inside *Lasius* nests. The emerging adults are tended by *Lasius*.

In different populations, *P. argus* eggs are significantly associated with different species of plants or combinations of plants and microhabitats (C.D. Thomas 1985a; Read 1985; Ravenscroft 1990; J.A. Thomas 1991; Jordano *et al.* in press; N. Armour-Chelu, pers. comm.): indeed, there are almost as many different plant associations as populations studied. In contrast, four studies all show an association of *P. argus* with *Lasius* ants (e.g. Ravenscroft 1990; N. Armour-Chelu, pers. comm.). Suitable conditions occur in Britain where there is a coincidence of young host plant foliage, warm conditions, and adequate densities of *Lasius*.

Threats: *P. argus* is threatened by biotope loss and fragmentation, caused by modern agriculture, afforestation, urbanisation, etc. For example, in one of the best remaining regions for heathland, the Poole Basin in Dorset, only 14.6% of the original heathland survived to 1978: 62% of the remaining fragments are of <1 ha, and 89% <10 ha (Webb and Haskins 1980). There has also been a reduction of the now uneconomic traditional farming activities (burning, cutting, grazing) which created and maintained the successional habitats required by *P. argus*. Unmanaged heathlands undergo succession, becoming birch, pine and eventually oak woodland.

The use of successional habitats means that *P. argus* must repeatedly colonise new patches of habitat, particularly on heathlands: the butterfly has a metapopulation structure in which long-term persistence is determined by the balance of local extinctions and colonisations (Thomas and Harrison 1992). This balance has been disrupted by changes in human land use patterns. *P. argus* can colonise new patches of habitat only if they occur within 1 km of existing colonies, and many biotope fragments are now more isolated than this. Thus, the persistence of the butterfly increasingly depends on its ability to survive **within** fragments, which is difficult because of the reduction in traditional management. *P. argus* will be eliminated from a biotope fragment when none of the habitat within it is in a suitable condition. However suitable the habitat within a biotope fragment becomes afterwards, *P. argus* is unlikely to recolonise if the fragment is too isolated. Thus, *P. argus* has been lost from biotope fragments, one-by-one, in regions which continuously contained **some** suitable habitat.

P. argus thrives where large areas (albeit much reduced) of biotope remain in a suitable condition. In very large heathland fragments, accidental fires and sporadic disturbances still provide a continuity of successional habitats.

Conservation: There is wide recognition of the need to conserve *P. argus* in Britain, in part because it exemplifies the problems arising from the fragmentation of threatened biotopes. Three approaches are needed to conserve *P. argus* in Britain. There has been partial implementation of each.

1. Biotope preservation. Long-term persistence is most likely to occur in the largest fragments of biotope (>100ha), where habitat continuity can be maintained relatively easily. Failing that, continuity may be achieved on a series of smaller (say 5ha) fragments provided that each is within 1km of another. Many large fragments are already protected. The Great Orme (*caernensis*) is a local nature reserve (Country Park), the sole mossland population is in sympathetic private ownership and is likely to become a nature reserve in future, and Portland Bill (*cretaceus*) colonies are predominantly in disused quarries, which are not immediately threatened. Heathlands are still under threat from development, but many are already reserves and progress continues to be made. For example, the RSPB has just obtained further large tracts of Dorset heathland, in part funded by British Petroleum who exploit oil from under the Poole Basin.

2. Habitat management. Unmanaged, *P. argus* is likely to become extinct from small (<5ha) and medium-sized (5–50ha) heathland fragments because habitat continuity will eventually be broken. *P. argus* can be maintained provided that conservationists actively continue traditional management. To date, the management of heathland reserves has been sporadic, but programmes which take account of the needs of *P. argus* are increasingly being established and carried out.

3. Introductions. One of the major impacts of humans on *P. argus* has been to disrupt its ability to disperse naturally to new patches of habitat as they become available. Introductions represent the restoration of that ability, and could be very successful. However, this requires a coordinated programme because the biotope fragments of a particular region will be under multiple ownership. Such a programme would monitor the distribution of *P. argus* and the creation of fresh habitat, and introduce *P. argus* when the fresh habitat was too isolated (>1km) to be colonised naturally. So far, introductions have not been coordinated, and have relied on the mercurial activities of a few individuals. Many of these introductions have been successful, demonstrating that this method of conservation can work for *P. argus* (Thomas and Harrison 1992: N. Ravenscroft pers. comm.): the most successful introduction has persisted for

nearly 50 years in a series of limestone habitat patches in the Dulas valley in north Wales.

Acknowledgements

I thank N. Armour-Chelu, D. Jordano and N. Ravenscroft for access to unpublished material.

References

DE WORMS, C.M.G. 1949. An account of some forms of *Plebejus argus* L. *Rpt. Raven Ent. Nat. Hist. Soc.* **1949**: 28–30.

HEATH, J., POLLARD, E. and THOMAS, J.A. 1984. *Atlas of Butterflies in Britain and Ireland*. Viking, Harmondsworth.

JORDANO, D., RODRÎGUEZ, J., THOMAS, C.D. and FERNÁNDEZ HAEGER, J. (in press). The distribution and density of a lycaenid butterfly in relation to *Lasius* ants. *Oecologia*.

JORDANO, D. and THOMAS, C.D. (in press). Specificity of an ant-lycaenid interaction. *Oecologia*.

RAVENSCROFT, N.O.M. 1986. *An investigation into the distribution and ecology of the silver-studded blue butterfly (*Plebejus argus *L.) in Suffolk: an interim report*. Suffolk Trust for Nature Conservation, Ipswich.

RAVENSCROFT, N.O.M. 1987. Plebejus argus *colony population estimates and changes in status in Suffolk 1985–1986*. Suffolk Trust for Nature Conservation, Ipswich.

RAVENSCROFT, N.O.M. 1990. The ecology and conservation of the silver-studded blue butterfly *Plebejus argus* L. on the Sandlings of East Anglia, England. *Biol. Conserv.* **53**: 21–36.

READ, M. 1985. *The silver-studded blue conservation report*. Msc thesis, Imperial College.

THOMAS, C.D. 1985a. Specialisations and polyphagy of *Plebejus argus* (Lepidoptera: Lycaenidae) in North Wales. *Ecol. Ent.* **10**: 325–340.

THOMAS, C.D. 1985b. The status and conservation of the butterfly *Plebejus argus* L. (Lepidoptera: Lycaenidae) in North West Britain. *Biol. Conserv.* **33**: 29–51.

THOMAS, C.D. 1991. Spatial and temporal variability in a butterfly population. *Oecologia* **87**: 577–580.

THOMAS, C.D. and HARRISON, S. 1992. Spatial dynamics of a patchily distributed butterfly species. *J. Anim. Ecol.* **61**:

THOMAS, J.A. 1991. Rare species conservation: case studies of European butterflies. *In:* I.F. Spellerberg, F.B. Goldsmith and M.G. Morris (Eds) *The scientific management of temperate communities for conservation.* BES Symp. **31**: 149–197.

THOMAS, J. and LEWINGTON, R. 1991. *The Butterflies of Britain and Ireland*. Dorling Kindersley, London.

WARREN, M.S. 1986. The status of the *cretaceus* race of the silver-studded blue butterfly, *Plebejus argus* L., on the Isle of Portland. *Proc. Dorset Nat. Hist. Arch. Soc.* **108**: 153–155.

WEBB, N.R. and HASKINS, L.E. 1980. A ecological survey of heathlands in the Poole Basin, Dorset, England, in 1978. *Biol. Conserv.* **17**: 281–296.

The Zephyr Blue, *Plebejus pylaon* (Fischer-Waldheim)

M.L. Munguira and J. Martin

Departamento de Biologia (Zoologia), Facultad de Ciencias, Universidad Autonoma de Madrid, Madrid, Spain

Area: Spain, Switzerland, Italy, Hungary, Bulgaria, Romania, Yugoslavia, Albania, Greece, Turkey, Russia and Asia Minor.

Status and Conservation Interest: Status – Hungary: endangered; Spain, Switzerland, Italy: vulnerable; other countries: indeterminate, (see Heath 1981; Munguira *et al.* 1991).

The species, known also as the 'nina del astragalo', is present over a wide area, but always local and isolated in several populations some of which form different subspecies (species for some authors, Kudrna 1986, Bálint and Kertész 1990). Nevertheless, young stages of all these different forms are dependent on *Astragalus* plants and live on dry steppe-like habitats. This makes the butterfly rare throughout its range. The species' biotopes are at present being altered as a result of the change from traditional land uses to more aggressive agricultural practices, or are being abandoned. The conservation of the species cannot be achieved by simply protecting the sites, due to the seral character of *P. pylaon* habitats, and would need certain management practices in order to maintain desirable ecological features.

Taxonomy and Description: The taxonomic level of the forms under consideration is not clear at the moment and needs further study. *Plebejus vogelii* Oberthür and particularly *P. martini* Allard, are true species for most of the authors due to their morphological and ecological features (Higgins and Hargreaves 1983, Bálint and Kertész 1990). Nevertheless, the taxa included under the name *pylaon* are treated by some authors as distinct species. Kudrna (1986) for example splits the group into four different species in Europe: *hesperica* Rambur, *pylaon, sephirus* and *trappi* Verity. Bálint and Kertész (op. cit.) group the European forms in these same four taxa, but they split each group into several biogeographical sub-groups without naming them as separate species. Within these so-called species a large number of subspecies have been described, but at least with the Spanish ones (group *hesperica* above) we consider all the subspecies as synonyms (Munguira 1989), and this certainly may be the case in other groups.

Distribution: The species is present from central Spain to the surroundings of the Baikal Lake. In Spain it lives in the central Plains, Iberian Mountains and near Sierra Nevada in Granada Province in a total of 37 UTM squares of 10 x 10km (Munguira 1989, Munguira and Martin 1989). In Italy and Switzerland subspecies *trappi* is also very local. In the last country it is only found in 16 UTM squares (Gonseth 1987) in the Valais. It is also very local in Hungary (Bálint and Kertész 1990) and only present in 22 UTM squares in Yugoslavia (Jaksic 1988).

Population Size: In Spain the populations are local but the number of adults is high. Many plants can have up to 20 eggs, giving adult yields in each population of several thousand individuals. After overwintering, larval numbers may reach the level of 2–3 per plant. Due to the local character of the populations, some localities are sensitive to extinction events. In Sierra de Alfcar, the type locality of Spanish *hesperica*, the butterfly has never been collected since its description in 1839. In central Spain a colony was partially destroyed by a limestone

Plebejus pylaon, **male, Camporeal (photo by M. Munguira).**

pit (Gomez-Bustillo 1981) but at present the species is still on the site although in reduced numbers. Other localities still support important numbers of the species but are vulnerable to human impacts.

Habitat and Ecology: The species always occurs on disturbed *Quercus rotundifolia* forests (encinares) in the Iberian Peninsula. Seral communities are maintained on dirt road verges, quarries, or on land disturbed by overgrazing. The geological substrate is clay or limestone. The soil is exposed in approximately 75% of the surface of the places where the foodplant (*Astragalus alopecuroides*) grows. The vegetation is formed by strong rooted perennials and shrubs specialised to live in habitats with very poor soil conditions. Altitude ranges from 400 to 1400m, and rainfall is always scarce (between 400 and 500mm per year) in every locality studied.

Eggs are laid on the leaflets of the foodplant in May or early June. After a week the first instar larvae begin to feed on the parenchyma of the leaves, leaving characteristic eye-like damage on the plant. At the beginning of July the larvae undergo the second moult and build a silken refuge on the base of the foodplant in which they spend all the rest of the summer and the winter (aestivating and overwintering). In the following March the larvae begin to feed on the young shoots of the plant and develop quickly until reaching the full-grown condition (fifth instar) in March–April. They pupate in the ground and emerge as adults 20 to 30 days later.

The last two larval instars are invariably tended by ants belonging to several species at each locality. We have found attending ants of eight different species of the genera *Formica, Camponotus, Crematogaster* and *Plagiolepis.* Larvae have dorsal nectary organs (Newcomer's gland) and tentacle organs. Tentacles are displayed when the larva is in danger, and the attending ants become excited and attack any potential enemy when this happens. This behaviour probably defends larvae against parasitoids and in fact, despite having reared almost 40 larvae to adults, we never obtained parasitoids from the species. Relationships with ants are facultative, and the whole life cycle can be completed without the ants' presence.

The butterfly is present in all the localities where we have seen its foodplant. Nevertheless, the plant also exists in southern France where *pylaon* has never been recorded. In the high altitude localities of the Iberian Mountains the foodplant is the Iberian-African *A. turolensis* (Sheldon 1913). The biology and ecology of subspecies *trappi* and *sephirus* are similar (SBN 1987; Bálint and Kertész 1990). The foodplant of *trappi* is *Astragalus exscapus*, and the butterfly appears a month later than in Spain, making the whole life cycle a month late. The habitat in the Valais consists of dry grasslands on rocky limestone slopes.

Habitat of *P. pylaon*, Camporeal, May 1991 (photo by M. Munguira).

Threats: Most lowland populations are endangered by urbanisation, because they live on flat areas suitable as building sites. In the Tagus Valley the species lives in surrounding small olive groves, and modern agriculture practices can also destroy this habitat, reducing headlands and hedges to a minimum as a consequence of management intensification. While small fields maximise the border area, increases in the grove area are reducing the headlands and hedges.

Some of the highland populations are threatened by road developments (SBN 1987), or because they are potential areas for pine plantations in the Spanish Iberian Mountains (Munguira 1989).

Most of the areas in which the butterfly lives have seral vegetation communities. Rabbit or sheep grazing is probably necessary to maintain the proper habitat in Spain (Munguira 1989). On the other hand in Switzerland, sheep overgrazing probably endangers the foodplant suitability (SBN 1987).

Conservation: The species is present at the moment in several Natural and National Parks: Tshatkal Reserve (Uzbekistan), Galicica National Park (southern Yugoslavia), Gran Paradiso National Park (Val d'Aosta, Italy) and El Regajal Reserve (Madrid, Spain). This by no means assures proper protection for the butterflies, because National Parks and Reserves are normally created to protect the larger mammals and birds. At least with these reserves, the four European subspecies are protected in theory. The **real** conservation of the species can only be achieved when proper management is maintained on at least several suitable hectares on each reserve. This management involves continuing with traditional land uses such as extensive grazing. Nevertheless, the exact grazing regime and the required sheep and goat stocking rates are not known properly, and require further study.

The Regajal Reserve, one of the Spanish localities where *pylaon* is present, illustrates the conflicts between insect conservation and development. The area was suggested as a Lepidoptera Reserve in the mid-seventies (Viedma and Gomez-Bustillo 1976). Later on a project to build a roundabout crossing the area was conceived, receiving the criticism of amateur and professional entomologists alike. The site is not only valuable for its rarities, but also because it has always been a collecting site for most of Spain's leading entomologists. The motorway was finally built in 1989, crossing the reserve through its very centre. The impact of the motorway is certainly serious: for example the rivers have changed their regime, causing several serious floods in 1990. The damage to insect populations will never be known because a suitable impact assessment was not done before building the motorway. After all these events, the area is receiving a protected status by regional authorities, and will probably be the first Spanish Reserve created mainly to protect Lepidoptera.

References

BÁLINT, Z. and KERTÉSZ, A. 1990. A survey of the subgenus *Plebejides* (Sauter, 1968) – preliminary revision. *Linn. Belg.* **12**: 190–224.

GOMEZ-BUSTILLO, M.R. 1981. Protection of Lepidoptera in Spain. *Beih. Veroff. Natursch. Landschaft. Bad.-Wurt.* **21**: 67–72.

GONSETH, Y. 1987. *Atlas de distribution des papillons diurnes de Suisse (Lepidoptera Rhopalocera).* CSCF, Neuchatel.

HEATH, J. 1981. *Threatened Rhopalocera (butterflies) in Europe.* Council of Europe, Strasbourg.

HIGGINS, L.G. and HARGREAVES, B. 1983. *The Butterflies of Britain and Europe.* Collins, London.

JAKSIC, P. 1988. *Provisional distribution maps of the butterflies of Yugoslavia (Lepidoptera, Rhopalocera).* Societas Entomologica Jugoslavica, Zagreb.

KUDRNA, O. 1986. *Butterflies of Europe. Vol. 8. Aspects of the Conservation of Butterflies in Europe.* Aula-Verlag, Wiesbaden.

MUNGUIRA, M.L. 1989. *Biologia y biogeografia de los licenidos ibericos en peligro de extincion (Lepidoptea, Lycaenidae).* Ediciones Universidad Autonoma de Madrid, Madrid, Spain.

MUNGUIRA, M.L. and MARTIN, J. 1989. Biology and conservation of the endangered lycaenid species of Sierra Nevada, Spain. *Nota lepid.* **12** (Suppl. **1**): 16–18.

MUNGUIRA, M.L., MARTIN, J. and REY, J.M. 1991. Use of UTM maps to detect endangered lycaenid species in the Iberian Peninsula. *Nota lepid.* Suppl. **2**: 45–55.

SBN. 1987. *Tagfalter und ihre Lebensraume.* Schweizerischer Bund fur Naturschutz, Basel.

SHELDON, W.G. 1913. Lepidoptera at Albarracin in May and June, 1913. *Entomologist* **46**: 283–9, 309–13, 328–32.

VIEDMA, M.G. and GOMEZ-BUSTILLO, M.R. 1976. *Libro Rojo de los lepidopteros ibericos.* ICONA, Madrid.

The Pannonian Zephyr Blue, *Plebejus sephirus kovacsi* Szabó

Z. BÁLINT

Zoological Department, Hungarian Natural History Museum, Baross utca 13, Budapest, H–1008, Hungary

Country: Hungary.

Status and Conservation Interest: Status – rare.

The butterfly was found in 1949, in the close vicinity of Budapest and it was thought that this population was the only Hungarian one. Several new colonies were discovered in the 1980s, but all were within a 30km radius of the first one. These colonies represent the most western as well as the most northern occurrences of the species. Very recently a new population has been found in northeast Hungary showing continuity towards the Transylvanian (Romania) colonies.

Taxonomy and Description: *P. sephirus* is a member of a western palaearctic group of lycaenids of central Asian xeromontane origin (Bálint and Kertész 1990a; Bálint 1991a). Several described subspecies of *sephirus* exist in the Carpathian Basin (central Hungary: ssp. *kovacsi* Szabó, 1954 (= *foticus* Szabó, 1956); Banat (Voivodina): ssp. *uhryki* Rebel, 1911; Transylvania: ssp. *proximus* Szabó, 1954), some which are most probably synonyms of the nominate subspecies *sephirus* Frivaldszky, 1835 occurring in the Balkans.

Distribution: Very restricted in two isolated parts of the country. Eight small colonies can be found north of Budapest, one in Tokaj, northeast Hungary, found very recently (1991) by Professor Varga.

Population Size: All colonies are strongly isolated, and the structure of the populations is closed. There is no possibility of interchange of adults even between the closest populations, whilst they are separated by heavily cultivated agricultural regions or human settlements. One small population which is divided by a double rail track was studied by the capture-recapture method. The results show that the adults are strongly stenochorous, with the life history of the species closely associated with the larval foodplant.

Two of the larger populations have been monitored during the last two years. All known colonies in the vicinity of Budapest have been estimated by counts of adults during the last three years. The major two colonies contained about 700–900 butterflies. Three smaller colonies had fewer than 100 individuals.

Habitat and Ecology: Colonies are strongly confined to the association *Astragalo-Festucetum rupicolae*, a typical habitat of forest steppe on loose calciferous soil. There is one generation each year with a very short flight period of adults from the middle of May to the beginning of June. Adults are active only when the air temperature is above 25°C, and the wind is not strong. Eggs are laid singly on the larval foodplant, *Astragalus exscapus* L. Caterpillars hatch after about ten days. After a short feeding period they retreat to ant chambers at the base of the plants. The diapause lasts from about the end of June (because of the long hot summer) to the middle of the following spring, about the middle of April. All older instars are tended by ants, so *Plebejus sephirus* is a steadily myrmecophilous species. The following ant species are involved: *Tetramorium* (*caespitum* gr.); *Formica pratensis*; *Camponotus aethiops*; and *Lasius* (*alienus* gr.) (Fiedler 1991). Caterpillars pupate in the upper end of the ant chambers. The pupal stage lasts about ten days and the pupae are also tended by ants. Adults of *P. sephirus* take nectar mainly from *Dianthus giganteiformis* Borb. ssp. *pontederae* Kern., endemic to the Pannonian region.

Threats: The present scattered Hungarian distribution of the species shows that current distribution is mainly the result of human activity: the loose soil of the central Carpathian Basin has been cultivated from early historical times. The major recent threats have been: (1) the establishment of new housing estates; (2) illegal rubbish heaps; (3) motor-cross activities; (4) afforestation; (5) natural succession; (6) overcollecting.

Conservation: The first discovered habitat of *P. sephirus*, namely Somlyóhegy near Fót, has been a nature reserve since 1953. Two larger areas, where the strongest colonies exist, will be protected in the very near future. The butterfly and its larval hostplant are protected by Hungarian law (Bálint and Kertész 1990b). A paper on the conservation and management of *P. sephirus* was ordered by the Hungarian authorities and was drawn up (Bálint 1991b), but there is no financial support to undertake the practical measures suggested to ensure good management. The recommendations for the *P. sephirus* populations in the Budapest area are as follows:

1. Protection of all colonies during the flight period of the species;
2. Monitoring of all populations;
3. Two important habitats with strong *P. sephirus* colonies could be attached to the Somlyohegy Nature Reserve, which could be a special reserve for *P. sephirus*, where it is necessary to arrest natural succession and negative human influences;
4. Stronger publicity for conservationist activities.

References

BÁLINT, Zs. 1991a. (A xeromontane lycaenid butterfly: *Plebejus pylaon* (F.W., 1832) and its relatives), I. *Jan. Pann. Múz. Évk.* **35**: 33–69 (in Hungarian).

BÁLINT, Zs. 1991b. (The ecology and conservation of *Plebejus sephirus* (Frivaldszky, 1835) in Hungary). Budapest (in Hungarian).

BÁLINT, Zs. and KERTÉSZ, A. 1990a. A survey of the subgenus *Plebejides* Sauter, 1968 – preliminary revision. *Linneana Belgica* **12**: 190–224.

BÁLINT, Zs. and KERTÉSZ, A. 1990b. The conservation of *Plebejus sephirus* (Frivaldszky, 1835) in Hungary. *Linneana Belgica* **12**: 254–273.

FIEDLER, K. 1991. Systematic, evolutionary, and ecological implications of myrmecophily within the Lycaenidae (Insecta: Lepidoptera: Papilionoidea). *Bonn. Zool. Monog.* **31**, 210 pp.

The threatened lycaenids of the Carpathian Basin, east-central Europe

Zsolt Bálint

Hungarian Natural History Museum, Zoological Department, Budapest, Baross utca 13. H–1008

The following species are notable Lycaenidae which occur in the region. Each is treated as a discrete account and these 17 taxa collectively indicate the main lycaenid conservation needs in the Carpathian Basin, and the eastern adjacent region of Romania. The references are given for the whole account rather than each species separately.

Aricia macedonica isskeutzi Balogh

Country: Hungary.

Status and Conservation Interest: Status – vulnerable.

A subspecies confined to a very small region of northern Hungary.

Taxonomy and Description: Close to *Aricia allous* (Geyer) (see Geiger 1988) but differing in some minor genitalic and superficial characters (Varga 1968).

Distribution: *Aricia macedonica* Verity distributed in the Balkans is an allopatric group of taxa, distinct from that of *A. artaxerxes* (Fabricius) (Britain), *A. allous* (Alps and central Europe) and *A. inhonora* (Jachontov) (Scandinavia, Russia). The subspecies *issekutzi* is the most northern and western representative of the *macedonica*-complex, and it can be found in the Karst of Torna (northern Hungary and southern Slovakia) and in the Bükk Mountains (northern Hungary).

Population Size and Status: Not known.

Habitat and Ecology: Xerothermophilous, univoltine (from late June to early August). Stenotopic, inhabiting clearings of forest steppes, rocky and dry grasslands. Caterpillar steadily myrmecophilous (Fiedler 1991). Larval foodplants *Helianthemum ovatum* (Viv.) Dunal and *Geranium sanguineum* L.

Threats: The populations are strongly isolated and threatened by intensification of grassland management, afforestation, urbanisation and tourism.

Conservation: Most of the Hungarian habitats can be found in the territories of Aggtelek National Park and Bükk National Park. Thorough ecological studies are necessary to continue the work of Varga (1968).

Aricia eumedon (Esper)

Country: Hungary.

Status and Conservation Interest: Status – vulnerable.

A protected species, which is only known from northern Hungary. The example recorded from Transdanubia (W. Hungary), collected at the beginning of the century, has never been confirmed.

Taxonomy and Description: All the central European populations are identical (see Geiger 1988).

Distribution: Transpalearctic. The species is widely distributed in the brook or river valleys of the Carpathians (Slovakia), but it is absent from the central part of this range.

Population Size and Status: Not known.

Habitat and Ecology: Hygrophilous, univoltine (mainly July). Stenotopic, the colonies can be found in wetlands along water courses with luxuriant vegetation of the larval foodplant *Geranium palustre* (L.). Caterpillars are steadily myrmecophilous (Fiedler 1991). The main nectar source of the adults is also the above-mentioned purple flowered *Geranium* species.

Threats: Natural succession, overcollecting.

Conservation: All the Hungarian colonies, which constitute a single metapopulation, are in a small mountain stream valley situated in the Aggtelek Natural Park. Patrolling of the known sites is needed along with a study of the ecosystem of the stream valley.

Cupido osiris (Meigen)

Country: Hungary.

Status and Conservation Interest: Status – endangered.

A protected species. Only three Hungarian sites are known, and these are the most northern permanent populations of this species.

Taxonomy and Description: The Hungarian populations do not differ from the central European ones (see Geiger 1988).

Distribution: Mediterranean. Very rare in Slovakia, several populations in Transylvanian Basin, Romania (Bálint 1985a).

Population Size and Status: Not known.

Habitat and Ecology: Xerothermophilous, stenotopic, probably bivoltine. The Hungarian habitats include abandoned orchards and vineyards. Caterpillars are steadily myrmecophilous (Fiedler 1991). Larval foodplants are *Colutea arborescens* (L.) and *Onobrychis viciaefolia* Scop..

Threats: Only one of the three populations has been monitored in the last years, most probably the most endangered one. Factors giving concern include: earthworks as a result of open-pit mining; air pollution from a lime factory; and the recultivation of abandoned orchards and vineyards.

Conservation: The conservation of the species in Hungary has not yet been achieved. Patrolling and study of the known populations, together with the monitoring of suitable habitats for new sites are urgently required.

Jolana iolas (Ochsenheimer)

Country: Hungary.

Status and Conservation Interest: Status – vulnerable.

A protected species, *J. iolas* was discovered in Hungary. The habitat of the original specimens was recently destroyed by urbanisation. Many known colonies have disappeared in recent decades.

Taxonomy and Description: The Hungarian populations do not differ from the Central European ones (Geiger 1988).

Distribution: Mediterranean. The northern limit of the species range can be found in Hungary. The southern Slovakian records have not been confirmed recently (Kulfan and Kulfan 1991).

Population Size and Status: Not known.

Habitat and Ecology: Xerothermophilous, univoltine (May–July), stenotopic. The known habitats are mainly abandoned vineyards or Pannonian karst oak-scrubs. Caterpillars are presumed to be moderately myrmecophilous (Fiedler 1991) and the larval foodplant is *Colutea arborescens* (L.) (Uhrik-Mészáros, 1948; Szabó, 1956). Adults fly around the bushes of the larval foodplant, which is also their main nectar source.

Threats: Afforestation (planting of *Pinus nigra* Arn.), urbanisation (a lot of habitats have been built upon) and overcollecting.

Conservation: Some colonies can be found in Landscape Protection Areas. Their habitats need full protection. The ecology of the species must be studied.

Maculinea alcon (Denis & Schiffermüller)

Country: Hungary.

Status and Conservation Interest: Status – endangered.

The Hungarian populations have almost totally disappeared and only a very few colonies remain in the western part of the country.

Taxonomy and Description: The Hungarian populations are identical with the European ones (see Geiger 1988).

Distribution: West Palaearctic. The most easterly populations can be found in Hungary and in Romania (Transylvania).

Population Size and Status: Not known.

Habitat and Ecology: Hygrophilous, univoltine (late July–beginning of August), stenotopic. Larval hostplant is *Gentiana pneumonanthe* (L.). Caterpillars are obligately myrmecophilous (Fiedler 1991). Other details concerning the Hungarian populations are not known.

Threats: Wetland drainage.

Conservation: All the remaining populations must be discovered and studied. Some already known colonies can be found in Landscape Protection Areas. The whole ecosystem (incorporating the effects of traditional agricultural practices) of the habitats must be protected.

Maculinea nausithous (Bergstrasser)

Country: Hungary.

Status and Conservation Interest: Status – endangered.

A protected species. Serious loss of habitat through wetland drainage and intensification of grassland management has taken place.

Taxonomy and Description: The Hungarian populations are identical with the European ones (see Geiger 1988).

Distribution: West Palaearctic. The most easterly populations can be found in the western part of the country (Transdanubia).

Population Size and Status: Not known.

Habitat and Ecology: Hygrophilous, univoltine (late July–beginning of August), presumed stenotopic. Larval hostplant is *Sanguisorba officinalis*(L.). Caterpillars are obligately myrmecophilous (Fiedler 1991). Other details concerning the Hungarian populations are not known.

Threats: Much of the suitable habitat for this species has become the victim of wetland drainage and intensification of grassland management.

Conservation: All the remaining populations must be documented and measured and the ecology of the species in Hungary must be studied. Some populations are in the Landscape Protection Area and in the Ferto-tó National Park, where the whole ecosystem must be protected effectively.

Maculinea sevastos limitanea Bálint

Country: Romania.

Status and Conservation Interest: Status – vulnerable.

Endemic to the eastern Carpathians. The populations are very scattered.

Taxonomy and Description: Resembles *Maculinea alcon*, but the wing shape is more expanded, and the underside darker brown somewhat similar to *M. nausithous* (Bálint 1986).

Distribution: An east Mediterranean species, its most western and northern populations can be found in Transylvania (Romania) (see Kudrna 1986).

Population Size and Status: Not known.

Habitat and Ecology: Xerothermophilous, univoltine (July). Caterpillars are presumed to be obligately myrmecophilous.

The larval hostplant is *Gentiana crutiata* (L.). The species occurs in the same habitats as *Parnassius apollo transylvanicus* (Schweitzer, 1912), and *Polyommatus dorylas magna* (Bálint 1985). Ecologically very similar to the transpalaearctic *M. xerophila* Berger.

Threats: Afforestation, intensification of grassland management and tourism.

Conservation: The unique ecosystem of Békás-szoros (Cheile Bicazului, the type locality of the subspecies) with its surroundings in the eastern Carpathians could be a National Park in Romania, where the traditional grassland and forest management could be maintained. Tourists could be restricted to indicated paths rather than be allowed to ramble freely.

Plebejus (Lycaeides) idas (L.)

Country: Hungary.

Status and Conservation Interest: Status – vulnerable.

The species is very little known in Hungary, and only scattered faunistic records exist. Its typical habitat (heath covered with *Calluna vulgaris* (L.) Hull. and *Vaccinium myrtillus* L.) is very rare.

Taxonomy and Description: The Hungarian populations belong to one of the central European subspecies described as *stempfferschmidti* Beuret, which is most probably identical with the German or the other central European populations (Geiger 1988). The species needs a comprehensive taxonomic revision.

Distribution: Holarctic. Most probably the Mediterranean (Balkans, Serbia, Croatia) '*idas*' populations represent another species, so the Hungarian colonies seem to be boundary populations.

Population Size and Status: Not known.

Habitat and Ecology: Xerothermophilous, bi- or trivoltine, presumed stenotopic. Caterpillars are regularly or obligately myrmecophilous (Fiedler 1991). Its typical habitat is heath covered with *Calluna vulgaris* (L.) Hull. and *Vaccinium myrtillus* L.). Other details (such as larval foodplants in other localities, etc.) are unknown from Hungary. *Sarothamnus scoparius* (L.) Wimm. is known as the larval foodplant in northeastern Hungary, on a site with atlantic influences.

Threats: Intensification of grassland and forestry management.

Conservation: Only one stable and strong population is known. It is situated on a xerophytic, silicate grass steppe of an acid mountain slope, partly covered with scrub (*Quercus cerris* L.

and *Q. petraea* (Mattuschka) Lieblein) in northeast Hungary (Bálint 1991). This unique habitat was strongly disturbed by the opening of a new forestry service road, the changing of the water-course system and the partial destruction of the grassland. Field research on this species is urgently required in Hungary to determine if it exists at other sites and to gather basic information on the species.

Polyommatus (Agrodiaetus) admetus (Esper)

Country: Hungary.

Status and Conservation Interest: Status – vulnerable.

The species was described on the basis of Hungarian specimens. A typical forest steppe species, many of its habitats were destroyed in the last decade. Very local in the country and in the Carpathian Basin.

Taxonomy and Description: The species is a member of the *ripartii* (Freyer)-group, which consists of many very closely related allopatric species (Geiger 1988). The group was analysed by De Lesse (1960).

Distribution: An east Mediterranean species. The species has the western and northern European limits of its range in Hungary.

Population Size and Status: Not known.

Habitat and Ecology: Xerothermophilous, univoltine (late June–July), stenotopic. Caterpillar presumed steadily myrmecophilous (Fiedler 1991). Larval hostplant in Hungary: *Onobrychis arenaria* (Kit.) DC. (Szabó 1956). Other details are not known.

Threats: Major threats are afforestation, recultivation, urbanisation and air pollution.

Many habitats have been lost through the recultivation of abandoned orchards and vineyards or were destroyed when built over very recently (especially in the area surrounding Budapest where the species is now extinct). Some colonies have disappeared because of artificially planted *Pinus nigra* Arn. (Pest County: Esztergom).

Conservation: Only two populations have been confirmed recently; one of them is situated in the territory of Aggtelek National Park. The second population is strongly threatened by a lime factory (Pest County: Vác). Since the ecology of the species is totally unknown, field studies are urgently required. Field surveys are also essential since it seems very likely that more populations exist.

Polyommatus (Agrodiaetus) damon (Denis & Schiffermüller)

Country: Hungary.

Status and Conservation Interest: Status – endangered.

The species has been recorded only from two Hungarian localities (Bálint 1991), and one of these has not been confirmed in recent years. The single remaining population is the only known confirmed one in the whole Carpathian Basin.

Taxonomy and Description: The Hungarian population is identical to those of central Europe (Geiger 1988, p.388).

Distribution: Transpalearctic (from Iberian peninsula to Mongolia), but the range consists of very scattered populations.

Population Size and Status: Not known.

Habitat and Ecology: Xerothermophilous, univoltine (July, beginning of August), stenotopic. Caterpillar nocturnal feeder, steadily myrmecophilous (Fiedler 1991). Larval hostplant *Onobrychis viciaefolia* L. (pers. obs.). Other details are not known.

Threats: The single remaining population is in the territory of Budapest, and this site is the most popular centre for picnics, weekend activities and winter sports. These recreational activities represent a serious threat to the species.

Conservation: Fencing off the habitat to safeguard the species is not possible in this area and the only long-term solution for the species in Hungary seems to be translocation to another suitable habitat (possibly in a protected area). Suggested field studies in conjunction with a proposal for the conservation of *P. damon* are under preparation.

Polyommatus (Vacciniina) optilete (L.)

Country: Slovakia.

Status and Conservation Interest: Status – endangered.

The only recently known population of the species in the Carpathian Basin can be found in northwest Slovakia.

Taxonomy and Description: The Slovakian populations do not differ from those of central Europe (Geiger 1988).

Distribution: Holarctic. It has been recorded from several northern Carpathian localities, but only one site has been confirmed recently (Kulfan and Kulfan 1991).

Population Size and Status: Not known.

Habitat and Ecology: Tyrpophil, univoltine (July), stenotopic. Caterpillar myrmecoxenous (Fiedler 1991). The larval hostplant in the Alps is mainly *Vaccinium* L. species (Geiger 1988). No details concerning the Slovakian populations are known.

Threats: Natural succession and wetland drainage.

Conservation: It would be important to protect the peat bogs and to study the ecology of the Slovakian populations.

Polyommatus eroides (Frivaldszky)

Country: Slovakia.

Status and Conservation Interest: Status – endangered.
In the Carpathians, records of the species exist only from Slovakia. The species has not been reported from Hungary, or even from Romania.

Taxonomy and Description: Resembling *Polyommatus eros* (Ochsenheimer) (Geiger 1988), but larger with a deeper blue upperside ground colour and a somewhat wider black border.

Distribution: An east Mediterranean species, perhaps endemic for the Balkans. The Slovakian populations were connected with the Moravian ones, but both of them have become strongly isolated in recent times and are very close to extinction, most probably by human influences (see Králicek and Povolny 1957).

Population Size and Status: Not known.

Habitat and Ecology: Xerothermophilous, univoltine (July), stenotopic. Caterpillar presumed to be steadily myrmecophilous (Fiedler 1991). Other aspects of the ecology of the species are totally unknown.

Threats: The records are very scattered, which suggests that the populations are on the way to disappearing. Kulfan and Kulfan (1991) grouped the species into a complex of xerothermophilous butterflies which are threatened by several harmful factors, including recultivation of their habitats (abandoned orchards and vineyards), burning fields, overgrazing, building-over, illegal rubbish-dumping, earthworks, afforestation and natural succession.

Conservation: Ecological and taxonomic investigations are urgently required.

Polyommatus dorylas magna (Bálint)

Country: Romania.

Status and Conservation Interest: Status – vulnerable.
Endemic to the eastern Carpathians.

Taxonomy and Description: Much larger than the nominate race, with a very wide and conspicuous antemarginal white border (Bálint 1985b).

Distribution: *P. dorylas* is distributed in the western Palaearctic region. This subspecies is known only in the mountain system of the eastern Carpathians (Romania and Carpat-Ukraine, ?Slovakia).

Population Size and Status: Not known.

Habitat and Ecology: Xerothermophilous, univoltine (July and beginning of August). Caterpillar steadily myrmecophilous (Fiedler 1991). Larval hostplant and main nectar source of the imagines: *Anthyllis vulneraria* L. (pers. obs.). The species lives in the same habitats as *Parnassius apollo transylvanicus* (Schweitzer, 1912) and *Maculinea sevastos limitanea* (Bálint 1985).

Threats: Afforestation, intensification of grassland management, tourism.

Conservation: The same suggestions as those advanced for *M. sevastos limitanea* apply equally to this taxon.

Lycaena helle (Denis & Schiffermüller)

Country: Romania.

Status and Conservation Interest: Status – endangered.
The species is endangered in the western part of its range.

Taxonomy and Description: The Romanian populations are identical to those of central Europe (Bálint and Szabó 1981).

Distribution: Transpalearctic. The European populations are very scattered (Meyer 1981–1982). Only three sites are known in Transylvania (western part of Romania). One of them was reported at the beginning of this century and has never been confirmed. The second record originates from the 1970s and this, also, has not been confirmed recently. Only the third, the most recently discovered site (in 1979, Szabó 1982), seems to be strong enough to survive.

Population Size and Status: Not known.

Habitat and Ecology: Hygrophilous, bivoltine (April, early May and July), stenotopic. Caterpillars myrmecoxenous (Fiedler 1991). The ecology of the Transylvanian populations is not known.

Threats: Wetland drainage, overcollecting.

Conservation: The habitat of the strongest population should urgently be declared a nature reserve and the whole ecosystem also needs protection. A part of the swamp has been destroyed already, and *Maculinea alcon* L. has disappeared. The butterfly must be protected by law, because it is the subject of intensive collecting.

Lycaena tityrus argentifex Bálint

Country: Romania.

Status and Conservation Interest: Status – vulnerable.
   Endemic to the alpine and subalpine zones of the eastern and southern Carpathians.

Taxonomy and Description: Somewhat similar to the taxon *subalpinus* Speyer, but the female often with submarginal orange lunules, and the underside ground colour deep silver grey with large spots.

Distribution: West Palaearctic species. The subspecies *argentifex* is confined to the eastern and southern Carpathians, occurring at the same elevations as *subalpinus* in the Alps (800–2000m).

Population Size and Status: Not known.

Habitat and Ecology: Alpicol, univoltine (July–August), presumed stenotopic. Caterpillar myrmecoxenous (Fiedler 1991). The habitats are mesophilous meadows, but other details concerning the ecology of the subspecies are not known.

Threats: Intensification of grassland management and wetland drainage. The known habitats are traditionally used by the native inhabitants as grassland. Any modification of the system by changes in the regime or the use of the meadows could be dangerous for the species.

Conservation: Establishment of natural reserves and the study of the ecology of the species are required.

Pseudophilotes bavius hungaricus (Diószeghy)

Country: Romania.

Status and Conservation Interest: Status – endangered.
   An endemic subspecies of the Transylvanian Basin (West Romania).

Taxonomy and Description: Close to *P. bavius* Eversmann, but differing in some minor characters (König 1988).

Distribution: An east Mediterranean species. The western limit of its range is represented by the populations of *hungaricus*. Only very few populations are known and they are very scattered (Szabó 1982). Very recently the species (most probably an undescribed subspecies) was found in Dobrogea, south Romania (Székely, pers. comm.).

Population Size and Status: Not known.

Habitat and Ecology: Xerothermophilous, univoltine (April), stenotopic. Caterpillar presumed weakly myrmecophilous (Fiedler 1991). Larval hostplant *Salvia nutans* L. The early stages were described and the ecology was partly studied by König (1988).

Threats: Intensification of grassland management, afforestation, earthworks, air pollution and overcollecting. Some habitats were overgrazed (Cluj Napoca-Kolozsvárl: Szénafüvek), or planted over by *Pinus nigra* Arn. or *Robinia pseudacacia* L. (Teuis-Tövis). Others are endangered by a chemical factory (close to Sibiu-Nagyszeben). A single colony in a nature reserve (Suat-Magyarszovát: Csigla domb) was most probably exterminated by the activities of the native collectors.

Conservation: Some habitats are protected by law, but the protection remains only on paper and has not been enforced. Very strict dispositions would be needed. Thorough ecological studies are necessary to continue the initial work of König (1988).

Tomares nogelii dobrogensis (Caradja)

Country: Romania.

Status and Conservation Interest: Status – endangered.
   Only a single population is known from Romania.

Taxonomy and Description: see Higgins and Riley (1983) and Hesselbarth and Schurian (1984).

Distribution: An east Mediterranean species. The Romanian locality in Dobrogea represents the most westerly one known.

Population Size and Status: Not known.

Habitat and Ecology: Xerothermophilous, univoltine (May). Caterpillar steadily myrmecophilous (Fiedler 1991). Other details concerning the Romanian populations are not known.

Threats: Overgrazing, overcollecting.

Conservation: The known site is very small and strongly disturbed by human activity. The habitat is well known amongst the Romanian lepidopterists, so overcollecting of the species is a real danger in spite of the fact that the habitat is a nature reserve. The Romanian population of *nogelii* has never been studied from the ecological point of view, and field studies of *nogelii dobrogensis* are urgently required.

References

BÁLINT, Zs. 1985a. *Cupido osiris* (Meigen, 1829) in the Carpathian Basin (Lepidoptera: Lycaenidae). *Folia ent. hung.* **46**: 256–257 (in Hungarian).

BÁLINT, Zs. 1985b. *Plebicula dorylas magna* nov. ssp. (Lep.: Lycaenidae) from the eastern Carpathians, Romania. *Neue Ent. Nachr.* **14**: 14–20.

BÁLINT, Zs. 1986. Further studies on *Maculinea alcon* (Den. & Schiff., 1775) (Lepidoptera: Lycaenidae). *Galathea, Nürnberg* **2**: 92–108.

BÁLINT, Zs. 1991. Conservation of butterflies in Hungary. *Oedippus* **3**: 5–36.

BÁLINT, Zs. and SZABÓ, Gy. 1981. The occurrence of *Lycaena helle* (Den. et Schiff., 1775) in the Szatmár lowland. *Folia ent. hung.* **42**: 235–236 (in Hungarian).

DE LESSE, H. 1960. Les nombres de chromosomes dans la classification du groupe d'*Agrodiaetus ripartii* Freyer (Lepidoptera, Lycaenidae). *Rev. franc. Ent.* **27**: 240–264.

FIEDLER, K. 1991. European and North West African Lycaenidae (Lepidoptera) and their associations with ants. *J. Lepid. Soc.* **28**: 239–257.

GEIGER, W. (Ed.) 1988. *Tagfalter und ihre Lebensräume. Arten. Gefährdung. Schutz.* Schweizerische Bund für Naturschutz, Basel, 2nd edn., *xi* + 516 pp.

HESSELBARTH, G. and SCHURIAN, K.G. 1984. Beitrag zur Taxonomie, Verbreitung und Biologie von *Tomares nogelii* (Herrich-Schäffer, 1851) in der Türkei (Lepidoptera, Lycaenidae). *Entomofauna* **5**: 243–250.

HIGGINS, L.G. and RILEY, N.D. 1983. *A Field Guide to the Butterflies of Britain and Europe.* Collins, London, 5th edn., 384 pp.

KÖNIG, F. 1988. Morphological, biological and ecological data on *Philotes bavius hungarica* Diószeghy, 1913 (Lepidoptera, Lycaenidae). *4th Nation. Conf. Entomol. Cluj-Napoca*, pp. 175–182. (in Romanian).

KRÁLICEK, M. and POVOLNÝ, D. 1957. *Polyommatus eros eroides* (Frivaldsky, 1837) (sic) in Czechoslovakia. *Acta Soc. ent. Czech.* **53**: 193–201 (in Czech.).

KUDRNA, O. 1986. *Aspects of the Conservation of Butterflies in Europe. Butterflies of Europe. Volume 8.* Aula-Verlag Wiesbaden, 323 pp.

KULFAN, J. and KULFAN, M. 1991. Die Tagfalterfauna der Slowakei und ihr Schutz unter besonderer Berücksichtigung der Gebirgökosysteme. *Oedippus* **3**: 75–102, 4 figs.

MEYER, M. 1981–1982. Revision systematique, chorologique et ecologique des populations europeennes de *Lycaena (Helleia) helle* Denis & Schiffermüller, 1775.

SZABÓ, A. 1982. Data to the Romanian distribution of the species *Lycaena helle* Schiff. and *Philotes bavius* Ev. (Lepidoptera, Lycaenidae). *Studii si Comunicari, Reghin* **2**: 299–306 (in Romanian).

SZABÓ, R. 1956. The Lycaenids of Hungary. *Folia ent. hung.* **9** (SN): 235–262.

UHRIK-MÉSZÂROS, 1948. Data on the knowledge of the life history of *Lycaena iolas* O. *Folia ent. hung.* **3** (SN): 5–8 (in Hungarian).

VARGA, Z. 1968. Bemerkungen und Ergänzungen zur taxonomishen Beurteilung und Ökologie der im Karpatenbecken vorkommenden Populationen von *Aricia artaxerxes* Fabr. *Acta biol. Debrecina* **6**: 171–185.

'Chosen-aka-shijimi', *Coreana raphaelis* Oberthur

T. Hirowatari

Entomological Laboratory, College of Agriculture, University of Osaka Prefecture, Sakai, Osaka 591, Japan

Country: Japan.

Status and Conservation Interest: Status – vulnerable.

In Japan, this species occurs only in very local areas of northern Honshu, and all the populations seem to be threatened with extinction. In most districts, positive actions by the residents in support of conservation are evident. This is one of the model cases of conservation in Japan (Sibatani 1989), and activities have included: (a) monitoring population size; (b) volunteer patrolling; (c) breeding of butterflies; (d) planting of foodplants; and (e) campaigns for public education in conservation awareness.

Taxonomy and Description: The genus *Coreana* Tutt is monotypic and one of the most primitive members of the tribe Theclini (sensu Eliot 1973). Representatives from Iwate Prefecture are treated as ssp. *yamamotoi* Okano (broader orange marking on upperside), and from Yamagata Prefecture as ssp. *ohruii* Shirozu (broader black border on hindwing upperside).

Distribution: Confined to northern Honshu Iwate Pref.: Kuji (40°11'N, 141°46'E) to Miyako (39°38'N, 141°59'E), around Sizukuishi (39°41'N, 140°59'E); Yamagata Pref.: Shinjo (38°45'N, 140°18'E) to Kawanishi (37°59'N, 140°02'E); Niigata Pref.: Asahi (38°15'N, 139°35'E), Sekikawa (36°06'N, 139°36'E).

Outside Japan, this species is distributed in some disjunct areas of Amur and southern Ussuri (southeastern Russia), northern China and the Korean Peninsula.

Habitat and Ecology: In northern Honshu the species occurs on the borders of woods, along creeks, in marshes near low hills where *Fraxinus* spp. (Oleaceae) grows, the foodplant of this species. There are many rural houses in this area which are surrounded by hedges of this plant, and such hedges are now the main habitat of this species.

The larvae mainly feed on *Fraxinus japonica*, and occasionally on *F. lanuginosa* and *F. mandshurica*. Eggs are laid in batches of several to 20 on the trunks of foodplants. Larvae hatch in April. Second instar larvae make simple shelters by spinning leaves. Third and 4th instar larvae nibble the stems of the leaves and sit on drooping leaves. Fourth (last) instar larvae are sometimes tended by ants (*Lasius* spp.). Pupae are found under fallen leaves, pieces of decayed wood or under stones (Fukuda *et al.* 1984).

There is one generation each year. Adults emerge in mid-June, and are seen until early August. The species overwinters as eggs.

Threats: Habitats of this species are being progressively destroyed by the development of housing sites, etc. Felling foodplants in the area along creeks or marshes near low hills is one of the main factors which reduces the population size. One further threat is the decrease in the number of hedges made of *Fraxinus* spp. which now seem to be essential for the species.

Conservation: This species has been strongly associated with rural human life in its range in Japan and its survival seems to depend on the future activities of the local communities.

In Kawanishi (Yamagata Pref.), this species was designated as a protected species of the Prefecture in 1977. However, in the absence of effective conservation measures, its habitats have been progressively destroyed. Nevertheless, local bodies began to promote conservation and urged the local government to take conservation measures. For example, in 1989, at the time of creek improvement in Kawanishi, the foodplants of *C. raphaelis* were transplanted to unoccupied ground (*c.* 600m) that had been taken over by the local government, and some of the plants were also transplanted to school grounds (Nagaoka amd Kusakari 1989).

In Iwate Pref., the butterfly is now designated a protected species in all the cities, towns and villages (Ogata *et al.* 1989). As in the case of Yamagata Pref., local governments as well as local bodies do recognize that prohibition of collecting without adequate management measures are not effective for real protection of butterflies, and they are now devising the following measures: (1) continuous monitoring of population size by local bodies and lepidopterists; (2) environmental protection by patrolling and by checking the urbanisation plans of the local governments; (3) breeding butterflies and planting of their foodplants in public places, such as school grounds or private housing sites; and (4) education for conservation awareness by holding lecture meetings and by producing public relations leaflets or videotapes.

References

FUKUDA, H., HAMA, E., KUZUYA, T., TAKAHASHI, A., TAKAHASHI, M., TANAKA, B., TANAKA, H., WAKABAYASHI, M. and WATANABE, Y. 1984. *The Life Histories of Butterflies in Japan* Vol. 3. Hoikusha, Osaka (in Japanese).

NAGAOKA, H. and K. KUSAKARI. 1989. Habitat status of *Coreana raphaelis* and conservation practice in Kawanisi-shi, Yamagata Prefecture. *In:* Hama, E., Ishii, M. and Sibatani, A. (Eds) *Decline and Conservation of Butterflies in Japan, I.* pp. 65–73. Lepidopterological Society of Japan, Osaka (in Japanese).

OGATA, Y., MIURA, H. and Y. MUROYA. 1989. Population status of *Coreana raphaelis* and the conservation practices in Iwate Prefecture. *In:* Hama, E., Ishii, M. and Sibatani, A. (Eds) *Decline and Conservation of Butterflies in Japan, I.* pp. 74–82 (in Japanese).

SIBATANI, A. 1989. Decline and conservation of butterflies in Japan. *In:* Hama, E., Ishii, M. and Sibatani, A. (Eds) *Decline and Conservation of Butterflies in Japan 1,* pp. 16–22. Lepidopterological Society of Japan, Osaka.

'Oruri-shijimi', *Shijimiaeoides divinus* Fixsen

T. HIROWATARI

Entomological Laboratory, College of Agriculture, University of Osaka Prefecture, Sakai, Osaka 591, Japan

Country: Japan.

Status and Conservation Interest: Status – vulnerable.

In Japan, this species occurs in very local and disjunct areas in Honshu and Kyushu. The populations of Honshu are feared extinct, especially in the northern district. In fact, the ones in Aomori Prefecture and Iwate Prefecture are thought to have been extinct since the late 1970s. No effective conservation measures have been taken by local governments in Kyushu except for the prohibition of collecting.

Taxonomy and Description: The genus *Shijimiaeoides* Beuret, related to *Maculinea* van Eecke and *Glaucopsyche* Scudder, contains two species, *lanty* Oberthur and *divinus* Fixsen, both occurring in eastern Asia. Representatives from Honshu and Kyushu are treated as ssp. *barine* Leech and *asonis* Matsumura, respectively of *S. divinus*. The nominotypical subspecies occurs in the Korean Peninsula, and also seems to be endangered (Fukuda *et al.* 1984).

Distribution: Very local, in disjunct areas of Honshu and Kyushu. The localities of known habitats consist of three groups: (1) northern Honshu: Aomori Pref., Iwate Pref. Morioka (39°41'N, 141°08'E); (2) central Honshu: Niigata, Nagano and Gunma Prefs.; and (3) Kyushu: Aso, Kuju. Outside Japan, this species is distributed in local areas of the Korean Peninsula.

Population Size: Population size of this species has never been estimated systematically. However, the decline of populations in northern Honshu seems to be obvious. In Aomori Pref. they began to decrease in the 1960s and became extinct by the second half of the 1970s (Muroya 1989). In Azumino, Nagano Pref., this species was widespread in the 1970s, but it is now on the brink of extinction (Kobayashi 1989). Exceptionally in Kyushu, populations of this species and their habitats seem to have been conserved during these decades.

Habitat and Ecology: Usually occurs on sunny grassland, river banks, degraded areas along railroads and, especially, on volcanic slopes.

Larvae obligately feed on the flowers and flowerbuds of *Sophora flavescens* (Leguminosae). In Kyushu (Aso, Kuju), volcanic slopes are used for pasture, and *S. flavescens* grows well in such grasslands, because cattle avoid grazing it.

There is one generation each year, with adults present in May in Kyushu, and in June in Honshu. Eggs are laid on a flowerbud. The larva is yellowish and milky white, attended by ants (not identified). The pupa is blackish and found on the ground near the foodplant.

Threats: Extinction of the northern Honshu population (Aomori, Iwate) is attributable to degradation of habitat caused by cultivation, alteration in land management practices, and urbanisation such as construction of golf courses, airport, and so on. The habitats of *S. divinus* are mostly grasslands, which may be easily cultivated or used in urban development. For example, at the foot of Mt. Iwaki (Aomori Pref.), exploitation by the national and local governments was carried out for seven years (1962–1968) during which time a total of 2155ha of grassland were cultivated, covering most of the habitats of the species. After that small populations that had survived in grasslands along creeks also became extinct in the late 1970s.

Alterations in land management practices, another of the main factors, has involved a decrease in the number of cattle and a resultant cessation of grass-cutting: this has led to successional changes which are not suitable for the growth of the foodplant.

Conservation: In spite of the decline in the 1960s in northern Honshu, no campaign was undertaken to save the species. Consequently, the populations of Aomori were eradicated in the late 1970s. The populations of central Honshu seem to be at a crucial stage at the present time but no conservation project has been undertaken, either. In Kyushu, the local governments prohibit collecting of the species, and local bodies are cooperating on a volunteer patrolling system. An essential measure would be to conserve the grassland and prevent any further alterations in land management practices. However, at this moment nothing has been done as a result of inadequate financial support.

References

FUKUDA, H., HAMA, E., KUZUYA, T., TAKAHASHI, A., TAKAHASHI, M., TANAKA, B., WAKABAYASHI, M. and WATANABE, Y. 1984. *The Life Histories of Butterflies in Japan,* Vol. 3. Hoikusha, Osaka (in Japanese).

KOBAYASHI, Y. 1989. Decline of *Shijimiaeoides divinus* populations in Azumino, Nagano Prefecture. pp. 97–98, in Hama, E., Ishii, M. and Sibatani, A. (Eds) *Decline and Conservation of Butterflies in Japan I.* Lepidopterological Society of Japan, Osaka (in Japanese).

MUROYA, Y. 1989. Decline of *Shijimiaeoides divinus* populations in Aomori Prefecture. *Ibid.*: 90–97 (in Japanese).

Lange's Metalmark, *Apodemia mormo langei* Comstock

Jerry A. Powell[1] and Michael W. Parker[2]

[1] *Department of Entomological Sciences, 201 Wellman Hall, University of California, Berkeley, California 94720-0001, U.S.A.*
[2] *U.S. Fish and Wildlife Service, San Francisco Bay National Wildlife Refuge Complex, Newark, CA 94560, U.S.A.*

Country: U.S.A.

Status and Conservation Interest: Status – possibly out of danger; endangered listing (USFWS).

This local subspecies was one of the first eight insects to be listed as an endangered species in 1976 under the Federal Endangered Species Act. Its remnant habitat was purchased by the U.S. Fish and Wildlife Service (USFWS) in 1980 and designated as the Antioch Dunes National Wildlife Refuge, the first such refuge in the country established to protect insects and plants. Population numbers of *Apodemia mormo langei* declined over a period of 50 years to a few hundred individuals in the early 1980s. During the past decade they have increased tenfold or more in response to recovery actions, which include exclusion of vehicular and most foot traffic, removal of exotic vegetation, and extensive outplanting of the larval host plant.

General accounts of the unique insect and plant communities and destruction of the Antioch dunes by sand mining and industrial development have been recorded (Howard 1983; Howard and Arnold 1980; Farb 1964; Powell 1981, 1983).

Taxonomy and Description: Considerable polytypy is expressed, often discordantly, in hostplant species, seasonal phenology and voltinism, and in size and colour pattern of the adults (Opler and Powell 1962; Powell 1975).

Distribution: *Apodemia mormo* (Felder & Felder) (Riodininae) is widely distributed in the western Nearctic and occurs in scattered, often isolated colonies. Some forms of the butterfly are quite limited in geographic distribution and may be separated by distances of only 15–20km from other populations that are easily distinguished phenotypically. *Apodemia mormo langei* was discovered in 1933, on the riverine sand dune system just east of Antioch, Contra Costa Co., California (Comstock 1938). This subspecies is represented by just one population (Opler and Powell 1962). The nearest known colonies of *Apodemia mormo* are located on the northwest slope of Mt. Diablo and on the hills northwest of Vallejo, Solano Co., which are respectively about 15km SW and 39km WNW of the *langei* site. These populations have appreciable differences in colour pattern from *langei*.

Population Size: U.S. Geological Survey topographical maps and aerial photographs that span 1905 to 1969, document the destruction of the Antioch sand dunes. At the turn of the century, after agricultural development of the region, they extended for 3–4km in a narrow band along the San Joaquin River and reached heights of 20–35m. Sand mining operations began prior to and during the 1920s (Howard and Arnold 1980). Although the installation of two powerline towers, in 1909 and 1927, resulted in habitat disturbance including building construction and introduction of exotic plants, today these Pacific Gas and Electric (P.G. & E.) towers stand on the two remaining remnants of sand hills.

By 1931, five huge sand pits, each with a railroad spur, were in operation, for the developing San Francisco Bay area. During post World War II years, massive industrial developments replaced the eastern half of the dunes, and in the 1950s sand mining moved to the western sector. A Kaiser Gypsum plant

Female Lange's Metalmark on flowers of *Senecio douglasii*.

was completed in 1956, and this isolated the two remaining remnants of the habitat, the Stamm Property (SP) to the west and the 'Little Corral' (LC) flanked by the P.G. & E. properties to the east (Figure 1).

Although its habitat was gradually restricted during the 40 years following discovery, the local abundance of *Apodemia mormo langei* remained high. Lepidopterists observed the butterflies by the hundreds and collected specimens at rates of 25–30 per hour in various seasons during 1947–1972. Even as late as 1972, three observers took 70 specimens one day and 50 more seven days later and estimated sighting 150–200 on each date.

Soon thereafter, however, the colonies were severely affected by increased sand-mining at the western parcel (SP), by rototilling on the P.G. & E. properties in compliance with a county ordinance for fire prevention, and by overgrazing by horses. Thus by 1976, when Powell began population census by transect counts, numbers of *langei* had dropped alarmingly. During mark-recapture monitoring by Arnold and Powell from 1977–1982, the maximum number of *langei* two persons could observe in 3.5–4.5 hour periods at the two sites was 45–55 (Arnold and Powell 1983; Powell unpubl. data). Total population numbers, calculated from daily Jolly-Seber and Manly-Parr estimates and the survival rates of individual butterflies, declined from more than 2000 in 1977 to fewer than 600 in 1982 (Arnold 1985 and unpubl. reports to USFWS).

The butterfly numbers stabilised and increased slightly in 1983–84 and then rose significantly as *langei* began to occupy *Eriogonum* in peripheral areas that had been both planted and colonised naturally. The estimated total population exceeded 1200 in 1985, the final year of Arnold's mark-recapture studies (Arnold, unpublished report to USFWS). Subsequently, single day sighting counts, made weekly by USFWS personnel, indicate that the numbers of *langei* have continued to climb dramatically. Seasonal peak numbers have risen from 168 in 1986 to more than 1900 in 1991. It is likely that the population has 10 to 20 times the number of butterflies that it was estimated to have contained 10 years ago (e.g. 6000 to 12,000).

Habitat and Ecology: Populations occur in close association with the larval foodplants, species of *Eriogonum* (Polygonaceae), typically in well drained semiarid sites, such as rocky desert slopes, sand dunes, or chaparral-covered hills, ranging from sea coast to timberline at 2750m. Colonies of *A. m. langei* are limited to dense or moderately dense patches of the larval foodplant, *Eriogonum nudum auriculatum* (Arnold and Powell 1983). Arnold and Powell believed that isolated or spindly, scattered plants fail to support colonies of the butterfly because early instar larvae derive insufficient protection for overwintering.

A. m. langei is univoltine, with adults flying for about 30 days beginning in early August. Males precede females by a few days, and peak numbers occur about two weeks after emergence begins. The eggs are deposited in clusters of 2–4 on withering foliage on the lower half of the plant. Eclosion of larvae takes place during winter, after rainfall and foliation begin. Feeding occurs by skeletonizing the leaf surfaces and the inflorescence stalks by later instars in June and July. Larvae feed in early morning and presumably evening and retreat to the base of the plants during the day. Pupation occurs in the litter

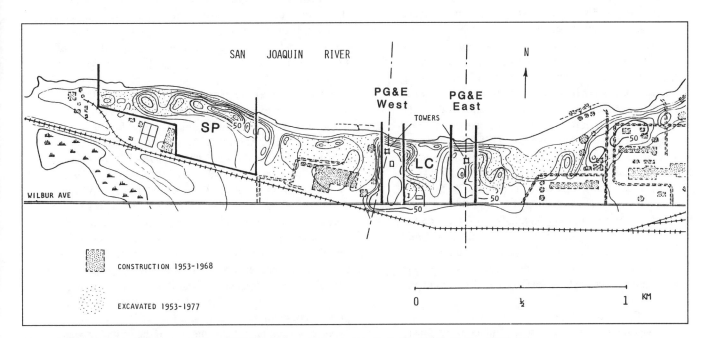

Figure 1. Map of the Antioch Dunes National Wildlife Refuge, just east of Antioch, Contra Costa Co., California.
Redrawn from Antioch North Quadrangle, U.S. Geological Survey topographic map, 1953. Shaded areas delineated by dotted lines indicate construction sites, 1953–1968, compiled from aerial photographs. Sparsely dotted areas depict sand-mining excavations during 1953–1967. The two corridors traversed by P.G. & E. powerlines are the only unexcavated hills that remain. Bold lines define the two parcels of the Refuge, "Stamm Property" (SP) and "Little Corral" (LC), the latter flanked by P.G. & E. properties.

at the base of the plant, in late July and early August (Arnold and Powell 1983).

Males tend to occupy restricted areas day after day, while females move greater distances. Mark-recapture data suggested that males live an average of about 12 days. Adults of both sexes forage for nectar; *Eriogonum* serves as the primary nectar source, at least in recent years, while occasional visits are made to *Gutierrezia* and *Senecio* (Asteracecae), both of which were formerly more abundant, and other plants (Arnold and Powell 1983).

Under natural circumstances, this variety of *Eriogonum nudum* probably lived as an edge species, occupying slip slopes of active sand in the hills that were stabilised by scattered oaks and a rich flora of desert affinities (Howard 1983). There is no doubt that the active sand habitat greatly increased during the 1920–1940 era of sand-mining. Thus, it is likely that, along with its larval host, *A. m. langei* had increased in population numbers by the time of its discovery in the early 1930s.

Conservation: Rehabilitation of habitat suitable for colonisation by *A. m. langei* began before acquisition of the Refuge lands by USFWS. Propagation and outplanting on the P.G. & E. properties began in 1979, following inadvertent rototilling of one of the primary stands of *Eriogonum*, despite efforts by the company to prevent such an accident. P.G. & E. contracted with Biosystems Analysis Inc. to develop a restoration plan, and about 450 seedlings were planted in March 1980 (Howard and Arnold 1980). Collective efforts during 1980–1984, which were orchestrated by Howard and Arnold, were financed by P.G. & E., grants from the California Native Plant Society, a USFWS contract, and assistance by the University of California, Berkeley undergraduate botany association and other volunteers (Arnold 1985). During the same years, the USFWS began planting *Eriogonum* at the western parcel (SP) by scarifying and seeding the excavated surface left bare by a final surge of sand-mining in 1978–79. In 1985 the USFWS entered a Cooperative Agreement with P.G. & E. that allows the Service to manage the additional 5ha owned by P.G. & E., which are contiguous with LC (Figure 1). In 1987, fencing of the lands was completed, and this virtually eliminated further human degradation of the habitat. Also in 1987 a vineyard to the south of the *Apodemia* colony at SP was removed and subsequently planted with 7000 *Eriogonum* seedlings. Small numbers of *langei* have begun to occupy that area (58 were observed in one day in 1991).

In 1991 a more ambitious cooperative restoration project was initiated to create new sand dunes in previously mined areas occupied by weedy vegetation. Low hills, consisting of sand mined from another P.G. & E. property up river, have been deposited and contoured on the LC and P.G. & E. western parcels. These were subsequently seeded and planted and now bear mantles of *Eriogonum* and *Senecio douglasii* seedlings, the latter a major nectar source for the butterflies, as well as two endangered plants, *Oenothera deltoides* var. *howelli* (Onagraceae) and *Erysimum capitatum* var. *angustatum* (Brassicaceae).

Altogether, we estimate that outplanted *Eriogonum* colonies that have reached densities believed to be sufficient to support *Apodemia* occupy areas of 9600m^2 at SP and 3200m^2 on the P.G. & E. properties, a total of nearly 1.3ha.

In 1979 the maximum distribution of the foodplant range (range width x range length, right angle) was estimated to be 2.3ha at LC and 1.5ha at SP, not more than one-third of which was suitable for *Apodemia* as judged by occurrence of adults (Arnold and Powell 1983). Hence, there was only about 1.3ha of viable *Eriogonum* habitat at its lowest ebb, and subsequent efforts have at least doubled that area. Several additional patches of the host plant, planted in recent years, are expected to develop into viable habitat within a few seasons.

Threats: Effects of weediness and possibility of fire are the principal threats to continued existence of *A. m. langei*. A standing crop of annual weeds poses a fire danger each year during the long dry season (May–October). The refuge is bordered inland by industrial development, and there are several small beaches that are accessible to recreational boat visits, so possible sources of human-initiated fires cannot be controlled.

Conservation and recovery efforts have been a dramatic success, increasing the population numbers from a perilously low level a decade ago. However, after 10–15 years *Eriogonum* host plants senesce, and they fail to reproduce in the absence of open, active sand. We have witnessed the growth and decline of *Eriogonum* and associated *langei* colonies in several areas during the past 15 years. For example, a robust colony developed in association with the foundations of a building that was removed after 1972 on P.G. & E. west; it was the home of a strong colony of *langei* during 1978–1982, but these plants were senescent by 1988 and have died out by 1992. The foundations protected the plants from rototilling during the 1970s, but competition with weeds prevented seedling growth. A similar fate can be predicted for most of the existing and recently planted patches of *Eriogonum*. Once a colony of the food plant is established, it is impractical to prevent a ground cover of weeds, especially annual exotic grasses, yellow star thistle, Russian thistle, and vetch, which does not kill mature *Eriogonum* but prevents development of its seedlings. Thus, it is easier to clear a site and plant new patches of the host plant than to maintain existing ones.

To be successful on a long term basis, the management plan needs to prescribe replacing senescent patches of *Eriogonum* on a continuing basis.

Acknowledgements

We thank Richard Arnold, Alice Howard, John Steiner, and Jean Takekawa for discussions and information regarding the recent and past history of the Antioch sand dunes and the flora; Arnold and Steiner reviewed a draft of the manuscript and offered useful criticisms.

References

ARNOLD, R.A. 1985. Private and government-funded conservation programs for endangered insects in California. *Nat. Areas J.* **5**: 28–39.

ARNOLD, R.A. and POWELL, J.A. 1983. *Apodemia mormo langei.* pp. 99–128. *In:* Arnold, R.A., Ecological studies of six endangered butterflies (Lepidoptera: Lycaenidae): Island biogeography, patch dynamics, and the design of habitats preserves. *Univ. Calif. Publns Entomol.* **99**.

COMSTOCK, J.A. 1938. A new Apodemia from California. *Bull. South Calif. Acad. Sci.* **37**: 129–132.

FARB, P. 1964. Insect city in the dunes. pp. 44–49. *In: The Land and Wildlife of North America.* Life Nature Library, Time-Life Books, New York.

HOWARD, A.Q. (Ed.) 1983. The Antioch dunes. A report to the U.S. Fish and Wildlife Service. Prepared under P.O. No. 11640-0333-1; 115 pp. + appendices.

HOWARD, A.Q. and ARNOLD, R.A. 1980. The Antioch dunes – safe at last? *Fremontia* **8**(3): 3–12.

OPLER, P.A. and POWELL, J.A. 1962. Taxonomic and distributional studies on the western components of the *Apodemia mormo* complex (Riodinidae). *J. Lepid. Soc.* **15**: 145–171.

POWELL, J.A. 1975. Riodinidae. The Metalmarks. pp. 259–272. *In:* Howe, W.H. (Ed.). *The Butterflies of North America.* Doubleday; Garden City, New York.

POWELL, J.A. 1981. Endangered habitats for insects: California coastal sand dunes. *Atala* **6**: 41–55 (1978).

POWELL, J.A. 1983. Changes in the insect fauna of a deteriorating riverine sand dune community during 50 years of human exploitation. Report to U.S. Fish and Wildlife Service. Prepared under P.O. no. 11640-0333-1; 78 pp.

The Hermes Copper, *Lycaena hermes* (Edwards)

D.K. Faulkner and J.W. Brown

Entomology Department, San Diego Natural History Museum, P.O. Box 1390, San Diego, California 92112, U.S.A.

Country: U.S.A.

Status and Conservation Interest: Status – rare; indeterminate (Red List).

The Hermes Copper is a remarkably distinct species, differing considerably from its congeners in both morphology and ecology. It has a highly restricted geographical distribution in the southwestern United States and adjacent northwestern Baja California, Mexico. Because of the widespread loss and fragmentation of its habitats, associated with urbanisation and other development, this species has lost a significant portion of its former range. Owing to its vulnerable nature, the Hermes Copper is recognized by the United States Fish and Wildlife Service as a 'category 2 candidate' species for listing as threatened or endangered.

Taxonomy and Description: The Hermes Copper was described as *Chrysophanus hermes* by W.H. Edwards (1870) from 'California'. Wright (1906) later described *Chrysophanus delsud* from San Diego County, California; the latter is a subjective synonym of *hermes*. The species has been included in the genera *Tharsalea* Scudder (e.g. Comstock 1927; Wright 1930) and *Lycaena* Fabricius (dos Passos 1964; Howe 1975). Miller and Brown (1979) placed *hermes* in the monotypic genus *Hermelycaena* Miller and Brown on the basis of its unique morphological and ecological characteristics. Currently, most taxonomists consider *hermes* to be a member of the Holarctic genus *Lycaena*.

Distribution: The Hermes Copper is a narrowly endemic species, restricted to western San Diego County, California, and a small portion of adjacent Baja California, Mexico (Brown 1980; Ehrlich and Ehrlich 1961; Emmel and Emmel 1973; Garth and Tilden 1986; Orsak 1977; Rindge 1948; Scott 1988). Its total range is approximately 250km from north to south (from about Fallbrook in San Diego County, California, to slightly south of Santa Tomas in Baja California, Mexico), and 50km from east to west (from near the coast, inland to about Pine Valley, California). Within this range it occurs in small, disjunct colonies.

In San Diego County, the Hermes Copper has been recorded from El Cajon, Santee, Flynn Springs, Blossom Valley, Tecate, Pine Valley, Guatay, and numerous other localities, many of which no longer support native vegetation.

Population Size: In the absence of focused studies on population size and vagility, information on these parameters is mostly anecdotal. The Hermes Copper has been collected at about 35 localities in the United States and four localities in Mexico. Most colonies are isolated from each other. Hence, gene flow between populations probably is rather low. In addition, adults exhibit limited vagility: they do not hilltop and they seldom are observed beyond the immediate vicinity of the larval host. Thorne (1963) indicated that colonies vary little in size from year to year, but there are few quantitative data to support this observation. It is likely that few colonies exceed 50 individuals.

Habitat and Ecology: This species occurs in coastal sage scrub and open southern mixed chaparral communities in which the larval host plant, redberry (*Rhamnus crocea* Nutt. in T. & G., Rhamnaceae) is a common component. In San Diego County, these habitat types range from near sea level along the coast to about 1250m at the western edge of the Laguna Mountains. The foodplant is a fairly common species, extending well beyond the range of the butterfly. Hence, the restricted distribution of the Hermes Copper is difficult to explain.

The Hermes Copper is univoltine, with adults present from mid-May through early July, depending upon elevation. The primary adult nectar source at most localities is flat-top buckwheat (*Eriogonum fasciculatum* Bentham; Polygonaceae), but *L. hermes* also has been observed to nectar on slender sunflower (*Helianthus gracilentus*) and a few other composites (Asteraceae). Males perch on vegetation along trails and openings, and confront other butterflies that pass by.

Eggs are laid singly on stems of the foodplant and overwinter until the following spring. The egg is white, echinoid, and covered with deep pits between high, irregular walls. The fully-grown larva is apple green, with a mid-dorsal band of darker green bordered with yellowish-green. Pupation occurs on the foodplant, and the pupa is attached by a cremaster and a silken girdle. Full details of the life history are presented by Comstock and Dammers (1935). Ballmer and Pratt (1989) indicate that the larvae of *Lycaena hermes* differ greatly from those of other *Lycaena* species in host preference and morphology. No parasitoids or predators are recorded.

Threats: Although declines have not been documented quantitatively, the Hermes Copper undoubtedly has suffered from loss and fragmentation of habitat as a result of urbanisation. As long ago as 1930, Wright (1930) reported 'Its trysting places are being rapidly taken over by realtors and the species may soon become extinct...' Indeed, much of the former range of *L. hermes* is presently occupied by urbanised portions of San Diego. As development in San Diego County extends eastward from the coast, the Hermes Copper is further threatened by habitat loss.

Conservation: Currently, the Hermes Copper receives minimal protection under the California Environmental Quality Act. Under this legislation, impacts to sensitive plants and animals and sensitive habitat types must be assessed to determine whether the adverse affects of habitat loss and fragmentation resulting from development are 'significant'. If they are determined to be significant, mitigation measures are required to reduce impacts below a level of significance. Unfortunately, because invertebrates typically receive little attention in the environmental review process, impacts to these species usually are undocumented.

Management recommendations for the Hermes Copper include increased awareness of this species, particularly for those individuals and agencies involved in the environmental review process, and protection of existing colonies from habitat loss and fragmentation associated with urbanisation. The Hermes Copper is presently recognized by the United States Fish and Wildlife Service as a category 2 candidate species for listing as endangered or threatened; the Service recently received a petition to list the species as threatened. Such a listing would increase significantly the protection afforded Hermes Copper.

References

BALMER, G. and PRATT, G. 1989 (1988). A survey of last instar larvae of the Lycaenidae of California. *J. Res. Lepid.* **27**: 1–70.

BROWN, J.W. 1980. Hermes copper. *Environment Southwest* **491**: 23. San Diego Natural History Museum.

COMSTOCK, J.A. 1927. *The Butterflies of California.* Published by the author. 227 pp.

COMSTOCK, J.A. and DAMMERS, C.M. 1935. Notes on the early stages of three butterflies and six moths from California. *Bull. South. Calif. Acad. Sci.* **34**: 120–141.

DOS PASSOS, C.F. 1964. A synonymic list of the Nearctic Rhopalocera. *Mem. Lepid. Soc.* **1**: 1–145.

EDWARDS, W.H. 1870. Description of a new species of Lepidoptera found within the United States. *Trans. Amer. Entomol. Soc.* **3**: 21.

EHRLICH, P.R. and EHRLICH, A.H. 1961. *How to Know the Butterflies.* Wm. C. Brown Co. Publ., Dubuque, Iowa. 262 pp.

EMMEL, T.C. and EMMEL, J.F. 1973. Butterflies of Southern California. *Nat. Hist. Mus. Los Angeles County, Sci. ser.* **26**: 1–148.

GARTH, J. and TILDEN, J.W. 1986. *California Butterflies.* University of California Press, Berkeley. 246 pp. + plates.

HOWE, W.H. 1975. *Butterflies of North America.* Doubleday and Co., Inc., Garden City, New York. 633pp.

MILLER, L.D. and BROWN, F.M. 1979. A revision of the American coppers (Lepidoptera: Lycaenidae). *Bull. Allyn Mus.* **51**: 22–23.

ORSAK, L.J. 1977. Butterflies of Orange County. *Univ. Calif. Irvine, Mus. Syst. Biol. Res. ser.* **4**. 349 pp.

RINDGE, F.H. 1948. Contributions toward a knowledge of the insect fauna of Lower California. No. 8. Lepidoptera: Rhopalocera. *Proc. Calif. Acad. Sci.* **24**: 303.

SCOTT, J.A. 1986. *The butterflies of North America.* Stanford University Press, Stanford, Calif. 583 pp.

THORNE, F.T. 1963. The distribution of an endemic butterfly, *Lycaena hermes. J. Res. Lepid.* **2**: 143–150.

WRIGHT, W.G. 1906. *Butterflies of the West Coast of the United States.* Whitaker and Ray Co., San Francisco, Calif. 257 pp.

WRIGHT, W.G. 1930. An annotated list of the butterflies of San Diego County, California. *Trans. San Diego Soc. Nat. Hist.* **6**: 1–40.

Thorne's Hairstreak, *Mitoura thornei* Brown

John W. Brown

Entomology Department, San Diego Natural History Museum, P.O. Box 1390, San Diego, California 92112, U.S.A.

Country: U.S.A.

Status and Conservation Interest: Status – possibly threatened.

Thorne's Hairstreak is a geographically isolated and ecologically distinct taxon that is restricted to a single mountain in southwestern San Diego County, California. Owing to its highly restricted distribution and the potential threats of habitat loss and degradation, Thorne's Hairstreak is recognized as a 'category 2 candidate' for listing as endangered or threatened by the United States Fish and Wildlife Service.

Taxonomy and Description: Thorne's Hairstreak was described by Brown (1983) as *Mitoura thornei*. Although most authors have treated it as a distinct species (e.g. Brown 1983; Garth and Tilden 1986; Ferris 1989; Ballmer and Pratt 1989), Shields (1984) suggests that it is a subspecies of *Mitoura loki* (Skinner), and Scott (1986) suggests that it is a subspecies of *Mitoura grynea* Huebner. Most likely, *M. thornei* is part of a 'superspecies' complex in which the degree of morphological divergence and genetic isolation among taxa do not conform well with our fixed system of binomial (or trinomial) nomenclature. Regardless of taxonomic opinion, Thorne's Hairstreak is ecologically distinct and geographically isolated from its nearest congeners.

The nearctic genus *Mitoura* Scudder frequently is considered a subgenus of *Callophrys* Billberg. Hence, Thorne's Hairstreak occasionally is referred to as *Callophrys* (*Mitoura*) *thornei*.

Distribution: Thorne's Hairstreak is restricted to Otay Mountain (= San Ysidro Mountains) in the southwestern portion of San Diego County, California. On Otay Mountain it is confined to places where the larval foodplant, Tecate cypress (*Cupressus forbesi*; Cupressaceae), grows. Although a significant stand of Tecate cypress occurs to the north in Coal Canyon, Orange County, California, and small populations are found to the south in northwestern Baja California, Mexico, Thorne's Hairstreak has not been documented from any of these localities (e.g. Orsak 1977; Brown 1983).

Population Size: Otay mountain undoubtedly supports an extensive, nearly contiguous population (or set of populations) of Thorne's Hairstreak, although no quantitative data are available. Most of the Tecate cypress on the mountain has not been subject to encroachment by development or other human activities that result in loss of habitat, although chaparral fires frequently reduce or eliminate stands of the trees.

Habitat and Ecology: Thorne's Hairstreak occurs only in southern interior cypress forest (Holland 1986) or where this habitat blends into other habitat types. The larval foodplant is Tecate cypress (*Cupressus forbesi*), a closed-cone conifer that occurs on mesic slopes and drainages in chaparral, and with which the adults are intimately associated. Thorne's Hairstreak is at least double brooded, with adults flying in late February through March, and again in June. Capture records indicate that the second brood may be only a partial one, as is the case with the closely related *Mitoura loki*. The emergence of laboratory reared individuals in August suggests the presence of a third brood in the fall, but this is yet to be documented in the field.

The early stages of *M. thornei* closely resemble those described for *M. siva* (Edwards) (Coolidge 1924), *M. loki* (Comstock and Dammers 1932a), and *M. nelsoni* (Boisduval) (Comstock and Dammers 1932b), (see Ballmer and Pratt 1989). The eggs are echinoid and light green, and are laid singly on the new growth of the host plant. The egg stage lasts 7 to 14 days. Newly hatched larvae initially bore into the young stems of the host but later become external feeders. The larvae closely resemble the terminal twigs upon which they feed. Complete larval development, from hatching to pupation, requires 26–35 days under laboratory conditions (Brown 1983). Pupation generally occurs in the duff or debris at the base of the host trees. No parasitoids or predators are recorded.

Threats: Fire is an integral element in the natural history of Tecate cypress as it is the major factor that initiates cone opening and subsequent seed dispersal (Zedler 1977). Chaparral fires undoubtedly have caused fluctuations in the populations of both the cypress and the associated butterfly. Zedler (1977) indicates that Tecate cypress requires approximately 25 years to reach reproductive maturity. Hence, an increase in the incidence of fire (i.e. a frequency of less than every 25 years) could severely affect the host trees. In recent years, chaparral fires have been common in the Otay Mountain area, usually as a result of carelessness by people. Chaparral fires probably represent the greatest threat to the cypress and its associated insect fauna, including Thorne's Hairstreak.

Conservation: Currently, Thorne's Hairstreak receives minimal protection under the California Environmental Quality Act. Under this legislation, impacts to sensitive plants and animals and sensitive habitat types that result from development activities, must be assessed to determine whether the adverse affects of habitat loss and fragmentation are 'significant'. If they are determined to be significant, mitigation measures are required to reduce impacts below a level of significance. Unfortunately, because invertebrates typically receive little attention in the environmental review process, these impacts typically are undocumented.

Management recommendations for Thorne's Hairstreak include increased awareness of this species, particularly to those individuals and agencies involved in the environmental review process, and increased fire control and fire management on Otay Mountain. Much of Otay Mountain is under the ownership of the United States Bureau of Land Management. Consequently, much of this land is likely to remain an open space. Thorne's Hairstreak presently is recognized by the United States Fish and Wildlife Service as a category 2 candidate species for listing as endangered or threatened; the Service recently received a petition to list the species as threatened. Such a listing would increase significantly the protection afforded this species.

References

BALLMER, G. and PRATT, G. 1989 (1988). A survey of last instar larvae of the Lycaenidae of California. *J. Res. Lepid.* **27**: 1–70.

BROWN, J.W. 1983. A new species of *Mitoura* Scudder from southern California. *J. Res. Lepid.* **21**: 245–254.

COMSTOCK, J.A. and DAMMERS, C.M. 1932a. Metamorphosis of five California diurnals (Lepidoptera). *Bull. South Calif. Acad. Sci.* **13**: 33–45.

COMSTOCK, J.A. and DAMMERS, C.M. 1932b. Metamorphosis of six California Lepidoptera. *Bull. South Calif. Acad. Sci.* **13**: 88–100.

COOLIDGE, K.R. 1924. The life history of *Mitoura loki* Skinner (Lepid.: Lycaenidae). *Entomol. News* **35**: 199–204.

FERRIS, C. 1989. Supplement to the catalogue/checklist of the butterflies of America north of Mexico. *Mem. Lepid. Soc.* **3**: 1–103.

GARTH, J. and TILDEN, J.W. 1986. *California Butterflies.* University of California Press, Berkeley. 246 pp.

HOLLAND, R. 1986. Preliminary descriptions of the terrestrial natural communities of California. State of California, Department of Fish and Game. 156 pp.

ORSAK, L.J. 1977. Butterflies of Orange County. *Univ. Calif. Irvine, Mus. Syst. Biol. Res. ser.* **4**. 349 pp.

SCOTT, J.A. 1986. *The Butterflies of North America.* Stanford University Press, Stanford, Calif. 583 pp.

SHIELDS, O. 1984. Comments on recent papers regarding western Cupressaceae-feeding *Callophrys (Mitoura). Utahensis* **4**: 51–56.

ZEDLER, P.H. 1977. Life history attributes of plants and fire cycles; a case study in chaparral dominated by *Cupressus forbesi*. pp. 451–458. *In:* Mooney, H.A. and L.E. Conrad (tech. coords.), *Proceedings of the Symposium on the Environmental Consequences of Fire and Fuel Management on Mediterranean Ecosystems.* Palo Alto, Calif.

Sweadner's Hairstreak, *Mitoura gryneus sweadneri* (Chermock)

Thomas C. Emmel

Department of Zoology, University of Florida, Gainesville, Florida 32611, U.S.A.

Country: U.S.A.

Status and Conservation Interest: Status – rare, threatened.

This local butterfly was described from the city of St. Augustine on the northeastern coast of Florida, a site which remains the centre of this rarity's distribution in the state. Virtually everywhere, it is threatened by reduced available habitat due to land clearing for housing and other development. In late 1986, after learning of the trend towards irreversible habitat loss for the Sweadner's Hairstreak, the mayor of St. Augustine led a drive to enact a city ordinance to protect the butterfly and its only known native foodplant. St. Augustine thus became the second city in the United States to protect a threatened butterfly site by law. (Pacific Grove on the central California coast protects the overwintering colonies of the common Monarch butterfly, *Danaus plexippus*.)

Taxonomy and Description: The butterfly was described in 1944 by noted lepidopterist Frank H. Chermock. Chermock named it as a distinct species, *Mitoura sweadneri*. A.B. Klots (1951) listed it as a subspecies of *M. gryneus* in his popular field guide, and it has been referred to as a subspecies ever since. In 1993, Emmel, Baggett and Fee will publish a paper elevating the taxon to full specific status again, based on life history characteristics, hybrid crossing studies, and genitalic differences.

Distribution: Sweadner's Hairstreak is considered very local and usually very rare. It has been found in several sites in the present city limits of Jacksonville, south through St. Augustine to New Smyrna Beach on the east coast of Florida, and several colonies are now known on the Gulf coast of Florida around Crystal River north to Cedar Key. Each colony is quite separated geographically from the others.

Population Size and Status: All colonies are very isolated and generally quite small in number (from 12 to 50 adults normally being present). The adults of both sexes appear to occupy a small home range, generally on a single large cedar tree or on several closely adjacent cedars. However, the males are strongly territorial and chase other adults that enter their defended areas.

Thus, a maximum of three or four adults may be found spaced around a single tree.

Habitat and Ecology: The butterfly lives in sandy coastal habitat occupied by its only known native foodplant, the Southern Red Cedar (*Juniperus silicicola*). These coniferous trees support both the immature stages and the adults, although the adults depend on locally growing wildflowers near the base of the trees for nectar.

The egg of Sweadner's Hairstreak is pale green, and the young larva is superbly coloured to match the plant and scale-like leaves of the cedar twig. The mature larva is flat and slug-like in shape, and has a deep green ground colour with pale green diagonal stripes high on the sides. The pupa is dark brown and serves as the hibernating stage for the species during the short north Florida winter. The species has three annual broods (spring, summer, fall).

For unknown reasons, the butterfly seems to be rather tightly adapted to coastal climates and is rarely found very far inland, despite the much wider inland distribution of Southern Red Cedars.

Threats: The greatest threat to the species is continued development of the coastal habitat for housing resulting from urban expansion and the desire for recreational beach homes. Other threats include road construction, dump clearing, and related land disturbances which have destroyed many of the formerly available habitats for the species. Finally, even if the red cedar trees are left in the area by the government ordinance requirements, the multiple-brooded adults may not survive if the proper wildflowers are not left in close association with the surviving trees. Without nectar, the adults die within a day or two, prior to reproducing.

Conservation: The conservation needs of Sweadner's Hairstreak lie not only in legal protection of its native foodplant but also in protecting strips of native vegetation associated with those Southern Red Cedar trees. The butterfly can survive in a remarkably small area (even 20m^2), as long as nectar sources are left in association with the red cedar trees. Popular support in the cities of Jacksonville, St. Augustine, and St. Augustine Beach has led to the passing of several civic ordinances since 1986 by those urban areas to preserve the butterfly and its foodplant. Additionally, the cities are reducing pesticide spraying for mosquito control in butterfly colony areas. There is considerable hope now that the loss of developmentally attractive coastal areas having Southern Red Cedar and Sweadner's Hairstreak colonies may be arrested (Emmel 1987).

References

EMMEL, T.C. 1987. Delicate balance: Sweadner's Hairstreak butterfly *(Mitoura gryneus sweadneri)*. *Florida Wildlife* **41** (2): 39.

KLOTS, A.B. 1951. *A Field Guide to the Butterflies*. Houghton Mifflin Co., Boston, Massachusetts. 349 pp.

Bartram's Hairstreak, *Strymon acis bartrami* (Comstock & Huntington)

Thomas C. EMMEL and Marc C. Minno

Department of Zoology, University of Florida, Gainesville, Florida 32611, U.S.A.

Country: U.S.A.

Status and Conservation Interest: Status – rare; indeterminate (Red List).

Bartram's hairstreak is classified as a threatened species because of its restricted distribution, low abundance, and recent loss of habitat.

Taxonomy and Description: This subspecies is restricted to Florida and was described in 1943 by Comstock & Huntington. It is characterised by the heaviest white markings of all the subspecies of *Strymon acis*. The species ranges from Florida throughout the West Indies to Dominica (Riley 1975). Typical *Strymon acis* from Antigua and Dominica form the largest race. *S. a. petioni* Comstock & Huntington occurs on Hispaniola and has gray undersides. *S. a. mars* Fabricius from the Virgin Islands, St. Kitts, and Puerto Rico has brown on the underside and a large orange area. *S. a. gossei* Comstock & Huntington from Jamaica and the Cayman Island resembles the last subspecies in the narrowness of the white bands, but the submarginal zone is broader. The Bahamas subspecies *armouri* Clench has narrow white bands and a narrow submarginal marking area. The Cuban subspecies *casasi* Comstock & Huntington is very similar to *bartrami* in Florida, with heavy white markings. The scientific and common name of Bartram's Hairstreak for the Florida population honours the memory of William Bartram, an early Florida naturalist whose journeys through the state first brought wide recognition of its unique natural history.

Distribution: This attractive little hairstreak is found only in southern Dade County, including the Everglades National Park, and on Big Pine Key in the Florida Keys. Hurricane Andrew may have severely impacted the mainland population of this butterfly on 24 August 1992, as it moved directly through the known colonies of this butterfly when crossing southern Dade County.

Population Size: Thirty field surveys, conducted by Hennessey and Habeck (1991) between 23 May and 16 December 1988, found an average of 0.5 adults per hectare in pineland habitats of the Everglades National Park and 0.3, 1.0 and 2.7 individuals per hectare at three locations on Big Pine Key. The status of mainland populations following Hurricane Andrew is not yet known at the time of writing (December 1992).

Habitat and Ecology: Bartram's Hairstreak is a small grayish butterfly with two pairs of delicate tails on the hindwings. The undersides of the hindwings have a highly distinctive pattern of white spots and lines, plus a red eyespot at the base of the tail. It occurs in open tropical pinelands that have an abundance of the larval hostplant. Females lay their eggs singly on the flowers of Woolly Croton, *Croton linearis*. The larvae feed on the flowers and leaves of the host. Adults frequently perch on Woolly Crotons and visit nearby flowers for nectar. Several generations are produced each year.

Threats: The primary threats to this species are housing developments and agricultural clearing in the heavily crowded southern Dade County area. However, the natural disaster presented by the tremendously destructive Hurricane Andrew winds, on 24 August 1992, may have destroyed or severely affected all the remaining habitat areas on the mainland. On both Big Pine Key in the Florida Keys and in southern Dade County, open tropical pinelands are also threatened periodically by fire.

Conservation: Additional surveys are badly needed now to monitor the abundance and distribution of Bartram's Hairstreak in both southern Dade County and the Florida Keys. Ecological studies should be conducted to identify the species' habitat requirements. Prescribed burning of pinelands may be necessary to maintain habitat for this species (Hennessey and Habeck 1991), but land managers should take care not to burn large tracts entirely, lest populations of Bartram's Hairstreak and other rare butterflies be destroyed by the fire. Careful management planning is needed for the remaining habitat in the Keys and in the Everglades National Park. The species is an attractive butterfly and could be used in publicity campaigns advocating preservation of these increasingly rare tropical pineland habitats in Florida (Minno and Emmel 1993).

References

HENNESSEY, M.K. and HABECK, D.H. 1991. Effects of mosquito adulticides on populations of non-target terrestrial arthropods in the Florida Keys. Unpublished final report. U.S. Fish and Wildlife Service and University of Florida Cooperative Wildlife Research Unit, Gainesville, Florida.

MINNO, M.C. and EMMEL, T.C. 1993. *Butterflies of the Florida Keys*. Scientific Publishers, Gainesville, Florida. 168 pp.

RILEY, N.D. 1975. *A Field Guide to the Butterflies of the West Indies*. Demeter Press, Inc., Boston, Massachusetts. 224 pp.

The Avalon Hairstreak, *Strymon avalona* (W.G. Wright)

Thomas C. EMMEL and John F. EMMEL

Department of Zoology, University of Florida, Gainesville, Florida 32611, U.S.A., and 26500 Rim Road, Hemet, California 92544, U.S.A.

Country: U.S.A.

Status and Conservation Interest: Status – insufficiently known (Wells *et al.* 1983, Red List).

This hairstreak is one of the world's most restricted species, being found only on Santa Catalina Island just slightly more than 20 miles off the coast from Los Angeles, southern California. The limited land available for development in southern California, including Santa Catalina, means that ultimately this species is threatened by development. Proximate dangers include overgrazing and other destruction by cattle and feral livestock such as goats.

Possible hybridisation with the related *S. melinus* (which was recorded from Santa Catalina for the first time in 1978) has been suggested, but such claims are probably inaccurate (Gall 1985; Gorelick 1987).

Taxonomy and Description: This species was described by W.G. Wright in 1905 from the vicinity of Avalon on Catalina Island. It does not occur on any of the other Channel Islands, where a related species, the Gray Hairstreak (*Strymon melinus* Hübner) may be found. No geographic variation has been noted in *Strymon avalona* on Santa Catalina Island.

Distribution: This species occurs only on Santa Catalina Island, off the coast of southern California.

Population Size: The Avalon Hairstreak is common in select localities such as the hills around Avalon. The butterfly is generally distributed in various localities from an elevational range of sea level to 65m. A number of colonies have been reported along the road to Renton Mine, Pebbly Beach, Jewfish Point, the Isthmus, and hills to the west of Avalon.

Habitat and Ecology: The species prefers chaparral and grass-covered slopes at relatively low elevations. Captures have been reported in every month of the year, with the first brood primarily occurring from mid-February through April, a second brood in July and August, and a third brood flying from September to November. The adults frequently perch on bushes and grassy areas in chaparral, and visit the flowers of common sumac (*Rhus alurina*) and the giant buckwheat (*Eriogonum giganteum* Wats.).

Eggs are laid singly, usually in the terminal buds or on immature flowers of the foodplant, *Lotus argophyllus* (Gray) Greene var. *ornithopus* (Greene) Ottley, and *Lotus scoparius* (Nutt.) Ottley, in the Leguminosae. Mature larvae show considerable variation in ground colour, ranging from a pale apple green to pale pink. The entire body of the larva, except the cervical shield, is covered with short white fine hairs. The pupa is pale pinkish-brown or wood brown with markings of various shades of olive-green. Pupation occurs at the base of the foodplant, with the usual support of a delicate silk girdle (Emmel, Emmel and Mattoon in press).

Threats: The species is not known to be endangered at the present time, although increased urbanisation or changes in vegetation cover due to overgrazing by domestic and feral livestock constitute potential threats every year. No special conservation measures have been taken on Santa Catalina Island for this butterfly.

Conservation: The widespread continental species *Strymon melinus* has not yet become successfully established on Santa Catalina Island. Likewise, this rare endemic *Strymon avalona* has not established itself on any of the other Channel Islands or on the mainland of North America. The situation should be monitored yearly to better understand why *Strymon melinus* in particular, has not managed to establish itself yet on Santa Catalina Island where many of its potential foodplants are growing.

References

EMMEL, T.C., EMMEL, J.F. and MATTOON, S.O. In press. *The Butterflies of California*. Stanford University Press, Stanford, California.

GALL, L.F. 1985. Santa Catalina's endemic Lepidoptera. II. The Avalon Hairstreak, *Strymon avalona*, and its interaction with the recently introduced Gray Hairstreak, *Strymon melinus* (Lycaenidae). *In:* Menke, A.S. and Miller, D.R. (Eds). *Proc. 1st Symposium on Entomology of the California Islands*. Santa Barbara Museum of Natural History, pp. 95–104.

GORELICK, G.A. 1987. Santa Catalina's endemic Lepidoptera. II. The Avalon Hairstreak, *Strymon avalona* (Lycaenidae): an ecological study. *Atala* 14 (1986): 1–12.

WELLS, S.M., PYLE, R.M. and COLLINS, N.M. 1983. *The IUCN Invertebrate Red Data Book*. IUCN, Gland, Switzerland.

The Atala Butterfly, *Eumaeus atala florida* (Röber)

Thomas C. EMMEL and Marc C. MINNO

Department of Zoology, University of Florida, Gainesville, Florida 32611, U.S.A.

Country: U.S.A.

Status and Conservation Interest: Status – out of danger; vulnerable (Red List).

The Atala butterfly is one of the most strikingly coloured butterflies in Florida and it is desirable to collectors. Its conservation interest arises from the fact that the species was feared extirpated in the early 1970s after the few known colonies died out, but then made a spectacular recovery starting in 1979 from a single small colony rediscovered in the Miami area. The species has recovered much of its former range and is now even considered a pest of ornamental cycad plantings! It is assessed as relatively common in parts of southern Florida (Bowers and Larin 1989; Minno and Emmel 1993).

This species was the subject of one of three full lycaenid entries in the IUCN Invertebrate Red Data Book (Wells *et al.* 1983), and one of six butterflies discussed in the Invertebrate volume of Franz (1982). It gave its name '*Atala*' to a journal published by the Xerces Society.

Taxonomy and Description: The subspecies was described by Röber in 1926, on the basis of having more extensive blue-green on the upper side and larger spots of that colour on the underside of the hindwings. The typical subspecies, *Eumaeus atala atala* Poey (1832), occurs in Cuba, on Andros Island, and on Great Abaco Island in the Bahamas (Riley 1975). Some lepidopterists have questioned if the Florida population is sufficiently distinct to be called a separate race (Clench 1977).

Distribution: The Atala Butterfly is found in southern Florida from Broward County in the vicinity of Fort Lauderdale south to southern Dade County, and it is recorded historically from Elliott Key and Key Largo (the most recent record for the latter Key being 5 June 1960). Most of the populations in southern Dade County were probably severely impacted by Hurricane Andrew on 24 August 1992.

Population Size: The Atala Butterfly was once abundant in the rimrock areas of the southern mainland of Florida, but large-scale harvesting of the host plant, coontie (*Zamia pumila*, Cycadaceae) for starch in the late 1800s greatly reduced the number of coontie plants. Urbanisation and development of the coastal habitat favoured by the Atala also had a large impact. By 1965, the Atala had been reduced to a single known population in Hugh Taylor Birch State Park. After this colony died out, the Atala was feared extirpated from Florida. However, in the late 1970s, another colony was found on Virginia Key in the Miami area. Conservationists such as Roger Hamler of Dade County Parks set out potted coontie plants on which females laid eggs. Plants with eggs were then moved to other locations and new colonies were started. Rawson (1961) demonstrated the possibility of translocating *E. atala* by liberating adults in a new site.

The Atala has made a spectacular recovery and is now found in urban and natural areas around Fort Lauderdale and Miami, and has been successfully introduced into the Everglades National Park. Some plant nurseries and botanical gardens currently consider the Atala a pest species, as the larvae are capable of defoliating *Zamia* species used in landscaping. It is not known whether our current population is of original Florida stock or the result of a new introduction from the Bahamas or Cuba.

The very few records of Atala from the Florida Keys include only Elliot Key and Key Largo (Schwartz 1888). Small (1913) listed coontie among the plants found in the Keys, but we have not encountered it on any of the islands. The early pioneers probably extirpated coontie (and thereby the butterfly) from the Keys, as it was a readily available source of starch. The only modern record of the Atala from the Keys is the single capture of a male on 5 June 1960 in the City of Key Largo. The status of the populations on the mainland was probably severely impacted by Hurricane Andrew on 24 August 1992, and subsequent surveys have not yet been done to ascertain the species' status on the mainland.

Habitat and Ecology: The Atala is found in tropical pinelands and hardwood hammocks in close association with the larval foodplant, coontie (*Zamia pumila*, Cycadaceae). The Atala adults are the largest lycaenids in Florida and occur all year round. It is one of the most strikingly coloured butterflies on its ventral surfaces, with jet black wings, iridescent blue spots and a red patch on the underside of the hindwings. The upper wings are black with iridescent green in males and iridescent blue in females, while the abdomen is bright red. The adults have a slow fluttering flight pattern. Males perch on the leaves of shrubs and make circular flights around the perch site like other hairstreaks. Both sexes often visit flowers.

The white eggs are laid in clusters on the young growth of coontie. Larvae are bright red with a yellow spot, and are probably distasteful to birds or other predators. Pupae are brown with small dark spots and hang from the substrate by a silk girdle. Droplets of bitter tasting liquid are exuded over the cuticle of the pupae.

Threats: The Atala is listed as a species of special concern in Florida because of its restricted distribution and cyclic fluctuations in abundance. This butterfly is currently known from more colonies on the mainland than were recorded before 1965, but the Atala has lost habitat areas formerly occupied in the Florida Keys. Hurricane Andrew probably severely impacted populations of the Atala in southern Dade County.
Continued threats occur in both wild and urban areas. The Atala occurs in tropical hardwood hammocks and pinelands in close association with the host plant. It also now uses some urban areas such as gardens and nurseries where the foodplant is grown as an ornamental. Thus this species is exposed to both habitat clearing and burning in the wild (although prescribed burning of pinelands may be necessary to maintain habitat). Spraying or other pest control measures in urban habitats pose another threat. For example, before Hurricane Andrew, Fairchild Botanical Garden in southern Dade County regularly used Bti sprays to control the infestation of the Atala Butterfly on its valuable cycad collection (from the 1980s through summer 1992).

Conservation: The unexpected occurrence of wide habitat destruction by Hurricane Andrew in the summer of 1992 necessitates new surveys to monitor the distribution and abundance of the Atala in Florida. Outside of the affected urban areas, prescribed burning of pinelands may be necessary to maintain habitat for Atalas in natural settings. The species is probably permanently lost from the Florida Keys, unless restoration plantings of the coontie host plants are done on Big Pine Key where some substantial tropical pinelands remain (there are no pinelands left on Elliot Key or Key Largo, its originally recorded habitat in the Florida Keys). Taxonomic studies should be conducted to determine if the current taxon present in south Florida is the same as that present before 1965, and to define the relationship of *E. atala florida* to *E. atala atala* in the Bahamas.

References

BOWERS, M.D. and LARIN, Z. 1989. Acquired chemical defense in the lycaenid butterfly, *Eumaeus atala. J. Chem. Ecol.* **15**: 1133–1146.

CLENCH, H.K. 1977. A list of the butterflies of Andros, Bahamas. *Ann. Carnegie Mus.* **46**: 173–194.

FRANZ, R. (Ed.) 1982. *Rare and Endangered Biota of Florida. 6. Invertebrates.* University Presses of Florida.

MINNO, M.C. and EMMEL, T.C. 1993. *Butterflies of the Florida Keys.* Scientific Publishers, Gainesville, Florida. 168 pp.

RAWSON, G.W. 1961. The recent rediscovery of *Eumaeus atala* (Lycaenidae) in southern Florida. *J. Lepid. Soc.* **15**: 237–244.

RILEY, N.D. 1975. *A Field Guide to the Butterflies of the West Indies.* Demeter Press, Inc., Boston, Massachusetts. 224 pp.

SCHWARTZ, E.A. 1888. Notes on *Eumaeus atala. Insect Life* **1**: 37–40.

SMALL, J.K. 1913. *Flora of the Florida Keys.* Published by the author, New York. 162 pp.

WELLS, S.M., PYLE, R.M. and COLLINS, N.M. 1983. *The IUCN Invertebrate Red Data Book.* IUCN, Gland.

Smith's Blue, *Euphilotes enoptes smithi* (Mattoni)

Thomas C. EMMEL and John F. EMMEL

Department of Zoology, University of Florida, Gainesville, Florida 32611, U.S.A., and 26500 Rim Road, Hemet, California 92544, U.S.A.

Country: U.S.A.

Status and Conservation Interest: Status – endangered (Red List).

This butterfly is known only from the coastal fog belt of Monterey County in California, where it inhabits the immediate coast of the Big Sur country. A member of a widely distributed western U.S. species, *Euphilotes enoptes smithi* is an endemic California subspecies whose coastal habitat has suffered a number of disturbances, including beach recreation and off-road vehicles. Montane habitats, in general, have suffered less (Arnold 1983a,b).

Taxonomy and Description: The subspecies was described (Mattoni 1954) as different from the numerous other subspecies of *Euphilotes enoptes* in part because of the broad black marginal borders on the lustrous blue upper wings of the males. Females are brown above, with a band of red-orange marks across the hindwings. The overall distinguishing features from other subspecies are the light undersurface ground colour and prominent black markings with a faint black terminal line (Emmel, Emmel and Mattoon in press).

The male is distinguished by the broad marginal border of the hindwings. The ventral surface of both males and females has a faint terminal line and a light ground colour with large prominent spots.

Distribution: This species is confined to coastal Monterey County from Big Sur and the mouth of the Salinas River southward to Del Rey Creek and an area several miles north of the San Luis Obispo County line. It ranges from near sea level to approximately 65m elevation. The type locality is at Burns Creek, State Highway 1, in Monterey County.

Population Size: Populations are small in number and probably have never been particularly large because of the relatively restricted habitat.

Habitat and Ecology: The Smith's Blue butterfly occurs on cliffs, steep slopes, and road cuts along the immediate coast, within the northern coastal scrub plant community. It also is found extensively on coastal and inland sand dunes, and occasionally on serpentine grassland.

The adults emerge between mid-June and early September, corresponding with the blooming of the buckwheat plants on which they feed, rest, sun, and mate. While each adult lives for only about one week, individual emergences are scattered over the extended flight period. Females deposit eggs singly in buckwheat flowers. Larvae hatch 4–8 days later and go through five instars before pupating in flowerheads or in the litter and sand at the base of the plant. Pupae hang in place from September until adults emerge the following year. The verified host plant for the larvae is *Eriogonum parvifolium* Sm. in Rees. (Pratt and Ballmer 1989). Larvae also feed on *E. latifolium*, and differences in plant phenology at different sites may represent a potential isolating mechanism for populations.

Threats: The primary threat to the conservation and recovery of the Smith's Blue butterfly is the wide variety of man-made disturbances of the coastal habitat. Dunes are widely threatened by beach recreation, off-road vehicles, housing developments, and road construction. Additionally, non-native plants such as iceplant and Holland dunegrass invade the dunes and displace native buckwheat. At Fort Ord, the sand dunes have been damaged by military vehicles and infantry exercises. At the Seaside-Marina dune system and the Del Monte Forest, their habitat has been destroyed by sand mining. More than half the dune habitat present at the turn of the century had been destroyed by about 1980 (Powell 1981).

Conservation: A conservation plan for Smith's Blue designed by Arnold (1983b) was one of the first detailed prescriptions for a North American lycaenid. Prevention of further habitat loss or change was the prime need, and Arnold's plan aimed to maintain known populations of *E. e. smithi* by coordinating habitat preservation, rehabilitation and management.

Five categories of action were proposed: (1) preservation and protection of existing habitats; (2) implementation of short-term and long-term management; (3) development of monitoring programmes to census selected populations annually to assess the effects of management efforts; (4) promotion of public awareness of the butterfly and its habitat, and (5) enforcement of laws and regulations to protect the butterfly.

This species was listed as Endangered on June 1, 1976. In 1977, the U.S. Army established a butterfly preserve at Fort Ord, and some of the non-native plants have been removed there as well as native plants re-established. For remnant sand dune habitats at Sand City in Monterey County, the city agreed to complete a conservation plan before proceeding with any work in the dune areas that have been zoned for housing development.

References

ARNOLD, R.A. 1983a. Ecological studies on six endangered butterflies (Lepidoptera: Lycaenidae): Island biogeography, patch dynamics, and the design of habitat preserves. *Univ. Calif. Publns Entomol.* **99**: 1–161.

ARNOLD, R.A. 1983b. Conservation and management of the endangered Smith's Blue Butterfly, *Euphilotes enoptes smithi* (Lepidoptera: Lycaenidae). *J. Res. Lepid.* **22**: 135–153.

EMMEL, T.C., EMMEL, J.F. and MATTOON, S.O. In press. *The Butterflies of California*. Stanford University Press, Stanford, California.

MATTONI, R.H.T. 1954. Notes on the genus *Philotes*. 1. Description of three new subspecies and a synoptic list. *Bull. South. Calif. Acad. Sci.* **53**: 157–165.

POWELL, J.A. 1981. Endangered habitats for insects: California coastal sand dunes. *Atala* **6**: 41–55.

PRATT, G.P. and BALLMER, G.R. 1989. A survey of the last instar larvae of the Lycaenidae (Lepidoptera) of California. *J. Res. Lepid.* **27**: 1–81.

The El Segundo Blue, *Euphilotes bernardino allyni* (Shields)

R.H.T. MATTONI

9620 Heather Road, Beverly Hills, California 90210, U.S.A.

Country: U.S.A.(California).

Status and Conservation Interest: Status – endangered (Red List).

This subspecies is a sand obligate ecotype found only on the El Segundo sand dune ecosystem of the coastal plain of western Los Angeles. Its remaining three discrete colonies are surrounded by a dense urban area that remains both a fast growing and fast denaturing area. As a federally listed endangered species, the El Segundo Blue (ESB) is significant in conferring an umbrella of protection on at least ten other species of plant and animals that are restricted to this sand dune system and to more than 20 species restricted to the coastal sand dunes of southern California and northern Baja California.

Taxonomy and Description: The subspecies was described by Shields (1975) from the El Segundo sand dunes of Los Angeles county just prior to its listing among the first group of butterflies to be legally recognised as endangered by the Endangered Species Act of 1973. The taxon was originally classified as a subspecies of *E. battoides*, but both Shields (Shields 1975, Reveal and Shields 1988) and Mattoni (1989) independently diagnosed *allyni* as more logically belonging to the *bernardino* group of four related but clearly separated subspecies which they recognised as a distinct species.

Distribution: The ESB was historically restricted to the El Segundo sand dunes that covered about 1200ha. Today three discrete colonies exist on fragments that still maintain some characteristics of the natural community.

Population Size: The largest population is on property of the Los Angeles International Airport (LAX), where 80ha were recently set aside by the city of Los Angeles as a biological preserve, in part to satisfy biotic requirements of the butterfly. When serious study started in 1984, total population size was about 500. Following restoration efforts the standing population in 1990 was about 4000 (Mattoni 1988, 1990a, b, 1992). The second largest colony is on a 0.6ha lot on the Chevron Oil refinery property. The population prior to study was about 2000 and has since decreased to under 500 (Arnold 1983, 1986). A small colony of a few hundred butterflies persists on a 0.2ha isolated dune fragment at Redondo Beach. The latter was discovered in 1984.

Habitat and Ecology: The species is sand obligate and adapted to a single foodplant, the coastal buckwheat, *Eriogonum parvifolium*, (Polygonaceae). It has one generation per year, adults appearing from June through mid-August. Excepting the fossorial diapausing pupal stage, the entire life cycle of the butterfly is associated with flowerheads of the buckwheat including egg deposition, larval growth, nectaring, mating and dying (Mattoni 1991). The larvae are ant associated, but the relationship is facultative and the only ant now noted in association is the exotic Argentine ant, *Iridomyrmex humilis*. Adult butterflies were highly sedentary at the tiny Chevron site (Arnold 1983), but nothing is known of movements at LAX beyond observed concentrations near dense patches of foodplant.

Threats: Pratt (1987) first recognised that the major threat to the ESB at LAX was the presence of a dense common buckwheat stand which had been planted during a poorly conceived restoration effort 20 years earlier. This earlier flowering species provided sustenance to a guild of non-diapausing Lepidoptera that later migrated to the flowering coastal buckwheat. Overwhelming numbers, cannibalism, and shared parasites devastated the ESB. Removal of part of the exotic plant biomass was believed a major cause of the recent resurgence of ESB populations (Mattoni 1991).

The ESB at the Chevron site, while serving as a linchpin in the oil company's advertising campaign to show its concern for nature, precipitously declined (Arnold 1986). The cause was probably an intensive mark-release programme to assess population size, coupled with extreme trampling across a small area. The Redondo Beach site is completely untended, but is not suitable for building development and is thus not threatened by developers.

Conservation: Listing the ESB under the federal Endangered Species Act provides one of the greatest success stories of that legislation. For the principal colony at LAX, the 1976 listing happened just in time to halt a plan to develop almost the entire

120ha of dunes as a golf course. Following a protracted planning and political process, the preserve area increased in size. Under leadership of the local Councilwoman, the Mayor and Airport Commission agreed to set aside 80ha of the highest quality land as a permanent preserve with the proviso that the golf course on the remaining 40ha be designed with all rough areas re-planted habitat.

In the meantime, the Airport Commission provided $180,000 to begin restoration of the dunes ecosystem. Work on the dunes is now in its third year.

By contrast, the Chevron company has emphasised creating conditions to maximise survival of the ESB, at the expense of the ecosystem. The main effort has been directed towards creating a butterfly garden; because the site is so small, this approach has some validity. On the other hand long-term stability would be better insured with a community mimicking that of the historic system, and not a near monoculture of the foodplant with more glamorous advertising potential. Oppewall (1975) documents efforts by local collectors who successfully convinced Chevron to set aside the area as a preserve. For this, the company is to be commended.

References

ARNOLD, R.A. 1983. Ecological studies of six endangered butterflies (Lepidoptera, Lycaenidae): Island biogeography, patch dynamics, and the design of habitat preserves. *Univ. Calif. Publns Entomol.* **99**. 161pp.

ARNOLD, R.A. 1986. Private and government funded conservation programs for endangered insects in California. *Natural Areas Journal* **5**: 28–39.

MATTONI, R.H.T. 1988. *Captive propagation of California endangered butterflies.* Report to Calif. Dept. Fish and Game. Contract C-1456.

MATTONI, R.H.T. 1989. The *Euphilotes battoides* complex: Recognition of a species and description of a new subspecies. *J. Res. Lepid.* **27**: 173–185.

MATTONI, R.H.T. 1990a. *Habitat evaluation and species diversity on the LAX El Segundo sand dunes.* Rept. to the LAX board of airport commissioners.

MATTONI, R.H.T. 1990b. *Unnatural acts: succession on the El Segundo sand dunes in California. In:* Hughes, H.G. and T.M. Bonnickson (Eds.) *Proc. first SER Conference, Berkeley, CA 1989.* Soc. Ecol. Restoration, Madison WI 53711.

MATTONI, R.H.T. 1992. The endangered El Segundo blue butterfly. *J. Res. Lepid.* **29**: 277–304 (1990).

OPPEWALL, J.C. 1975. The saving of the El Segundo Blue. *Atala* **3**: 25–8.

PRATT, G. 1987. Competition as a controlling factor of *Euphilotes battoides allyni* larval abundance. *Atala* **15**: 1–9.

SHIELDS, O. 1975. Studies on North American *Philotes* IV. Taxonomic and biological notes and new subspecies. *Bull. Allyn Museum* No. **28**. 36pp.

SHIELDS, O. and REVEAL, J. 1988. Sequential evolution of *Euphilotes* (Lycaenidae, Scolitantidini) on their plant host *Eriogonum* (Polygonaceae, Eriogonoideae). *J. Linn. Soc.* **33**: 51–91.

The Palos Verdes Blue, *Glaucopsyche lygdamus palosverdesensis* Perkins and Emmel

R.H.T. Mattoni

9620 Heather Road, Beverly Hills, California 90210, U.S.A.

Country: U.S.A. (California)

Status and Conservation Interest: Status – probably extinct (Red List).

The subspecies, now certainly extinct, was a coastal bluff ecotype found only on the southern half of the Palos Verdes peninsula in southern Los Angeles county. The species has high conservation value, nonetheless, as it has not been officially delisted under the theory that extinction is not certain. Hence all building projects in the species distribution area – and there are many – must recognise habitat value. At least one major development is currently stalled waiting approval of a plan to protect foodplants. The great benefit of the situation is provision of protection to other endangered species, now unlisted, occurring in the habitat.

Taxonomy and Description: The subspecies was described by Perkins and Emmel (1977) from Los Angeles county just prior to its listing among the second group of butterflies to be legally recognised as endangered by the Endangered Species Act. The taxon was diagnosed as a subspecies distinct from, *Glaucopsyche lygdamus australis*, the southern blue, by exclusive use of the milk vetch *Astragalus leucopsis*, very fast flight, and several wing characteristics.

Distribution. By the time of its discovery by Perkins in the early 1970s, the Palos Verdes Blue (PVB) was already restricted to a few fragments retaining some natural characteristics. In 1977 at least nine discrete colonies existed. The last known occurrence was in 1983.

Population Size: The largest populations known during the brief time span the PVB was extant were at Atala Vista Terrace (type locality) and in the scrub extending from Palos Verdes Drive east to Friendship Park. The former locality was built over in 1978. Population sizes were never estimated and by the early 1980s numbers were extremely low, probably less than 100 adults among all the remaining fragments at that time (Arnold 1985). In spring of 1982 at Hesse Park, I counted six adults on the best day, with some 20 plants. Each plant had at least 100 eggs, and one plant over 500. Foodplant availability was limiting, probably due to spring disking for fire control.

Habitat and Ecology: The PVB was a coastal, sage-associated ecotype, restricted in foodplant use to the milk vetch. The vetch is restricted to the fog belt across southern exposures at elevations between 100 and 300 metres. The historical area probably occupied by the PVB was no more than 4000ha. The flora of the northwest slopes of the peninsula included the low shrub legume, *Lotus scoparious*, foodplant of the sister subspecies, *G. lygdamus australis*. Whether *australis* was parapatric to *palosverdesensis* is unknown.

The butterfly was single brooded with adult flight in February and March. Eggs were usually laid on flowerheads of the foodplant, but when foodplant numbers were diminished just prior to extinction, eggs were laid over the entire plant. Larvae usually fed on seed within developing seedpods of the vetch and were ant tended in the last two instars. The final known generation, observed at Hesse Park, had larvae feeding on leaves as well since the flowerheads and seeds were exhausted. Three other Lycaenid butterflies were associated with the flowerhead/seedpod guild: *Strymon melinus; Leptotes marina;* and *Everes amyntula*. The first two are polyphagous, have many alternative foodplants, and are widespread species. The latter, with the PVB is a monophage restricted to the vetch. It has been extirpated from the Palos Verdes peninsula, although the last specimens were sighted in 1986 (Jess Morton, Tony Leigh, pers. comm.).

Threats Leading to Extinction. Arnold (1986) reported the decline of the species and speculated that it had become extinct. Intensive search has been conducted by several local lepidopterists every year since 1983 without success. The proximate cause of extinction was denaturing of the land by development and fire suppression tactics. The historic population must have been continuous over the 4000ha coastal scrub habitat. With intensive development from 1950 the habitat was fragmented, although one 500ha section remains. Clearing practice so degraded this that the construction at Hesse Park in 1982, performed by the city of Rancho Palos Verdes in violation of the federal Endangered Species Act, destroyed the last remaining colony. The city was subsequently sued by the federal government, but this legal action was dismissed under the theory that the city could not be held liable.

Conservation. Ironically, a simple captive breeding method was developed in 1983 using the southern blue as a surrogate (Mattoni 1988). Had the technique been available the previous year, it would have been possible to have saved the species by captive breeding for later re-introduction into the habitat. Unfortunately the foodplant stands were continually being cleared for fire prevention and few plants now remain. It has been suggested (Mattoni unpublished) that an effort be implemented to release numbers of the southern blue, preadapted to feeding on vetch by captive mass rearing, into sites to be heavily restocked with vetch. This action would again grace the area with a butterfly that may evolve characteristics of its extinct relative. In addition to restoring natural biodiversity the plan would provide a demonstration of adaptive processes in a restored environment.

References

ARNOLD, R.A. 1985. *Palos Verdes blue butterfly management plan.* U.S.F. and W.S. informal report. 37pp.

ARNOLD, R.A. 1986. Decline of the endangered Palos Verdes blue butterfly in California. *Biol. Conserv.* **40**: 203–217.

MATTONI, R.H.T. 1988. *1988 report to California Department of Fish and Game, Contract C-1456.*

PERKINS, E.M. and EMMEL, J.F. 1977. A new subspecies of *Glaucopsyche lygdamus* from California (Lepidoptera: Lycaenidae). *Proc. Ent. Soc. Wash.* **79**: 468–471.

The Xerces Blue, *Glaucopsyche xerces* (Boisduval)

Thomas C. EMMEL and John F. EMMEL

Department of Zoology, University of Florida, Gainesville, Florida 32611, U.S.A., and 26500 Rim Road, Hemet, California 92544, U.S.A.

Country: U.S.A.

Status and Conservation Interest: Status – extinct (Red List).

The Xerces Blue, a former resident of the sand dunes in San Francisco, was the first butterfly species in North America to become extinct through human interference. (Two satyrines in the genus *Cercyonis* were the first subspecies of wider ranging U.S. species to disappear in historic times.) Today, an international organization devoted to the conservation of invertebrates, The Xerces Society, is named for this diminutive creature, a butterfly which has achieved fame far beyond its size and former restricted geographic distribution. From a scientific viewpoint, it was one of the most variable butterflies known and it would have made a unique tool for research on the effects of population size and geographic distribution on infra-specific variation. But for its untimely extinction, *G. xerces* would have contributed greatly to human knowledge in ecology and evolutionary biology.

Taxonomy and Description: The species was first described by Boisduval (1852) from one male and two females taken within the area now occupied by the city of San Francisco, in San Francisco County, California. These specimens were collected by Pierre Joseph Michel Lorquin, a French gold seeker and naturalist who arrived in San Francisco in late 1849 or early 1850 and apparently made his first shipment of specimens to Boisduval in the fall of 1851. Thus he had only two seasons at the most to collect the first set of specimens that he sent to Boisduval. While the species was extraordinarily variable, and several forms were named (originally thought to be separate species), all are presently referred to the nominotypical subspecies (Emmel, Emmel and Mattoon in press) and no geographic subspecies are recognized.

The closest living relative of the Xerces may well be a newly recognized subspecies of *Glaucopsyche lygdamus* residing on Santa Rosa Island, off the coast of southern California (Emmel and Emmel in press). The extraordinary phenotypic resemblance of the wing maculation of this new subspecies to that of *G. xerces* suggests a close phylogenetic relationship. The genitalia of *G. xerces* are very similar to those of *G. lygdamus*, and on the basis of male genitalia alone, the Xerces

Blue would have been assigned subspecific status under *lygdamus*. However, Downey and Lange (1956) pointed out considerable differences between these species in larval stages, adult wing maculation, and ecology. Additionally, the two species were once sympatric in San Francisco and hybrids were never detected.

Distribution: All recorded specimens are from San Francisco, and include the area presently covered by the city. The distribution on the San Francisco Peninsula ranged from near Twin Peaks to North Beach, and from the Presidio on the Bay southward to Lake Merced. Lone Mountain, formerly an isolated, sandy hill, was the classical locality for Xerces in the early 1900s.

Population Size: The only known colonies were in the San Francisco Bay area. No estimates of population size have come down to us in the early literature, but by comparison with the closely related *G. lygdamus* colonies in the area, we can guess that the typical size was several hundred individuals in a colony. By the year 1919, the only known population remaining was flying in a limited area west of the Marine Hospital, at the Presidio, San Francisco. The same area was still inhabited on March 23, 1941. The butterflies were then limited to a small area 21m wide by 46m long, in which *Lotus scoparius* was found. The last known specimens of Xerces were collected at the Presidio during May 1941 (Downey and Lange 1956), and many later visits to the area in search of the butterfly were fruitless.

Habitat and Ecology: The habitat of the PVB was sandy areas where a prostrate dune ecotype of the perennial legume, *Lotus scoparius* (Nutt.) Ottley, occurred. The butterfly typically occurred around patches of *Lotus* that grew in the partial shade of the Monterey Cypress (*Cupressus macrocarpa* Hartw.) in well-drained, sandy soil. *Lupinus arboreus* Sims, which also served the *Xerces* females as a hostplant for oviposition and larval growth, was widely distributed among the *Lotus*, and had a wider range than that of the *Lotus* and the butterflies. In 1956, the same association of plants at the last colony site remained essentially unchanged from 1941, and was also observed by the authors in 1963–67 in essentially unchanged condition. To the north, similar sandy areas with these *Lotus* and *Lupinus* species occur in Marin County, but the Monterey Cypress does not occur there. It appears that the expansion of the city of San Francisco into the natural sand dune habitat formerly available to *Glaucopsyche xerces* (and the other insects of the region) had destroyed too much of the habitat for the butterfly to continue to support a sustainable population beyond 1941.

The adults of Xerces flew in a single brood from about March 10 to April 15. However, specimens were taken from as early as late February to as late as early June. The flight, mating behaviour, and oviposition behaviour of Xerces were apparently similar to that of the other *Glaucopsyche* species of California. The female laid eggs singly in the small depression at the base of the leaflet on *Lupinus arboreus*, or laid eggs on new growth near the tips of the leaflets on *Lotus scoparius*. In 1939, it was observed that as many as nine eggs were laid per plant, and that the *Lotus* was slightly favoured by the females, with an average of 3–4 eggs per plant compared to 2 eggs per plant for the *Lupinus*.

The butterflies were associated with ants in their natural habitat although the ant associates were never identified. In the laboratory, larvae were fed substitute foodplants (*Lupinus micranthus* Dougl. and *Astragalus menziessii* Gray), and the captive larvae were raised without any ants so the species was not completely dependent on ants for successful maturation and pupation. The pale green larvae had long hairs on each side of the dorsal surface, and the whole body was covered with a whitish pile. The general colouration and pattern were variable, a trait found in other nearctic blue species today. The pupal colouration was highly variable. Diapause was in the pupal stage, with the length of that stage averaging from 10 to 11 months.

Threats: The decline of this fascinating butterfly and its final extinction in 1941 appears to be attributable solely to the expansion of the City of San Francisco in the preceding 60–80 years. This resulted in the removal of the native vegetation in the dunes and reduction of the remaining habitat areas to an unsustainable size. In such small populations, a minor change in climate or other environmental factor could prove devastating, especially to a species that flew in a single annual brood and had no options to react, little time or space, and a small genetic pool of variability. Collecting might have been detrimental also as the populations declined.

While a live Xerces Blue will never be seen again on Earth, the species has served as a remarkably effective symbol for the fragility of nature among American citizens and conservationists around the world. Scientific analysis of 344 historical specimens (Downey and Lange 1956) offer a hint as to the remarkable variation in this species and the annual changes of the frequency of pattern forms in the population.

References

BOISDUVAL, J.B.A.D. de. 1852. Lepidoptères de la Californie. *Ann. Soc. Entomol. France* (Series 2) **10**: 275–324.

DOWNEY, J.C. and LANGE, JR., W.H. 1956. Analysis of variation in a recently extinct polymorphic Lycaenid butterfly, *Glaucopsyche xerces* (Bdv.), with notes on its biology and taxonomy. *Bull. South. Calif. Acad. Sci.* **55** (3): 153–207.

EMMEL, T.C. and EMMEL, J.F. In press. A new *xerces*-like subspecies of *Glaucopsyche* (Lycaenidae) from Santa Rosa Island, California. *Systematics of Western North American Butterflies*. Scientific Publishers, Gainesville, Florida.

EMMEL, T.C., EMMEL, J.F. and MATTOON, S.O. In press. *The Butterflies of California*. Stanford University Press, Stanford, California.

The Mission Blue, *Plebejus icarioides missionensis* Hovanitz

J. Hall Cushman

Center for Conservation Biology, Department of Biological Sciences, Stanford University, Stanford, CA 94305, U.S.A.

Country: U.S.A.

Status and Conservation Interest: Status – endangered (Red List).

In 1976, the Mission Blue was officially listed as an endangered species by the U.S. Fish and Wildlife Service. The subspecies is also listed as endangered with the California Department of Fish and Game and almost all of its habitat protected as park land.

Taxonomy and Description: The Mission Blue is one of 12 recognized subspecies of the highly variable *Plebejus icarioides* and was first described by Hovanitz (1937).

Distribution: While *Plebejus icarioides* as a whole is patchily distributed throughout western North America, the present-day distribution of the Mission Blue subspecies is restricted to four known areas on the northern tip of San Francisco Peninsula. Although it is impossible to document the historical distribution of this subspecies, the Mission Blue almost certainly occurred throughout much of the coastal scrub habitat of the northern peninsula (Reid and Murphy 1986).

Population Size: The largest known Mission Blue population is on San Bruno Mountain (San Mateo Co.) and is estimated to consist of 18,000 adults. A substantial population is also found at Fort Baker (Marin Co.), although a precise estimate of its size is not available. Significantly smaller populations are found on Twin Peaks (San Francisco Co.) and the Skyline Ridges (San Mateo Co.), with estimates of 500 and 2000 adults, respectively (Reid and Murphy 1986).

Habitat and ecology: The Mission Blue has one generation per year, and adults fly from mid-April to mid-June. Adults live for up to one week, remain close to the larval host plant, and feed on nectar from a wide variety of plants, including *Eriogonum* (Polygonaceae) and numerous composites. Females oviposit on three lupine species, *Lupinus albifrons, L. formosus,* and *L. varicolor,* which are found in areas of recent disturbance and attain highest densities in grasslands on thin, rocky soils (Arnold 1983; Reid and Murphy 1986).

Females lay eggs on the leaves, stems, flowers, and seed pods of *Lupinus* hosts. The eggs are usually deposited singly and hatch in 4–10 days. After about three weeks, the second-instar larvae enter an obligatory diapause from which they emerge the following spring. These post-diapause larvae subsequently complete their development to adult in four to five weeks (Arnold 1983; Reid and Murphy 1986; Newcomer 1911).

The cryptically coloured larvae may exhibit significant age-specific differences in feeding behaviour. Downey (1962) noted that older larvae are most commonly found at the base of food plants while the younger larvae are substantially higher up on the host. Because of this, he postulated that the majority of mature larvae in this species are nocturnal feeders.

Juvenile stages of the Mission Blue are attacked by a variety of natural enemies. Arnold (1983) reported that 'Approximately 35% of field collected eggs were parasitised by an unidentified encyrtid wasp.' In addition, Newcomer (1911) and Downey (1962) both reported that the larval stages of *P. icarioides* were parasitized by various braconid and tachinid species.

As with many other lycaenid species, Mission Blue larvae are tended by ants. These associations have not received much attention (although see Downey 1962), and are thus poorly understood. However, the larvae are known to possess abdominal nectary glands which become active in the third or fourth instar and attract ants. Downey (1962) found that the butterfly could be reared successfully in the laboratory without ants, but makes no statements about how often older larvae are ant-tended in the field. Clearly, the importance of ants to the development and survival of Mission Blue larvae is very much an open question and requires further study.

Threats: Agricultural and urban expansion have resulted in the progressive loss of native grassland habitat and reduced exchange among existing Mission Blue populations. These major threats have been significantly reduced due to the habitat conservation plan mentioned in the following section. However, a remaining threat is the invasion of grassland habitats by non-native plant species. While lupine, the Mission Blue host plant, is relatively resistant to invasions of non-native grasses, it is quite susceptible to the invasion of woody species which create too much shade.

The major culprits in this regard are gorse (*Ulex europeaus*), blue gum (*Eucalyptus globulus*) and broom (*Cytisus* spp.), all of which are on the increase in grassland areas such as those on San Bruno Mountain.

Conservation: Concern about this subspecies, as well as the San Bruno Elfin (*Callophrys mossi bayensis*) and Callippe Silverspot (*Speyeria callippe*), was instrumental in leading to the formation of the U.S.A.'s first habitat conservation plan in 1983. The plan created the San Bruno Mountain County Park, an extensive area encompassing the largest existing butterfly population. Considerable effort has been made to annually monitor the size of adult populations and initiate management activities such as the control of invasive species (see Reid and Murphy 1986, and Bean *et al.* 1991 for details).

References

ARNOLD, R.A. 1983. Ecological studies of six endangered butterflies (Lepidoptera, Lycaenidae): island biogeography, patch dynamics, and design of habitat preserves. *Univ. Calif. Publns Entomol.* **99**: 1–161.

BEAN, M., FITZGERALD, S. and O'CONNOR, M. 1991. The San Bruno habitat conservation plan. *In: Reconciling conflicts under the endangered species act World Wildlife Fund,* Washington, D.C. pp. 52–65.

DOWNEY, J.C. 1962. Myrmecophily in *Plebejus (Icaricia) icarioides* (Lepidoptera: Lycaenidae). *Entomol. News* **73**: 57–66.

HOVANITZ, W. 1937. Concerning the *Plebejus icarioides* Rassenkreis (Lepidoptera: Lycaenidae). *Pan-Pacific Entomol.* **13**: 184–189.

NEWCOMER, E.J. 1911. The life histories of two lycaenid butterflies. *Can. Ent.* **43**: 83–88.

REID, T.S. and MURPHY, D.D. 1986. The endangered Mission Blue butterfly, *Plebejus icarioides missionensis. In:* B.A. Wilcox, P.F. Brussard and B.G. Marcot (Eds). *The management of viable populations: theory, applications, and case studies.* Center for Conservation Biology, Stanford, California. pp. 147–167.

The San Bruno Elfin, *Incisalia mossii bayensis* (Brown)

Stuart B. Weiss

Center for Conservation Biology, Department of Biological Sciences, Stanford University, Stanford, CA 94305, U.S.A.

Country: U.S.A.

Status and Conservation Interest: Status – endangered (Red List).

This subspecies is endemic to the northern San Francisco Peninsula, California. It was one of the first butterflies protected under the U.S. Endangered Species Act in 1976. As a local endemic in a highly urbanised region, threats to the San Bruno Elfin include land development and invasive introduced plant species.

Taxonomy and Description: The subspecies was discovered rather late, in 1962 (MacNeill 1963), and described by Brown (1969a). It was originally described as *Callophrys fotis bayensis*, but was later recognized to be in the species *C. mossii* (Edwards) (now genus *Incisalia*, which occurs from Vancouver Island along the coast range to near Los Angeles). Populations to the north in Marin County are recognized as a different subspecies, those to the south in the Santa Lucia Range are ssp. *doudoroffi*.

Distribution: The subspecies is restricted to three distinct areas on the northern San Francisco peninsula: Montara Mountain; Milagra Ridge; and San Bruno Mountain. Each of these localities supports an array of highly local demographic units tied together by occasional adult migration. Populations probably once existed within San Francisco at Twin Peaks and Mount Davidson, but have disappeared with urbanisation (Emmel and Ferris 1972).

Population Size: The San Bruno Elfin was never common, because of specialized habitat requirements (see below). The butterfly exists in local discrete populations of ten to several hundred adults at higher altitudes. A thousand or more adults may exist in about 15 total subpopulations on San Bruno Mountain in a good year. Montara Mountain supports about 10 local populations, and Milagra Ridge supports about four. Virtually all of the existing habitat is now protected as parkland, and numerous populations have been qualitatively monitored since 1982. Colonies noted by Arnold (1984) occupied small areas (0.15–8.0ha) on steep, north-facing slopes.

Habitat and ecology: The distribution of the butterfly closely follows the narrow, fragmented distribution of its larval hostplant, stonecrop, *Sedum spathulifolium* (Brown 1969b). This succulent plant grows in abundance only on thin-soiled or rocky north-facing slopes within the coastal fog belt. *Sedum* occurs in both short-statured coastal scrub and grassland vegetation types, and is most common near the summits of coastal mountains and around rocky outcrops on lower slopes. *Sedum* readily invades roadcuts and old quarry faces provided the aspect is correct. Local populations of the Elfin correspond closely to these patches of the larval hostplant, which range from a hundred square meters to several hectares in extent.

San Bruno Elfin adults fly from February into April, during the latter part of the rainy season in northern California, but before the onset of persistent summer fog. Adults usually appear after the first extended warm sunny period of the season, as early as the first week in February, or as late as April. The window of sunny, calm conditions during the flight season is highly variable from year to year, and adults run the risk of being grounded by inclement weather for weeks on end. Populations were greatly reduced during and after near record rainfall in 1983, but appear to be less affected by recent drought conditions (San Bruno Mountain Conservation Plan Monitoring Reports, 1982–1991).

Habitat topography may be limiting for Elfin populations in certain cases. Because of low winter sun angles, the steepest habitat areas may be in deep shade for much of the day, limiting access by adults (Weiss and Murphy 1991). While natural contours are rarely shaded all day even in February, roadcuts and quarry faces may face severe shading limitations. Steep (>40°) north-facing slopes provide minimal solar exposure even in March, and are rarely occupied by Elfin. Equally steep northeast-facing slopes receive direct morning light when winds are calm, and provide excellent Elfin habitat. Elfin activity on steep northwest-facing slopes, however, may be limited by strong afternoon winds.

Adults are highly sedentary, typically moving less than 100 metres (Arnold 1983), with a maximum recorded movement of about 800m (Arnold 1984). Males perch on rocks and vegetation, and dart out at passing insects; females spend much of their time crawling among the foodplants (Emmel and Ferris 1972; Arnold

1983). Both sexes visit flowers (especially *Lomatium utriculatum*, but also other early blooming coastal species) when plants are available, but a number of local Elfin populations on Montara Mountain exist where nectar resources are astonishingly sparse.

The butterfly is univoltine. Females oviposit on *Sedum* rosettes. Early instars feed on the fleshy leaves, but third and fourth instars feed on the flowers when they appear. Third and fourth instars are easily observed basking and feeding on *Sedum* flowerheads, and exhibit a continuous colour polymorphism ranging from deep red (the colour of *Sedum* foliage) through orange to bright yellow (the colours of *Sedum* flowers); larvae may change colour morph over a few days (Orsak and Whitman 1986). Larvae may be tended by ants of up to nine different species, but the relationship appears facultative (Arnold 1983). However, most larvae in the field are observed without ants (Emmel and Ferris 1972, S.B. Weiss pers. obs.). Larvae are parasitized by a tachinid, *Aplomya theclarum* that emerges from the fourth instar Elfin larvae. Parasitisation rates of reared larvae and collected pupae are high, of the order of 50–80% (Arnold 1983). Given the high densities of larvae observed (one or more per square meter), such high mortality appears necessary to produce the typically low density of adults the following year. The fourth instar caterpillar pupates in the duff immediately below the hostplants, and diapause lasts through the summer, fall and early winter.

Threats: Because the vast majority of San Bruno Elfin populations are on public land (including San Bruno Mountain County Park, Golden Gate National Recreation Area, and McNee Ranch State Park) further opportunities for habitat conversion are limited. A proposed six lane road would skirt a population on Montara Mountain, but that construction has been challenged on a host of environmental and development issues other than the San Bruno Elfin. Continued expansion of a quarry on San Bruno Mountain could destroy some habitat on that property; however, the quarry is scheduled to be shut down within a decade. The prohibitions of the Endangered Species Act and park rules provide a strong deterrent against overcollecting by both amateurs and scientists. Wildfires may threaten in more heavily vegetated areas, but the thin vegetation on rocky outcrops is relatively safe from fires. Vegetation succession also appears unimportant, given the thin soils and windswept conditions of the habitat. Invasive introduced species such as gorse (*Ulex europeaus*), brooms (*Cytisus* spp.), pampas grass, ice plant (*Mesembryanthemum* spp.), and blue gum (*Eucalyptus globulus*) are encroaching on some local populations.

Conservation: Since most of the habitat is already protected, conservation prescriptions for the San Bruno Mountain fall under the jurisdiction of the San Bruno Mountain Habitat Conservation Plan, 1982 (Bean *et al.* 1991), which includes yearly monitoring of adult numbers and management activities.

Elements of a Recovery Plan (Arnold 1984) included: (1) protection of essential habitat (which was designated on each site), through a range of strategies including cooperative agreements, easements and others; (2) prevention of further habitat degradation, and habitat enhancement where possible, through minimising toxin use, removal of weeds, control of off-road vehicles and revegetating with native flora; (3) development and implementation of management plans for extant colonies by utilising annual surveys and fostering autecological studies; (4) re-establishment of the species in restored sites within its historical range; (5) increase in public awareness; and (6) enforcement and evaluation of protective laws and regulations at all levels.

Control of invasive species is currently under way at Milagra Ridge and San Bruno Mountain. Large areas of *Sedum* along Wolf Ridge in Marin County (just outside the historical range of the Elfin) are presently unoccupied by the butterfly, raising the possibility of an introduction attempt there. Revegetating abandoned quarry faces on San Bruno Mountain would provide a great opportunity to increase the habitat of the San Bruno Elfin, because *Sedum* will rapidly invade bare rock surfaces. The quarry configuration would provide large areas of appropriate solar exposure (especially northeast-facing slopes and flat benches) if restoration were attempted (Weiss and Murphy 1991).

References

ARNOLD, R.A. 1983. Ecological studies of six endangered butterflies (Lepidoptera, Lycaenidae): island biogeography, patch dynamics, and design of habitat preserves. *Univ. Calif. Publns Entomol.* **99**: 1–161.

ARNOLD, R.A. 1984. (Main author of) *U.S. Fish and Wildlife Service. 1984. Recovery plan for the San Bruno Elfin and Mission Blue butterflies.* U.S. Fish and Wildlife Service, Portland, Oregon.

BEAN, M., FITZGERALD, S. and O'CONNOR, M. 1991. The San Bruno habitat conservation plan. *In: Reconciling Conflicts under the Endangered Species Act.* World Wildlife Fund, pp. 52–65.

BROWN, R.M. 1969a. A new subspecies of *Callophrys fotis* from the San Francisco Bay Area. *J. Lepid. Soc.* **23**: 95–96.

BROWN, R.M. 1969b. Larva and habitat of *Callophrys fotis bayensis. J. Res. Lepid.* **8**: 49–50.

EMMEL, J.F. and FERRIS, C.D. 1972. The biology of *Callophrys fotis bayensis. J. Lepid. Soc.* **26**: 237–244.

MACNEILL, C.D. 1963. *Callophrys fotis* (Strecker) from the San Francisco Bay area. *Pan-Pacific Entomologist* **39**: 60.

ORSAK, L. and WHITMAN, D.W. 1986. Chromatic color polymorphism in *Callophrys mossii bayensis* larvae (Lycaenidae): spectral characteristics, short-term color shifts, and natural morph frequencies. *J. Res. Lepid.* **25**: 188–201.

WEISS, S.B. and MURPHY, D.D. 1991. Thermal microenvironments and the restoration of rare butterfly habitat. *In:* J. Berger (Ed.) *Environmental Restoration.* Island Press, Covelo, California, pp. 50–60.

The Lotis Blue, *Lycaeides idas lotis* (Lintner)

R.A. ARNOLD

Entomological Consulting Services Limited, 104 Mountain View Court, Pleasant Hill, CA 94523, U.S.A.

Country: U.S.A.

Status and Conservation Interest: Status – probably extinct; endangered (Red List).

The Lotis Blue was regarded by Arnold (1985) as probably the rarest resident butterfly in the continental United States. Historically, it was probably restricted to just a few localised colonies in coastal northern California. Although it was listed as an endangered species in 1976, today it is feared to be extinct.

Taxonomy and Description: The Lotis Blue was formerly considered to be a subspecies of *Lycaeides argyrognomon* (Bergstrasser), and was listed as endangered under the name *L. argyrognomon lotis*. However, European butterfly taxonomists have recently examined the types of *L. argyrognomom* and *L. idas*. They concluded that all North American taxa, which were formerly called *L. argyrognomon*, should now be called *L. idas*. Hence, the Lotis Blue is now referred to as *L. idas lotis*. Twelve subspecies of *L. idas* (Linneaus) have been described from North America (Downey 1975). The Lotis Blue is one of the larger subspecies of *L. idas*. It is also separable from other described species by its wing colours and markings.

Distribution: Nearly all collections or sightings of the Lotis Blue since 1933 have been from a single location, near the town of Mendocino in Mendocino County, California (Arnold 1991). This location is a Sphagnum bog situated in the right-of-way for the Elk-Fort Bragg 60-kV transmission line, operated by the Pacific Gas and Electric Company (P.G. & E). The bog is about 1ha in size and is surrounded by Red Alder (*Alnus rubra*) riparian forest, Northern Bishop Pine (*Pinus muricata*) forest, and Mendocino Pygmy Cypress (*Cupressus pygmaea*) forest. Characteristic understory vegetation includes various ericaceous shrubs, sedges, and ferns.

Historical records of the Lotis Blue reveal that it was known from only a few other locations, between Point Arena and Fort Bragg in coastal Mendocino County. Reports of the butterfly's probable occurrence in Sonoma and northern Marin counties by Tilden (1965) are unsubstantiated by any specimens. Because of substantial differences in the types of vegetation that occur in these areas, it is doubtful that the butterfly ever occurred outside of coastal Mendocino County. Fewer than 75 specimens are housed in North American entomological collections (Arnold 1991).

In 1990, P.G. & E. sponsored an extensive survey of the butterfly and its suspected larval foodplant at 23 locations in coastal Mendocino County, the historical geographic range of the Lotis Blue. Unfortunately, no specimens of the Lotis Blue were found; indeed, none have been seen since 1983 and the negative results of this survey suggest that the butterfly may now be extinct (Arnold 1991).

Population Size: On June 19th and 20th, 1953, J.W. Tilden collected at least 26 adults of the Lotis Blue from the bog population of the eventual P.G. & E. transmission line, which are preserved in North American entomological collections. During 1977–1989, Arnold saw only 26 adult butterflies during 67 days of field work at the P.G. & E. location, and none after 1983. Because of the small size of the butterfly's habitat, its population numbers probably were never greater than a few hundred individuals per season at the powerline bog. The butterfly's very rarity has precluded detailed investigations about its population size and structure, as have been obtained for other endangered lycaenids that occur in California (Arnold 1983).

Habitat and ecology: Because of the Lotis Blue's rarity, little is known about its specific habitat requirements and ecology. In northern California, other subspecific taxa of *Lycaeides idas* typically occur in wet meadows, bogs, seeps or springs, and along streamsides. Populations of these butterflies are typically associated with small, and often isolated, patches of their larval foodplants. Known larval foodplants include legumes that grow in these wet habitats, in particular *Lotus oblongifolius*, *Lupinus polyphyllus* and *Astragalus whitneyi* (A. Shapiro, pers. comm.).

Four legume species have been observed growing in or very near the bog at the primary Lotis Blue population site along the transmission line. Of these legumes, *Lotus formosissimus* (Coast Trefoil) is the most likely candidate to be the butterfly's larval foodplant, since it grows in the bog where most specimens of the Lotis Blue have been observed. Also, a female was observed

(J.F. Emmel, cited in Arnold 1985) attempting to oviposit on this plant.

A hypothetical life cycle and natural history of the Lotis Blue can be surmised based on circumstantial evidence from related taxa whose biologies are better known. Like other taxa of *L. idas* in northern California, the Lotis Blue is probably univoltine. Historical collection records indicate that adults may be present from mid-May through mid-July. Eggs are laid throughout the adult flight season and newly hatched larvae probably begin to feed immediately. Partially grown larvae, probably second instars, diapause until the following spring, when larval development is completed in about four to six weeks after feeding resumes. Presumably, the pupal stage lasts no more than a few weeks.

Threats: Because of the butterfly's extremely limited geographical range, and the small size of its only known habitat, the Lotis Blue is extremely vulnerable to any type of habitat loss or alteration. Collecting of specimens could also be detrimental. Arnold (1985) speculated that drought may have previously affected the butterfly's habitat by decreasing water levels in the bog. However, more recent information suggests that successional changes in the vegetation at the transmission line site, and at other potential population sites, are probably responsible for the recently observed decline of the butterfly.

The leguminous foodplants of other northern California populations of *L. idas* generally grow in small patches in wet habitats that are at the early stages of vegetation succession. Circumstantial evidence from the 1990 P.G. & E. sponsored study suggests that *Lotus formosissimus*, the suspected larval foodplant of the Lotis Blue, also grows in greatest abundance in the early successional stages of wet areas, such as bogs, plus the headwaters and shorelines of streams (Arnold 1991). Furthermore, examination of field notes from cadastral surveys and maps prepared by the U.S. Coast and Geodetic Survey, during the late 1800s and early 1900s indicate that the transmission line site and much of the coastal area within the butterfly's historic range were logged then. Indeed, many areas, including the transmission line bog, which today support dense forest vegetation, were open fields a century ago. Thus, the forests surrounding the transmission line bog represent regrowth rather than natural habitat. Comparison of a series of aerial photos covering the past several decades depict how rapidly the vegetation has changed from a more open area to a dense forest with a closed canopy in many places. Presumably, as the successional changes have proceeded, the increasing density of the vegetation gradually choked out the suspected larval foodplant of the butterfly, which prefers open areas. By 1990, only 15 specimens of *L. formosissimus* were observed at two locations in or near the transmission line bog (Arnold 1991), and only two specimens were observed growing in the bog during 1992 (Arnold, unpublished data).

Conservation: Clearly, basic ecological and natural history information about the butterfly is needed to identify potential habitat sites within its historic range and to manage these areas to benefit the Lotis Blue. Confirmation of the butterfly's larval foodplant is essential to identify its breeding habitat. Because of the butterfly's dubious status, surveys should be undertaken to determine if it even still exists.

Objectives of the butterfly's recovery plan (Arnold 1985) are to: (1) protect the butterfly and its habitat at the only known site; (2) establish three new viable populations at different sites; and (3) determine the extent of the population and size of secure habitats needed so the butterfly can be reclassified as 'threatened' rather than 'endangered'. However, until the basic biological information about the butterfly is obtained, the objectives of the recovery plan probably cannot be achieved.

References

ARNOLD, R.A. 1983. Ecological studies of six endangered butterflies (Lepidoptera: Lycaenidae): island biogeography, patch dynamics, and the design of habitat preserves. *Univ. Calif. Publns Entomol.* **99**: 1–161.

ARNOLD, R.A. 1985. (Main author of) U.S. Fish & Wildlife Service. *Lotis Blue butterfly recovery plan.* U.S. Fish & Wildlife Service. Portland, Oregon. 46pp.

ARNOLD, R.A. 1991. *Biological studies of the endangered Lotis Blue butterfly for P.G. & E.'s Elk-Fort 60kV transmission line.* Pacific Gas & Electric Company. San Ramon, California. 46pp. and appendices.

DOWNEY, J.C. 1975. Genus *Plebejus* Kluk. *In:* Howe, W.H. (Ed.). *The Butterflies of North America.* Doubleday. Garden City, New York. pp. 337–350.

TILDEN, J.W. 1965. *Butterflies of the San Francisco Bay Region.* Univ. of Calif. Press. Berkeley, California. 88pp.

Additional taxa of concern in southern California

R.H.T. Mattoni

9620 Heather Road, Beverly Hills, California 90210, U.S.A.

Three additional lycaenid butterflies of conservation interest occur in southern California:

The Human Folly Blue, *Philotes sonorensis extinctis* Mattoni

The subspecies occurred across a 1000ha site in the upper San Gabriel river wash. It has been extinct since 1968, having been eliminated by the activities of the U.S. Army Corps of Engineers to provide a spreading basin for subsurface water recharge. Ironically the Corps is today charged with the responsibility of protecting wetlands and species. Details of this subspecies can be found in Mattoni (1991).

Reference

MATTONI, R.H.T. 1991. An unrecognised, now extinct, Los Angeles area butterfly (Lycaenidae). *J. Res. Lepid.* **28**: 297–309 (1989).

The Santa Monica Mountains Hairstreak, *Satyrium auretorum fumosum* Emmel & Mattoni

This hairstreak is only known from a few localities within a circumscribed area of about 25,000ha in the western Santa Monica mountains. The range is completely surrounded by urban development and itself is being further fragmented by developments. Battlelines between environmentalists and developers have been drawn to define the future of the mountains. The compromises finally reached regarding habitat preservation of the area may serve as a model for the rest of the United States. With land values in the order of one million dollars per hectare, economic pressures even affect biologist consultants. An effort to federally list the species is underway.

The San Gabriel Blue, *Plebejus saepiolus* undescribed subspecies

This is another extinct taxon. Known only from a few meadows in the Big Pine recreation area on the north slope of the San Gabriel mountains it was last seen in the mid 1980s. Its distribution was very limited, since its wet meadow habitat, necessary to support the clover foodplant, is very restricted across the dry north slope. Extinction was brought on by draining of the limited meadow habitats by the U.S. Forestry Service.

Selected Neotropical species

Departamento de Zoologia, Instituto de Biologia, Universidade Estadual de Campinas, C.P. 6109, Campinas, São Paulo, 13.081, Brazil

Styx infernalis Staudinger

Country: Peru.

Status and Conservation Interest: Status – vulnerable.

This species is probably the most primitive of the Riodininae, confined to a very small region of high species diversity and endemicity. It is very rarely observed.

Taxonomy and Description: A medium-sized, dirty transparent grey butterfly with narrow wings and a heavy black body, seeming rather like a Geometrid or Lymantriid moth. It has short antennae.

Distribution: *S. infernalis* is known only from central and southern Peru, at elevations between 1000 and 1600m (Figure 1).

Population Size: Not known.

Habitat and Ecology: This species inhabits primeval cloud forest with steep slopes and torrents. It is active in sun patches near midday, with a weak, almost gliding flight, in small aggregations near rushing streams. The early stages are unknown.

Threats: Habitat conversion for coffee or other plantations (very scattered colonies).

Conservation: The main need is to locate colonies and secure large tracts of undisturbed cloud forest.

Nirodia belphegor (Westwood)

Country: Brazil.

Status and Conservation Interest: Status – vulnerable.

Nirodia is a monotypic genus (very close to *Rhetus*, composed of common tropical species), whose only species is confined to high-altitude rockfields in a very ancient environment. It has

been observed fewer than ten times since its original description 140 years ago in spite of extensive human activity in the region.

Taxonomy and Description: *N. belphegor* is a medium-small, yellow-spotted, dark blue butterfly with pointed forewings and a short broad tail on the hindwings (Figure 1d of regional account), strongly reminiscent of *Rhetus periander* (Cramer). It seems quite close to a fossil riodinine from the Eocene (Durden and Rose 1978).

Distribution: It is known from only four localities in the Serras do Espinhaço and Cipó in central Minas Gerais, Brazil, at elevations above 1000m (Figure 1) where it is seen very sporadically.

Population Size: Not known.

Habitat and Ecology: It inhabits 'campo rupestre', a xeric system on rocky soils at about 1000m elevation, characterised by strong endemism in plants (Velloziaceae, Eriocaulaceae, Xyridaceae) and animals (including amphibians), with ancient affinities to similar systems in Africa. Males are seen resting on the ground with wings outspread (like *Rhetus*) drinking water beside small creeks rushing down through rockfields. They make short sallies out from perching places on sunlit rocks and dart irregularly about as if defending a territory in that space (fide Ivan Sazima). Early stages are unknown, as are any further biological details on the species.

Threats: The 'campo rupestre' system, restricted in area, is under very heavy pressure from removal and exportation of dried plants, and is subject to extensive burning and trampling.

Conservation: The species should be preserved in the recently declared Serra do Cipó National Park, and the proposed Caraça Natural Park.

Reference

DURDEN, C.J. and ROSE, H. 1978. Butterflies from the middle Eocene: the earliest occurrence of Fossil Papilionoidea (Lepidoptera). *Pearce-Sellards Series, Texas Memorial Museum* 29: 1–25.

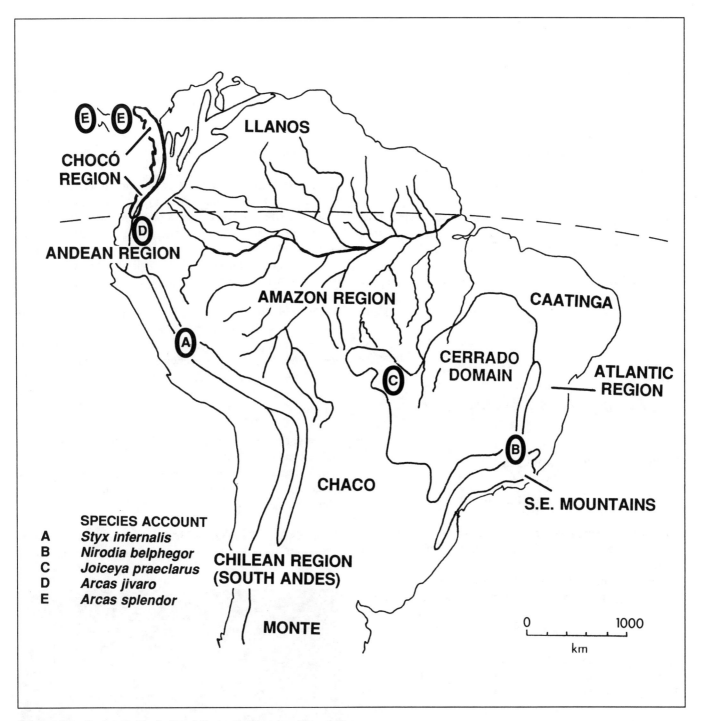

Figure 1. Distribution (A–E) of selected Neotropical species of Lycaenidae.

SPECIES ACCOUNT
A *Styx infernalis*
B *Nirodia belphegor*
C *Joiceya praeclarus*
D *Arcas jivaro*
E *Arcas splendor*

Joiceya praeclarus Talbot

Country: Brazil.

Status and Conservation Interest: Status – endangered.

Joiceya is a monotypic genus known only from the type series, from a small, heavily collected and increasingly converted region.

Taxonomy and Description: A '*Setabis alcmaeon* (Lewis 1973, plate 77: Figure 5) -like' pattern: small, with a pointed forewing and elongated hindwing; dull grey-brown underside with faint distal lines; strong blue upperside with a black base-to-margin line on the hindwing; and a black area between forewing base and submarginal spots. It is like no other species or genus.

Distribution: *J. praeclarus* is known only from an original collection in central Mato Grosso (Cuiabá and Tombador), Brazil (Figure 1). It has not been collected in intensive recent work in the region.

Population Size: Not known.

Habitat and Ecology: The ecology of this species is not known, but it probably inhabits the understorey of isolated humid headwater or spring-fed forests in strongly scarped regions within the cerrado landscape (chapadas).

Threats: The area is being used intensively for colonisation, ranching, hydroelectric projects, mines, and industrial farms, with removal of all original vegetation in parts.

Conservation: The species may be present in the new Chapada dos Guimarães National Park and other small reserves in the region, but it needs to be relocated and colonies specifically saved.

Reference

LEWIS, H.L. 1973. *Butterflies of the World.* Follett, Chicago.

Arcas, five rarer species

Countries: Panama, Ecuador, Peru, Brazil.

Status and Conservation Interest: Status – rare or vulnerable (with the exception of *A. imperialis* which is not considered threatened).

These are the most exquisite of all neotropical Theclinae, typical of large areas of virgin wet forest and usually disappearing in disturbed areas. They are easy to find when present and are thus good indicators of undisturbed forest systems.

Taxonomy and Description: These are largish, two-tailed species with an additional well-separated long anal lobe of the hindwing (thus flashing six mobile 'antennae' to the false head). They are brilliant striated green on the ventral surface (often with additional nuances of rose and chrome yellow) and iridescent blue or green above. The genus was revised by Nicolay (1971). Illustrations of at least *A. imperialis* appear in most popular butterfly books, and *A. ducalis* has been called the most beautiful small butterfly in the neotropics.

Distribution: The non-threatened *A. imperialis* (Cramer) occurs from Mexico to southern Brazil, with northerly females sometimes showing much rose colour ventrally. *A. cypria* (Geyer) is infrequent from Mexico to western Colombia, and *A. ducalis* (Westwood) is very local in southeastern Brazilian mountains. The *A. tuneta* superspecies (*delphia* Nicolay in

Costa Rica, and *tuneta* (Hewitson) from Peru to southeastern Brazil) are very rarely encountered. *A. jivaro* Nicolay is known only from the two types in a single locality, in eastern Ecuador and *A. splendor* (Druce), not seen for 110 years after its original collection, is restricted to scattered cloud forest localities from Costa Rica to W. Ecuador (Figure 1). Further taxa may still be found.

Population Size: Not known.

Habitat and Ecology: *Arcas* males are most often seen in early afternoon on forested hilltops or ridges, where they sit high (5–10m) in the trees in the sun, looking out from leaves over a green sunlit space. They vigorously defend this space against other males while waiting for a female to arrive. Mated females are found lower down, inspecting growing tips of the foodplants (Annonaceae: *Rollinia*, and Lauraceae for *A. ducalis*). Two or three species can be found on a single hilltop in Panama or southeastern Brazil, but such favoured sites are very rarely found. Flower visiting is infrequent, mostly before midday, but may be prolonged. Flight is very rapid, a brilliant green swirl accompanied by blue flashes, with the insect returning to the same or a nearby perch. Most populations occur throughout the year but the insects are commoner on sunny days in the rainier seasons.

Threats: Moderate modification of the habitat may eliminate male perching sites and prevent the sexes from meeting and mating, in the sparse populations of these species. Two of the species are known from very few localities and may easily be eliminated.

Conservation: For the rarest of these species, *A. jivaro* and *A. splendor*, further localities should be looked for and protected

Arcas ducalis (photo by K.S. Brown, Jr.).

wherever possible. Three of the more widespread species (*cypria*, *ducalis*, and *tuneta*), though known from more areas, are still very rarely encountered. Along with the more frequently encountered *A. imperialis,* they should be reported and monitored as good indicators of the health of intact, rich tropical wet forest ecosystems.

Reference

NICOLAY, S.S. 1971. A review of the genus *Arcas* with descriptions of new species (Lycaenidae, Strymonini). *J. Lepid. Soc.* **25**: 87–108.

Arawacus aethesa (Hewitson)

Country: Brazil.

Status and Conservation Interest: Status – vulnerable.

This species is endemic to wet forests in a restricted area of the Atlantic lowlands of southeastern Brazil. Since the building of a major new highway twenty years ago, over 90% of the vegetation has been cut over, greatly disturbed or removed.

Taxonomy and Description: *A. aethesa* is closely related to *A. aetolus* (= *linus* Auctt.), the classical 'false head' phenotype which is very widespread in the neotropics, with convergent black lines on the cubital spot of the hindwing margin, from the forewing costa. It is easily distinguished by its smoky brown undersurface, with a yellow submarginal band.

Distribution: It is known only from southern Bahia, northern Espírito Santo, and eastern Minas Gerais, in the Atlantic forests of eastern Brazil.

Population Size: Not known.

Habitat and Ecology: It has been observed in sunlit columns in the interior of wet lowland forest. The foodplant is almost surely *Solanum* leaves.

Threats: Habitat reduction is the primary threat to this species and many others endemic to Atlantic lowland forest.

Conservation: The species exists in several reserves within its range, but needs to be specially protected as it uses secondary-succession plants in a forest biome.

Cyanophrys bertha (Jones)

Country: Brazil.

Status and Conservation Interest: Status – vulnerable.

A very rarely seen (only the single type existed among collections in all American and European museums until very recently) and spectacular species typical of large, species-rich, high-elevation sites in the coastal mountains, where many other unusual and little-known species occur.

Taxonomy and Description: Like other *Cyanophrys*, it is blue above and pea-green below, but in contrast to them it has a white stripe across both wings on the underside, bordered basally with diffuse blue-white blotches.

Distribution: The species is known in Brazilian collections from over 1000m elevation in the mountains of Minas Gerais (Pocos de Caldas, Barbacena), Rio de Janeiro (Petrópolis), São Paulo (Serra do Japi, where quite frequent at times), and Paraná from a total of fewer than 20 specimens.

Population Size: Not known.

Habitat and Ecology: Males frequent hilltops in the early afternoon, where they perch in the crowns (not usually the highest points) of tall scraggly trees, changing perches every few minutes or when approached. Both sexes can be found on flowers in the morning, and females frequent sunny glades on hillsides. Early stages are still unknown. It is associated with *C. herodotus* (F.), *C. amyntor* (Cramer), *C. acaste* (Prittwitz), *C. remus* (Hewitson) and *C.* nr. *pseudolongula* (Clench), the last three often perching on the same high-elevation hilltop trees.

Threats: Like many highly localised and rarely seen Theclinae, it can be eliminated from the few local colonies by minor habitat alteration.

Conservation: The species should be preserved in a number of parks and inaccessible areas.

Neotropical Lycaenidae endemic to high elevations in SE Brazil

K.S. Brown, Jr.

Departamento de Zoologia, Instituto de Biologia, Universidade Estadual de Campinas, C.P. 6109, São Paulo, 13. 081, Brazil

Country: Brazil.

Status and Conservation Interest: Status – threatened community.

These are rarely observed, often very specialised species and genera, in very local habitats in a strongly heterogeneous landscape. The area is subject to intensive human activity and there is considerable modification of the vegetation.

Taxonomy and Description: In the Riodininae the community includes: three monotypic genera: *Nirodia belphegor* (discussed under 'Selected Neotropical Species'); *Eucorna sanarita* (Schaus), dark with a 'fuzzy' pattern; *Petrocerus catiena* (Hewitson), similar to a dark *Calydna*; isolated species of *Mesosemia* (?) (*M.? acuta* Hewitson, beige with a falcate forewing); *Calydna* (a still undescribed species, very small with orange spots and a falcate forewing); *Crocozona* (?) (*C.? croceifasciata* Zikán, small with a transverse orange band across both wings); a species of *Mesenopsis* (*M. albivitta* (Lathy), imitating common Dioptid moths with orange bars on each wing (see next account); *Panara ovifera* Seitz; *Mycastor leucarpis* (Stichel); *Argyrogrammana caesarion* Rebillard and a number of species of *Napaea* (all dark brown).

Endemic theclines are many, though not equal to the high-altitude groups in the Andes; some are more 'furry' than their lower-altitude congeners (due to the cold?) and many have rather sombre patterns (but see *Cyanophrys bertha*, Brown, this volume).

Distribution: The above groups are found in the Serras do Mar and da Mantiqueira, from the interior of Bahia and Espírito Santo south to Santa Catarina and northern Rio Grande do Sul. They are most common in very high areas in Rio de Janeiro/Minas Gerais/São Paulo.

Population Sizes: Not known.

Habitat and Ecology: The species fly rarely, but have been noted flying in sunny weather near midday, in variable seasons and habitats. Most have been found too sporadically to make any generalisations, but as a rule they are likely to be in wet habitats or bamboo forests, not rare when found, occasionally partial to hilltops, and probably tightly associated with special host plants or ants.

Threats: The exceedingly heterogeneous habitats are full of small micro-islands of different vegetation (often no more than a few hundred square metres on a hilltop, hillside or gully) whose destruction leads to extinction of the populations.

Conservation: Although many large, inaccessible areas still exist in these regions, some of them officially preserved, little information is available about the presence of these rare species, and possibly other Lycaenidae still undescribed. Much exploration is needed to establish the localities of colonies and preserve them.

Riodininae: Amazonian genera with most species very rare or local

K.S. Brown, Jr.

Departamento de Zoologia, Instituto de Biologia, Universidade Estadual de Campinas, C.P. 6109, São Paulo, 13. 081, Brazil

Country: Brazil.

Status and Conservation Interest: Status – threatened community.

There are a number of forest species that are very rarely seen, concentrated in compact taxonomic groups, whose local colonies, often very far apart, may be eliminated easily by modest alteration of the habitat.

Description: The group includes:
- four species of *Alesa* (*telephae* Boisduval, *fournierae* Rebillard, *neagra* Röber, *thelydryas* Bates, known from very few specimens but not *A. prema* Godart or *A. amesis* Cramer),
- *Mimocastnia rothschildi* Seitz (a hypertrophic representative of the same phenotype and lineage);
- both species of *Colaciticus*;
- three species of *Mesenopsis* (a fourth is montane in SE Brazil, see preceding account);
- all species of *Xenandra* including *X. pulcherrima* (Herrich-Schäffer) (usually placed in *Melanis*);
- most species of *Esthemopsis* and *Symmachia;*
- *Zelotaea phasma* Bates;
- all species of *Dysmathia.*

The species vary from uniformly dingy (the last genus) to uniformly white (penultimate), with many having strong colours of yellow, orange and red or green; all are small except for *Mimocastnia.*

Population Sizes: Not known.

Habitat and Ecology: They are typically found as isolated males in very high-diversity hilltops or clearings, very occasionally on flowers or in small assemblages. These species all inhabit the deep forest; some may be canopy dwellers, but most just seem to be very rare and sporadic in occurrence, presumably due to excessively narrow ecological tolerances.

Threats: The very rarefied distributions indicate that the conversion of small areas may eliminate local colonies which will not be re-established in nearby intact habitat.

Conservation: Wherever colonies are known, they should be protected by moderate-sized reserves which can maintain natural processes and heterogeneity.

Theclinae endemic to the Cerrado vegetation (central Brazil)

K.S. Brown, Jr.

Departamento de Zoologia, Instituto de Biologia, Universidade Estadual de Campinas, C.P. 6109, São Paulo, 13. 081, Brazil

Country: Brazil.

Status and Conservation Interest: Status – threatened community.

These are very local species that are indicators of healthy and diverse, well-watered cerrado habitats which contain the full range of microenvironments and successional vegetation typical of the region.

Taxonomy and Description: Coming from many groups and genera in the Theclinae, most of the characteristic 'cerrado species' have large red markings or blotches on the underside, almost as if they formed an environment-mediated mimicry ring. Typical representatives are *Arawacus tarania* (Hewitson), *Strymon tegaea* (Hewitson), *S. ohausi* (Spitz), *S.* sp. (*ziba*-group), *'Thecla' mantica* Druce, *Magnastigma julia* Nicolay, *'Thecla' socia* Hewitson, and *'Thecla' bagrada* Hewitson. All are distinctive and restricted to the cerrado domain and its peripheries.

Distribution: Central Brazil Plateau in Goiás, Distrito Federal, Minas Gerais, Mato Grosso, Mato Grosso do Sul, and parts of Bahia, São Paulo and Paraná, in the cerrado.

Population Sizes: Not known.

Habitat and Ecology: The habitats of the group are variable: *S. tegaea* prefers wet grasslands by headwater woods, while the minute *S. ohausi* is restricted to tiny grassy marshes in small sinkholes within the cerrado. *A. tarania* is more widespread in scrub with a grassy understorey, the juveniles feeding on small Leguminosae (K. Ebert, pers. comm.); *'Th.' mantica* and *M. julia* prefer bushy cerrado, the larvae of the former living on Chrysobalanaceae (K. Ebert, pers. comm.). The other three *'Thecla'*, are often found perched in medium-sized trees, near the end of the afternoon. Most are scarce.

Threats: Large areas of cerrado are being occupied by intensive, mechanised and chemical agriculture, completely destroying and poisoning the diverse and complex natural systems. As several of these species are intensely localised and occupy rare, scattered and very specific habitats, their few local populations are especially vulnerable.

Conservation: A number of preserved areas in the cerrado region probably include the commoner species of Theclinae endemic to this biome, but colonies of the rarer ones such as *S. ohausi* and *M. julia* need to be localised and specifically protected. The latter has not been seen since the 1969 collecting trip that led to its discovery and description, when it was found in only three localities, all of precarious preservation today.

Neotropical Riodininae endemic to the Chocó region of western Colombia

C.J. CALLAGHAN

Louis Berger International Inc., 100 Halsted Street, P.O. Box 270, East Orange, N.J. 07019, U.S.A.

Country: Colombia.

Status and Conservation Interest: Status – threatened community.

The area supports a high number of rare, specialised species of riodinine butterflies, all very sensitive to alterations in vegetation patterns. The area is currently under pressure from human activity, especially logging of pulp-wood for paper mills.

Taxonomy and Description: The fauna is taxonomically poorly known, so that future study may well reveal additional species or genera which are endemic to the region. Preliminary work by Callaghan (1985) suggests that 33 (36%) of a total of 91 species of the known Riodininae are endemic. Among these are *Euselasia rhodogyne* (Godman), *E. violacea* Lathy, two undescribed *Euselasia*, *Mesosemia asa iphigenia* Stichel, *M. sibyllina* Staudinger, *Eurybia juturna cyclopia* Stichel, *Lucillella* sp. nov., *Calospila rubrica* (Stichel), *C. asteria* (Stichel), *C. caligata* (Stichel), *Nymphidium balbinus* Staudinger, and *Stalachtis magdalenae cleove* Staudinger. In addition to these endemics, the Chocó above 1000m also forms the last refuge for *Mesosemia mehida* Hewitson and *M. bifasciata* Hewitson, described from western Ecuador.

Distribution: The Chocó region extends from north of Quibdó south along the western slopes of the Cordillera Occidental to northwestern Ecuador. The fauna shows strongest affinities with Panamá/Costa Rica, with which it shares 58% of its Riodininae. Because of this shared influence from Panamá, 43% of the Chocó fauna is also found in the Cauca Valley to the east of the Cordillera; but from there eastwards, the faunal similarities drop rapidly. Only 17% of the taxa are also encountered on the eastern (Amazonian) slope of the Cordillera Oriental.

Population Sizes: Not known.

Habitat and Ecology: The characteristic of the Chocó is its high rainfall, as much as 13 metres a year east of Quibdó. The rain is nearly constant, though slightly less in January–February and July–August, and often mostly in the afternoon and evening. The butterflies take to the wing during short intervals of sun, usually in the morning and early afternoon. Most species concentrate on hilltops, although many are found in the forests along trails and streams, often deeply cut into the weathered soil.

Threats: Nearly all species are very sensitive to habitat alteration, particularly cutting of the rain forest. A significant fall in the number of hilltopping species has been seen as a function of the cutting of larger trees on the slopes.

Conservation: Reserves in the Chocó are few and only established with great difficulty due to the conflicting economic interests, particularly from the paper industry. However, due to the uniqueness of the habitat and its high endemism, combined with the rudimentary level of existing knowledge, every effort should be made to support the investigation and establishment of sustainable reserves in the Chocó.

Reference

CALLAGHAN, C.J. 1985. Notes on the zoogeographic distribution of butterflies in the subfamily Riodininae in Colombia. *In:* Proc. 2nd Symp. Neotropical Lepidoptera. *J. Res. Lep.* Supplement **1**: 50–69.

Aloeides dentatis dentatis (Swierstra), *Aloeides dentatis maseruna* (Riley); Subfamily Theclinae, Tribe Aphnaeini

S.F. Henning[1], G.A. Henning[2] and M.J. Samways[3]

[1] 5 Alexander St., Florida 1709, South Africa
[2] 17 Sonerend St., Helderdruin 1724, South Africa
[3] Department of Zoology and Entomology, University of Natal, Pietermaritzburg 3200, South Africa

Country: South Africa.

Status and Conservation Interest: Status – *A. d. dentatis*: rare; *A. d. maseruna*: indeterminate; rare (Red List).

These two subspecies are highly localised endemics from the central grassland savannah of southern Africa. Earlier recorded sites for both butterflies have been damaged, with localised loss of the species.

Taxonomy and Description. The upperside of *A. d. dentatis* is orange, with narrow black margins and apical patches (Murray 1935, Pennington 1978). The basal half of the forewing costa is orange. The underside of the hindwing is crimson-red with silvery white and black markings. The diagnostic feature is a medial series of small dentate markings with black along their outer edge. There is also a form with a pale brown rather than crimson ground colour, and with indistinct markings. The female is similar to the male but has more rounded wings. Forewing lengths: male 14–18mm; female 15–19mm.

A. d. maseruna has a pale tawny-orange upperside with a dark grey border. The underside of the hindwing is pale brown or pinkish-red with the silvery dentate band more extensive than in the nominate subspecies. Forewing lengths: male 13.5–18.5mm; female 15–19mm.

Distribution. *A. d. dentatis* occurs on the highveld of the Transvaal, at Waterval Onder, Ruimsig, Pretoria, Springs, Alberton and Suikerbosrand.

A. dentatis maseruna was originally recorded from Maseru in Lesotho. Other localities in the Orange Free State and the Western Transvaal are now also known.

Population Size: From mark-recapture data collected at the Ruimsig Reserve in 1989/1990, it was estimated that the population size of *A. d. dentatis* was 400 specimens on the wing. The population size of other populations of *A. d. dentatis* is not known. There is no information available on the sizes of the known colonies of *A. dentatis maseruna*.

Habitat and Ecology: *A. d. dentatis* occurs in highveld grassland. The adults do not range far from the host plants and ants. The males maintain small territories, on sandy patches among the foodplants, in which they can be found throughout most of the day. The females fly randomly throughout the area, and are as common as the males. During partly cloudy days, *A. d. dentatis* has been seen to bask on a rock by lying sideways.

It feeds on a variety of flowers, and its foodplant at Ruimsig is *Hermannia depressa* (Sterculiaceae) at an elevation of 1500m. The eggs are laid in pairs on the underside of the leaves of the foodplant. In the Suikerbosrand Nature Reserve, at 1900m, the foodplant is *Lotononis erianthe* (Fabaceae), and the eggs are laid on the stems. At Ruimsig, the larvae shelter during the day in the nest of the widespread ant *Acantholepis capensis* Mayr. The larvae apparently release a pheromone which appears to mimic the brood pheromone of the ant, causing the ant to treat the larvae as its brood. At night, the larvae emerge from the nest to feed on the foodplant. During these journeys, they apparently release a pheromone which imitates the alarm pheromone of the ant. This excites the attendant ants and partially protects the larvae while they feed. The larvae pupate within the ants' nests. When they emerge from the pupae, the adults run along the tunnels in the nest with wings still unexpanded, only expanding them once outside the nest.

The eggs of *A. d. dentatis* are 0.8mm in diameter and 0.5 mm high. They are bun-shaped, with a bold network of ridges. The colour is creamy-white at first, becoming purple-brown with development. All six larval instars are similar in appearance. The head is dark brown with light brown setae. The broad neck-shield and small rounded anal shield are dark brown. The body is grey with longitudinal streaks and markings of reddish-brown. The tubercle cases on the eighth segment are black and bear the characteristic protective spines. The retractile tubercles are white. The honey gland is absent. Maximum length of the final instar larva is 18–19mm. The pupa is 12–13mm long, golden-brown and rounded (Henning 1983a,b, 1984a,b, 1987; Tite and Dickson 1968a,b).

Adults are on the wing from August to April with a peak from October to December (Henning1983a,b, 1984a, 1987; Tite and Dickson 1968b).

A. d. maseruna inhabits flat grassveld, usually near water or marshy areas. The habitats are sparsely grassed, the ground being sandy with gravel. The adults sit on sand or gravel patches, the males establishing territories from which to chase intraspecific intruders and court females. The males fly low and fast, and in wide circles, generally returning to their original spots. The females fly slowly about in the same areas. When a female enters the territory, the male approaches from the rear and 'shimmies' just behind her. When unresponsive, she flies off. Alternatively, when responsive, she immediately settles. The male settles beside her and sidles up, but if she is not ready to mate, she turns away from him in a 'rejection posture', causing him to fly off. The actual mating has not yet been recorded. The fertilised female then spends her time searching for the foodplant *Hermannia jacobifolia* (Sterculiaceae) on which to lay eggs. The female alights on the plant and immediately begins searching with her antennae for ant pheromone trails. The ant species has not yet been recorded. The female will search the 200mm plant from top to bottom and even the ground around the base. When she is appropriately stimulated, she usually lays two eggs, side by side, on the stem of the foodplant.

The egg of *A. d. maseruna* is also bun-shaped with a pronounced network of ridges. Initially, the egg is greyish-white, becoming purple-brown. The remainder of the life history is unrecorded.

A. d. maseruna is on the wing from November to February (Henning and Henning 1989).

Threats. The establishment of the butterfly reserve at Ruimsig, specifically for *A. d. dentatis*, and its presence in the Suikerbosrand Nature Reserve suggests that this butterfly is no longer under immediate threat. However, it is essential to continue monitoring this subspecies, especially as the Ruimsig population is so small (Henning and Henning 1985, 1989). Towards this end, over a two week period in December 1989 and January 1990, an estimation was made of the population size at the Ruimsig Reserve. By using a mark-recapture method it was estimated that the population size was about 400 specimens on the wing. This was far greater than was expected. This study will be continued on an annual basis to determine whether the management methods at the reserve are successful or not.

Recent records for *A. d. maseruna* from Maseru are sparse. The most suitable habitats have been used for farming, or washed away by erosion. Another recorded locality is Ladybrand, apparently along the banks of a river where it has not been seen in recent times. A new locality is at Heilbron, where it has been found next to a dam in the town and also 10km further north on a slight slope above a stream. The locality next to the dam is in the grounds of a recently erected old age home, and as this development continues, the colony may well disappear. The other locality north of Heilbron is apparently safe, as is the Boons locality, which is in a large, flat, marshy area.

Conservation: In 1985 the Roodepoort City Council established a 12ha reserve at Ruimsig for *A. d. dentatis*. The butterfly is also found in the Suikerbosrand Nature Reserve.

No conservation measures are currently in force for *A. d. maseruna*.

References

HENNING, S.F. 1983a. Biological groups within the Lycaenidae (Lepidoptera). *J. ent. Soc. S. Afr.* **46**: 65–85.

HENNING, S.F. 1983b. Chemical communication between lycaenid larvae (Lepidoptera: Lycaenidae) and ants (Hymenoptera: Formicidae). *J. ent. Soc. S. Afr.* **46**: 341–366.

HENNING, S.F. 1984a. The effect of ant association on lycaenid larval duration (Lepidoptera: Lycaenidae). *Ent. Rec. J. Variation* **96**: 99–102.

HENNING, S.F. 1984b. *Southern African Butterflies*, with illustrations by Clare Abbott. Macmillan South Africa, Johannesburg.

HENNING, S.F. 1987. Myrmecophily in lycaenid butterflies (Lepidoptera: Lycaenidae). *Ent. Rec. J. Variation* **99**: 215–222.

HENNING, S.F. and HENNING, G.A. 1985. South Africa's endangered butterflies. *Quagga* **10**: 16–17.

HENNING, S.F. and HENNING, G.A. 1989. *South African Red Data Book – Butterflies*. South African National Scientific Programmes Report No. **158**, Council for Scientific and Industrial Research, Pretoria, 175 pp.

MURRAY, D.P. 1935. *South African Butterflies: A Monograph of the Family Lycaenidae*. John Bale, Sons and Danielsson, London.

PENNINGTON, K.M. 1978. *Pennington's Butterflies of Southern Africa*. Ed. by C.G.C. Dickson, with the collaboration of D.M. Kroon. Ad. Donker, Johannesburg.

TITE, G.E. and DICKSON, C.G.C. 1968a. The *Aloeides thyra* complex (Lepidoptera: Lycaenidae). *Bull. Brit. Mus. (Nat. Hist.) Ent.* **21**: 367–388.

TITE, G.E. and DICKSON, C.G.C. 1968b. The genus *Aloeides* and allied genera (Lepidoptera: Lycaenidae). *Bull. Brit. Mus. (Nat. Hist.) Ent.* **29**: 225–280.

Erikssonia acraeina Trimen; Subfamily Theclinae, Tribe Aphnaeini

S.F. Henning[1], G.A. Henning[2] and M.J. Samways[3]

[1] 5 Alexander St., Florida 1709, South Africa
[2] 17 Sonerend St., Helderdruin 1724, South Africa
[3] Department of Zoology and Entomology, University of Natal, Pietermaritzburg 3200, South Africa

Countries: South Africa, Namibia, Zaire, Zambia.

Status and Conservation Interest: Status – vulnerable; rare (Red List).

There are no recent reports of known colonies except for the South African colony, which is thriving on a private farm. This colony is presently being investigated by the Transvaal Nature Conservation Department, with a view to circumventing the threat of agricultural development destroying the colony. No conservation measures are being taken to preserve the other colonies.

Taxonomy and Description: The upperside is orange with a narrow, black marginal border, a black, subcostal, discal patch on the forewing and a thin, black, post-discal band on the hindwing (Pennington 1978). The underside is orange with thin, post-discal, black lines and scattered black spots. The female is similar to the male but with a more rounded wing shape. Forewing lengths: male 15–18mm; female 16–21mm.

Distribution: This species has a scattered distribution, occurring in Ovamboland in Namibia, and the Waterberg Mountains (1700m) west of Nylstroom in the western Transvaal. It has also been recorded from Mongu (Barotse Province, Zambia) and in Zaire.

Population Size: The Waterberg colony in South Africa is thought to be strong although no figures on population size are available. There are no recent reports from the Zambian colony, and it has not been recorded from Ovamboland, Namibia since the type was collected.

Habitat and Ecology: *E. acraeina* flies in open, grassy savannah with sandy soil, in occasional localities where its foodplant *Gnidia kraussiana* (Thymelaeaceae) and host ant (*Acantholepis* sp.) occur together. It does not range far from its host plant and ant. The males establish small territories among the foodplants in which they can be found throughout most of the day. The females fly randomly within the area, and are as common as the males. When basking on a sandy patch in the sunshine, individuals have been seen to lie down on their side maximising exposure. They settle on the ground, on small plants or on grass. Individuals are often seen feeding on flowers. *E. acraeina* flies slowly and weakly, the bright colour and slow flight indicate that the species is probably unpalatable through sequestering toxins from its foodplant. It does not mimic an *Acraea* as the name implies but has developed aposematic colouring independently. The most closely related genus is probably *Aloeides*, of which most species have tawny-orange colouring.

The eggs are laid in coarse sand at the base of the foodplant near the entrance to the ants' nest. The egg is dome-shaped with irregular raised convolutions, giving a truffle-like appearance. Convolutions are absent at the micropyle, which is large, round and deeply indented. When first laid it is yellowish-ochre, later darkening to grey or greyish brown.

The larva shelters in the nest during the day, emerging at night to feed on the foodplant. All instars appear similar. The body is pinkish-grey with a maroon longitudinal line down the centre of the dorsal surface, flanked on either side by a bluish-green area. Laterally, the larvae are marked with regular reddish-brown markings. The honey gland on the seventh segment is well developed and the retractile tubercles on the eighth are white. The sixth (final) instar reaches a maximum length of 35mm.

Pupation takes place within the ants' nest. The pupa is at first bright yellow darkening to a deep ochre with a brownish dorsal line within 48 hours. Pupal length is about 15mm (Henning 1984).

Adults are on the wing from November to February (Henning 1984; Henning and Henning 1989).

Threats: The Waterberg colony, although strong, is on a private farm, and therefore may be susceptible to agricultural development in the long term. There are no recent reports from the colonies in Zaire or Namibia. Similarly, threats to the Zairean colony are unknown (Henning and Henning 1989).

Conservation: The status of this species is currently being investigated by the Transvaal Nature Conservation Department with assistance from the Lepidopterists' Society of Southern Africa. No conservation measures are being taken to conserve the species at the other localities.

References

HENNING, S.F. 1984. Life history and behaviour of *Erikssonia acraeina* Trimen (Lepidoptera: Lycaenidae). *J. ent. Soc. S. Afr.* **47**: 337–342.

HENNING, S.F. and HENNING, G.A. 1989. *South African Red Data Book – Butterflies.* South African National Scientific Programmes Report No. **158**, Council for Scientific and Industrial Research, Pretoria, 175 pp.

PENNINGTON, K.M. 1978. *Pennington's Butterflies of Southern Africa.* Ed. by C.G.C. Dickson, with the collaboration of D.M. Kroon. Ad. Donker, Johannesburg.

Alaena margaritacea Eltringham; Subfamily Lipteninae, Tribe Pentilini

S.F. Henning[1], G.A. Henning[2] and M.J. Samways[3]

[1] 5 Alexander St., Florida 1709, South Africa
[2] 17 Sonerend St., Helderdruin 1724, South Africa
[3] Department of Zoology and Entomology, University of Natal, Pietermaritzburg 3200, South Africa

Country: South Africa.

Status and Conservation Interest: Status – vulnerable (Red List).

This liptenine is endemic to one locality in the northeastern Transvaal. Two colonies are known high in the Strydpoort Mountains where the butterfly inhabits the steep grassy slopes and lichen-covered rocks 400m from the summit. Planting of stands of pine trees in the area poses a threat, although the Transvaal Nature Conservation Department is aware of the situation.

Taxonomy and Description: This is a small species (Clark and Dickson 1971; Murray 1935; Pennington 1978) with elongated forewings. The upperside is black with a broad orange band, which is very broad in the female, almost reaching the base. The underside of the hindwing is creamy white with an intricate, lace-like pattern of thin black lines. Forewing lengths: male 12–13.5mm; female 14–15mm.

Distribution: *A. margaritacea* is endemic to South Africa, and is known only from one locality near Haenertsburg in the northeastern Transvaal (Henning and Henning 1989).

Population Size: Although the two colonies near Haenertsburg only cover an area of about 1ha, there can be numerous individuals.

Habitat and Ecology: Two secluded colonies are known from the slopes of the Strydpoort Mountains about 400m below the peaks. *A. margaritacea* flies on the steep grassy slopes with large lichen-covered rocks (Swanepoel 1953). Near midday, the males have been recorded ascending almost to the mountain tops, where they establish small territories at the base of rocky ridges just below the peaks. *A. margaritacea* has a weak fluttering flight, and when disturbed, it flies a few metres before settling again on a grass stem. If repeatedly disturbed, it may fly for a hundred metres before settling again. The males normally establish territories in the breeding area, perching on grass stalks and fluttering around the grass. When another male enters its territory, it sometimes chases the intruder away. The female flutters slowly throughout the breeding area, searching for suitable lichen on which to lay her eggs.

The foodplant is probably rock lichen, although the female sometimes lays on rocks and stones supporting only a little lichen. The eggs are laid singly or in small clusters. The eggs are 0.9mm in diameter, 0.4mm high, and purple-brown. There are four rings of 14, round indentations on each egg. Those at the micropyle are narrow and elongated. Nothing is known of larval behaviour. The first instar is purple-brown with a pale yellow neck-shield and white humps which bear the outer dorsal and lateral setae. The head is purple-brown. The subsequent instars and pupa are unrecorded.

The adult is on the wing in December and January, with a peak towards the end of December.

Threats: The planting of plantation pine trees is a serious threat to this species.

Conservation: The Transvaal Nature Conservation Department is aware of the threats to this species, and is currently monitoring it.

References

CLARK, G.C. and DICKSON, C.G.C. 1971. *Life Histories of the South African Lycaenid Butterflies.* Purnell and Sons, Cape Town.
HENNING, S.F. and HENNING, G.A. 1989. *South African Red Data Book – Butterflies.* South African National Scientific Programmes Report No. **158**, Council for Scientific and Industrial Research, Pretoria, 175 pp.
MURRAY, D.P. 1935. *South African Butterflies: A Monograph of the Family Lycaenidae.* John Bale, Sons and Danielsson, London.
PENNINGTON, K.M. 1978. *Pennington's Butterflies of Southern Africa.* Ed. by C.G.C. Dickson, with the collaboration of D.M. Kroon. Ad. Donker, Johannesburg.
SWANEPOEL, D.A. 1953. *Butterflies of South Africa: Where, When and How they Fly.* Maskew Miller, Cape Town.

Orachrysops (Lepidochrysops) ariadne (Butler); Subfamily Polyommatinae, Tribe Polyommatini

S.F. Henning[1], G.A. Henning[2] and M.J. Samways[3]

[1] *5 Alexander St., Florida 1709, South Africa*
[2] *17 Sonerend St., Helderdruin 1724, South Africa*
[3] *Department of Zoology and Entomology, University of Natal, Pietermaritzburg 3200, South Africa*

Country: South Africa.

Status and Conservation Interest: Status – rare; endangered (Red List).

O. ariadne is a highly localised Natal endemic. One of the two recorded colonies has become extinct, and the other occupies 1 hectare on private land. Neglectful management of the site is posing a serious threat. Much more biological information on the species is required, as is a management plan for its protection.

Taxonomy and Description: This species has rounded wings. The males are dull violaceous-blue on the upperside with narrow dark brown margins. The underside is dark greyish-brown with black spots and a distinct line of clearly-defined white post-discal marks. The female is brown on the upperside with blue areas reduced to the basal half of the wings; the underside is similar to that of the male. Forewing lengths: male 13–17 mm; female 13–19 mm.

Distribution: *O. ariadne* is endemic to Natal (Henning and Henning 1989). It has only been found in the Karkloof District, although previously it was recorded nearby at Balgowan. A few specimens which could represent this species have been recorded from Nkandla near Eshowe.

Population Size: The population size of the only confirmed colony (at Karkloof Falls) is not known.

Habitat and Ecology: *O. ariadne* inhabits a one hectare area of steep grassy slopes adjacent to forests (Pennington 1978). It occurs in tall grass on the north side of the stream running down to the top of the Karkloof Falls. On the south-facing steep slope, among the tall *Hyparrhenia* spp. grasses, the foodplant *Indigofera astragalina* (Fabaceae) is found (Swanepoel 1953).

O. ariadne is a fast, low flier, but may fly to a height of two metres to clear the tall grassheads. The males patrol up and down the valley, dodging in and out of the tall grass, sometimes venturing into the adjacent valley across the stream, but always returning to where the foodplant grows. They do not appear to be strongly territorial.

This species is on the wing from 1000h to 1430h. The females spend much time looking for the foodplant on which to lay their eggs. They fly more slowly than the males, and are always found in the vicinity. Little is known of the life-history, although early instars have been seen to feed on the foodplant before going down, as third instars, into an unidentified ant nest to feed on the brood.

Threats: The habitat is being overgrown. In the past, vertebrate herbivores and natural fires kept the site in a more open, earlier successional stage suitable for the foodplant and ant host.

Conservation: Careful monitoring of the site and active management is advisable to prevent the colony disappearing. No formal conservation measures are currently in force, aside from some interest by the owners of the land.

References

HENNING, S.F and HENNING, G.A. 1989. *South African Red Data Book – Butterflies*. South African National Scientific Programmes Report No. **158**, Council for Scientific and Industrial Research, Pretoria. 175 pp.

PENNINGTON, K.M. 1978. *Pennington's Butterflies of Southern Africa*. Ed. by C.G.C. Dickson, with the collaboration of D.M. Kroon. Ad. Donker, Johannesburg.

SWANEPOEL, D.A. 1953. *Butterflies of South Africa: Where, When and How they Fly*. Maskew Miller, Cape Town.

Hypochrysops C. and R. Felder

D.P.A. SANDS

Division of Entomology, CSIRO, Meiers Road, Indooroopilly, Queensland 4068, Australia

Country: Australia

Status and Conservation Interest: Status – several species endangered or rare.

Habitat destruction has affected seven species whose survival is now considered to be threatened in four Australian States (Table 1, last column). The most threatened species in the genus, *H. piceatus*, is only known from two localities in southern Queensland, one formerly at Millmerran but now cleared for farming and the other consisting of a few kilometres of roadside savannah near Leyburn. Together with *Paralucia spinifera* Edwards & Common, these two butterflies are the most 'at risk' of all the Australian butterflies. It is possible that other localities will be found for *H. piceatus* but none has yet been discovered despite searches of suitable intact open forest containing the foodplant, *Casuarina luehmannii*. Fortunately, the butterflies are not uncommon in some years and have maintained their abundance despite heavy collecting at times by amateurs.

Taxonomy and Description: Species of *Hypochrysops* are renowned among lepidopterists for the distinctive and beautiful patterns on the undersides of their wings. Unlike the closely related genus *Philiris* Rober, most species of *Hypochrysops* are easily distinguished and were described before the turn of the century. All except one (*H. piceatus* Kerr, Macqueen & Sands) of the species occurring in Australia were described by the time Waterhouse's *'What Butterfly is That?'* (1932) was published. However, the specific and subspecific status of some populations has been reviewed recently (Sands 1986) and some taxonomic identities changed.

Distribution: The majority of the 57 species recognised (Sands 1986), occur on the neighbouring islands north of Australia and only one (*H. coelisparsus* [Butler]) occurs west of Wallace's line. Six of the 18 species of *Hypochrysops* in Australia are endemic while the remainder are also found on mainland New Guinea.

Population Size: Not known.

Habitat and Ecology: The life history of *H. ignitus ignitus* (Leach) was described by Waterhouse (1932) and it differs only slightly for subspecies *erythrinus*. Adults oviposit on small (up to 2m) plants of *Eucalyptus confertiflora* or *Acacia* spp. and their larvae shelter by day in byres of the attendant ant, *Iridomyrmex nitidus*, constructed on the stems and trunk of the foodplant. At the end of the wet season populations normally stabilise after the dry season stress – a time when much of their habitat is now burnt intentionally as a precaution against wild fires.

Threats: Not all species 'hilltop' but for those that do, human activities such as clearing and installation for radio and television equipment, forestry observation towers and mining of rock outcrops often result in destruction of the hilltop habitats and local extinctions. The most susceptible to these activities are the subspecies of *H. delicia* Hewitson and *H. ignitus* (Leach).

It is likely that the intentional annual burning of savannah in the Northern Territory near Darwin contributes to the extreme rarity of *H. ignitus erythrinus* (Waterhouse & Lyell). The firing is carried out by conservation authorities in the belief that the original inhabitants did so as a method for hunting wildlife. However, these fires now started at the end of every wet season are quite devastating to several insect species and particularly to *H. ignitus erythrinus*.

At the end of the wet season populations of *H. ignitus ignitus* normally stabilise after the dry season stress. The abundance of this subspecies, dependant on suckers and low regrowth of the larval foodplants, has been dramatically reduced since routine fuel reduction burning began. It is said that vertebrates are not affected by these 'slow burns' since they are sufficiently mobile to escape from the advancing flames. Immature stages of arthropods, on the other hand, are incinerated when surrounded by combustible materials close to the ground. There is an urgent need to review these burn policies and to take account of sessile organisms, perhaps by providing fire-free areas where dry country habitats of rare insect fauna are allowed to stabilise.

The Australian species of *Hypochrysops* are local, uncommon or rare, occurring in undisturbed habitats and very few if any are able to adapt to encroaching urbanisation. *H.*

pythias (Felder & Felder) occurs at times in hundreds in Papua New Guinea, especially where its foodplant *Commersonia bartramia* has regrown after human disturbance, but the Australian subspecies *euclides* has never been observed in such numbers even though the food plant is the same and often a predominant regrowth plant. It is an unusual species as adults are known to aggregate in large numbers at night in Papua New Guinea.

For those species that congregate on undisturbed hilltops males are sometimes seen in numbers but the females are always uncommon. Hilltops are selected as locations where unmated female adults can, with a degree of certainty, find a mate among the competing males.

Australian tropical and subtropical rainforests have been depleted to a fraction of their original area, and conservation of the remainder is essential if the survival of several species of *Hypochrysops* is not to be threatened. The fringing rainforests along the Rocky River have suffered from gold mining activities placing at risk survival of the unique *H. theon cretatus* Sands. Nowhere else is this recently-described subspecies known to occur. It is the most southern population of a species found throughout mainland New Guinea and is the most distinctive of all of the seven subspecies recognised (Sands 1986). Fortunately, much of the habitat for another subspecies, *H. theon medocus* (Fruhstorfer), and the related *H. hippuris nebulosis* Sands is not at risk. However, the rainforest margin species, *H. miskini miskini* (Waterhouse) is seriously threatened by habitat

destruction in southeastern Queensland. Formerly common near Burleigh Heads, on the Coomera River and near Rainbow Beach, the species has disappeared from most localities and is becoming rare at the remainder. Although slightly different in morphology from the southern populations, populations of *H. miskini* from the northern localities are not so threatened.

At the edge of its range in northern NSW, *H. digglesii* (Hewitson) is now confined mainly to moist savannah near Broken Head. Unfortunately, although most of the nearby rainforest is included in a National Park, the breeding sites for this species are at present threatened by local development proposals.

It is important to note that this is the only locality remaining intact for this species in NSW and that it differs quite considerably in appearance from the more abundant populations in Queensland.

Coastal paperbark (*Melaleuca* spp.) swamps are habitats for several species destroyed on a large scale in recent years. *H. apollo apollo* Miskin was once quite abundant at a few paperbark localities including Cardwell, the southern edge of its range and at Port Douglas, northern Queensland. However, forestry activities, mainly clearing and planting with *Pinus* sp. and earth works for a canal development at the first locality and clearing for a golflinks at the second, have seriously damaged the major breeding sites for this unusual butterfly. *H. apollo apollo* has suffered from clearing of the paperbark swamps that support the epiphytic plant, *Myrmecodia beccari*, the larval foodplant.

Table 1. *Hypochrysops* spp. currently known to survive at five or fewer localities in States where they were formerly widely distributed.

Taxon	State[†] with nos localities intact		Present elsewhere (state[†])	Habitats	
				Type*	At risk (+/−)
H. apelles apelles	NSW	*c.* 4	Q, NT	MG	+
H. apollo apollo	Q	*c.* 5	−	SV	+
H. byzos byzos	Q	*c.* 3	NSW	SV	−
H. cleon	Q	1	−	RF	−
H. digglesii	NSW	1	Q	SV	+
H. epicurus	NSW	*c.* 5	Q	MG	+
H. hippuris nebulosus	Q	1	−	RF	−
H. ignitus ignitus	SA	1	Q, V, NSW	SV	+
H. ignitus erythrinus	NT	2	WA	SV	+
H. piceatus	Q	1	−	SV	+
H. theon cretatus	Q	1	−	RF	+

Key

†	NSW	New South Wales	*	MG	mangroves
	Q	Queensland		SV	savannah
	NT	Northern Territory		RF	rainforest
	SA	South Australia			
	V	Victoria			
	WA	Western Australia			

Another factor that is decreasing the abundance of the butterfly is removal of the bulbous foodplants by collectors and who cut them up in search of pupae. Colonisation of the bulbs by the exotic ant *Pheidole megacephala* may also affect survival of *H. apollo* since it displaces the native *Iridomyrmex cordatus*, the natural bulb inhabitant. Indeed, *P. megacephala* may eventually threaten the survival of ant plants, as it is known to destroy the developing seeds. This is probably one of the very few examples of a conservation issue for Australian butterflies involving threat to the breeding sites by collectors. The same habitat is shared with the much more abundant *H. narcissus narcissus* (F.) which breeds on mistletoes, a species also present in and breeding on mangroves in northern Queensland.

Mangroves are important breeding sites for a number of interesting lycaenid butterflies. In southeastern Queensland and northern NSW, the coppery *H. apelles apelles* (F.) only occurs near saltwater swamps where the larvae feed on several species of mangroves. The species was once very common near Southport and on the Tweed River but its numbers have declined in recent years and it has disappeared from several localities. Housing developments, clearing of mangroves and possibly, spraying with insecticides have resulted in the species becoming scarce in NSW and uncommon in southern Queensland. Further north in Queensland a wide range of plants are food for larvae and the species is not at risk. Another species, *H. epicurus* Miskin, has suffered from similar destruction of its only mangrove (*Avicennia marina*) habitat in southeastern Queensland and NSW. This species has become quite rare at localities where it was formerly very common due to habitat interference.

References

SANDS, D.P.A. 1986. A revision of the genus *Hypochrysops* C. & R. Felder (Lepidoptera: Lycaenidae). *Entomonograph* No. 7. E.J. Brill, Leiden.

WATERHOUSE, G.A. 1932. *What Butterfly is That?* Angus & Robertson, Sydney.

Illidge's Ant-Blue, *Acrodipsas illidgei* (Waterhouse and Lyell)

P.R. SAMSON

Bureau of Sugar Experiment Stations, P.O. Box 651, Bundaberg, Queensland 4650, Australia

Country: Australia.

Status and Conservation Interest: Status – rare (Common and Waterhouse 1981).

Its life cycle is unusual, larvae being obligate myrmecophages. It has a restricted distribution and occurs almost exclusively among mangroves, a habitat which is under threat from development in the populous area where the species is known. A proposal for a canal estate and residential subdivision was rejected in a local government court decision in Brisbane in 1989, based in part on the need to preserve colonies of *A. illidgei* occurring in the area. In July 1990, *A. illidgei* became the first butterfly to be designated as 'Permanently Protected Fauna' in Queensland.

Taxonomy and Description: *A. illidgei* was originally described as a subspecies of *A. myrmecophylla* (Waterhouse & Lyell), from which it differs by its larger size, the broader markings beneath the wings and the male genitalia (Kerr, Macqueen and Sands 1968).

Acrodipsas Sands contains seven described species, all endemic to Australia (Common and Waterhouse 1981). They were previously referred to as *Pseudodipsas* C. and R. Felder. Four species have been described since 1965. Two more probable species await description (D. Sands, pers. comm.). All species except *A. illidgei* are known mostly from males collected on hilltops in open *Eucalyptus* forest. The life histories are poorly understood, and only *A. illidgei* and two others have been reared from the immature stages.

Distribution: *A. illidgei* is restricted to coastal areas, mostly in mangrove habitats. For many years the species had only been recorded between Brisbane and Burleigh Heads in southern Queensland, but there are recent records from Mary River Heads near Maryborough, Queensland (Manskie and Manskie 1989) and Brunswick Heads, New South Wales (G. Miller pers. comm.).

Population Size: Almost all recent specimens have been collected at Burleigh Heads or at Redland Bay near Brisbane. There are no estimates of the population sizes at these sites.

Newly-emerged female of *Acrodipsas illidgei* (photo by P.R. Samson).

Final instar larva of *Acrodipsas illidgei* with associated ants and brood (photo by P.R. Samson).

Habitat and Ecology: The colonies at Burleigh and Redland Bay occur in communities dominated by the grey mangrove *Avicennia marina*. Other records from Mary River Heads, Hay's Inlet near Brisbane, and Brunswick Heads are also from mangrove areas.

Adults of *A. illidgei* are small and inconspicuous, and are not easy to see among the dense mangrove vegetation. My observations at Redland Bay suggest that breeding occurs in patches of trees. I have found 25 eggs laid on a single mangrove tree with smaller numbers on adjacent trees. On that occasion the vast majority of trees apparently carried no eggs, despite the presence of ant colonies in some of them. Whether these patches remain stable over time is unknown.

Of the immature stages, only the eggs are in exposed positions, and they are difficult to locate. Eggs are laid on branches or under loose bark of trees colonised by the associated ants. Eggs are aggregated on the particular trees used for breeding. They hatch in about one week during summer.

The first instar larvae are carried into ant nests by the small ant, *Crematogaster* sp. (*laeviceps* group) (Samson 1987, 1989). The nests occur in cavities (mostly in borer holes) in the wood of living trees. There, the larvae prey on the ant brood throughout their development. Pupae also occur inside the nest and several larvae or pupae may be found together in a hollow branch. Larvae and pupae occurring in these nests can only be found by destroying the branches and ant colonies in which they live. Almost all have been found inside nests in *A. marina*. However, several have been found beneath bark of *Eucalyptus* (Smales and Ledward 1942), indicating that there is no special relationship with *Avicennia*.

Collecting records suggest that there are at least two generations each year, with maximum frequency of capture in September and December to February: no adults have been taken during the colder months of May through July.

Adults have been seen feeding at flowers (Hagan 1980). Like some other species of *Acrodipsas*, females possess many fully developed eggs at emergence from the pupa (Sands 1979).

Another lycaenid, *Hypochrysops apelles* (Fabricius), has an obligate relationship with *Crematogaster* sp. (*laeviceps* group) in southern Queensland. That butterfly occurs continuously along the coast to northern Queensland (Common and Waterhouse 1981), probably attended by the same ant. It is surprising, therefore, that *A. illidgei* has such a restricted distribution.

Threats: Survival of *A. illidgei* is threatened by the loss of mangroves to residential development. The species' distribution coincides with the most populous region of Queensland, where coastal development is proceeding at a rapid rate. Fogging with insecticides to control biting insects that breed in mangroves may also threaten *A. illidgei*.

Collecting poses little threat to the species. Only a small number of collectors have visited the breeding sites. The butterflies do not have a sharply defined flight period and are very difficult to find and capture in the habitat. Collecting of immature stages destroys the ant galleries that are searched.

However, it is only the galleries in the smaller, dead branches of the mangroves that are readily opened up by collectors: the greater part of the ant nests in the large branches and trunks of the mangroves are inaccessible.

Conservation: Part of the habitat of *A. illidgei* at Burleigh Heads is protected within an environmental park established to preserve what little remains of mangroves in the area. Whether *A. illidgei* still breeds within the park is not known.

Recently, approval for a canal estate proposal at Point Halloran, Redland Bay was rejected because of deleterious effects on the environment. The proposed development was to have included 610 residential allotments of which 385 were to have canal frontages on 106ha. The presence of *A. illidgei* in the area was one factor in the court's decision to reject the proposal (The Courier Mail, 17 June 1989). A small part of this area has since been rezoned for residential development, but the remainder is likely to become an environmental park.

The colony at Redland Bay that is most often visited by lepidopterists is near to, but not contained within, the development proposal. There is at present no habitat protection afforded to this site.

The mangrove habitat of *A. illidgei* at Mary River Heads is part of an area nominated for world heritage listing. A request from local residents for insecticidal fogging to control biting midges has been denied because of possible harm to the butterflies (The Courier Mail, 2 May 1992).

The designation of *A. illidgei* as 'Permanently Protected Fauna' under the Queensland Fauna Conservation Act 1974–79 on July 21, 1990 gives it an unusually high and controversial status (Monteith 1990). This status has otherwise been accorded to a few high-profile vertebrates, such as the koala and platypus. Permits are needed to keep specimens in private collections, and a separate permit is required in order to move specimens to different premises, or interstate. Permits may be obtained for scientific study of the species but a fear is that the degree of formality imposed is likely to deter the interest of enthusiastic amateurs who have contributed so much to knowledge of Australian Lycaenidae.

References

COMMON, I.F.B. and WATERHOUSE, D.F. 1981. *Butterflies of Australia*. (2nd edn.) Angus and Robertson, Sydney.

HAGAN, C.E. 1980. Recent records of *Acrodipsas illidgei* (Waterhouse and Lyell) (Lepidoptera: Lycaenidae) from the Brisbane area, Queensland. *Aust. ent. Mag.* 7: 39.

KERR, J.F.R., MACQUEEN, J. and SANDS, D.P. 1968. The specific status of *Pseudodipsas illidgei* Waterhouse and Lyell stat. n. (Lepidoptera: Lycaenidae). *J. Aust. ent. Soc.* 7: 28.

MANSKIE, R.C. and MANSKIE, N. 1989. New distribution records for four Queensland Lycaenidae (Lepidoptera). *Aust. ent. Mag.* 16: 98.

MONTEITH, G. 1990. Another butterfly protected in Queensland. *Myrmecia* **August 1990**: 153–154.

SAMSON, P.R. 1987. The blue connection: butterflies, ants and mangroves. *Aust. nat. Hist.* 22: 177–181.

SAMSON, P.R. 1989. Morphology and biology of *Acrodipsas illidgei* (Waterhouse and Lyell), a myrmecophagous lycaenid (Lepidoptera: Lycaenidae: Theclinae). *J. Aust. ent. Soc.* **28**: 161–168.

SANDS, D.P.A. 1979. A new genus, *Acrodipsas*, for a group of Lycaenidae (Lepidoptera) previously referred to *Pseudodipsas* C. & R. Felder, with descriptions of two new species from northern Queensland. *J. Aust. ent. Soc.* **18**: 251–265.

SMALES, M. and LEDWARD, C.P. 1942. Notes on the life-histories of some lycaenid butterflies – Part I. *Qd. Nat.* **12**: 14–18.

The Eltham Copper, *Paralucia pyrodiscus lucida* Crosby

T.R. New

Department of Zoology, La Trobe University, Bundoora, Victoria 3083, Australia

Country: Australia.

Status and Conservation Interest: Status – rare, vulnerable.

This local subspecies was feared to be extinct in the Melbourne area of southeastern Australia before a thriving colony was found in January 1987 on land already subdivided for imminent housing development. A major campaign was undertaken to (a) acquire and reserve the habitat, (b) search for other colonies and (c) design a management plan for the butterfly. This case broke new ground in increasing invertebrate conservation awareness in Victoria.

Taxonomy and Description: The subspecies was described (Crosby 1951) from the Eltham (37°43'S, 149°09'E) / Greensborough area of outer northeastern Melbourne, and differs in the amount of copper scaling from the nominate subspecies, *P. p. pyrodiscus* (Doubleday) which occurs in parts of eastern Australia as far north as southern Queensland. Colonies around Kiata (36°22'S, 141°48'E) and Castlemaine (37°04'S, 144°13'E) are also at present referred to this subspecies. The extra-Victorian limits of the subspecies are not wholly clear: at present no other populations are referred to *lucida* formally.

Paralucia Waterhouse and Turner contains three species, all endemic to Australia. One, *P. aurifera* (Blanchard), is widespread but local and the other two are rare.

Distribution: The subspecies is very restricted in isolated parts of Victoria. Eight discrete colonies are known around Eltham; the subspecies otherwise occurs only at Kiata (six colonies within 3km of each other; one at nearby Salisbury) and Castlemaine (a single colony only) (Braby *et al.* 1992).

Population Size: *P. p. lucida* was discovered near Melbourne in 1938. Accumulated collector wisdom shows that it was taken more or less regularly over the following decade or so but declined markedly from about 1950 onwards and thereafter became extremely rare. It was believed to be extinct in recent years until the discovery of a thriving colony near Melbourne in 1987.

All presently known colonies are very isolated, and the population structure is essentially closed. There is very little possibility of interchange of adults between most nearby suburban colonies, and none over the broader scale of distribution. Most of the Eltham colonies are small and seem unlikely to be viable in the long term. Population sizes have been estimated both by counts of adult butterflies during the flight season and nocturnal counts of feeding caterpillars (Vaughan 1987, 1988) and as the largest (presumed viable) colonies occupy only a few hundred square metres, these counts are likely to be reasonably accurate. The major Eltham colony, on the subdivision land, contained an estimated 300–500 larvae. At the other extreme only six butterflies were observed in a colony on private land. Several intermediate sized colonies each had populations estimated at 100–150 individuals. In contrast, the Kiata colonies contained 'many hundreds' of individuals, and there are 100–200 at Castlemaine. In 1988, the State population of the Eltham Copper was about 2600 individuals (Braby and Crosby in prep.).

Habitat and Ecology: Some colonies are confined to open forest areas, generally on north to west-facing slopes, and others occur on highly degraded areas such as roadsides. The life cycle appears to be limited obligatorily to a spiny dwarfed form of Sweet Bursaria (*Bursaria spinosa*: Pittosporaceae) as the sole larval foodplant, and to plants associated with nest chambers of the ant genus *Notoncus*. There is one major generation each year, with adults present from late November to early February, and a possible small, partial second generation represented by a few adults in March (Braby 1990).

Eggs are laid singly or in small groups on or near the larval foodplant. Caterpillars hatch after about two weeks and are nocturnal feeders: they retreat to *Notoncus* chambers at the base of the plants during the daytime and are regularly tended by the ants, these being *N. enormis* Szabo at Eltham but *N. ectatommoides* (Forel) at Kiata. Caterpillars pupate in the ant chambers after five instars, and the pupal stage of the major generation lasts about a month.

Adult *P. p. lucida* take nectar from various flowers, including *Bursaria*. They seem to be aggressive to other butterflies, and males actively pursue females.

Both the stunted *Bursaria* and *Notoncus* ants are widespread in Victoria, and there is seemingly no shortage of sites suitable for *P. p. lucida*. Its restricted distribution is at present difficult to explain.

Threats: Recent declines appear to be attributable solely to urbanisation, with associated removal of native vegetation, fragmentation and destruction. The habitats of some former colonies near Eltham are now housing estates and this was clearly the major threat to the newly discovered colonies. The largest colony was reduced substantially during 1988–89. The very small colony noted above was in a suburban garden, but many such gardens are rapidly converted to exotic plant species rather than fostering native flora. Four of the Kiata colonies are within an 80ha Native Plant and Wildlife Reserve. Encroachment of exotic weeds on the site of the sole Castlemaine colony, which is not protected, may be a concern (Braby and Crosby in prep.). Sheep grazing has apparently reduced the number of host plants in one degraded Kiata colony.

Conservation: The need for conservation of *P. p. lucida* became both apparent and urgent because of the imminent subdivision of the major site on which the butterfly was fortuitously discovered. A briefing paper to the State Minister for Conservation, Forests and Land led to negotiations with the developers, who agreed to a moratorium on development until the feasibility of purchasing the site as a 'Butterfly Reserve' could be investigated. The total cost of this was projected at A$1 million. The State Government contributed A$250,000 and the Eltham Shire Council committed A$125,000. A highly organized public appeal during the next year raised a further $56,000 and during that time the 'Eltham Copper' became an important local emblem. The total of some A$426,000 is by far the largest sum ever committed to conservation of an invertebrate species/subspecies in Australia and a major part of the prime colony site (0.7ha) was purchased in early 1989. This was augmented substantially by the State Government transferring to the butterfly reserve an area (*c.* 2.6ha) of Education Department land adjacent to this which supported a further important colony.

This case did much to increase public awareness of butterfly conservation and the general importance of invertebrates in the environment. Following initial assessment of conservation status (Crosby 1987), a management plan for *P. p. lucida* has been prepared (Vaughan 1987, 1988). The habitats reserved, though only a few hectares in extent, should be sufficient to sustain the populations at Eltham with adequate management.

Management recommendations for these remnant urban populations include:

i) protection of all existing colonies from threatening processes associated with urbanisation including: human activity (trampling, slashing or burning vegetation, dumping of garbage, sullage overflow and changes to drainage patterns, potential overcollection); weed invasion; overgrowth of food plants; and activities of other species of animals;

ii) provision for expansion of the habitat by prompting natural regeneration of *Bursaria* and propagation from seeds or cuttings, or transplanting plants from any sites to be destroyed by development;

iii) provision for a ranger to foster practical management activities and monitor the effects of these.

Listing of the subspecies under the Victorian Flora and Fauna Guarantee Act is controversial, although full provision for invertebrates is included in this pioneering legislation. A requirement of the Flora and Fauna Guarantee Act listing is the preparation of an Action Statement from the earlier management plan. This statement, detailing steps needed to ensure the butterfly's long-term survival, is at present in draft form (Webster 1993). A further leaflet on the Eltham Copper has been issued recently to encourage its well being by habitat protection (Ahern 1993), and a Coordinating Group of scientists is overseeing the developing management plan. The Entomological Society of Victoria has placed *P. p. lucida* on its list of butterflies to which a Voluntary Restricted Collecting Code applies.

Current concerns include destruction of some of the small (unreserved) Eltham colonies and the coordination of effective measures to conserve the butterfly in other parts of Victoria. Attempts are being made, using the facilities of the 'Butterfly House' at the Royal Melbourne Zoological Gardens, to establish captive stock for future reintroduction to the wild.

Acknowledgements

M. Braby, D. Crosby and P. Vaughan are thanked for information additional to that included in the published reports.

References

AHERN, L. 1993. Eltham Copper Butterfly 'The People's choice'. *Land for Wildlife Note No. 21.* Department of Conservation and Natural Resources, Victoria.

BRABY, M.F. 1990. The life history and biology of *Paralucia pyrodiscus lucida* Crosby (Lepidoptera: Lycaenidae). *J. Aust. ent. Soc.* **29**: 41–51.

BRABY, M.F. and CROSBY, D.F. In prep. The status and conservation of the Eltham Copper Butterfly, *Paralucia pyrodiscus lucida* Crosby, in Victoria, Australia.

BRABY, M.F., CROSBY, D.F. and VAUGHAN, P.J. 1992. Distribution and range reduction in Victoria of the Eltham Copper butterfly *Paralucia pyrodiscus lucida* Crosby. *Vict. Nat.* **109**: 154–161.

CROSBY, D.F. 1951. A new geographical race of an Australian butterfly. *Vict. Nat.* **67**: 225–227.

CROSBY, D.F. 1987. *The conservation status of the Eltham Copper Butterfly* (Paralucia pyrodiscus lucida *Crosby*) *(Lepidoptera: Lycaenidae).* Arthur Rylah Institute for Environmental Research. Tech. Rpt. No. **8**, Melbourne.

VAUGHAN, P.J. 1987. (1988). *The Eltham Copper Butterfly draft management plan.* Arthur Rylah Institute for Environmental Research. Tech. Rpt. No. **57**, Melbourne.

VAUGHAN, P.J. 1988. *Management plan for the Eltham Copper Butterfly* (Paralucia pyrodiscus lucida *Crosby*) *(Lepidoptera: Lycaenidae).* Arthur Rylah Institute for Environmental Research. Tech. Rpt. No. **79**, Melbourne.

WEBSTER, A. 1993. Eltham Copper Butterfly, *Paralucia pyrodiscus lucida.* Action Statement No. 39. (draft). Department of Conservation and Natural Resources, Victoria.

The Bathurst Copper, *Paralucia spinifera* Edwards and Common

E.M. Dexter and R.L. Kitching

Department of Ecosystem Management, University of New England, Armidale, NSW 2351, Australia

Country: Australia

Status and Conservation Interest: Status – endangered (Common and Waterhouse 1981).

The species, endemic to Australia, is known only from three localities all within 50km of each other. The populations are highly fragmented and are subject to various threats including grazing, pasture improvements and establishment of forestry plantations.

Taxonomy and Description: The Australian endemic genus *Paralucia* Waterhouse and Turner contains three species, *P. spinifera*, *P. aurifera* and *P. pyrodiscus*.

The first specimen of *P. spinifera* was collected in October 1964 at Yetholme (33°27'S 149°48'E) New South Wales, by I.F.B. Common and M.S. Upton. Despite subsequent searches, the species was not found again until October 1977 and it was officially described and named by Edwards and Common (1978). Apart from the difference in size, shape and colour of the wing, Edwards and Common (1978) distinguished *P. spinifera* from its congeners *P. aurifera* (Blanchard) and *P. pyrodiscus* (Rosenstock) by its spine-like process that extends over the base of the tarsus on the tip of each fore tibia. Both sexes have this feature.

Distribution: *P. spinifera* is known to occur at three main localities which are all within 50km of each other. The populations are highly fragmented both naturally, by occurring on ridges above 900m in altitude, and artificially, by pine plantations and areas of improved pasture.

Population Size: Site A (see below) has the highest population of *P. spinifera* amounting to approximately 1120 individuals sighted over an eight-week period. Population sizes at the other two localities are smaller.

Habitat and ecology: The three known localities for the species are remarkably uniform in geography, which suggests that the species has very specific microhabitat requirements. This has been confirmed by later studies (Dexter and Kitching unpublished).

All sites are on the edge of open eucalypt woodland (Specht 1981) and usually on west to north-west facing slopes. The density of *P. spinifera* differs markedly in the three areas and is correlated with a spatial pattern of the larval food plant, native blackthorn *Bursaria spinosa* Cav. (Pittosporaceae).

The butterfly has a mutualistic relationship with the ant *Anonychomyrma itinerans*. Ant surveys of known *P. spinifera* localities repeatedly yielded other ant species which may be important to the butterfly's life history. These were *Iridomyrmex sp. 1,2,3, I. purpureus, I. rufoniger* group 1 and 2, and *Ochetellus* sp.

Ant surveys were also done in nearby areas, some only metres away, which appeared to be suitable habitat but lacked *P. spinifera*, and on every occasion the attendant ant was absent. One population which was high in numbers in 1989 crashed in 1991. A follow-up survey showed that *A. itinerans* was not present.

Athough *A. itinerans* has a wider distribution than *P. spinifera*, it too is restricted to regions above 900m in altitude. Apart from the central tablelands, *A. itinerans* is also found at Piccadilly Circus (35°22'S 148°49'E) (Australian Capital Territory), Barrington Tops (31°59'S 151°27'E) and Brown Mountain (36°36'S 149°23'E) in New South Wales.

P. spinifera is univoltine and has a very early flight season which starts in the last week of September and finishes in mid-November. During this period the adult emergence is scattered and matings occur throughout the eight-week period.

After mating, the female oviposits on bushes with ants, presumably detected using olfactory cues, and lays singletons or groups of up to four white eggs which darken to green with maturity. The egg group size of *P. spinifera* is considerably smaller than that of the closely related *P. aurifera* and *P. pyrodiscus* which are 15 and 12 eggs respectively (Braby 1990). Eggs are laid on the lower third of the bush and are positioned on either the underside of leaves on the main trunk or on debris at the base of the plant. Eggs take approximately 15 days to hatch. During the egg phase, the attendant ants are constantly searching the host plant, possibly seeking newly hatched larvae.

After hatching, first instar larvae are immediately attended by one ant, which is curious as the early instar larvae do not have ant-attracting organs. From instars one to three the larvae and ants are diurnal, feeding in both morning and afternoon and retreating to the nest at midday and dusk. After the third instar, the larvae and ants become nocturnal. The larvae of *P. spinifera* can have up to eight instars and can take between 60 and 70 days to pupate in laboratory conditions without ants.

Preliminary laboratory studies (Dexter and Kitching, unpublished) have shown that larvae without ants remain on the bush permanently whilst larvae with ants return to the base of the plant during daylight hours. Larvae reared without ants are also considerably smaller at pupation than larvae which have been reared with ants.

Threats: The three main localities, which for the purposes of this paper are termed sites A, B and C, differ greatly in the degree of habitat degradation and thus level of threat, which appears to be a reflection of the land tenure.

Site A, which has the highest population of *P. spinifera*, is closest to the 'natural state' with a high level of plant diversity and a large community of ants present. This land is owned by the Department of Defence with restricted access, has not been burnt for 17 years, and has never been grazed by livestock. Site A also includes a nearby smaller site which is similar in condition to the main block described above.

Site B supports five fragmented subpopulations and, although together the populations occupy an area of 5km^2, a mark-recapture study (Dexter and Kitching, unpublished) showed that the subpopulations do not intermingle and that the vagility of the adults is low. These sites are all on private land and have been or are still subject to grazing.

Site C occurs within a nature reserve where it is fully protected by law. However, the population at this site is probably the most threatened of all. The site is heavily infested with blackberry, *Rubus* sp., is disturbed by feral pigs and threatened by fire control burns. Unfortunately the managing body is required to burn the area to reduce the risk of wildfire spreading from within the reserve to the neighbouring pine plantation.

Unlike some lycaenids, for which grazing seems to be beneficial to the butterfly, grazing is detrimental to this species, as livestock trample and eat the seedlings of *B. spinosa*. This in turn inhibits juvenile recruitment of *B. spinosa* and can cause changes in the spatial pattern of the plant, leading to plant isolation. Larvae which occur on isolated bushes usually deplete their food supply so heavily that they starve or pupate prematurely. If larvae pupate at a smaller body size, the emerging adult will also be small and this can affect reproductive fitness because fecundity in butterflies is positively correlated with body size (Gilbert 1984).

One sympathetic landholder is actively involved in managing her *P. spinifera* populations and provides hungry larvae with new bushes which ants and larvae colonise. It should be noted that for this management strategy to be successful the branches need to be entwined, as larvae do not seem to move across the ground.

Overall the main threats to the survival of this species are:
- ignorance of its existence and habitat degradation. The type

locality narrowly avoided being cleared during installation of a major power line, with no local appreciation of the butterfly's existence whatsoever.
- grazing by cattle, sheep and goats, either by direct impact on the food plants or by use of pasture fertilisation to improve fodder quality.
- clearing for establishment of forestry plantations. Along with pasture improvement, this process has probably produced the current highly fragmented distribution of the species in the area, although it must always have been a very local species. Clearing and habitat change were of course carried out in ignorance of the existence of the species.
- all sites are under some threat from exotic weeds, the most significant being blackberry (*Rubus* spp.) and scotch broom (*Cytisus scoparius*). At one site, the *Bursaria* is in danger of being completely overgrown by the broom and at the only protected site (Winburndale Nature Reserve) uncontrolled spread of blackberries is a threat to part of the site at least.

Conservation: *Paralucia spinifera* encapsulates many of the problems associated with the conservation of lycaenids. The scatter of highly restricted sites each with a different set of actual and potential problems and the relatively small changes that would be required to actually eliminate whole populations make generalisations difficult. Crucial to any management of the species is local awareness and sympathy and that has been created over the last few years. Only those who have regular, albeit casual, contact with the sites concerned can monitor day to day changes.

Some general threats, particularly overgrowth by noxious weeds and damage to hostplants by feral animals, should be controlled by application of existing programmmes in National Parks and other public lands. Sites on private land need to be monitored for these impacts and the impact of stock, particularly goats, which may browse upon the host plants, and cattle which can produce soil impaction and other disturbance inimical to ant populations.

Major land use changes involving clearing for conifer plantations and fertilisation for pasture 'improvement' are probably responsible for the present limited distribution of the species and obviously any further changes present additional threats. The occurrence of some butterfly populations on protected land is encouraging although other sites need to be monitored in this connection. One site is being proposed for listing under National Estate regulations because of the presence of this butterfly.

There is circumstantial evidence for one site that overcollecting has severely reduced the population. The short flight period, very restricted areas in which populations occur, and a tendency by collectors to take long series for no justifiable reason may have contributed to making this species more sensitive than most to collecting pressures. Lepidopterists have argued vigorously for a self-regulatory approach to butterfly conservation rather than one driven by species-specific legislation. Collectors need to be very aware of the sensitivity of species like *Paralucia spinifera* for which self-regulation does not appear to have worked. The case could certainly be made for total protection of the species.

References

BRABY, M.F. 1990. The life history and biology of *Paralucia pyrodiscus lucida* Crosby (Lepidoptera: Lycaenidae). *J. Aust. ent. Soc.* **29**: 41–51.

COMMON, I.F.B. and WATERHOUSE, D.F. 1981. *Butterflies of Australia*. Angus and Robertson, Sydney.

EDWARDS, E.D. and COMMON, I.F.B. 1978. A new species of *Paralucia* Waterhouse and Turner from New South Wales (Lepidoptera: Lycaenidae). *Aust. ent. Mag.* **5** (4): 65–70.

GILBERT, N. 1984. Control of fecundity in *Pieris rapae* I. The problem. *J. Anim. Ecol.* **53**: 581–588.

SPECHT, R.L. 1981. Foliage projective cover and standing biomass. *In:* Gillison, A.N. and Anderson, D.J. (Eds). *Vegetation classification in Australia*. CSIRO and ANU Press, Canberra.

The Australian Hairstreak, *Pseudalmenus chlorinda* (Blanchard)

G.B. PRINCE

Department of Parks, Wildlife and Heritage, 134 Mrs. Macquarie's Road, Hobart, Tasmania 7001, Australia

Country: Australia.

Status and Conservation Interest: Status – Mainland subspecies: *P. c. chloris*, rare; *P. c. fisheri* and *P.c. barringtonensis*, vulnerable; *P. c. zephyrus*, not threatened. Tasmanian subspecies: *P. c. conara* and *P. c. chlorinda*, vulnerable (both indeterminate: Red List); *P. c. myrsilus* and the un-named *P. c. zephyrus*-like form, endangered.

Several of the subspecies of *P. chlorinda* are extremely localised, particularly in Tasmania where most conservation attention to this species has been paid. Several forms of the Hairstreak in Tasmania were stated by Couchman and Couchman (1977) 'to have suffered more than any local species of butterfly', and much suitable habitat has been destroyed. The Couchmans expressed grave concern for the butterfly's future in Tasmania, and a more recent survey (Prince 1988) also stressed the need for conservation measures. Many colonies have become extinct, and most of the remainder face threats to their continued well being. The species as a whole in Tasmania is considered vulnerable.

Taxonomy and Description: *P. chlorinda* is the sole species of the endemic Australian thecline genus *Pseudalmenus* Druce, and is known from southeastern mainland Australia and Tasmania. It shows substantial geographical variation (Figure 1) and seven named subspecies are widely recognised (Common and Waterhouse 1981), together with at least one other Tasmanian form. Couchman and Couchman (1977) noted another two Tasmanian forms which were by then extinct. Collectively, these forms constitute one of the most diverse polytypic Lycaenidae in Australia, probably representing incipient speciation, and of considerable evolutionary interest.

Distribution: All eight subspecies have highly circumscribed distributions (see Figure 1) and only one, *P. c. zephyrus*, can be considered to be reasonably widespread. *P. c. chloris* is regarded as rare and local in New South Wales and the other mainland subspecies, *P. c. fisheri* and *P. c. barringtonensis* , are highly localised in the Grampians Mountains, Victoria and Barrington Tops, New South Wales, respectively. Of the Tasmanian taxa, *P. c. chlorinda* is found from Hobart to north of Swansea and

westward to the South Esk and Upper Tamar Valleys, *P. c. conara* is known from the midlands and *P. c. myrsilus* from the Tasman and Forestier Peninsulas and a small part of the east coast. The un-named *P. c. zephyrus*-like form is known from the northeast of Tasmania. The recent discovery of the species in western Tasmania suggests the likelihood that other colonies may exist in that remote area: that race has been referred tentatively to *P. c. chlorinda*, but specimens are not available.

Population Size: Most subspecies are clearly very localised but little information is available on population size, especially for the mainland taxa. Many of the Tasmanian sites surveyed by Prince (1988) had very low 'occupation rates' of suitable eucalypt trees, with few hairstreak pupae recorded from them. Many populations may, indeed, be confined to single eucalypt trees in very small isolated patches of habitat, from which recolonisation is probably unlikely. Detailed information on *Pseudalmenus* dispersal is not available, but it is believed to be largely sedentary in habit.

Habitat and Ecology: Eggs are laid singly or in small groups on young twigs of a larval foodplant, *Acacia*. In Tasmania, the usual foodplant is the bipinnate *A. dealbata* (80% of Prince's records), with the closely related *A. mearnsii* (9%) also utilised. Other acacias, particularly the phyllodinous *A. melanoxylon*, have also been recorded, more especially for the mainland subspecies. Larvae feed on the *Acacia* foliage and are attended by small, black ants (*Iridomyrmex foetans*). The role of the ants is not clear, but they appear to be essential, and probably protect the caterpillars from parasitoids. Caterpillars pupate under the loose bark of nearby eucalypts, predominantly *Eucalyptus viminalis* (92% of pupae) in Tasmania, growing within a few metres of the acacias. Most (77%) grew within 2m, and few pupae were found on eucalypts only 10m from larval foodplants. The most frequently selected eucalypts were 15–18m tall, with diameters of 75–150cm. Pupae occurred up to around 2m from the ground, and most were on the northern half of the tree.

Adults fly in spring and early summer, with slight differences in flight period between subspecies, and most forms are univoltine. A partial second generation has been suggested for *P. c. fisheri* (Common and Waterhouse 1981) but otherwise the

171

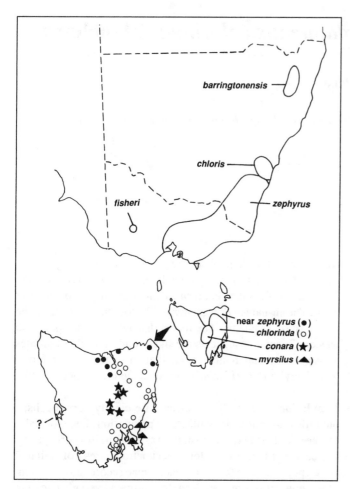

Figure 1. Distribution of subspecies of *Pseudalmenus chlorinda* in southeastern Australia, with details of Tasmanian subspecies. Mainland data after Common and Waterhouse (1981).

period from December to at least August or September is passed as pupae. This stage therefore constitutes a suitable one for monitoring population sizes of *Pseudalmenus*. Pupae are often on trees occupied by *I. foetans*, and the scent of the ants might influence selection of host trees (Prince 1988). The ant can also be abundant on trees lacking *Pseudalmenus*.

Threats: At many sites in Tasmania where *P. chlorinda* has become extinct, the habitat has been destroyed or severely disturbed. Pastoral clearing (52%) and fire (direct implication in loss of 24% of sites, contributory to the loss of a further 20%) were the predominant factors involved, and grazing, forestry (clearing for timber and woodchips) and housing subdivisions

accounted for the remainder. For extant colonies, Prince (1988) assessed fire as the most common threat (31%) though clearing and subdivision are also significant.

Pupae were recorded in the mid-1980s at only 15 of the 43 sites noted by earlier workers, but some new sites were also found. Of 66 locations recorded for *P. chlorinda* in Tasmania, only 12 of the 40 which still support the hairstreak were considered to be reasonably secure (Prince 1988). *P. c. myrsilus* is especially restricted, and *P. c.* near *zephyrus* was found in only four areas. Most known sites are small and threatened. At many, pupae were found only on a single tree. Couchman and Couchman (in Prince 1988) observed instances where a single tree had supported a population of *P. chlorinda* for many years, and that population had disappeared once the tree had been cut down.

Conservation: Couchman and Couchman (1977) emphasised the threefold needs of *P. chlorinda*: the close associations of a suitable *Eucalyptus*; a suitable *Acacia*; and the specific ant. They emphasised that the destruction of any of these might lead to the butterfly's local extermination. Protection of these resources in suitable habitats is clearly the major conservation need for *P. chlorinda*, both in terms of reservation of habitat and management within reserves and on private land. Many of the populations are in reserved sites, but some of these have been subject to clearing and fire. Protection of habitats on private land may be feasible in some instances, but sites close to urban centres are under considerable pressure from urban expansion. Increased community awareness of the butterfly is also needed.

Active management, for example guarding against clearing of acacias near eucalypts, merits promotion, and a trial reported by Prince (1988) suggests that translocation of the butterfly to new suitable habitats might be feasible as a management tool. Studies of the status of mainland subspecies are also a priority for this species, together with clarification of the status of populations in western Tasmania.

References

COMMON, I.F.B. and WATERHOUSE, D.F. 1981. *Butterflies of Australia.* (2nd edn.) Angus & Robertson, Sydney.

COUCHMAN, L.E. and COUCHMAN, R. 1977. The butterflies of Tasmania. *Tasmanian Year Book* (**1977**): 66–96.

PRINCE, G.B. 1988. The conservation status of the Hairstreak Butterfly *Pseudalmenus chlorinda* Blanchard in Tasmania (report to Department of Lands, Parks and Wildlife, Tasmania).

APPENDIX 1

IUCN Red Data Book categories

Many of the species discussed in this book have been allocated, sometimes tentatively, to the traditional IUCN Red Data Book categories. They are subject to revision of status as new information is incorporated. The categories are defined as follows:

Extinct (Ex)

Species not definitely located in the wild during the past 50 years (criterion as used in the Convention on International Trade in Endangered Species of Wild Fauna and Flora). (For some butterflies, the status is applied to taxa which are known to have become extinct by, for example, destruction of the last or only known colony, without regard to the 50 year period: TRN.)

Endangered (E)

Taxa in danger of extinction and whose survival is unlikely if the causal factors continue to operate. These include species whose habitats or numbers have been reduced drastically and may be in danger of imminent extinction. The category also includes taxa which are probably already extinct, but which have been seen during the last 50 years (see comment in parentheses, above: 'Endangered' implies some uncertainty over whether or not the species is extinct: TRN).

Vulnerable (V)

Taxa believed likely to become Endangered in the near future if causal factors continue to operate. A wide range of threats is included, from habitat destruction to overexploitation, and other environmental disturbances. The taxa need not, necessarily, be rare if threats operate over a large range.

Rare (R)

Taxa with small world populations which are not at present Endangered or Vulnerable, but are at risk. They are usually in limited geographical areas or habitats, or in low numbers over a more extensive range.

Indeterminate (I)

Taxa known to be Endangered, Vulnerable, or Rare, but for which there is insufficient information to determine which of these is the appropriate category.

Out of Danger (O)

Taxa formerly in one of the above categories but which are now considered relatively secure because of effective conservation measures and/or removal of previous threats to their survival.

'Threatened' is a general term to denote species which are Endangered, Vulnerable, Rare, or Indeterminate.

A 'Threatened Community' is a group of ecologically linked taxa occurring within a defined area, which are all under the same threat and require similar conservation measures.